THE WORLD'S
WORST
DISASTERS
& MISTAKES

THE WORLD'S

WORST

DISASTERS & MISTAKES

Bounty
Books

This collection first published in 2014 by Bounty Books,
a division of Octopus Publishing Group Ltd,
Endeavour House, 189 Shaftesbury Avenue,
London WC2H 8JY
www.octopusbooks.co.uk

An Hachette UK company
www.hachette.co.uk

The material in this book originally appeared in three
separate titles:
The World's Worst Disasters of the Twentieth Century
by Roger Boar &Nigel Blundell
The World's Greatest Mistakes by Nigel Blundell
The World's Greatest Blunders by Sue Blackhall

ISBN: 978-0-753727-94-2

Printed and bound by CPI Group (UK) Ltd, Croydon, CR0 4YY

THE WORLD'S

WORST

DISASTERS
& MISTAKES

The World's WORST DISASTERS of the TWENTIETH CENTURY

Acknowledgements

The publishers would like to thank the following organisations and individuals for their kind permission to reproduce the photographs in this book:

Irish Times 171, Keystone Press Agency 2 below, 25 inset, 34, 42, 62–3, 69, 72, 75, 78, 83, 84, 90, 97, 156, Popperfoto 2 middle right, 46, 115, 116, 121, 129, 132, 136, 151, Press Association 109, Radio Times Hulton Picture Library 49, Topham 2 above, middle left, 10, 11, 17, 19, 22, 23, 25, 30, Wide World Photos 142, 158, 176, 178–9. News Ltd 188-9.

Contents

The Mont Pelée Volcano (1902)

It may not be good for the tourist trade to call some of the Lesser Antilles the Volcanic Caribees, but that is what they are. Stretching in an arc from the Virgin Islands in the north to Grenada in the south, the Windward and the Leeward Islands have been built up from the ocean floor by volcanic action. On some the volcanoes are extinct, on others, still active. Only two have erupted in historic times, Mont Pelée on Martinique and La Soufrière on St Vincent.

Martinique is now a Department of France, so firmly integrated that when someone says '*Je vais en métropole*' he means he is going to Paris, not Fort de France, the island's capital. But in 1902 the most important commercial centre was St Pierre, a town of 26,000 inhabitants, lying in a mile-long, crescent-shaped strip on the north-west coast, below ravines rising steeply towards Mont Pelée ('bald mountain') which reared, 4,430 feet above sea level, five miles away, almost due north.

Sugar, rum and bananas were the basis of the island's prosperity. St Pierre was a gay town – people called it the Paris of the West Indies – with riotous tropical vegetation, a mixed population of whites, mulattos and blacks, and strongly contrasting wealth and poverty.

Mont Pelée steamed and puffed occasionally, rather like an old man smoking his pipe. The main crater had remained dormant for ages, although there had been a minor eruption in the volcano 50 years earlier. For as long as anyone could remember there had been a lake there called *L'Etang des Palmistes*, and it was a favourite picnic spot. The only other eruption recorded had been in 1792 and that, too, had been insignificant.

On the south side of the mountain, facing St Pierre, there was a dry secondary crater, *L'Etang Sec*, with steep flanks unbroken except at one point, where, also on the south side, a gash in the rim led into a ravine called *La Rivière Blanche* which extended right to the coast. In the rainy season flood water flowing down this and other ravines could cause considerable damage.

On 2 April 1902, fresh steaming vent-holes were noticed in the upper part of *La Rivière Blanche*. Three weeks later, a small amount of volcanic ash floated down on to the streets of St Pierre and there were a few earth tremors, just enough to upset crockery. In the following days the situation became more ominous. There were explosions in the secondary crater which hurled up rocks and clouds of ash. Then a lake formed there, 200 yards across, and also a cinder cone as high as a house, with steam spurting from the top. Soon ash was falling more heavily, mantling and muffling the town, seeping into shops and houses, killing birds and animals and bringing with it the nauseating stench of sulphur. Mrs Prentiss, wife of the American consul, wrote: 'The smell is so strong that horses in the street stop and snort, and some of them drop dead in their harness.'

In response to the considerable alarm caused by these events, Louis Mouttet, Governor of Martinique, appointed a commission to assess the situation and he visited the town. It was the last trip he ever made. Incredibly, the commission reported no immediate danger and while Mouttet maintained a studied air of calm the local newspaper, *Les Colonies*, backed him up with soothing editorials. The extraordinary complacency of all three has been ascribed to political collusion: important elections were due to be held on 10 May and Mouttet was anxious not to let his supporters disperse.

As ash continued to fall, St Pierre began to look like a body drained of blood. Deep rumblings could be heard coming from the belly of the mountain. Despite troops brought in by the Governor, law and order became difficult to maintain. Shops and businesses closed. Terrified villagers from the mountain slopes burst into bars and hotels demanding refuge. From the other end of the town, people were pouring southwards, swelling the population of St Pierre to 30,000. On 5 May came a foretaste of what Pelée could do. The cleft in its side becoming blocked with ash, massive quantities of rain water had collected in *L'Etang Sec*, been heated by volcanic action and now burst out in a seething torrent of boiling mud to hurtle down the mountain side. The tide engulfed a sugar-mill on the coast north of St Pierre, killing over 100 people, then plunged into the sea, causing a huge wave which swamped the lower parts of the town. *Les Colonies* reported 'the entire city afoot' and 'a flood of humanity pouring up from the low point of the anchorage, not knowing where to turn.'

Far worse was to come. On 6 May Pelée's rumblings turned to a steady roar interspersed with explosions which threw up masses of red-hot cinders. And the Governor did something unforgivable: he stationed troops on the roads to stop people leaving the town. *Les Colonies* found a disreputable professor to declare: 'Mont Pelée is no more to be feared than Vesuvius is feared by Naples. Where could one be better off than in St Pierre?' In a proclamation the Mayor gave his support: 'Please allow us to advise you to return to your normal occupations.'

All through Wednesday 7 May the roaring and the explosions continued.

THE MONT PELÉE VOLCANO

View of St Pierre

Heavy rain sent more torrents of mud down the mountain carrying huge boulders many tons in weight. Mingled with water, the ash gave the town a top-coating of hot sticky paste. There was only one slender ray of hope for the 30,000 residents: La Soufrière on St Vincent was reported to be in eruption. Perhaps that would relieve the pressure.

Thursday dawned clear and sunny. The people glanced apprehensively upwards to Pelée, and were relieved to see only a vapour column of unusual height. At 6.30 a.m. a passenger ship, the S.S. *Roraima*, arrived in port and tied up alongside 17 other vessels. By then the scene was dramatically different. 'For hours before we entered the roadstead,' said Assistant Purser Thompson, 'we could see flames and smoke rising from Mont Pelée. No one on board had any idea of danger. As we approached we could distinguish the rolling and leaping red flames that belched from the mountain in huge volume and gushed high in the sky. Enormous clouds of black smoke hung over the volcano. The flames were then spurting straight up in the air, now and then waving to one side or the other a moment, and again suddenly leaping higher up. There was a constant muffled roar. It was like the biggest oil refinery in the world burning up on the mountain top.'

Thompson thought the spectacle magnificent. Almost everyone on board was watching. There were no premonitions, except perhaps on the part of the Captain, who told a passenger: 'I am not going to stay any longer than I can help.'

But he stayed too long. The mountain-side facing the town was already glowing red-hot and at 7.52 a.m. exactly (the time was recorded on the military hospital clock which somehow escaped destruction) it exploded. 'There was no warning,' wrote Thompson. 'The side of the volcano was ripped out and there hurled towards us a solid wall of flame. It sounded like a thousand cannons. The wave of fire was on us and over us like a lightning flash, a hurricane of fire which rolled in mass straight down on St Pierre and the shipping. The town vanished before our eyes . . .'

In fact there were two explosions, one which shot upwards from the main crater in a dense black cloud pierced with lightning flashes and the other which blew out sideways from *L'Etang Sec*. Expanding sulphurous gases had shattered lava into fragments and now, through the gaping cleft in the secondary crater, a murderous avalanche of white-hot particles mixed with gas and superheated steam tore down *La Rivière Blanche* at hurricane speed.

From its effect on metals it has been calculated that the temperature of the blast was around 1,000°C. People died almost instantaneously wherever they happened to be, with hardly a struggle or a movement, from the inhalation of the fiery gases or from burns, some stripped of all clothing by

Mont Pelée

THE MONT PELÉE VOLCANO

the blast. Of the entire population of 30,000 only two men survived. Thompson recalled: 'After the explosion not one living being was seen on land.' The town was reduced to a heap of smoking rubble. Walls were torn down, metal roofs ripped off and crumpled like paper, trees stripped to the bare trunks. Within seconds, as the blast passed over, St Pierre reappeared as an ancient ruin, stripped of every mark that had given it identity, like something from pre-history unearthed by archaeologists, though here no digging was necessary. There was no lava crust as at Pompeii, only ash. Searching the ruins later, rescue workers could barely recognize even well-known streets.

The situation in the harbour was little better. The *nuée ardente*, or 'glowing cloud' had caused a tidal wave which capsized or badly damaged every ship, and only one managed to escape to St Lucia with 22 of her crew dead or severely burned. 'Wherever the fire struck the sea,' said Thompson, 'the water boiled and sent up great clouds of steam. The blast shrivelled and set fire to everything it touched. Only 25 of those on the *Roraima* out of 68 were left after the first flash. The fire swept off the ship's masts and smoke-stack as if they had been cut by a knife.'

Thompson saved his life by burying himself under bedding in his cabin. The *Roraima* was in no state to put to sea. One passenger who survived, a Barbadian nurse, described how ash poured in through a skylight in 'boiling splashes' as she and their mother were dressing three children for breakfast. The cabin was filling up with the scalding stuff when the first engineer heard their screams and helped them to the forward deck. By then one little boy was dead and a baby was dying. Parts of the ship were on fire and now the whole town was 'one mass of roaring flames'. 'My mistress lay on the deck in a collapsed state. The lady was collected and resigned, handed me some money, told me to take Rita (the surviving child) to her aunt, and sucked a piece of ice before she died.' On the other ships the boiling ash stuck to men's clothing, coating them from head to foot and baking them alive. Some were seen crawling about the decks, charred beyond recognition. Many jumped overboard and 'their scorched flesh sizzled as it entered the water.'

One of the two survivors in St Pierre was a Negro shoemaker, Léon Compère-Léandre, aged 28. He was sitting on his doorstep when disaster struck. 'All of a sudden I felt a terrible wind blowing, the earth began to tremble and the sky suddenly became dark. I turned to go into the house, made with great difficulty the three or four steps that separated me from my room, and felt my arms and legs burning, also my body. I collapsed over a table.' Others came into the room, 'crying and writhing with pain, although their clothes showed no sign of having been touched by flame.' Very soon all were dead, also an old man that Léandre found in the house. 'He was purple and inflated, but the clothing was intact. . . . Crazed and almost overcome, I threw myself on a bed, inert and awaiting death. My senses returned to me in perhaps an hour, when I saw that the roof was on fire.' Léandre owed his life to an incredible fluke. Out of all those people, for reasons which will never be known, his lungs escaped fatal damage.

The other survivor was Auguste Ciparis, a 25-year-old Negro stevedore, who was due to be hanged for murder. He was lodged in a structure almost certainly unique in the entire town, a condemned cell, reminiscent of the modern Nissen hut, in the shape of a bisected circle, resting against the outer wall of the local prison. At the front was an aperture blocked by a solid door so low that it could only be entered on all-fours. Above it was a small, heavily grated window. Massively constructed to prevent prisoners getting out, the cell protected Ciparis from the full blast.

Dressed in shirt, trousers and hat, he was waiting for his breakfast when the window suddenly darkened and he was struck by searing heat. At the same moment there was a resounding crash as the prison wall collapsed on the roof. Then, as ash blocked out the window entirely, Ciparis found himself in total darkness. 'I smelled nothing but my own body burning,' he said later. 'Soon I heard nothing but my own unanswered cries for help.'

Three days later, when the town could be entered by rescuers, Ciparis was released, horribly burnt but coherent. He was reprived, with a suspended sentence, and lived until 1929, earning a living as a side-show attraction in a circus: the Prisoner of St Pierre, complete with a replica of his cell.

On 20 May 1902, another eruption of Pelée combined with an earthquake drove many people from Martinique for ever: 2,000 were killed and several villages destroyed. More violent eruptions occurred on 26 May, 6 June, 9 July, and 30 August. There was a pause until September 1929, when once again the terrible *nuée ardente* roared down, with its super-heated steam, gases and incandescent particles, and tore up the modest structures of a new town which 1,000 intrepid citizens had struggled to build. This time Pelée was too late to catch a living soul: the inhabitants had read the signs and had gone. And this time no Governor tried to stop them.

San Francisco Earthquake (1906)

The sounds preceding an earthquake can be as terrifying as the event itself, particularly when they come to the ears of people dazed with sleep. Sometimes there is a boom like distant gunfire, or a sharp, snapping sound. There may be a rumbling noise like heavy traffic moving over cobbled streets. As they move forward, shock waves oscillate with a pull-and-push motion while others called 'strike waves' mingle with them, throwing off impulses at right angles. The total effect is like a clod of earth being shaken in a sieve.

The citizens of San Francisco heard a low and ominous rumble at twelve and a half minutes past five o'clock on the morning of Wednesday, 18 April 1906. A few seconds later came the first shock. William James (brother of novelist Henry James), was in a hotel bedroom with his wife. As the furniture began to rock and dance he stayed remarkably calm. 'This is an earthquake', he said to his trembling spouse, 'there is no cause for alarm' – and proceeded to dress with careful deliberation. The whole hotel now seemed to be bumping about.

Most of the 340,000 population were not so detached, though they had experienced lesser earthquakes before, the most recent in 1898 and 1900. This one was much more severe, more ruthless. There were three shocks, separated by only a few seconds and the third was by far the heaviest. One city official later reported watching horror-struck as a massive oak wardrobe in his bedroom tipped sideways, backwards and sideways again before being hurled forward and splintering into pieces. A local businessman wrote: 'I was awakened by a very severe shock. The shaking was so violent that it nearly threw me out of bed.' A bookcase was thrown off the wall, everything on tables and the mantelpiece was swept off as in a sudden roll at sea and the floor was littered with smashed china and glass.

Another man in a lodging-house bedroom saw chunks of plaster falling from the ceiling. Then through a gap a child's foot appeared. The next moment, the whole building gave a lurch, the gap closed under violent compression and the foot was severed in a gush of blood. At that point the man panicked and jumped through an open window, just in time to escape from the collapsing house.

A few people were out of doors when the earthquake struck. One was the editor of the *San Francisco Examiner*. He had just left his office with some of the staff and was chatting with them on a side-walk when the ground started rocking violently and they were thrown off their feet. All around, buildings were swaying and tipping under the shocks, throwing down showers of glass, bricks and masonry in a cloud of dust. Tram-lines were snapping under the pressure and reared up like thick metal snakes, short-circuiting in blinding sparks as overhead cables fell on them. Ominously the men could smell gas.

Two young men, Fred Walker and his friend Carlos, had arrived in the city that evening for a sight-seeing tour, coming by sea through the Golden Gate, the passage that links the land-locked Bay with the Pacific. (There was no bridge in those days; it was opened in 1937.) They had put up in a good-class hotel in the north-east corner of the oblong peninsula on which the city stands, not far from the area known as Chinatown, then as now the biggest Chinese settlement outside the Orient.

If the next day had not brought a different scene, the young men might have noted the city's breathtakingly beautiful setting on its hilly strip of land bounded on three sides by water, met some of its robust, independent-minded citizens, and seen one thing more which summed up San Francisco's flamboyant optimism: the $7,000,000 Palace Hotel. Enrico Caruso had arrived to sing with the Metropolitan Opera in *Carmen* and was staying there that night.

Fred and Carlos felt drawn to Chinatown. Its opium dens, gaming saloons, twisting alleys, and grubby, vicious, colourful life drew them like a magnet and they explored it for hours, until nearly 5.00 a.m.

Twelve minutes later, as they were walking back to their hotel, came the rumbling sounds, then the first shock. Fred was thrown against a wall, while buildings all around began to heave. As terrified people in their night clothes rushed screaming into the streets the two hurried on and found their hotel had become a pile of rubble with no sign of a single survivor.

While the Palace Hotel was rocking Caruso is said to have sung a few notes through an open window to make sure he had not lost his voice. Then he went out and sat on his suitcase in the street until someone took him to another hotel. There, pampered but resolute, he swore never to come back to San Francisco. He never did.

Meanwhile, the shocks had toppled some of the fine mansions and left others leaning at an angle of 15 degrees from the vertical. Most of the buildings in Market Street, bisecting the wealthy north from the poorer south part of the city, had been shaken to pieces as well as, except for its massive domed tower, the huge City Hall, only recently completed and supposed to be shock-proof. Elsewhere in the smart quarter a hotel in Valencia Street had

Capital city destroyed

An earthquake only days before Christmas virtually wiped the Nicaraguan capital of Managua off the map in 1972. The two jolts, lasting only seconds, came at 12.28 a.m. on 22 December. An eye-witness said: 'I saw dust rise like a blanket being lifted across the city. Then I saw nothing but fires.' Between 11,000 and 12,000 people died, hundreds of them hawkers sleeping under the central market building. Seventy five others died – 17 of them babies – when the city's general hospital collapsed, but doctors set up emergency operating theatres in the grounds, and asked car drivers to shine their lights as medical staff treated 5,000 casualties. All fire-fighting equipment was lost under rubble, and it was dawn before a fire-engine arrived after a six-hour race from neighbouring Costa Rica. More than 300,000 people – 75 per cent of the capital's population – were homeless by then, and refugees were already streaming out of the city. Among them was a pale, thin man who had been staying at the Intercontinental Hotel. Billionaire recluse Howard Hughes had been flushed out into the open briefly, before being whisked away in a private jet.

gently subsided like a deflating balloon, ending up with the fourth floor at ground level from which the people emerged unharmed.

The worst damage from earthquake alone was in the downtown area, near the site of the original Spanish settlement, Mission Dolores. But loss of life was comparatively small and within a couple of hours many citizens could be seen with utensils salvaged from their shattered homes cheerfully cooking breakfast in the streets. Things could have been worse, they were saying.

Then came the fire. Throughout the city, fires started in dozens of different places, in abandoned buildings from heaters left burning, from hearths, kitchen-ranges, or sparked by electricity or the ignition of gas escaping from broken mains. One housewife struck a match in what had been her kitchen and caused an explosion which ended in hundreds of houses being burned to the ground.

Months before, Fire Chief Danny Sullivan had warned city officials that his Service might be unable to cope with a serious conflagration. Now his words proved horribly true. For 52 fires there were only 38 horse-drawn fire-engines. Great fissures in the streets had fractured every single water main. Except from artesian wells here and there, or from the sea in fires close to the shore, there was not a drop of water to pour on the blaze.

Fanned and driven forward by a stiff breeze the fires were beginning to coalesce into a single inferno and a refugee described the sight from one of the city's many hills. 'Looking down we saw the great tide of fire roaring in the hollow, burning so steadily yet so fast that it had the effect of immense deliberation; roaring on towards miles of uninhabited dwellings so lately emptied of life that they appeared consciously to await their immolation.' He saw roofs and hilltops standing out starkly against the glare of the flames and 'sparks belching like the spray of bursting seas'.

By noon on that first day the fire was totally out of control. Federal troops summoned by the one telegraph wire still intact were on the way, as were units of the National Guard and 600 helpers from the University of California at Berkeley on the east side of the harbour. On the spot, amid the inferno, only two things could be attempted: to save as many lives as possible and blast a gap in the path of the flames. All that afternoon and through the red-glowing night, as the whole of Chinatown was being reduced to ashes, as well as the Palace Hotel, every house but one on Nob Hill, and thousands of houses, shacks, sheds and shanties in the rest of the city, the Navy ferried streams of refugees across the Bay to Oakland on the eastern shore while volunteers strove desperately to keep embarkation points clear of fire. For many there could be no rescue; they had been burned to death where they lay

San Francisco, devastated by the earthquake

Southern Italy devastated by earthquakes

Six violent earthquakes hit Southern Italy on 23 November 1980, killing 2,614 people, 47 of them worshippers in a church at Balvano. Further tremors hit the area, between Naples and Salerno, in the next few days, and on 26 November Interior Minister Virginio Rognoni offered his resignation after a row over 'slow action' by the government, but his offer was rejected. On 23 January 1981, the area was hit by severe blizzards, and a month later another 'quake killed eight more people.

---

trapped beneath the rubble of their homes. Eighty died in this way in one hotel. As the flames came closer, one man, who was trapped, persuaded a policeman to shoot him.

Attempts to create fire-breaks by dynamiting buildings failed. The explosive charges, laid by inexperienced men, were mostly too heavy, making buildings blow outwards instead of collapsing, so starting new fires. On the morning of the second day, Brigadier Funston, commanding federal troops, wired Washington: 'San Francisco practically destroyed. You cannot send too many tents and rations. 200,000 homeless.'

The fires were still raging when a tide of frantic people who had lost everything they possessed began looting. Mayor Schmitz issued a proclamation: 'The Federal Troops . . . have been authorized by me to KILL any and all persons found engaged in looting or in the commission of any other crime.' At the same time soup-kitchens were started and hordes of refugees were fed. One thing was certain: San Franciscans might die from a bullet, but once over the initial shock would never succumb to despair. Some of the accompanying photographs illustrate the resilience required of most San Franciscans.

Fringe areas of the city were saved, but by the Saturday, when the fires were at last burning themselves out, four square miles had been annihilated: 514 blocks containing 28,000 buildings, 450 people had been killed. Loss from earthquake was assessed later at £7 million; from fire no less than £140 million.

Recovery was a daunting prospect, but led by their level-headed Mayor the citizens rallied extraordinarily, helped by a flood of assistance from outside and also by their innate ruggedness and optimism. Many of them were descended from those tough individualists who had come halfway across the world to take part in the 1848 gold rush. Since then there had been many fires and several earthquakes, but every challenge had been met. Now

Many buildings which escaped the earthquake were destroyed by raging fires

this new one, great as it was, found them undaunted, their civic pride profoundly touched. Even while the fires were still raging orders were being placed for new tram-lines and other equipment. Within two days enough rail track had been repaired for trains to start taking out people whose homes were in other states. Electricity was restored in two weeks.

Proudly, or arrogantly, according to the point of view, San Francisco calls itself 'the city that knows how', but at least the title is deserved. Within three years, while thousands of the victims awaited resettlement in tented camps, more than a third of the city was rebuilt, not simply as a repetition of the old but on new plans with many buildings made earthquake- and fire-resistant. In 1911 the seal on total recovery was set when Congress approved San Francisco as the location of a world's fair to commemorate the opening of the Panama Canal. As if recovery from disaster was not enough, a 650-acre site was then reclaimed from tidal land stretching down from the Golden Gate, covered with landscaped gardens, pavilions, miniature palaces, and the Panama Pacific International Exposition was opened in February 1915. By the time it closed in December, 19,000,000 people had been through the gates.

Nine years had passed since that afternoon when the *Evening World Herald* of Omaha, Nebraska, had reported: '3.45 p.m. EXTRA. San Francisco wrecked and helpless.' Now every trace of that disaster had been obliterated, every connection except one: the cause. That crack in the earth's crust known as the San Andreas Fault had been the culprit, when movement occurred in the rocks on either side. The fault runs for 600 miles from Cape Mendocino in the north to the Colorado Desert, under the sea west of the Golden Gate and down the centre of the peninsula on which San Francisco stands. Along that whole length shifts in the land mass occur frequently, though none has been as severe as in 1906. They cannot be controlled; the most to be hoped for is that some day they will be predicted with greater accuracy. Meanwhile, San Francisco, one of the world's greatest seaports and trading centres, lives on, with its 2,000,000 inhabitants, beautiful, tough, cosmopolitan, energetic, disaster-prone – the city that has known how to survive.

The Titanic
(1912)

Even at the outset, the *Titanic*'s maiden voyage was marked by near-tragedy. As the immense 46,329-ton vessel moved majestically from her berth at Southampton, she came abreast of a moored liner, the *New York*. Suddenly there came a number of loud reports as the other's thick mooring-ropes snapped like string, and then the two ships began to be drawn irresistibly together. The *Titanic* was stopped, just in time, the strange 'suction' ceased, and tugs nosed the *New York* back to her berth. An identical situation arose a few minutes later when the *Teutonic* also strained at her ropes and heeled over several degrees until the *Titanic* had slid past.

Then the liner was lifting to the surge of the open sea and her crew relaxed. High on the liner's bridge Captain Edward Smith relaxed with them. Beneath his feet, the deck trembling almost imperceptibly with the thrust of her massive turbines, was the largest, the finest and the safest ship that had ever been built. To guarantee that safety, 15 transverse bulkheads sub-divided her from stem to stern; a double bottom was a further guarantee against accident. She was, in the mind of everyone ashore and afloat, the ultimate – the unsinkable ship.

After a brief call at Cherbourg, the *Titanic* left Queenstown (now Cobh) in Ireland during the evening of Thursday, 11 April 1912 and headed out into the Atlantic and waters which the veteran Captain Smith knew well. She steamed steadily westwards, without further incident; the sea was calm, the weather clear and brilliantly bright but very cold. Indeed, the temperature dropped dramatically during the morning of Sunday, 14 April and radio messages received by the *Titanic*'s Marconi man warned of the danger of icebergs.

The ship continued to race on at full speed, her lights twinkling on the dark still water, her engines thrusting her forward at a steady 22 knots. Then, just before midnight, a look-out suddenly screamed, 'Iceberg right ahead!'

Frantic orders were given which would have swung the liner's bows to port, but it was too late. As they began the swing an immense iceberg scraped along her starboard side then slipped astern into the night. Captain Smith was on the bridge almost before his First Officer Murdoch could ring 'Stop engines!' He ordered all watertight doors to be closed then turned to Fourth Officer Boxhall to order him to take soundings. Even as the young officer turned to go, however, the ship's carpenter arrived on the bridge to report 'She's making water fast'.

Far Left: views
of the luxurious
interior of the *Titanic*.
Left: Artist's
impression of the
boat tilting into the
Atlantic

THE TITANIC

Those of the passengers still awake were unaware that anything had occurred, for the impact had been slight. Lawrence Beesley, one of the survivors, stated that there was 'no sound of a crash or of anything else; no sense of shock, no jar that felt like one heavy body meeting another . . .'

Up on deck, despite the bitter cold, some energetic passengers were actually having a 'snowball' fight, using the ice that the deadly berg had deposited during the brief encounter, while one, obviously a wag and not wishing to leave the comfort of the lounge, held out his glass and asked a friend to 'see if any ice has come aboard; I would like some for this.'

A few passengers asked stewards why the engines had stopped, and were assured that there was nothing wrong. The stewards were acting in good faith – at that moment they truly believed that nothing *was* wrong. Down below, however, it was a different story. The men in the foremost boiler-room found themselves swimming as tons of water began to thrust through a great rent in the ship's side. They managed to struggle into the next boiler-room, and then the next, to reach No. 4 which was nearly amidships but still dry.

Realizing that the damage was severe, Captain Smith went to the radio-room where the two Marconi men Jack Phillips and Harold Bride were now on stand-by, to tell them that the ship had struck an iceberg and he wished them to be ready to send out a distress call.

By the time he had regained the bridge it was obvious that the *Titanic* was slowly sinking. The berg had ripped a jagged gash along the liner's starboard bow for one-third of her length, and the ice-cold Atlantic water was pouring in. At 0025, some 25 minutes after the collision, Captain Smith ordered the boats to be uncovered. Ten minutes later he returned to the radio-room to order the operators to start transmitting, adding grimly: 'It may be your last chance.' Immediately the urgent call was crackling into the night, stating what had happened, giving the ship's call-sign MGY and her position, and asking for immediate help.

It was picked up by two liners, the *Frankfort* and the *Carpathia*, although the captain of the latter twice asked his operator if he had read the message

Sabotage on luxury liner

On her maiden voyage, the sumptuous French liner, the *Georges Philippar* was completely destroyed by fires which apparently broke out simultaneously in several parts of the vessel. Sabotage was blamed for the mysterious disaster, which occurred in the Red Sea in May 1930 and claimed 53 lives.

The *Titanic* being towed out of Southampton Port on its departure for New York. Inset: Millionaire, John Jacob Astor, one of the 1,403 people who perished

correctly, not believing that the unsinkable *Titanic* could be in such trouble. When reassured that it was, he ordered his operator to reply that he would be coming to the rescue at full speed, and asked his engineers to give him 'everything that they had'.

Meanwhile the *Titanic*'s stewards were going from cabin to cabin, tapping on the doors and almost apologetically asking the occupants to put on warm clothing and go to their boat stations, taking their life-belts with them. Still unaware of the seriousness of the situation, most of the passengers did as they were asked although some refused to leave the warmth of their cabins merely for an unexpected and very inconsiderate drill.

The boats were swung out and the order was passed: 'Women and children only'. At first there was great reluctance to leave the ship for she seemed so safe, so permanent, compared to the frail-looking boats. As Beesley was to state later: 'The sea was as calm as an inland lake save for the

Tragedy of the 'boat people'

Nearly 700 Vietnamese refugees died in a series of disasters off the Malaysian coast during 1978 and 1979. An overloaded ship sank on 26 July 1978, killing 217 people. On 22 November 1979, a trawler hit a sandbar in the Tregganu estuary after being refused permission to land, and 200 of the 254 aboard drowned. Another 250 'boat people' died in three further disasters in the following month.

gentle swell which could impart no motion to a ship the size of the *Titanic*. To stand on the deck many feet above the water lapping idly against her sides, gave one a sense of wonderful security . . .'

Everyone was behaving in a calm, almost detached manner. There was none of the panic which was to cause loss of life in other ships under similar circumstances, although a brief and ugly scene among the steerage passengers was quickly quelled by the officers.

At last the boats began to be loaded and then slowly lowered, but not actually dropped into the sea. This was because Captain Smith had been told of the replies to his distress signal, especially that from the *Carpathia* which had stated that she was only 60 miles away and would be with them within four hours. But the captain soon realized that his ship was sinking lower with every passing minute, and as her bows went deeper and her stern rose from the water it would be more difficult to lower the boats. Some were still only half-filled, many women refusing to leave their husbands. Mrs Isador Strauss was one, saying firmly, 'Where you go, I go.' They stayed together – and died together.

As the boats splashed down, the strains of 'Nearer my God to Thee' drifted into the night from a group of the ship's musicians who had gathered on deck with their instruments. Some of the male passengers joined in the singing, others stared over the ship's side for a last lingering look at the faces of their loved ones before they became indistinguishable in the darkness. The crews of the boats were mainly stewards and stokers, for every officer and nearly every seaman stayed on board to help those who remained.

Two hours after the liner had been struck Captain Smith ordered 'Abandon ship! Every man for himself!' He remained on his bridge and was never seen again. Despite this order, Phillips and Bride were still transmitting, urging the ships that were straining to their rescue to hurry. Then their power failed and they went on deck.

Those in the lifeboats looked back at the sinking liner. The ship, nearly a

26

sixth of a mile long with four towering funnels and still brilliant with light that gleamed from portholes and saloons, was now down by the bows and sinking slowly but discernibly. The angle became wider as her stern lifted, then she tilted to attain an almost vertically upright position and remained thus, motionless. As she swung all her lights were suddenly extinguished and there came a deep rumble as tons of machinery broke loose and fell towards the bows. Then the great liner slid forwards and down, the waters closing over her like a shroud.

Soon after 0400 hours the *Carpathia*, having raced through dangerous waters at (for her) a hitherto unknown speed of 17 knots, arrived on the scene and by 0800 hours had rescued every boatload. With her was the *California*, a liner that had stopped during the night less than 10 miles from the *Titanic* and whose captain was subsequently severely criticized for not observing the stricken vessel's distress rockets.

The whole world was stunned when the final accounting was released. Of the 2,206 people on board, 1,403 were lost, mostly crew and male passengers. Yet out of the greatest sea disaster of all time came good. The inquiry resulted in the formation of the International Ice Patrol and also stricter Board of Trade regulations regarding the provision of sufficient lifeboats to carry everyone on board ships.

Tokyo Earthquake (1923)

On Sunday, 2 September 1923, a news report came via Shanghai from Osaka, Japan. It read: 'Yesterday, Yokohama and most of Tokyo totally destroyed in devastating earthquake followed by fire. Heavy loss of life.'

For some days, because of shattered communications, news of what had happened reached the outside world only in fragments.

On 3 September, more reports trickled through: '100,000 people reported killed, 200,000 buildings destroyed, including all Tokyo's business quarter and most government offices. A power station collapsed, killing 600. Tokyo arsenal exploded. Water system completely destroyed. Food warehouses burned to the ground. Fires still raging.'

On 4 September: 'Casualties mounting, possibly 150,000 killed. Railway station in ruins; Japan's longest tunnel at Sasako caved in, suffocating a trainload of passengers. Sumida River burst its banks, drowning hundreds. All bridges down. Almost all schools, hospitals, factories wrecked. Summer resorts on Sagami Bay (20 miles south-west of Tokyo) obliterated.'

On 5 September: 'Many passenger and goods trains derailed with heavy loss of life. Tidal waves, 40 feet high, swamped Sagami Bay, causing massive destruction, then receded, baring the ocean floor. Oil-storage tanks at Yokohama exploded. 40,000 people burned to death by fire cyclone in Tokyo park. 1,600 crushed, then burned in subsequent fire when Fuji cotton mill collapsed. American hospital thrown bodily with all its inmates from cliffs above Yokohama. Count Yamamoto, recently appointed Prime Minister, was attempting to form a cabinet at Tokyo Naval Club when the floor gave way, killing 20 of his colleagues. Estimated casualties: 500,000 homeless of whom many injured. Total dead, in population of 3,000,000, unknown. 1,500 prisoners released from the Ichigaya prison, Tokyo, when the building was threatened with collapse and more have broken out from other prisons. There is now widespread robbery with violence, looting of abandoned premises, rape and motiveless murder. This has been blamed, apparently unjustly, on several thousand Korean immigrants living in the city and some hundreds have been lynched. Martial law has been declared.'

By 6 September, the London *Times* correspondent reported that Yokohama had been 'wiped off the map'. In Tokyo there were now one and a half million homeless. 'The difficulty of telling such a vast story is to know where to begin.'

The horror had begun at 10 minutes before noon on the hot, sunlit morning of Saturday when the first earthquake shock, more powerful than any felt in 70 years, struck Tokyo and the port of Yokohama, eight miles to the south-west of the outer fringe of the city on the shore of Tokyo Bay.

The islands of Japan, lying within the south-east Asian seismic belt and perched on the edge of the great Pacific trench known as the Tuscarora Deep, suffered thousands of shocks every year and building methods had been adapted accordingly. In Tokyo in 1923 there were some western-style ferro-concrete buildings linked by broad roads near the centre, but the rest of the city was still one gigantic village with narrow twisting paths running between small, one-storey homes clustered closely together and made in a traditional style of lightweight timber, paper and thatch. The beams in these houses were not nailed but dove-tailed together so that when earth-tremors became heavy the inhabitants could simply dismantle the structure.

But in 1923 disaster was beyond control. In Tokyo, the first shock, followed by two others equally massive, destroyed even newer buildings and left the terrain like a corrugated roof with the raised parts eight or nine feet above the normal level. Huge chasms opened in the streets swallowing up people, even tram-cars, then closing on them like a giant mouth. Telephone wires and overhead electric cables were snapped like string, people tripping over them in their panic being electrocuted; an entire tram-load died in this way, struck rigid, according to an eye-witness, as they had been in their last moment of life. 'We saw them sitting in their seats, all in natural attitudes. One woman's hand was held out with a coin as though she had been on the point of paying her fare.'

China rocked by earthquakes

An estimated 1,400,000 people died in 1976 when earthquakes shattered one of China's most densely-populated regions. The first shock, at 3.42 a.m. on 28 July, was measured at 8.2 on the Richter scale, equal to 10,000 Hiroshima atom bombs. The shock waves were felt 3,500 miles away in Alaska. A second major quake 15 hours later was followed by 125 tremors over the next three months. The industrial city of Tangshan was totally destroyed, with 655,000 dead and 780,000 injured. Two-thirds of the buildings in Tientsin were either demolished or too dangerous to re-occupy. In Peking, many buildings were damaged, and up to 100 people died. Four hundred years earlier, China's Shensi province suffered the world's record losses from a single 'quake. A total of 830,000 people perished in a two-hour shock on 23 January 1556.

TOKYO EARTHQUAKE

Above: huge craters appeared as a
result of the earthquake
Left: The flimsy structure of the
buildings meant that homes were
completely flattened

The earthquake was not the deadliest killer. Fire, caused largely by exploding gas-mains, destroyed thousands more. Driven by a strong wind the flames were soon roaring through the city. Hordes of terrified people tried to escape into the large grounds surrounding the Imperial Palace, even into canals where they stood for hours, only to be found later dead, their heads charred beyond recognition and the rest of their bodies intact. One woman was lucky: she stood neck-high in water with a baby on her head for a whole day, and both survived. Elsewhere some young girls were found cowering inside a large drain-pipe. Others had thought themselves safe in Tokyo's many parks but freak conditions produced whirling funnels of flame which swept across great distances to snatch hundreds of victims high in the air and fling them incinerated to earth again.

For the first 36 hours, people could do no more than try to survive. Large numbers of troops for clearance work, military engineers and relief supplies were on the way, but help from beyond Japan took time to organize. Meanwhile the fires could not be stopped, even by blowing up buildings in their path, and on the Saturday night, beneath a sky that itself seemed on fire in a dome of scarlet and orange above the stricken city, pathetic groups huddled wherever they could find space to breathe, clutching the few belongings they had managed to salvage. Some wandered about near where their homes had been with the names of missing children, relatives and friends scrawled on bits of paper which they held out to strangers or hung from their necks, because their throats were too parched to be able to speak. On the following night, Sunday, when the fires were dying for lack of fuel, people were seen still searching, groping about with little paper lanterns on poles, their mouths covered against clouds of choking white dust that the wind was whipping across smouldering ruins.

In Yokohama the scene was equally horrifying. Yet the purely physical destruction was not as tragic as in Tokyo which, under its former name of Edo, had been inhabited for 4,000 years and contained many cultural treasures. Seventeen libraries were destroyed in the fire, including that of the Imperial Palace, as well as 151 Shinto shrines, 633 Buddhist temples and

---

Horror in Chile

Four thousand people died when earthquakes hit southern Chile on 21 May 1960, and partly demolished the town of Concepción for the fifth time in its history. Tidal waves caused by the seismic upheaval also drowned 180 people and caused millions of pounds worth of damage in Japan, 10,000 miles away.

TOKYO EARTHQUAKE

many beautiful gardens brought to perfection by that particular Japanese talent for creating a botanical paradise.

Yokohama, a modern, struggling port with hardly anything old or picturesque about it, but economically most important, was also struck by the earthquake and fire which occurred almost simultaneously. The first great shock which sent the American hospital and many luxurious homes toppling from The Bluff also buckled the quays into snake-like convolutions, wrecked a long pier stretching out into the Bay, destroyed the customs house at its head, tore chasms in the streets, shattered bridges, demolished the two big hotels burying 180 guests, and ripped open the oil tanks.

As the second and third shocks quickly followed, crowds of terrified people stampeded to the shore expecting to find safety in small boats, only to see a wall of blazing oil spreading inexorably towards them across the water. Many were burned, others rowed frantically towards the *Empress of Australia*, at that moment being drawn by tugs out of the Bay, and ultimately 12,000 were picked up by the liner. 21,000 died in Yokohama that day.

Final estimates of the total dead in both cities were around 150,000, and of the severely injured, 100,000. Apart from larger buildings, some of which

Soldiers serving rations to starving survivors

Earthquake in Rumania
**More than 1,500 people died when an earthquake hit the
Transylvania region of Rumania, north of Bucharest, on 4 March
1977. But one 19-year-old boy was rescued alive in Bucharest after
being entombed by rubble for ten days.**

had stood up well, 700,000 small homes had been destroyed. No one even
tried to assess the financial and economic loss. The rescue services,
principally the army, and the survivors themselves fought back strongly. At
first, there was only a handful of rice for each person each day, and one
correspondent noted that a man he knew to have been 'worth millions' was
grateful to get even that. But supplies from outlying districts built up
quickly and until the telephone system was restored the army ran a carrier-
pigeon service with other cities to make known the local needs. Thousands
of the homeless were evacuated; tents were provided for the remainder.
Within days some water mains had been repaired and in the following
weeks, helped by a government scheme for compensation, many small
businessmen were back, setting up shop again.

Massive aid came from many countries, including Britain and U.S.A., in
money, emergency supplies and medical teams, and within seven years
Tokyo and Yokohama had been completely rebuilt. By 1930 they were new
cities with barely a scar.

Today, having risen once more phoenix-like from their ashes, the capital
city and its port are only part of a continuous urban-industrial belt
containing the largest concentration of population in Japan. Experts say that
even reasonable safety from earthquakes has not yet been achieved – and
perhaps it never will be.

The R101 (1930) and the Hindenburg (1937)

T he airship industry is probably the only industry to die in modern times because of disasters, although it experienced only two, the *R101* and the *Hindenberg*, which had a combined death-toll of less than 100. There have been much worse disasters, on land, at sea and in the air, but none has brought to such an abrupt halt the industry from which it evolved. Perhaps the seeds of disaster lay not in its flying machines, but in the industry itself, with its vulnerable technology resting upon politics.

It was not a young industry: the rigid airship evolved from the non-rigid blimp, and that in turn came from the ordinary balloon. Manned balloons were used by the French more than 200 years ago, and in wartime had obvious reconnaissance functions, but as they were largely at the mercy of the wind it became obvious that an elongated envelope propelled by an engine was essential if such dirigibles were to prove tactically useful.

The first truly successful airship, designed by Frenchman H. Giffard, was steam-powered and could offer a speed of 5 mph in still air. A more practical electrically-powered machine named *La France* took to the air in 1884. From then on designs improved until, in the period 1910 to World War I, the German Zeppelin pioneered air travel by safely carrying some tens of thousands of passengers over a distance of several million miles.

Although progress was made mainly by Germany and France, Britain had produced a few non-rigid airships (the first rigid machine, *The Mayflower*, crashed on its maiden flight). World War I demonstrated the success of the Zeppelin in air raids, but also its weaknesses (in particular the use of hydrogen as a lifting gas as the U.S.A. would not export non-inflammable helium), but it was from a forced-down Zeppelin in 1916 that Britain, copying the basic design, started serious work on its own rigid airships. Meanwhile the much smaller blimp had become fashionable as an observation post, especially for submarine detection. By the end of the war the airship industry had a rather healthy look about it.

By 1919 Britain had built two rigid airships – the *R33* and the *R34*. Defeated Germany was prevented from making any more Zeppelins until 1926, but had nevertheless been studying some of the more sophisticated problems involved.

Then came the two disasters – seven years apart – that virtually put a stop to airship manufacture in every country in the world. In 1930 came the destruction of Britain's *R101* (47 dead) followed, in 1937, by the more dramatically publicized *Hindenberg* disaster (36 dead). Germany kept its *Graf Zeppelin* in passenger service for another year, but World War II was imminent and it was already obvious that the battlefield of the air would in future be dominated by the much faster and more manoeuverable heavier-than-air machines, and that bombers, as they were made bigger and adapted for troop transport, would form the nucleus of civil aviation to come.

Although the use of airships as a slow-speed form of transportation for

The Wreckage of the R101

THE R101 AND THE HINDENBERG

Diagram of the R101

heavy freight today has its protagonists, most people regard the 'gasbag' era as dead. The process of dying began with the *R101* and the subsequent breaking-up for scrap of the better-designed *R100*.

In 1924 the British Government decided to stop toying with airships and moved seriously into the industry with the construction of the *R100* and the *R101*. The *R100* would be built by the Airship Guarantee Company, a subsidiary of Vickers at Howden in Yorkshire, while the *R101* was to be manufactured by the Air Ministry itself, at Cardington in Bedfordshire. The *R100*'s builders were short of cash but long on expertise, being able to call on Dr Barnes Wallis of subsequent 'Dam-buster' fame, and many other top-ranking scientists and engineers including Nevile Shute (*No Highway*) Norway, whose first two names became a household word.

The Ministry, however, suffered from lack of designing talent, as many of its experienced men had been killed in the war. It also suffered from over-exposure in the press as, with taxpayers' money involved, every stage in the work at Cardington had to be publicized. Thus, errors which the Airship Guarantee Company was able to rectify in silence had to be retained – for example, the too-heavy British diesel engines which the A.G.C. quietly swopped for lighter, petrol-driven power units.

Troubles and arguments, both technical and political, ended with the *R101* slower by 10 mph at 71 mph and, at 25 tons, with only half the disposable lift of her sister ship. The airship was flown to the Hendon Air Display in the summer of 1930 to let the public admire her, but only experts could have known she was losing gas and that she would only be able to return to Cardington by throwing out huge amounts of ballast. It was there that drastic and, in the event, foolish action was prescribed: instead of taking steps to reduce weight it was decided to increase it by cutting the airship in half, inserting a new metal bay (thus adding to her length) and putting in more bags of hydrogen for lift.

A photograph of the R101, swinging from the mooring-mast at Cardington

While all this was going on, the privately built *R100* made a very successful flight to Canada. Air Minister Lord Thompson, perhaps somewhat put out, decreed brusquely that *R101* would leave for India via Egypt on 4 October, with himself on board. By then the airship would be 'safe as a house, save for the millionth chance' – and anyway, he had to get back on time for a meeting. This was all very impressive, though it is not known to what extent Thomson's enthusiasm was generally shared.

The largely untested *R101* left its Cardington mast on the ordained date with 54 people aboard, of whom only six were passengers. In these days of plastic synthetics it is difficult to realize that the dural frame contained 17 hydrogen-filled gasbags made from the membrane of bullocks' intestines, held in position by hundreds of wires. New valves were fitted to control the gas, but they tended to 'over-react' causing them to release gas at an unexpected air turbulence, thus releasing gas prematurely. This was one of many control problems.

Despite efforts to save overall weight, no limit was placed on personal luggage; Lord Thompson's private effects weighed as much as 24 people. The airship's fittings included silver cutlery, potted palms and 600 feet of heavy Axminster carpeting. Supplies of food and drink were lavish, as there was to be an aerial state banquet over Ismailia, with Egyptian notables and other distinguished figures as guests. Because of the inconvenience of refuelling during a banquet (no smoking, etc.) the ship was carrying nine more tons of diesel oil than she needed to reach her destination.

Small wonder that the *R101* shuddered painfully into the sky that evening. A resident of Hitchin later told the *Daily Express* that she had run out of her house to find everything lit by 'a ghastly red and green light . . . there was the *R101* heading straight for the house . . . she cleared the trees of our drive and the house by the smallest margin . . . as the green and red tail-lights moved away up the drive horror descended on us all.'

THE R101 AND THE HINDENBERG

A few hours later Le Bourget airport in France confirmed that the airship was one kilometre north of Beauvais. After 2.07 a.m. the *R101* stopped replying to wireless messages, and by 2.08 horrified villagers had been woken by the noise and then the inferno. Le Bourget's operator tapped out the words, '*G-FAAW a pris feu*'.

G-FAAW – *R101* – had indeed caught fire, as a result of not clearing a low hill at Beauvais. It was all over in minutes. Unlike the more fortunate *Hindenburg*, there was no chance for passengers and most of the crew, for they were sleeping. Seven crew members survived.

No one knows for certain why the *R101* hit the ground at Beauvais. Perhaps she broke up under aerodynamic stress, perhaps a gas bag punctured, perhaps she simply lacked sufficient lift. Whatever the cause, it ended Britain's contribution to the development of the airship. *R100* was immediately grounded, then broken up for scrap.

That was almost the death of the airship industry as a whole, but not quite. The Germans continued, and by 1936 had completed the *Hindenberg* to join its sister ship *Graf Zeppelin*. With a length of rather more than 800 feet, she was the biggest airship ever built. Power came from four mighty Daimler diesel engines driving propellers in separate gondolas under the great gas-lifted hull. As with all airships, the gas was contained in a quantity of separate bags, or cells. Today, those would be made completely gas-tight, but in 1937 a slow seepage was expected and allowed for.

This brought with it the danger of fire, but designers had perfected the interior passenger quarters, with their 25 two-berth cabins, spacious dining-room, saloon and reading-room, so that there was almost no risk of hydrogen entering. Smoking was confined to one absolutely safe room, with double-doors and an ingenious method of keeping its air pressure higher than elsewhere, so that no gas could possibly enter. Passengers could smoke freely here, though the cigarette-lighters were chained to tables to prevent the absent-minded taking them to their bedrooms.

Plane explodes

An airliner exploded 9,000 feet over the Peruvian jungle on 24 December 1971, causing the deaths of 91 passengers and crew. There was only one survivor. Seventeen-year-old Juliane Keopcke was trapped in a section of the plane which, as it fell to earth, was caught in the strong updraught of a tropical storm. Her landing being cushioned, she escaped death and survived ten days before being discovered by natives.

Air crash above San Diego

One hundred and fifty people died when a Pacific South-West Airlines Boeing 727 approaching Lindbergh Field collided with a light Cessna 172 plane 3,000 feet above San Diego, California, on 25 September 1978. Fifteen homes were set ablaze by falling wreckage.

Elsewhere, in this ingenious, luxurious ship, was a baby grand piano, made of aluminium. On either side were promenade decks from which passengers could look out and down through big sloping windows.

The *Hindenberg* made a number of flights to the United States and to Brazil during 1936–37, and May 1937 brought yet another scheduled departure from Frankfurt to the American terminus at Lakehurst. Nothing could have been more routine; no German passenger airship or Zeppelin had yet crashed. From those first flights in 1910, many thousands of people had been carried safely to their destinations.

Slowly she rose into Frankfurt's sky on the evening of 3 May. Her passenger accommodation was half empty (though it was almost fully booked for the return trip) and the 36 on board, with a standard crew, totalled 97. Estimated time of arrival at Lakehurst was 8 a.m. on the 6th, but very soon Captain Max Pruss realized that strong headwinds were going to upset the schedule.

It was already 15.30 on the 6th when *Hindenberg* passed over New York's Empire State Building – a regular practice, to advertise Germany and her great airship to the people below, and give passengers an exciting, unfamiliar, look at the city. However, what interest there might have been in the arrival of another airship flight was diminished, rather than heightened, by its lateness. Apart from passengers' friends and relatives, few people were heading for Lakehurst. Hardly any of the press were turning out; one radio company had sent a commentator, Herb Morrison, with a portable recorder.

Bad weather made Pruss delay his arrival still further, and it was not until 7.00 p.m. that he began his approach to the Lakehurst mooring-mast.

The first lines were dropped to the ground crew at 7.25 p.m. A slightly bored Herb Morrison began his commentary, unaware that it would become one of the most moving records of human anguish.

There was a flame, and Morrison's voice, abruptly kindling with it to hysteria, sobbed, 'It's broken into flames, it's flashing, flashing, flashing terribly, it's bursting into flames!'

Those inside were the last to know, and to this day no one can be sure what

The *Hindenburg* burning fiercely on the landing field at Lakehurst

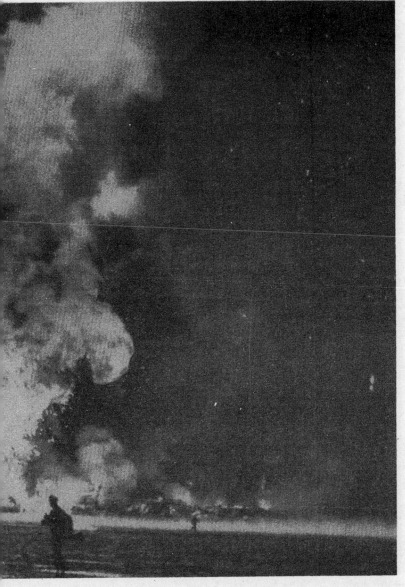

THE R101 AND THE HINDENBERG

The *Hindenberg* passing over New York City

caused that flame. Miraculously, with seven million cubic feet of incandescent hydrogen about them, only 36 died out of *Hindenburg*'s airborne total of 97. Much credit for this must go to officers and men at Lakehurst, who risked death to lead shocked, hurt, passengers and crew out of the holocaust.

So ended the day of the passenger airship. The rest of the world, including Britain, which had been watching the Germans with interest, gave up hope that these monsters of the sky would ever be safe and practical. There were undoubtedly other unspoken considerations, for no industry could die with such a small casualty list. The Germans withdrew the perfectly safe *Graf Zeppelin* in 1938, and in retrospect the reason is obvious. Zeppelins were not war machines. Balloons and blimps continued, however, while the real hardware of fighters and bombers took over.

There remains the possible return of the airship for freight transportation. Independent of land or sea it can travel 'as the crow flies', which offers advantages. In the long term, the issue will be decided by sheer economics, for a freight airship must make a profit if it is to survive – or even become a reality.

The Morro Castle (1934)

The *Morro Castle* was a vessel of 11,520 tons, pride of the Ward Line of America, dignified and stately, beautifully furnished and equipped, and only four years old. Although originally designed as a 'ferry' running between New York and Havana, she had become a popular cruising liner for those seeking sun, sea and relaxation and also an escape from the rigours of prohibition of the time. For no illicit speak-easy 'bathtub' liquor was drunk on board *her*. Everything – spirits, wines and liqueurs – was imported and was the real thing. Consequently the trip to Havana and back was, as many regulars agreed, 'one helluva cruise.'

The final night of each voyage was inevitably the wildest and noisiest of them all with everyone making the most of the last night of riotous freedom before arriving in New York at eight o'clock on the following morning.

Even the repeal of prohibition in the previous year made no difference – the last night in the *Morro Castle* was, by tradition, an abandoned, uninhibited affair and this particular night of Friday 7 September 1934 was no exception. Many of the passengers had been having last-minute parties in their cabins and were arriving in the warm, perfumed and rich-food-scented atmosphere of the main dining-room. Only at the captain's table where a number of the privileged had assembled was there a slight note of discord. The guests were there, but where was their host, Captain Robert Willmott? While they waited, undecided whether to start without him, a page-boy arrived with the captain's apologies – he could not attend for the moment. Actually the popular, English-born captain was already dead from a heart attack and had been found a little earlier by his second-in-command, Chief Officer William Warms, lying slumped, half-dressed, over his bath.

The inevitable rumours began to spread around the room until an officer announced what had happened and that Warms had taken over command of the ship. The sad news effectively ended the evening's festivities. The orchestra left the stand, lights were dimmed and the public rooms slowly emptied, although parties still continued in the cabins. It was said later that several girls had to be carried back, insensible, to their own cabins and that some members of the crew were fired for being drunk.

Up on the bridge, Warms stared into the night, conscious of the responsibility of this, his first command. A strong north-easter was building up, rain was lashing across the decks and vivid lightning was illuminating the dark, churning waves. At 2.00 a.m. the ship altered course for the Ambrose Light and New York harbour and Warms relaxed; another six hours would see the ship at Pier 13 and the present ordeal over.

Then with terrifying suddenness, a report reached the bridge from a night watchman who had seen smoke drifting from a ventilator. An officer sent to investigate returned white-faced and shaken. A fierce fire was already raging in the ship's library and a steward, opening a locker, had staggered back as a great gout of flame leaped from its interior. He had then run to one of the levers which controlled the ship's elaborate fire-control system and pulled hard. Nothing happened.

From that moment the liner was doomed.

Even as the alarm was being raised, a great mushroom of smoke and flame was rising high above the ship's superstructure, sparks and cinders raining down upon her decks. For the most part the ship's crew was unable to cope with the situation. A good number were stewards – ship-borne waiters – many of whom used the liner as an easy way of life, some even for a little lucrative smuggling on the side, and their first thought was for themselves. It turned out later that in the first six lifeboats, with a total capacity of more than 400, which pulled into Spring Lake, New Jersey, there were only 85 survivors, of whom 80 were members of the crew. Among them was the ship's chief engineer, Eben Abbott, whose immediate responsibility should have been to see that the hoses had ample power to operate. Instead, he was away in the very first boat.

For those experienced officers and seamen who remained, the subsequent hours became an unbelievable nightmare. Panic had spread amongst the passengers who refused, for the most part, to obey orders and make for the boats. A crew member said later, 'They wouldn't leave. We pleaded with them. We tried to herd them together. Many tried to fight their way past us and get down the ladder to the lower deck. At last we were forced to leave without them, as sparks and cinders were burning the ropes . . . I told the passengers plainly that they must run the risk of getting singed in going to the boats. They did not seem to understand. We got the boats away in the nick of time, or we should all have been burned.'

But as they rowed away in the near-empty lifeboats they left the confused and panic-stricken passengers to fend for themselves. The scenes were indescribable in their horror. Men, women and children milled about the deck in a bizarre variety of clothing. Some were in pyjamas and nightgowns, others, who a little while before had been enjoying some private party, were in evening attire, the women in elegant gowns and with jewels that sparkled in the glow of the fire. They began to huddle together as the flames drew closer and then, as the pitch between the deck planking began to bubble with

THE MORRO CASTLE

The Doomed *Morro Castle*, beached and on fire at Asbury Port, New Jersey

the heat, began to perform a grotesque *danse macabre* before finally plunging over the side with cries of utter despair.

Soon the flame-lit, heaving water around the liner seemed filled with passengers, mixed in utter confusion, clinging to wreckage or to the few rafts that had been launched. On one occasion a lifeboat, manned by only eight of the crew, passed through a group of men and women who shouted for help and clutched desperately at the gunwales, but the boat moved relentlessly on to disappear into the darkness. Of the 318 passengers, 90 were to die; of the 231 crew, 44.

George Rogers, the chief radio operator, was seated at his instrument, desperately awaiting the return of his first assistant, George Alagna, whom he had sent to the bridge for permission to start transmitting an SOS. As he sat, a wet towel over his face, he watched as paint began to peel off the walls and as a curtain caught fire and dropped down, setting fire to a settee. Soon he could hardly breathe. Finally, after Alagna had returned with a negative and had been sent back again, he tapped out the CQ (Stand by) then continued his agonizing wait. At last Alagna staggered back into the radio cabin and said, 'Okay chief, start sending.'

This was half-an-hour after the fire had first been reported. Precious time had been lost.

Rogers began to tap out his distress call: SOS. SOS. KGOV. TWENTY

MILES SOUTH OF SCOTLAND LIGHT. Halfway through a repeat of this message, an explosion rocked the cabin as the batteries blew out, filling the room with fumes of sulphuric acid. Coughing and spluttering, he managed to turn on his auxiliary generator and then tapped out: SOS TWENTY MILES SOUTH OF SCOTLAND LIGHT. CANNOT WORK MUCH LONGER. FIRE DIRECTLY UNDER RADIO. NEED ASSISTANCE IMMEDIATELY.

Another explosion effectively ended all further transmission but the message had been received by several ships in the vicinity and dawn revealed the great bulk of the *Monarch of Bermuda*, together with the *City of Savannah*, *Andrea F. Luckenbach* and others, all answering the call. The *Monarch of Bermuda* was the nearest vessel and her captain, Albert Francis 'saw a lot of men on the poop deck of the *Morro Castle* hanging over the side and yelling for assistance.' He and others on his ship also saw an incredible sight. Many of the *Morro Castle*'s passengers, trapped in their cabins, had tried to escape by squeezing through the portholes. These were far too small, however, and most of the desperate people had become helplessly stuck, the expressions on their faces revealing the agony of being burnt alive. As a passenger on the *Monarch of Bermuda* said: 'The grimaces made by the people in agony at the portholes was something that I shall never forget. On the deck we saw a young fellow with his wife. She fainted in his arms, and a huge tongue of flame popped out from the wall and sucked them in. We saw a man in pyjamas go up like a torch . . .'

By noon the only signs of life aboard the fiercely burning liner was in her bows where Warms and a few of his men were now stationed. A coastguard cutter, the *Tampa*, nosed as near as it dared and offered to take them off, but Warms refused – his ship was still afloat, he said. This offer was repeated several times but each time Warms replied, 'Not until the *Morro Castle* is in tow.'

The ship was held by an anchor which had been dropped to stop her colliding with rescue ships and this had to be weighed before the ship could be towed away, but there was no power, no winches. Two of Warm's men, however, had small hacksaws in their pockets, and for the next five hours they laboriously sawed through the three-inch anchor-cable, finally freeing the vessel. A hawser was then passed across but snapped as the storm increased.

One by one, the 14 crewmen, including a 14-year-old bell-boy who had elected to stay with them, were finally taken off. At last Warms also agreed to leave his ship and board the *Tampa*, but only after the commander had threatened to use force. Another hawser was passed and the tow began. At first all went well, the cutter towing ahead and a pilot boat acting as a jury rudder astern, but when both ropes parted the liner was abandoned to slowly drift shorewards, still burning furiously, with her paint peeling off in swathes from her once glossy sides, listing at an angle of 30 degrees. Narrowly missing a pier, she came to rest near the broadwalk at Asbury Park, between New York and Atlantic City, a popular convention and 'fun' town on the Atlantic seaboard.

News of the disaster had already been heard on the radio and by first light a dense crowd of sightseers had assembled to stare seawards as the flame and smoke-blackened liner drifted towards the shore. By noon, owners of ice-cream stalls, hot-dog and frozen-custard stands were eagerly coaxing every cent from this out-of-season show; families stood watching, while bodies were carried up the beach as they were washed ashore. Hawkers also moved amongst the steadily increasing crowds selling pieces of 'genuine' wreckage at a dollar a time.

By early afternoon the crowd had increased to a quarter of a million people and squads of regular soldiers, armed with rifles, were rushed to the scene to drive the mob like sheep before them and establish safety zones around the place where the ship lay beached. Scores of reporters also arrived and the stories they gathered were extremely harrowing.

An inquiry was soon opened before a Federal Grand Jury and proved to be a particularly outspoken one. Warms faced a number of charges, including failure to exercize discipline and control; to arouse the passengers or provide them with lifebelts; to organize the crew to escort the passengers to the boats; to fight the fire; and failure to send out the SOS promptly. He also came in for special criticism when it was disclosed that the liner had been allowed to steam at full speed into a steady head wind which helped fan the flames. Warms, Chief Engineer Abbott and Henry E. Cabaud, executive vice-president of the Ward Line, were arrested, found guilty and sentenced to imprisonment. This sentence, however, was set aside on appeal. The Line itself was fined $10,000 and also had to settle claims amounting to nearly a million dollars.

The inquiry did not establish the cause of the fire. Most experts agreed that a carelessly dropped cigarette had been responsible; others believed that the funnel passing close behind the library walls had overheated them. The loss of life was more simply explained. It was due to naked, uncontrollable panic. On the part of the passengers this was understandable: thrust suddenly into a situation where a horrible death threatened from red fire or black water, their loss of control was excusable.

For Warms, an experienced seaman, there was no such excuse. Faced with sudden responsibility involving his first command and the lives of his passengers and crew, he also cracked, but in a less obvious way. Alagna said

Acting Commander, R. W. Hodge brings the body of a young boy to shore

at the trial that Warms was 'behaving like a madman'. When the crisis came, he was unable to cope.

That was not the end of the story. The 'hero', Rogers, for a time earned his living recounting the events of that fateful night in vaudeville theatres throughout the U.S.A., but was later convicted of attempted murder and died in gaol. His assistant, Alagna, whose evidence against Warms helped convict that unfortunate officer, later tried to commit suicide.

Not long afterwards the once majestic vessel was towed to Baltimore to be scrapped. She had originally cost five million dollars; she was sold for less than $34,000. Her name passed into history as the principal in one of the ghastliest sea tragedies of all time.

Naples Black Market Express (1944)

World War II provided the most bizarre railway catastrophe of all time. Train No. 8017, which ran between Naples and Lucania every Thursday night, was known as the Black Market Express. It carried 520 passengers, most of them the professional black marketeers of Naples who made this regular journey to fill their bags with meats, grains, vegetables, oils, tobacco and sweets for Naples, then (in March 1944) occupied by the Allied Forces.

Although *la borsa nera* (the black market) was prohibited, the Allied Military Government and the Italian officials realized that if these black marketeers did not use Train 8017 to bring in illegal supplies, there would be hardly enough food available for the million inhabitants of Naples.

On the night of 2 March 1944, the train pulled out of Naples with 521 passengers and six railway workers: the 8017 had 42 box-cars (empty), two steam-engines, four coaches and one caboose. On all its previous trips two engines had been used, as the total weight of the train had never exceeded 500 tons but, on this fateful journey, medical students from Bari were returning from a hospital field exercise. Total weight touched 511 tons – 11 tons over the maximum for a two-engine pull.

The 8017 might have got away with the overloading, but some parts of the Naples-Lucania line had stretches of ice-coated upgrade rails. If it had not attempted to hit top speed on these stretches the chances were that the slippery tracks would have proved impassable.

After it pulled out of Balvano-Ricigliano station on the Apennine Mountain chain, the station-master said goodnight to his staff and left some instructions with his assistant, Giuseppe Salonia, for his spell of duty. These done, Salonia curled up with his newspaper for the next hour or so. Just before the next train was scheduled to enter Balvano, he remembered that he had not received any ticker-tape message about the 8017's arrival at Bella-Muro, its next stop nearly four miles further on, thus telling Salonia that the single track would be all clear for use.

Instead, Salonia was told by the Bella-Muro station that the 8017 was running nearly two hours late. He replied that he would hold the 8025 at Balvano and would check the single track himself with a free locomotive. At 2.40 a.m. the 8025 rumbled into the station. Salonia ordered two trackmen,

Caponegro and Biondi, to detach the engine from the train so that he could inspect the track leading to Bella-Muro.

The big mystery was the fate of the 8017 from the time it left Balvano station. Moments before it drew out, the train's chief engineer, Gigliani, in the leading engine had ordered his fireman, Rosario Barbato, to shovel a particularly large dosage of coal into the engine's furnace – 'We'll need it for these upgradients later', he had said.

The train had no trouble making the incline within the first tunnel, and puffed through the second reasonably well. Then it emerged on to a snaky viaduct about 25 yards long which fed into a forest-girt S-curve tunnel, the Galleria delle Armi, two miles long. At this disaster-point no-one can be 100 per cent sure what happened. It has been reasoned that the man at the throttle was worried by the high reading on his furnace-pressure gauge which apparently did not correspond with the engine speed, and the train must have been slowing badly in the damp narrow tunnel with its steep incline.

When all the cars, except the caboose, had entered the underground passageway, the 8017 groaned to a standstill under the excess weight on icy rails. Meanwhile, in the caboose brakeman Michele Palo was trying to keep himself warm; the engineer had not pulled the whistle-cord to give warning that anything was amiss so Palo assumed that the train had stopped for a signal of some kind – by no means an unusual event on a railway . . .

Finally he decided to take some action. He forced open a lower window and stuck his head out, but the whole train seemed to be encased in the black hole that bored through the hillside. The brakeman drew on his gloves and swung down from his caboose to find out what was holding things up. He had gone no further than a few yards into the black hole when he realized what had happened.

At once he turned round and ran along the track towards the Balvano

---

Tragedy on the underground

Forty one people died and more than 50 were badly hurt when the 8.37 a.m. Northern Line Tube train from Drayton Park crashed through buffers at Moorgate Station, London, on 28 February 1978, and thundered into the brick wall of a dead-end tunnel. It took rescuers three days to cut their way through the compressed sandwich of twisted metal 200 feet below the City streets, and reach the body of driver Leslie Newson, 58. The 50-foot first carriage of the train was crushed to just a third of its normal length.

Crash in Chicago

Forty five passengers died in a web of tangled steel and 300 more were hurt, many seriously, when a local train which had missed its stop began reversing to the platform at Chicago rail station and was hit from behind by a speeding express. The disaster, on 30 October 1972, was the worst in the history of the American mid-west city.

---

depot two miles away downhill. He hoped to arrive in about an hour and get help for some of those aboard 8017. But his nightmare jog-trot took him much, much longer than that – most of the time he found himself forced down on hands and knees. It was 2.50 a.m. when he came within sight of Balvano – at about the same time as Salonia had boarded the engine and started it up. Palo swung his red lantern from the mouth of the Balvano tunnel and yelled: 'Up the track!' 'Up the track!' When Salonia reached Palo he had collapsed on the line, and was moaning '*Sono tutti morti!*' ('They're all dead!')

Salonia had heard no crash, saw no evidence of an accident. Could the 8017 have left the rails? Not possible, Salonia decided, or some noise would have been heard in that snow-hushed countryside. He concluded that Palo had taken leave of his senses – the man was sobbing bitterly and every now and then buried his face in Salonia's jacket. Salonia picked the distraught railwayman up in his arms and carried him to the station where he was gently coaxed to relate what he could remember.

It was now almost 4.00 a.m. Despite the hour, everyone of importance in the town of Balvano was aroused. Salonia edged the 8025 engine slowly up the track to the tunnel Galleria delle Armi. He stopped the 8025 and, in the early morning mist, he made his way on foot to the last car of the 8017 which was held in the tunnel.

There was no sign of an accident, only an eerie, unnatural silence. Salonia slid open the door of one car and entered, lighting the interior with his lantern. Passengers were seated and sprawled in postures of utter relaxation. They looked as if they were asleep, but were all dead. In every car Salonia entered, the scene was repeated: not one of the 500 showed the slightest flicker of life. The men in the cab were dead too, the engineer still at his throttle with his head rested on the side of the window-pane.

Salonia broke down, hardly able to bear the evidence of his eyes. He took a grip of himself, undid the brakes and backed the 8017 to the engine of his 8025, hitched the engine to the 8017 caboose, and towed the train of peaceful death back to Balvano. The police took over the macabre duty of carrying out the dead and laying them side by side on the station platform for future identification.

In all, 521 people died in the eeriest railway disaster of the century. The Italian State police had the task of reconstructing what must have happened inside the mountain. The 8017 could not have gone very far into the tunnel before its wheels began to slide. Chief engineer Gigliani could easily have backed the train downhill out of the tunnel and on to the viaduct. Instead he chose to press on in a bid to get over the gradient that impeded the train's forward impetus. The four crewmen in the two locomotive compartments – Gigliani and stoker Barbato in the leading engine, throttler Senatore and foreman Ronga in the second cab – set about scooping coal into the firebox. They worked like men possessed, yet the huge wheels, having lost all grip of the rails, simply spun faster and faster over the slippery track, and the train stayed on the same spot.

As the roaring fires devoured the emergency supply of soft coal, not one of the sweating crewmen realized that the fuel was producing lethal carbon-monoxide gas. The passengers – most of whom were asleep – did not worry because the train had stopped within a mountain. The carbon-monoxide took the lives of the four men in the engines, then worked its deadly way through the lungs of the conductor and 516 passengers.

Police, checking every detail, found that five passengers had not been suffocated by the gas; three were black marketeers who were brought to the station-master's office for medical treatment. Later they disappeared discreetly to avoid the questioning which would certainly have exposed their illegal activities, so they were of no help to the police in tackling the mysteries surrounding the 8017.

One survivor, an olive-oil salesman named Domenico Miele, was to prove of great value. He reported that he had stepped off the train at Balvano to stretch his legs for a few minutes. Finding the cold air too much for him, he took a scarf from his luggage, an action which was to save his life. When the train came to dead stop inside the tunnel, Miele was one of the few who had not dropped off to sleep.

When the carbon-monoxide gas reached him, it started him coughing. Miele wrapped his scarf round his mouth as a filter, got off the train and made an unsteady way out of the tunnel. He did not guess that there was killer gas about because he climbed into the next, and last, coach to find another seat, but only reached the vestibule where he fainted and remained prostrate until he was picked up by two policemen who presumed him dead and carried him off to the improvised mortuary on the Balvano station platform.

NAPLES BLACK MARKET EXPRESS

As a result of partial gas poisoning Miele's hair (so says the official police report on the tragedy) turned from a rich black colour to a soapy grey.

The other surviving passenger was a small dealer named Luigi Cozzolino, but he suffered such severe brain damage that he did not realize what had happened, not even that his wife and eight-year-old son died on that ill-fated 8017.

Because of wartime censorship only one newspaper was allowed to publish a short official notice about the 'mishap'. All lawsuits were ruled out of order because the Allied Military Government had been technically in charge of Italy's railway system and could not be held accountable in law for a 'wartime accident'.

The London Pea-Soupers (1952)

In the old days, they called them 'pea-soupers' – stifling, blanketing fogs which reduced visibility to barely a few feet and invaded the lungs with damp, polluted air. For days at a time, the smog, thick with fumes from industrial waste, would hang over London. For decades, they had been an unpleasant feature of inner-city life. Half-way through this century, they were all but a thing of the past. . . .

Then, in December, 1952 – still many years before today's strict, anti-pollution rules – the unimaginable happened. In the wake of an influenza epidemic which was sweeping the country and terrible floods which hit many coastal areas, killing more than 300 people, a dense, dark cloud began to envelop the capital. It was more than fog or smog; it was worse than any 'pea-souper'. Within a fortnight, more than 4,000 had died in the worst fog and pollution disaster the world has ever witnessed.

Swirling, chill winds failed to disperse the choking smog which brought the city to a standstill; they merely helped spread the highly concentrated sulphur dioxide fumes that pervaded the fog. Dozens of people were killed in road accidents, but the vast majority perished from lung and pollution-related diseases; victims of a nightmare which combined freak weather conditions with poison waste which for decades had been pumping from the chimneys of industrial sites and factories unchecked.

People of all ages, from infants to old-age-pensioners, became tragic statistics in a death toll which swiftly rocketed to alarming proportions. In adults, those most at risk appeared to be in the over 45 age group. The scale of the disaster is best illustrated by the fact that the combined death toll of the two previous worst fog catastrophes, in Donora and the Meuse Valley, was 84 . . . virtually one-fiftieth of the victims of London, 1952.

An analysis of the tragedy by a leading American research professor, Philip Drinker, revealed that sulphur dioxide levels in the fog were 1.3 parts per million which is much lower than levels accepted in factories at the time, but high enough to affect ordinary human beings. Throughout the city, the grim picture was the same. The old and the infirm and even those previously in good health simply died from the pungent fumes which hung in the mist-filled air.

In desperation, thousands of people stayed shut in their homes as the fog

Above: Brixton market, shrouded in
smog. Below: Piccadilly Circus at
mid-morning

Year's rainfall falls in one day

More than 150 people died and another 20,000 were made homeless when savage thunderstorms hit southern Spain on the night of Thursday, 18 October 1973. A cold front from the North Atlantic met warm Mediterranean air flows, and created massive thunderclouds, 30,000 feet high, which crashed against the Sierra Nevada range of mountains behind Spain's tourist spots. The towns of La Rabita, where a year's normal rainfall, 8 inches, fell in one hour, and Puerto Lumbreras were worst hit, but fruit and wine crops throughout the provinces of Murcia, Almeria and Granada were devastated in what the authorities called 'the worst economic disaster in south-eastern Spain for 35 years.'

continued to cast a shadow of death across the city, refusing to venture into the perilous streets where, at times, it was impossible to see inches, let alone feet, ahead. Transport services and entire industries ground to a halt in the appalling conditions and, under cover of the pungent fog blanket, thieves went on a massive crime spree, looting shops and properties of tens of thousands of pounds.

The British Government was stunned by the disaster. Already, there was growing concern about pollution and a spiralling increase in associated diseases such as silicosis, asbestosis and pneumoconiosis. But the tragedy that fell on London prompted immediate action.

Parliament immediately voted to set up an emergency Atmospheric Pollution Committee to examine the nature, causes and effects of air pollution. Given wide-ranging powers, the committee was also to examine the then almost non-existent anti-pollution controls and propose ways of tightening them to ensure that disaster on such a scale was never repeated. The findings of that committee were to lead to legislation still in force today.

One man who saw friends and neighbours die as the killer fog gripped London, told newspapers at the time: 'There were days during that first fortnight when you just couldn't see your own hand stretched out in front of you. At times, the streets were deserted, save for the villains who made rich pickings. It seemed like the entire city was one giant morgue. If you wanted to remain safe, you just stayed indoors.' 'It was a nightmare that seemed to last an eternity. To walk out was foolish – but to venture onto the roads in a car was suicidal. There were literally hundreds of accidents, some of them fatal. If you did have to go out, you could almost cut through the air with a knife. The stench of sulphur was unbelievable; every time you took a breath you were left gasping or thrown into a convulsive fit of coughing. In every street, it seemed, there was someone who died, or someone whose friends and relatives had died. Mothers were terrified to go out with their babies. Apart from those who died, the number of people who fell ill – many with severe bronchial complaints – was incalculable. It was like living in a nightmare – you couldn't go anywhere and there was nothing you could do to get rid of the problem. You just had to hope and pray that one morning you would wake up and see the sky again.'

Another fog-bound Londoner who lived through the disaster said later: 'People were dropping like flies. When it was all over I was genuinely surprised that no more than slightly over 4,000 had died. It seemed that the only business in the city which had not come to a complete halt was that of the undertaker. Every street had its share of mourners. Day and night it was just the same; you were a prisoner in your own home, helplessly trapped by the fog. If you did go out, and survived the atmosphere, you would have been in real trouble in the event of an accident. The emergency services were totally unable to cope – they just couldn't find their way to the scenes of accidents or even hope to get there in time to the ones they were informed of.'

Within three weeks, the fog had begun to lift and slowly, very slowly, London life began to return to normal as its inhabitants picked up the pieces. Tens of thousands of pounds was pilfered by looters. A trail of devastation lay strewn across the capital. And more than 4,000 people lay dead . . . victims of the killer fog.

Le Mans
(1955)

L e Mans as we know it is the scene of the world-famous classic
motor racing event, the French Grand Prix d'Endurance, a 24-hour
non-stop event which has converted this ancient town into a gallic
Brands Hatch.

The town-hall is built on the site of a former castle, and the town itself,
which lies about 100 miles south-west of Paris, is the seat of a bishopric
dating back to the third century A.D. King Henry II of England was born
here, and its cathedral houses the tomb of Berengaria of Navarre, wife of
England's Richard Coeur de Lion.

Today, Le Mans is synonymous with the best in motor-racing, and it has
its own history, of which the most dramatic episode occurred in just a few
seconds on Saturday, 11 June 1955. In that instant a Mercedes car,
momentarily out of control, rocketed off the track into a part of the crowd of
more than a quarter of a million spectators, cut a swathe through them,
bounced and then exploded in an incandescent star-burst. In less time than
it takes to relate, it killed 82 people and seriously injured more than 100
others.

Shock, frenzy, horror? Certainly, and in full numbing measure – but the
officials, with a curious *sang froid*, insisted that the race should continue,
complete with its attendant fairground carnival music and amusements,
while the police, doctors and ambulancemen gathered the seriously injured,
the dead and fragments of the dead, and took them away with speedy
efficiency to nearby hospitals and mortuaries.

This particular Le Mans Grand Prix had aroused an enormous amount of
international interest. World champion Fangio was competing, and new
cars with famous drivers were expected to establish new speed records at, as
one newspaper reported, 'a pace never seen here before'. Entrants included
Mercedes-Benz of West Germany, the Italian Ferraris and Maseratis, the
Gordinis of France, British Jaguars, Aston Martins and so on. It was the
days when Fangio, Castelotti and Mike Hawthorn were virtually household
names, even among the non-aficianados of the sport.

The weather was sunny and hot, and even though some rain was forecast a
carnival atmosphere abounded. It was a kind of Royal Ascot of the internal-
combustion engine. In the surrounding fairground and bars business
boomed as the race got under way in the late afternoon. Bunched together,
the leading cars took the bends at 150 mph, and then Fangio and Hawthorn

began to break lap records, building up to an average lap speed of 120 mph – as fast as the fastest of any previous Grand Prix. It was exciting and spellbinding for the first two hours, at which point horror struck like a thunderbolt. One of the Mercedes cars slewed from the track, bounced over the earth safety-bank, rocketed through the massed spectators and finally exploded at a cost of nearly 100 lives, and many injured. Time taken – a matter of two or three seconds.

Precisely how this came about has since been a subject of unending controversy. At the time the contest was running well. The attention of the crowd was centred on Mike Hawthorn in a new D-type Jaguar who was seriously challenging world champion Fangio in his silver Mercedes-Benz. Both had gained a lap on Pierre Levegh, the Frenchman in the Mercedes No. 3 team car. No hazard was evident – the cars were 'all systems go' and the drivers in good trim.

Then Mike Hawthorn began to brake and slow down to pull into his pit on the right so that his co-driver, Londoner Ivor Bueb, could take over. During the subsequent inquiry, and some years later in a letter to *The Times*, Hawthorn was quoted as insisting that he had given the prescribed hand signal in accordance with accepted racing practice. As he slowed and pulled over towards his pit, Levegh's Mercedes came up from behind to pass at around 180 mph. In the resulting swerve the Mercedes touched the rear of a British Austin-Healey driven by Lance Macklin.

All motion is relative. That 'touch' at 180 mph hurled the Austin-Healey into a frantic broadside skid 100 yards long, but it ended safely enough and few paid much attention. All eyes were on Levegh's Mercedes. The car skewed and ran into the six-foot-thick earth safety-bank designed to function as an exterior brake and divert the driver back on to the track. This time, however, the reverse happened. The earth bank seemed to lift the car into a somersault so that it soared rocket-like into the air, somersaulted again before falling among the spectators, bounced once more and finally exploded into white-hot component parts, like shrapnel from an anti-personnel bomb.

Those few moments brought for many the instant eternity of death, including the driver himself whose body, thrown from the disintegrating car, was found dead near the roadside.

The shock was immediate but localized, and it is quite likely that only a tiny proportion of the crowd realized that anything at all had happened. It was, perhaps, to isolate those near the scene of death and destruction – a relatively small area – that the *gendarmes* moved in to set up a human barrier that could be penetrated only by doctors, firemen and professionally qualified helpers to speed up rescue work. For the same reason, perhaps, the

The blazing wreckage of the Mercedes car, driven by Pierre Levegh. Inset: the twisted debris of bodies and cars litter the enclosure

Tanker explodes

A tanker loaded with liquid gas exploded as it was driven along the coast road near Tortosa, Spain. The burning tanker crashed through the perimeter wall of Los Alfaques campsite and flung blazing gas over a quarter-mile radius, incinerating tents, caravans and holidaymakers. The disaster, on 11 June 1978, claimed 180 lives, many of them children.

decision was made at a high level to let the show continue – race, music and amusements.

The media were quickly on the spot and the disaster was soon being reported from every angle by international journalists, radio, television and newsreel men. To call it a field-day would be a misnomer; indeed, some film and television reports were so sickening that astonished producers and film editors, despite their love of the sensational, found themselves obliged to make cuts and fades. Even the printed word had to be moderated in many newspapers.

According to one reporter, 'the engine and back axle of the Mercedes sliced like a razor through the packed spectators. Some were decapitated, and for 100 yards along the straight the scene was like a bloodstained battlefield. Wailing men and women tried frantically to find out whether their friends or relations were among the victims. Women's screams rose above the roar of the cars as they continued round the course.'

A seasoned cameraman commented: 'I've covered wars and just about every type of horror job you can think of, but the stuff I've got here in the can is so appalling that it would make people sick to see it. There are kiddies with their heads sliced off – and their hands still gripping the ice-cream cornets they'd been sucking only seconds before. There was one father, mad with grief, refusing to believe that his son was dead and trying to carry him away to safety . . .'

Bodies lay everywhere. Many died en route to hospital. Ironically, those already dead were grotesquely covered with torn-down advertisement banners. Many had been charred by the fuel-fed flames of the Mercedes, whose engine contained a high proportion of weight-saving magnesium – an element well known for its explosive inflammability. Like an incendiary bomb, it defied the firemen and simply burned itself out.

Two English doctors worked alongside their French colleagues at the death site, although they had gone to Le Mans merely to see the race. With the approach of night came rain and a new crisis. The local hospital at Le

Mans, after carrying out more than 80 transfusions, was rapidly running out of blood supplies. More was needed – much more – and urgently.

For the first time since the tragedy, the fairground music was silenced while doctors used the loudspeaker system to make urgent appeals for blood donors. There was no lack of response. Donors queued at waiting ambulances, then, having given blood, went back to watch the race which was still in progress, or to the funfair stalls which were still open for business.

Overcynical? Who can say? Perhaps it was the emotive reaction of the time, but on the other side of the coin the deliberate continuation of the race and funfair avoided possible chaos and obstruction to the essential rescue work in progress. The effect of a quarter of a million visitors trying to leave the ground at the same time can well be imagined.

The competitors themselves were obliged to drive lap after lap around the floodlit track when all of them wished to withdraw from what had become a fiasco. It was now a race in which there could be no true winner, but the sponsors were divided in their reactions. Mercedes, taking a very firm line, desperately tried to contact the firm's directors at Stuttgart for permission to pull out their cars, but the telephone lines were frantically busy and communication was subject to long delays. In the end the West German Federal Government at Bonn intervened. Although the Le Mans organizers wanted the Germans to continue, at 1.45 a.m. on the Sunday the German team manager, Alfred Neubauer, received authority to flag in his two remaining cars which were running first and third, with Britain's Mike Hawthorn lying between.

The head of Jaguar, Mr William Lyons, also debated the abandonment of the race, but circumstances were rather different; his own son had been killed while driving a Jaguar to watch the race. He said, 'I can imagine nothing further from my son's wishes,' adding, without reference to the Mercedes withdrawal, 'racing in that respect is like flying. The risks are acknowledged and respected. But how can we be other than very grieved when a tragedy of this magnitude shadows the sport?'

The 1955 Le Mans Grand Prix was won, if the word has any meaning in retrospect, by Britain's Mike Hawthorn at an average speed of just over 107 mph. He commented after the event: 'It was the one time in my career I'd have been equally glad to lose.'

Hawthorn was naturally the target for criticism, especially in France, for it was his move into the pit that had triggered the subsequent horror. In press correspondence it was alleged that he had failed to give the requisite hand signal to warn the following drivers of his intended move, and that he had misjudged the distance to his pit, overshooting it by some 80 yards. Both

LE MANS

Macklin and Fangio echoed these criticisms some years later, although Hawthorn had been exonerated in the official inquiry following the disaster. Perhaps only Hawthorn himself knew the full truth, but he was killed a few years later (1959) in an ordinary road accident.

The French Government wasted no time in taking action. First, all motor racing was banned until new safety rules had been agreed and established. Second, after due deliberation, the new proposed safety regulations were put forward for international agreement.

Three main points emerged. The first was a ban on all racing events in which both high- and low-powered cars could compete simultaneously (it had been concluded that the relatively slow speed of Lance Macklin's Austin-Healey, hit by the much faster Mercedes, had been largely responsible for the catastrophe). Secondly, it was recommended that public stands on the course should be moved further away from the track, so reducing, if not totally eliminating, hazards to spectators. Finally, the pits, where cars were fuelled and maintained, should be moved over to a special side track well away from the public stands. These changes were internationally accepted and duly put into effect.

Agadir Earthquake (1960)

To the people of Agadir and to the several thousand tourists enjoying its winter sunshine, 2 March 1960 had been just another day. Now, half an hour to midnight and with a high, bright moon looking down on the drowsy city enveloped in the warm clinging darkness of a Moroccan evening, that day was almost over.

In the big, modern hotels near the sea, the lights were going out one by one. The children, tired from a day's ceaseless activity on the magnificent beaches of golden sand and from the continuous excitement of new sights and sounds, had long been asleep. Many of their elders had followed their example, tired from another day of continual sunshine, of excursions to the four-centuries-old Casbah, and of an orgy of writing 'Having a wonderful time, wish you were here' postcards to less fortunate friends who were combating the chill of winter.

Some, of course, remained very much awake. The popular bar at the huge Saada Hotel, just off the main sea-front, still had its fringe of dedicated drinkers; the card salon of nearby Gauthier's had its nightly collection of bridge players who rarely looked up from their cards or score-sheets to gaze out across the hotel's boasted 'panoramic view of the bay'. Away from the hotel area, some of the tourists were sampling the more dubious pleasures of the mainly Muslim quarter of Talbordj lying to the north-west, where cabarets with a 'native' flavour, including the commercialized exotic dances of old Morocco, had their admiring semi-circles of European patrons. Otherwise the whole city was still.

A casual talking point had been the three earth tremors that had shaken the city during the week, but they had been so slight that they had passed almost unnoticed, although some of those at the Saada bar had wittily suggested that their duty-free drinks had more of a 'kick' than usual.

But those tremors had been a promise of more to come.

At 11.39 p.m. there came a fourth, a shock which lasted for nearly 10 whole seconds – an unusually long time – to become the worst earthquake tremor ever recorded in Morocco. The whole of the city and the surrounding countryside trembled and shook with the immeasurable power of that subterranean movement. That comparatively brief moment of time seemed an eternity to everyone in Agadir that night. To many it seemed like the end of the world. To several thousand it *was* the end of their world.

At 11.40 p.m. the moon illuminated a scene of utter, terrifying chaos. The

67

AGADIR EARTHQUAKE

Agadir, before the horrifying earthquake

great ultra-modern hotels that had been built to satisfy the demand of the
post-war tourist boom had suddenly become grotesque heaps of shapeless,
dust-covered rubble. Every street was now littered with great piles of stones,
masonry and plaster that had spilled across them, to block nearly every road
from the shoreline to Talbordj where, a few moments before, many multi-
storied blocks of flats had been silhouetted against the night sky. Now they,
too, lay in piles of utter ruin. Only one road to this quarter was still open, and
that had a huge gaping crack right across it.

As the rumbling and crashing came to an end, a ghastly screaming and
shouting arose which developed into hysterical pandemonium as the
survivors began to claw their way free of masonry and stones. Agadir had
almost ceased to exist; even the ancient Casbah was destroyed, only a few
dazed inhabitants, grey with dust and shock, groped their way from the
ruins that had been their homes to stagger, shaking and sobbing, across the
high pile of masonry that had formerly been the protecting wall to reach the
fresh air and comparative quiet of the countryside.

Helpers search the ruins for bodies

With every line of communication cut, it was some time before news of the extent of the disaster was received in the French naval and air base which was still at Agadir (although France had recognized Morocco as an independent kingdom some four years earlier), but little could be done until dawn except alert other cities throughout the country, asking for urgent aid.

Dawn revealed an almost unbelievable sight. Nearly every hotel had been flattened, while damage in the thickly-populated Talbordj quarter had been as much as 90 per cent and some 80 per cent in the 'new town' nearby. Wherever the rescue teams looked they saw ruins with parked cars now shattered and half-buried with masonry. In some hotels, walls had crumbled away to reveal beds, some still sheltering the bodies of unfortunates who had been crushed in their sleep, hanging precariously and almost obscenely from the parapets of tottering walls, while the terrible screaming and moaning of the trapped or cries for help in a variety of languages rose on all sides.

The airport had escaped damage and was turned into a clearing house for the casualties. Aircraft began to arrive to carry the injured to Marrakesh,

69

Rabat, and other cities which had escaped the effects of the earthquake, although Mogador, 100 miles to the north, had also suffered some damage from the fringes of the earthquake.

A group of sailors was put to work on what had been the imposing Saada Hotel. They struggled desperately against time, their uniforms dusty and torn, but for the most part they only uncovered the crushed bodies of tourists and hotel staff. Even so, they had some success. One group heard the voice of a child calling for its mother, apparently coming from deep below a huge mound of stones that had previously formed part of the façade of the hotel. They dug down, first with spades and picks and then, more gently, with bare hands, until they came upon the child, miraculously alive, trapped in a slight hollow beneath great stones and beams.

But that was to be one of their few successes, for out of the hotel's guest-list of more than 150, only 20 survived.

There was no electricity to light up darkened holes beneath the rubble that might shield a body and no water to dampen the flames which licked at shattered woodwork. Initially, every effort was devoted to finding and then removing the injured to safety and quickly burying the dead to avoid the risk of infection – always a danger to those living in hot climates. Three thousand men of the Moroccan army were rushed to Agadir and then sent to patrol the whole area where the earthquake had also caused much damage. In the Moorish town of Inezgane, some seven miles away, damage was estimated at 30 per cent of the buildings.

A French naval squadron including an aircraft-carrier arrived off the coast; Dutch and Spanish warships joined it; Britain sent aircraft from Gibraltar to land at Agadir's airport. Soon a fleet of some 80 aircraft was operating a shuttle service to airlift the injured. More than 2,000 people were thus evacuated.

There was a number of British tourists in Agadir's hotels, and all of those who survived had alarming stories to tell. Alan Birtles of Warwickshire, for example, recalled that he and his wife were asleep in bed when there was a frightful rushing noise and a lot of crashing and screaming. It was pitch dark, which made matters worse. He tried the bedside light but the electricity cables had been ruptured. As he and his wife lurched about the

Earthquake in Iran

More than 26,000 people died when an earthquake destroyed 40 villages in north-east Iran on 19 September 1978. In one village, Tabas, only 2,000 of the 13,000 residents survived.

Tornado destroys Navy

One of the American Navy's greatest losses during World War II was inflicted not by the Japanese, but by the weather. On the evening of 17 December 1944, destroyers, cruisers and aircraft carriers of the Third Fleet Task Force 38 were replenishing stocks of food, fuel and ammunition during a sea rendezvous with support ships when a savage tornado struck the Philippine Sea. One of the commanders said later: 'My ship was riding as though caught in some giant washing machine. We were rolling between heaving cliffs of water, caught in so strong a vice of wind and sea that our 50,000 horse-power engines were helpless.' It was nine hours before he regained control of his ship, after the fleet had bobbed like helpless shuttlecocks, unable to prevent collisions in the sledgehammer waves. A total of 790 officers and men were lost overboard, killed at their stations or went down with their ships. Eighty more were badly hurt. Three destroyers were lost, five other ships had suffered major damage, and 146 aircraft were either lost or unflyable. Admiral Chester Nimitz, commander-in-chief of the Pacific Fleet, said: 'It is the greatest loss we have taken in the Pacific without compensatory return since the first Battle of Savo.'

room they found that the earthquake had brought all the drawers tumbling from the furniture, and they soon realized that the plaster from the ceiling overhead was still falling about them. He managed to find a cigarette-lighter and by its meagre light they struggled into some clothes. Then, going to the door, they found it had jammed and they had to break it down before they could escape. 'We broke down the doors of other rooms in the corridor to help people out', he concluded.

Richard Waddington who had been staying at the Marhaba Hotel, one of the few large buildings that had not collapsed completely, stated that the most awful thing about the disaster was 'the terrible screaming and shouting from people trapped under the rubble; but you could not do anything about it.' He went on: 'I was fortunate, I suppose, because I was under only six feet of rubble and they got me out in six hours. My father was 16 feet down. It took 22 hours to free him. My mother was farther down still. She was dead when they got to her.'

At the end of that first day the authorities ordered the complete evacuation of Agadir, then sealed off the whole area except for essential services. The Crown Prince of Morocco held a Press Conference to announce that the death-roll had risen to 10,000. That figure included 4,000 dead already

AGADIR EARTHQUAKE

One of the badly damaged buildings in Agadir

found, with an estimated 6,000 still buried beneath the ruins. Some 20,000 people had escaped unhurt, he said, and the 2,000 injured had already been evacuated. Final figures were never accurately established, and other sources quoted widely differing statistics.

The rescue work went on, although by now it had developed into a search for bodies. So much quicklime had been scattered about to prevent infection that one observer said that parts of the city resembled snow-covered fields.

Yet there were miraculous survivals. On 9 March, a week after the earthquake, three Moroccans were rescued quite unscathed. A father and his 10-year-old son had been dug out alive and rescue workers began to search around the same area until, led by weak cries, they found another man. On the following day, eight more were rescued. Rescue workers listening and calling among the débris were answered by feeble cries on 11 March and during that day they dug out a man of 24, three women and a family of three Jewish children, two girls and a boy of six. The following day two more were rescued, one a 28-year-old Muslim, the other, as it happened, the father of the three children rescued the previous day. The two girls, Alice and Jacqueline Kalfon, related how they had told stories and sung to their little brother Armand during their ordeal beneath the débris of their house. All were rushed to hospital, where Armand died a few hours later.

Rescue work was also going on in the remote areas of the Atlas Mountains where nearly 600 were reported dead and more than 2,000 homeless.

Helicopters circling over the devastated areas reported that in some instances the ground had opened like giant jaws and swallowed villagers 'by the dozen'.

The earthquake had a strange effect upon the Atlantic coastline and seabed which made an extensive hydrographic survey essential. At one place where the water had been charted at 1,200 feet, soundings showed that it was now only 45 feet. This was not only inshore; for nine miles from the coastline soundings showed a depth of 1,200 feet instead of the previous 4,500 feet.

The Vaiont Dam (1963)

In the north-eastern corner of Italy, where the Italian Alps merge with those of Switzerland and Jugoslavia, there are many rivers which are the source of water and hydro-electric power for northern Italy. Across the valleys dams have been built and reservoirs created.

The Vaiont Dam formed part of a complex of five dams, which together made up the north-west-Piave hydro-electric scheme. When it was opened in 1960 it was the third highest concrete dam in the world, its wedge-shaped wall towering 873 feet above the Piave river and the valley below. In this valley, on the banks of the river, lay a number of small villages. Closest to the dam was Longarone, a village of less than 2,000 people, and a number of outlying hamlets.

The autumn of 1963 was unusually wet. Rain had loosened the rocks and earth of the mountain slopes which formed the shores of the reservoir. One of these, Mount Toc, which rises steeply to a height of 6,000 feet, had caused such apprehension that on 8 October a mayor in the district issued a warning to fishermen and others who might venture on the lake shores of the possibility of landslides causing dangerous waves.

Anybody who lives close to a dam is aware of the possibility of a fault and the disaster that could follow. The people in the district of Longarone were no exception, but they had no apprehension of danger on the night of Wednesday, 9 October 1963. At 11.00 p.m. they were all at home, either in bed or watching television. Fifteen minutes later a vast avalanche swept down the slopes of Mount Toc and thousands of tons of rocks, mud, earth and uprooted trees tumbled into the lake. The effect was that of throwing a large stone into a basin of water. Although the reservoir was by no means full it promptly overflowed, spilling over the top of the dam and pouring into the valley below.

The few survivors said later they heard that fearful sound which is so often described as the first intimation of disaster – a noise like thunder. They assumed at once that the dam had given way and, pausing only to gather up those nearest to them, they fled, but only the people whose houses lay close to the high ground at the edge of the valley had any chance. Over the lip of the dam poured a torrent of water, mud, rock and timber, creating a towering wall which swept along the valley below, swirled up the hillside and engulfed villages in a horrifying, overwhelming tide.

The natural assumption that both survivors and the authorities initially

74

One of the many victims of the collapse of the Vaiont Dam

Eight villages destroyed

For days, the 30,000 inhabitants of the Peruvian city of Huaraz
had basked in scorching sunshine, with the temperature reaching
84°F. But on Saturday, 13 December 1941, that sunshine cost 7,000
of them their lives. At 6.45 that morning, the tongue of a glacier
on snowcapped Mount Palcaraju, towering 20,575 feet above the
town, snapped off and crashed into one of the two catchment lakes
below. It was already full with ice melted over the previous days.
Tons of displaced water fell into the second, lower lake, which
breeched its natural moraine dam with a hideous explosion. Eight
villages were obliterated as a 50-foot wall of water crushed houses
like cardboard cartons. Then the flood careered through Huaraz,
disintegrating everything in its path, before plunging onwards,
carving a 135-mile path of destruction until it roared into the
Pacific at Chimbote.

---

made – that the dam had burst – was not corrected until the dawn. The night
had been chaos and pandemonium: the sun rose to reveal a macabre scene – a
vast, silent desert of rock and mud and rubble, with here and there the
remains of a building. Longarone, four-fifths destroyed, was a heap of
stones; so were the nearby hamlets of Faè and Pirago, where all the
inhabitants died. Two other hamlets, Codissago and Castellavazzo, lost half
their population; the two on the lake were wiped out, with three-quarters of
the population missing.

It took time to establish these facts, for communications were destroyed.
Telephone and telegraph lines were cut; railway lines turned and twisted in
crazy spirals of buckled steel; and roads leading into the devastated villages
were unidentifiable swamps. When the Italian Minister of Public Works
visited the scene he described it as 'a truly biblical disaster . . . like Pompeii
before the excavations began.'

With daylight came the first of the helpers, ploughing through the morass
in the valley below the dam, where the river was swollen to twice its natural
size by the waters pouring into it. Throughout the day bodies were washed
up as workers struggled to reach the stricken villages in a frantic search for
survivors. The final approaches to Longarone, now quagmires blocked with
rubble and timber and the bodies of dead cattle, became choked with
soldiers, ambulances, lorries and people desperately hoping for news of
friends or relatives.

There was little hope for those who had not managed to escape to the high
ground. The force of the great wave could be seen in the twisted pieces of

metal, the total destruction, the bodies found hurled high into trees. The problem of extricating the bodies was immense: the municipal authorities at Belluno immediately ordered 500 coffins but as the days passed it became apparent that these would not be enough. Five days later rescuers were still digging for bodies and the problems of identification grew. Many were disfigured and denuded of clothing: whole families had died and there was nobody left to identify them. Eventually many were buried, unknown, although occasionally one of the thousands of helpers would find himself facing and able to identify someone he once knew.

The gruesome task was soon well organized. Bodies were extracted, sprayed with disinfectant, put in plastic shrouds and into simple coffins away from the warm sun as quickly as possible. A helicopter service was established and bodies arrived heaped on lorries, or carried, roughly-covered, on stretchers from the helicopters. The final death-toll totalled 1,189, although possibly some were not found. But on the morning of 12 October, two children were discovered, still alive, in the cellar under the débris of their home. While there was still hope of survivors, the rescue work continued at full intensity.

An urgent inquiry was made into the safety of the dam. It was inspected and found to have suffered only some damage to the top of its retaining wall. The vast extent of the landslide could be judged from the fact that little over a third of the original reservoir remained. Instead, a new mountain filled the centre of the dam, some grass and lopsided trees still covering its surface.

Almost immediately the cause of the disaster became a political issue and

Dam collapses

Uneasy residents had tried in vain to block the building of the Teton Dam in eastern Idaho, 50 miles from Yellowstone Park. They feared the structure, taller than a 30-storey building, would be undermined by channels, caverns and fissures in the volcanic rock of the canyon walls at each side. At 11.57 a.m. on 5 June 1976, their worst fears were realized. Erosion on the north side of the dam started the structure crumbling, and the crushing weight of 275 million tons of water plunged through the cavity created, sending a 100-foot wall of water cascading towards the small towns in the flood plain. More than 2,500 homes were destroyed, 17,000 head of livestock drowned, 100,000 acres of farmland were buried by sand and gravel silt, and property damage totalled £200,000,000. More than 2,000 people were hurt, but miraculously only 11 died. Had the dam broken at night, said Governor Cecil Andrus, thousands would have been lost.

THE VAIONT DAM

Above: soldiers search the Piove
River for bodies

Left: Victims were buried
in enormous mass graves

Thames floods
The River Thames and its estuary broke its banks on 31 January 1953, flooding large areas of Kent and Essex. The death toll was 307. There was also extensive flooding of the Continental coast, particularly in Holland, raising the total of dead to more than 2,000.

the subject of exhaustive inquiries. Rock-falls and small earth movements of the mountain were known to have occurred. The crucial question was: should a dam have been built in that situation in the first place? Three years after its completion it came to light that research was still being made into the suitability of its location.

A court of inquiry was set up to consider a number of questions and to establish whether the disaster could have been avoided. It had to consider various aspects: Was the location badly chosen? Was the dam badly designed? Was the area, and in particular the hazard constituted by the mountain, monitored frequently enough? Had the local authorities taken sufficient care in the warnings they issued? A minor earth tremor had been recorded in the mountain about half an hour before the landslide occurred. It was stated that the strength of the seismic waves showed that strain had been building up inside the mountain for some time. Could the people have been warned in time of the possibility of an earth-fall?

Although the court had been involved as a result of Communist pressure upon the Government whom they accused of negligence, it soon became apparent that there were grounds for such an inquiry; when its findings were eventually published there seemed little doubt that, with more care and more exhaustive enquiries into its potential dangers, the site would never have been chosen. The nationalized Italian electricity industry, which was responsible for the hydro-electric scheme, was found to be at fault. Builders and civil engineers were also found to carry some of the blame for a

One million people dead in Pakistan
The most devastating cyclone and tidal wave ever recorded hit east Pakistan on 12 and 13 November 1970. The final death toll, announced after the country became Bangladesh in December 1971, was over one million, and more than half the 1.4 million population of four islands, Bhola, Charjabbar, Hatia and Ramagati, was wiped out.

construction unsuitable to its particular site. It was common knowledge that there had been concern over the safety of the mountain. When the dam was being built and the reservoir filled, a series of landslides and cracks had appeared in the mountain, which had had to be reinforced with concrete to a depth of several feet on either side of the dam. Instruments recorded stresses and strains on the rock face, and the reservoir was not completely filled until two years after the dam had been completed. At the time of the flood all the men working at the dam were killed, but one who had worked on the original construction claimed that the technicians were waiting for such a disaster from one day to the next.

The local authorities, said the inquiry, must have known of this situation. Why did they do no more than warn the local inhabitants of the dangers on the lake itself? Some communities living around the lake and on Mount Toc had been evacuated. Should not the inhabitants of the valley also have been evacuated? Or at least warned of the possible dangers in strong terms?

As a direct result of the inquiry, the ill-conceived Vaiont Dam was closed down. The devastated villages were rebuilt and new factories sited in the valley.

The Florence Floods (1966)

In the late autumn of 1966 exceptionally severe weather with gales and frequent cloud-bursts struck almost the whole of Europe, raging for several days from Poland across Germany to the shores of the North Sea, down the coast into Holland and across France and Switzerland. In these areas the storms led to some loss of life, considerable damage and great inconvenience. But in Italy they spawned a disaster.

Because of its physical features many parts of Italy have always been subject to heavy flooding. As distinct from Britain, for instance, where the source of most rivers is only slightly above downstream areas, in Italy they rise in many cases thousands of feet above the plains, in the Western Alps, in the Dolomites to the north-east, and in the Apennines, the central ridge which runs like a backbone down the peninsula. In times of heavy rainfall these rivers, reinforced from innumerable mountain streams, pour down at tremendous speed, bringing with them masses of rock and other débris, particularly in the Dolomites where the higher slopes are very unstable. Certain precautions can be taken, of course, dredging river beds, building up banks, but there are times when Nature mocks these efforts.

Such was the case in 1966. Winds rising sometimes to hurricane force swept through the whole length of Italy and brought with them rains of an enormous intensity. It was as though, after weeks of intermittent rain, the sky had suddenly become an ocean which was now falling in a solid mass on the land.

The deluge lasted for two days and in some places, notably the Dolomites, six months' average rainfall came down in 24 hours. This alone would have flooded the northern plains to a depth of several feet, but at least the water would have been fairly stagnant. However, a swirling, destructive tide was created by the rivers swollen yet further by snow melted by warm mountain winds, which burst their banks and roared down at terrifying speed, sweeping aside great stretches of forest that lay in their path and carrying with them an ever-increasing load of rock and débris.

In Friuli-Venezia-Giulia, the north-eastern province at the head of the Adriatic, scores of farms with all their livestock were overwhelmed by floods, avalanches, mud-slides and giant boulders, while in many villages and towns, Trento, for instance, Merano and Bressanone, the streets were submerged in mud to a depth which swallowed up cars and buses. Long sections of road surfaces were completely carried away, railway lines were

Town disappears in liquid landslide

The earth literally opened up and swallowed a town in Canada in 1971. Saint-Jean-Vianney was a prosperous, well-kept community of 1,308 people, 135 miles north of Quebec. But it was built on treacherous soil – soluble clay with pockets of sand. On the grey, rainy evening of 4 May, the saturated pockets of sand started liquifying the clay, and quickly a brown river, 60 feet deep, began to flow as the soil vanished to a depth of 100 feet. Homes and people were sucked into the liquid landslide. When the clay began to solidify again, at midnight, 31 men, women and children had vanished for ever, and 38 houses had disappeared. Survivors were resettled in near-by Arvida, and Saint-Jean-Vianney was wiped off all maps.

cut, bridges demolished and so much wreckage was deposited in river beds that their level in some places rose many feet above roads running alongside.

For a while the north-east provinces were completely cut off except by radio, and an exhausted messenger who reached Venice over mountain tracks from the Dolomites was regarded as a curiosity. He said: 'For days we have been fighting against the fury of rivers without ceasing.'

One third of Italy was stricken by floods which Interior Minister Taviani described as the worst in history. The Po valley was flooded from both ends, by the overflowing river and by salt water when raging seas broke through dykes protecting the delta. Here one third of the population had to be evacuated, including 12,000 from the island of Donzella lying between two branches of the river.

In Venice sea and sky together produced the worst floods in a thousand years, the main danger coming from the sea. The fate of the city still depended on a system of dykes more than 400 years old which linked the islands separating the Lagoon from the Adriatic. Their upkeep had been neglected, especially during World War II, and early in November exceptionally rough seas combined with gales broke through a section of dyke at the island of Pellestrina. Immediately a wall of water poured into the city, rising to a height of seven feet in some streets and five feet in St Mark's Square, including the cathedral. For 48 hours, until repairs could be carried out and the flood began to subside, life was completely paralyzed.

The London *Times* correspondent reported that Venice was like a gigantic, half-sunken boat. He should have said 'a torpedoed tanker'. Oil storage tanks used for central heating had burst spreading slicks over the flood, and it was this oil-scummed water that ruined the stocks of 4,000

A wrecked car in a Florence Piazza

Clearing up after the flood

shops, an immense amount of private property and the ground-floor contents of half the city's hotels. Fortunately there was little damage to art treasures. If the gale had continued for only a few more hours, however, the city centre with its magnificent heritage would have been destroyed. Even so, the damage caused was astronomical.

The shops could be restocked, but it would not be so easy to restore agriculture. Before the war, the fertile area of Tuscany known as the Maremma had been largely marshland infested by malaria. Much of it had been reclaimed and the malaria eradicated, and a thriving industry started based on dairy farming and the production of fruit and vegetables for export. All this was ruined by the floods which submerged four-fifths of the town of Grosetto lying at the centre of the area, 80 per cent of the livestock was destroyed and damage caused exceeded that in the entire province of Venezia.

The heaviest cultural blow was struck at Florence and this aspect of Italy's disaster above all others caught the horrified imagination of the world. Cradle of the Italian Renaissance, a major shrine of western civilization, with its palaces, magnificent Romanesque buildings, and 40 museums housing many of the world's greatest art treasures, Florence was to suffer the fate of Venice – and worse.

On 4 November, the River Arno traversing the oldest part of the city burst its banks. Normally a man running can keep pace with the fastest flowing river, but on this day the Arno in a huge ungovernable flood surged forward at 40 miles an hour (a film made on the spot shows a car being hurled down the Via Formabuoni at just this speed). For several hours the torrent poured through the city spreading ever wider, flooding buildings and rising in places, including the Cathedral Square and the famous eleventh-century Baptistry, to over 15 feet. The best that anyone could do was to save a few possessions and escape drowning. Twenty-four hours later the deluge began to abate, leaving behind a massive residue of glutinous yellow mud, and in the following days it was possible to start surveying the damage. Final estimates showed 17 people dead, 45,000 homeless (a tenth of the population), 40,000 cars wrecked as well as 18,000 shops, including the workshops of some of the goldsmiths and leather-workers for which Florence was famous.

The loss and damage were enormous. Again, oil from burst tanks, and in some places naphtha, mixed with the flood and added to its destructiveness. Many famous buildings were swamped, among them the Medici Chapel, the San Firenzi Palace, the Casa di Dante, the Capella del Pazzi at Santa Croce and the church of Santa Maria Novella. Six hundred paintings by well-known masters were under water for hours when the basement of the famous

Horrific dam-burst

The world's worst dam-burst disaster happened in Morvi, Gujarat, India, on 11 August 1979. More than 5,000 people perished when the Manchhu River dam gave way.

Uffizi Gallery was flooded. Totally destroyed at the same time were 130,000 photographic negatives of Florentine art, many of them irreplaceable.

Elsewhere in the city there were other heavy casualties: the entire State Records of Tuscany from the fourteenth century to 1860, nineteenth-century newspaper files – a loss now making a detailed history of the Risorgimento impossible, Etruscan collections in the Archaeological Museum, the musical scores of Scarlatti, the private papers of Amerigo Vespucci (the Italian explorer who gave his name to America) and the earliest painting in Western art, the 'Cruxifixion' by Cimabue (1240–1302).

Worst hit of all were the libraries. For days more than 6,000,000 volumes, a great many of them unique, lay submerged under water and murky sludge in the State Archives and the vaults of the Biblioteca Nazionale, the equivalent of the British Museum Library – a potential loss which would have had a shattering effect on every aspect of future study and research. At once, a massive international rescue operation was set in motion, with experts from all over Europe coming to advise and help. Even so, the restoration, wherever possible, of these works and the paintings was to take years. Owing to the dissolvance of glue used in bindings and size in the paper, many books when salvaged were as solid as bricks. Each volume had to be cleaned, dried, treated with chemicals to prevent fungus and the pages cautiously prised apart. Finally each volume had to be rebound.

Every job of restoration had to be done as soon as possible to avoid rapid deterioration and speed was achieved by giving crash courses to teams of students and then putting them under the supervision of a single expert. All

Sacred mountain explodes

The Indonesian island paradise of Bali was plunged into hellish nightmare in April 1964 when Gunung Agung, regarded by natives as their holiest mountain, blew its volcanic cone. More than 1,500 people died and 87,000 were made homeless by choking ash from the 10,309 feet peak.

this caught the attention of the outside world, but naturally the people involved in the 36,000 square miles of Italy that had been devastated were more interested in obtaining credit to get on their feet again. There had been damage in 800 municipalities; 22,000 farms and private homes had suffered; 50,000 animals had been lost, thousands of tractors made useless. Total damage was estimated at £575 million ($1,090 million). The death-toll in all Italy was 112.

In Florence, a fortnight after the disaster, the people were working hard to succour the homeless, start business again and clean up their beautiful city. They were not relying much on government help; they knew official red tape too well. Enthusiasm bursting through his sober prose, the London *Times* correspondent noted: 'Tuscan sturdiness has risen above the ruin of the city's delicate grace.' He noticed an interesting point: it was the 'beatniks', so criticized by their elders as useless drop-outs, who were flinging themselves into relief work with the most astonishing energy. 'Beatniks', he added, 'are better than bureaucrats.'

A year later the people were back in their homes and at work again. Museums, galleries and libraries had re-opened and it was said that: 'The golden city of the Renaissance glitters again.' But despite intensive work on the river-bed and its banks, and the organization of a flood early-warning system, anxiety must remain. Asked what would happen if it rained like *that* again, a city official replied: 'We must just hope that it won't.'

Astronauts and Cosmonauts (1967 and 1971)

It was the disaster which had to happen.

Until 27 January 1967, the safest form of transport known to man had been the space capsule. Dozens of American astronauts and Soviet cosmonauts had ridden into space in giant rockets, fuelled by an explosive mixture of liquid oxygen and hydrogen. They had spun around the earth, covering millions of miles. They had walked in space with only the thin layers of the fabric of their pressurized suits separating them from instant death. They had ridden back to earth in the fireballs of their capsules, splashing down in oceans with pinpoint accuracy.

Their space machines were seemingly infallible, a technological marvel of new metals and electronic circuitry which had come straight from a designer's drawing board.

They were pushing science through new barriers every day and they boasted their biggest fear was running the same risk as a weekend amateur skydiver, that the simple technology of a nylon parachute would fail them on the last few thousand feet of their return to earth.

No effort of technical talent or expense had been spared to make America's space exploration programme statistically safer than driving on the nation's freeways in the rush hour. There had not been a single fatality in space, although ironically three of America's astronauts had died in the past year in off-duty plane crashes.

The crew of the Apollo One spacecraft, Virgil 'Gus' Grissom, Ed White and Roger Chaffee, were highly skilled fliers and supremely confident members of the National Aeronautics and Space Administration astronaut corps. They were members of the Apollo project to place the first men safely on the moon.

All three men were requested to report for duty on Launch Pad 34 of the Kennedy Space Center near Cocoa Beach, Florida, for yet another series of tedious rehearsals inside their cramped command module. They would spend a whole day in their space suits, strapped uncomfortably lying on their backs in the capsule, repeating over and over again the routine of cockpit drill. The thrill of the thundering acceleration of lift-off was not due for another month.

For five repetitive hours they ran through the drill. Gus Grissom, a 40-year-old Air Force pilot, a Korean war ace and veteran of two previous space missions, called out the crisp responses to the ground control's requests for the information displayed on his control console computer and instrumental panel.

A ground control technician was first to notice the malfunction. His television monitor, linked to a camera inside the Apollo capsule suddenly flashed pure white and then darkened. Puzzled, he leaned over to adjust the brightness and contrast controls.

As he did so, an anguished voice screeched through the ground control loudspeakers and headphones: 'Fire . . . I smell fire . . .' There were three seconds of silence then the voice of Ed White: 'Fire in the cockpit . . .'

Tape recorders in ground control picked up seven seconds of 'clawing and pounding to open the hatch' then the voice of Roger Chaffee pleading: 'We're on fire . . . get us out of here . . .'

Then there was silence.

In just four minutes an emergency crew had sprinted from the ground level concrete blast-proof control room and reached the top of the gantry by high-speed elevator. Their hands blistering from the scorching surface of the capsule, two of them wrenched open the main hatch. It was already too late. The crew of Apollo One were dead. They had been killed in a matter of seconds, sprawled lifeless in their take-off positions, on top of a three stage empty rocket, perched motionless just 218 feet off the ground.

The world had suffered its first space exploration disaster, right here on earth.

The leading members of the rescue squad began to reel back from the hatch, blinded by smoke, choking and inhaling searing gases from the oxygen rich blast of flame which roared from the twisted hatch. Their pure white overalls blackened and charred, the emergency team were forced to retreat along the catwalk from the gantry.

In the control room at ground level the pictures on the television cameras cleared as the swirling black smoke billowed out of the moon-ship. The bodies of the three astronauts were clearly visible, killed almost instantly by the ferocity of the inferno, their heat resistant space suits smouldering. As all external power supplies to Apollo One were cut off, the launch control director Dr Kurt Debus ordered the emergency teams: 'Stay away from the capsule. There is nothing you can do for them now.'

For the next six hours the unblinking eye of the television camera and its wide angle lens impassively relayed the scene of the horror to the control room as the bodies of the astronauts remained strapped in their seats. Few of the men in the control room could bring themselves to look.

ASTRONAUTS AND COSMONAUTS

At midnight, under the cold glare of floodlights, the medical teams, many of them with tears in their eyes, gently lifted the three bodies from the gutted remains of Apollo One.

Then began the inquest to find out what had caused the fatal spark which had turned the rich, life-giving oxygen of the space capsule into a killer gas, fuelling a tiny flame into a roaring holocaust within seconds. Experts began to recall that there had been several previous warnings of the potentially fatal risks of using pure oxygen in the NASA space vehicles.

Oxygen is the gas in our atmosphere which allows us to breathe, and allows burning to take place. It makes up only about one-fifth of our air. The remaining four-fifths is mainly nitrogen, unbreathable and not capable of supporting a flame.

The Soviet space technicians who designed the cosmonaut carrying Soyuz

Virgil Grissom, Edward White and Roger Chaffee during their Apollo Project training

Cable car plummets

Forty two people died when a cable car plunged to earth at the north Italian ski resort of Cavalese on 9 March 1976.

---

space capsules, boosted into their orbit by truly awesome rocket power, preferred to use a cumbersome but safe oxygen and nitrogen gas mixture. They knew that they could save precious payload weight by using pure oxygen, but the sheer power of their rockets gave them an enormous advantage over their American rivals.

The oxygen-nitrogen mixing system was weighty but simple technology. The American space programme controllers had to concede that even their mighty Saturn rockets could not match the brute power of the Soviet boosters. They had been set a challenge by the late President John F. Kennedy after whom their space centre was named. America's prestige as the world's most technologically advanced nation had been severely dented in the early days of the 'space race' as the Soviets piled up one pioneering space achievement after another. The President's challenge had been to put a man on the moon and return him safely to earth before the decade of the Sixties ended.

To meet that deadline NASA had to squeeze every ounce of power from their rocket boosters and save every possible ounce of weight in the capsules and command modules which were to be lifted into space. So they chose an atmosphere of pure oxygen inside the Apollo capsules, dispensing with the need for heavy mixing equipment and bulky nitrogen cylinders. Soviet technology, many NASA scientists explained, could throw iron-clad monster spaceships into orbit. The Americans would close the gap in the space race with the superior sophistication of their machines.

But many worried experts in the U.S. space programme had warned of the risks of using an oxygen-rich atmosphere in space cabins. Only two years before the Apollo One disaster, NASA's chief medical adviser Dr. Randolph Lovelace had handed the Agency a grim report on 'the potential dangers of 100 per cent oxygen atmosphere'.

Dr Lovelace reported that in one incident in a space cabin being tested inside an aircraft at 33,000 feet, a tube in a television monitor had overheated, causing hot plastic to drip on to a control panel. The crew were alerted by the fumes. 'Instead of focussing attention on the hazards of fire', he claimed, 'this accident gave a false sense of security.' A second fire had broken out inside a spaceship simulator at Brooks Air Force Base in Texas.

ASTRONAUTS AND COSMONAUTS

Two crewmen in space suits were practising a mission when one spotted a glow from behind an instrument panel. Within seconds part of the panel had burst into flames. The cause of the fire was never discovered.

The most dangerous fire had happened at the Naval Air Center in Philadelphia in a chamber containing pure oxygen at only one-third of the pressure of the Apollo capsule. A light bulb in the chamber burned out and a crewman replacing it caused a tiny spark as he screwed a new bulb into the socket. In the instantaneous flash fire which followed, the clothing of the four men inside the chamber immediately caught fire and they were all severely burned.

But other scientists at the Manned Spacecraft Center in Houston, Texas, came up with the comforting re-assurance that, even in a pure oxygen atmosphere, a fire in a spacecraft would simply smother itself – if it was orbiting in space. A fire spread, they explained, because a current of oxygen keeps it fed. The oxygen heated by the flame becomes lighter and rises up, letting fresh, cold oxygen in to keep the fire spreading. But in space there is no gravity, no up and no down. The burnt out oxygen would not rise, it would choke the flames.

Apollo One commander Gus Grissom certainly knew and accepted the risks of being a spaceman. He had only recently attended a hearing of the U.S. Congressional Space Committee with fellow astronaut John Glenn. Grissom had nodded his agreement when Glenn had told the Congressmen: 'You may as well realise now that some future space flight will fail, probably with the loss of life. There will be failures, there will be sacrifices, there will be times when we are not riding on such a crest of happiness as we are now.'

Grissom, the spaceman who was to die in a simple rehearsal in an earth-bound rocket, had been strongly tipped for captaincy of the first flight to the moon.

He had made two previous flights into orbit and had faced death on his first space mission – he almost drowned. His complex Mercury space capsule had performed perfectly in orbit but on splashdown in the Pacific his escape hatch had accidentally jettisoned. Grissom, weighed down by his bulky space suit, had to be rescued by NASA scuba divers as the capsule, the Liberty Bell 7, filled with water and sank.

Elevator tragedy

The world's worst elevator disaster happened at Vaal Reefs gold mine in South Africa on 27 March 1980. The cage plunged 1.2 miles down the liftshaft, killing all 23 passengers.

ASTRONAUTS AND COSMONAUTS

Major Ed White, 36, had been the second American to walk in space when he stepped out of his Gemini Four spacecraft 150 miles above the Gulf of Mexico and drifted alongside the capsule for fourteen minutes.

He said prophetically after that flight: 'As we fly more and more spacecraft we are going to have one come down and probably going to lose somebody. But I wouldn't want that to hold up the space programme.'

Roger Chaffee, 31, a navy lieutenant commander, was the new boy to the astronaut trio, eager for his first taste of space adventure.

The probable cause of the fire which killed Gus Grissom, Ed White and Roger Chaffee was a loose wire which would have sparked harmlessly behind the control panel but which turned into the fuse of an atmospheric firebomb in the rich oxygen of their cabin.

The Apollo One disaster set the U.S. manned space programme back by 18 months, until the capsule interior was re-designed with spark-proof electrical insulation and a new quick release which could easily be opened by astronauts from the inside.

On 19 April 1971 the permanent space station, Salyut One was launched into orbit. It was thrust into space by the Proton booster rocket, Russia's most powerful. The Soyuz Ten capsule docked with Salyut a few days later but technical problems with the airlock prevented the crew boarding the orbiting station.

On 6 June, a successful docking was made by Soyuz Eleven and its three cosmonauts, Georgi Dobrovolsky, 43, the commander, Viktor Patsayev, 38, a test engineer and Vladislav Volkov, 35, the flight engineer.

The three jubilant cosmonauts spent a record 23 days aboard Salyut while in ground control anxious Soviet doctors monitored the medical condition of the men. They were concerned as to what prolonged weightlessness would do to their physical condition. Within ten days the men had weakened alarmingly, losing much of their muscle power as they floated through space.

Without the force of gravity to make them expend energy, their muscles became flabby. But that was no great problem. In the zero gravity of space the cosmonauts had no difficulty in moving bulky telescope and camera equipment with their fingertips and performing amazing feats of 'weight lifting'.

Patsayev, the test engineer, even busied himself planting seedlings in the space station for mankind's first space garden.

On 30 June, after a flawless space mission, Commander Dobrovolsky disengaged his Soyuz from the space station and fired his retro-rockets for precisely two and a half minutes to start the slow, controlled descent to earth.

In the ground control room the medical specialists began to fuss over their

ASTRONAUTS AND COSMONAUTS

three record-breaking men, warning them by radio not to try to leave their capsule on landing because they would not have the strength to stand on their own two feet. They would have to be carried out like babies until the muscle power returned to their limbs. Floating effortlessly in space, Dobrovolsky laughed: 'We will just sit back and let you do all the work.'

As the craft seared its way back to earth, radio contact was lost, a routine breakdown of radio signals caused by the violent heat and static electricity experienced by all spacecraft burning their way back through the earth's atmosphere.

At 23,000 feet, the recovery parachutes blossomed open and Soyuz drifted towards the ground. Twenty feet above the soil of Kazakhstan, powerful rockets gave one final braking blast and Soyuz made a feather-light touchdown. The recovery crew opened the hatch, ready to lift the returning heroes to the waiting helicopters.

Inside, the three men were dead.

The small explosive bolts which had been detonated in space to separate Soyuz from the Salyut space station had jarred open an air valve in the main hatch. As the capsule began its return to earth, the cosmonauts slowly began to suffocate as their precious air leaked away into the fringes of space.

His reflexes slowed and his muscles wasted by more than three weeks of weightlessness, Commander Dobrovolsky had been too weak to raise his arm against the force of deceleration to close the valve.

Less than six weeks later, the memories of the American astronauts and the Soviet cosmonauts, were commemorated in a fitting tribute. Not just the crews of Apollo One and Soyuz Eleven, but also the spacemen who had died in plane crashes and training missions.

Apollo Fifteen mission commander David Scott had touched down on the surface of the moon on 30 July 1971, just two years after lunar pioneer Neil Armstrong. The most sophisticated part of his equipment was the Lunar Rover, a battery powered car which allowed him and his crewman Jim Irwin to drive for miles over the moon's surface. They drove to the edge of the lunar chasm, the Hadley Rille, overlooking a ridge 1,200 feet high.

There they placed a small metal figure of a fallen spaceman, and a plaque listing in alphabetical order, regardless of nationality, the names of eight astronauts and six cosmonauts who had given their lives for space exploration.

Peru Earthquake (1970)

In those parts of the world which, through faults in the earth's crust, are particularly susceptible to earthquakes, the people learn to live with the risk and to accept it as part of their lives, in the same way that people who live in the northern hemisphere accept the probability of snow in winter.

Peruvians have been aware of the likelihood of earthquakes throughout the centuries (the recorded history of earthquakes in Peru dates back to the Spanish chroniclers of 1619) and have learned to accept them philosophically. Few, however, imagined such a devastating earthquake as the one which occurred on Sunday, 1 May 1970, affecting 600 miles of the Peruvian coast and a vast hinterland, leaving dozens of towns in ruins or totally obliterated, and killing a staggering total of at least 50,000 people.

Peruvians are ardent football fans, and at 3.00 that afternoon most of them had settled down at home to watch the first match of the World Cup series on television. Twenty-three minutes later, out at sea, 50 miles west of the thriving fishing town of Chimbote with its population of 200,000, the ocean bed cracked and heaved. The earth, tortured by stress, sought to find for itself a more comfortable position, like an old man turning in bed; and all along a 250-mile stretch of coastline, bounded by Trujillo in the north and Lima, the capital, in the south, the ground heaved and shook in a mighty earthquake which achieved an intensity of between seven and eight degrees on the Richter scale. For many hundreds of miles north, south and east across the land, the shock was felt.

At first the magnitude of the disaster was not appreciated. In Lima, people rushed into the streets, but the capital was fortunate and escaped without damage. Not for some hours, for all communications had been cut, was it learned that the full force of this 'act of God' had been felt by Chimbote, which lay on the narrow coastal plain, and by the towns and villages inland, in the foothills of the Andean mountain range.

Early reports, even then, seriously underestimated the magnitude of the disaster. They spoke of '250 killed in Chimbote' and '140 in Huaraz'. Slowly the shocking truth emerged: Chimbote lay in ruins and an estimated 2,700 people had died. Casma, Huanmey and all the towns along the coast had suffered to a greater or lesser extent, and unknown thousands of people had been killed. It was quite impossible to discover what had happened inland, in the district of Callejón de Huaylas, a popular tourist area known as the 'Switzerland of Peru', where lay hundreds of mountain towns and small villages.

95

PERU EARTHQUAKE

Hurricanes batter Caribbean

At least 1,100 died and 150,000 were made homeless when
Hurricane David lashed the Dominican Republic on 1 September
1979, with winds gusting to 150 mph. Nearly 12 months later, on 5
August 1980, another hurricane battered the Caribbean.
Hurricane Allen caused nearly 100 deaths, mainly on the island of
St Lucia.

Radio communication was silenced as a result of damage to the hydro-electric station at Huallanca; roads were impassable through landslides and subsidence; and when, next day, helicopters attempted to reconnoitre, the pilots' view was obscured by mist and huge clouds of dust rising thousands of feet into the air. Nobody knew what had happened in an area the size of Scotland, dominated by the 22,205-feet-high peak of Mount Huascaran.

An hour after the earthquake it was already apparent that the magnitude of the disaster was far greater than the authorities in Lima had originally imagined. The President of Peru, General Velasco, set sail in a naval vessel for Chimbote (for the coastal roads were blocked by landslides, the airfields were unusable and there was always the fear of further tremors) with various senior officials. The next morning he inspected the ruined town and neighbouring Casma and Coishco, and visited the injured at an emergency hospital. Before he returned to Lima – bringing some of the injured on the ship with him – in order to direct rescue operations, he attempted to visit the mountainous Callejón de Huaylas, but it was still impossible.

At Chimbote, General Velasco had found a town in ruins; 60–70 per cent of the buildings were destroyed, the old part of the town, where many buildings were in poor condition, being the worst affected. Almost nothing, whether concrete or adobe, had escaped damage. Despite the efforts of the rescue parties, dozens of people still lay under the rubble, injured and perhaps dying. Many hundreds more camped in the streets; some had no roof beneath which to shelter, others were afraid of further earth tremors.

From the Callejón de Huaylas, isolated behind rock-barred roads, confused and unconfirmed reports suggested even worse destruction. Aircraft were still hampered by bad visibility and vast dust-clouds. Eventually an amateur radio operator from within the mountain fastnesses managed to make contact and, with his plea 'Don't forget us!', the world first learned that the town of Yungay and a part of nearby Ranrahirca had completely disappeared under a landslide from Huascaran. Later, the Air Force confirmed this news: a vast wall of mud and snow had swept down the

Above: Survivors search for belongings.
Below: A campsite for the homeless

mountainside and, divided by a spur of hills, swallowed the two small towns.

Of Yungay, where the few survivors had managed to flee to the cemetery on the edge of the town, all that could be seen were the tips of the 100-feet-high palm trees which had stood in the main square. A helicopter pilot reported that he had counted a dozen more towns, each of between two and three thousand inhabitants, which were now merely heaps of stones.

For two and a half days no helicopter was able to land in the Andes region because of the continuing bad visibility. Until a hundred parachutists managed to land, the only contact with these isolated regions came from the desperate, pleading voice of the radio amateur.

The very size of the area of devastation meant that much of it was inaccessible, and it was many days before relief-workers – their resources stretched to the utmost – managed to reach remoter parts. One of the problems was to know just what supplies were needed. In the mountain villages hundreds of thousands of Indian peasants remained without heating, food or shelter for almost a week. Throughout the area survivors poured on to the passable roads on foot, in carts and lorries, desperately seeking help and refuge. Distracted people made for the nearest towns – often to find, like the two injured village policemen who staggered into Huaraz three days after the earthquake, that the hoped-for sources of assistance were themselves in desperate straits. Without the much-needed help the death-toll mounted steeply.

On the coastal plain rescue operations continued, and relief-workers and aid of all kinds poured in from all over the world. So great was the task in this region, scattered with huge *haciendas* farming sugar or maize, that in Chimbote, despite the all-pervading smell of fish-meal from the damaged factory, five days after the earthquake rescue workers could still use their noses to find more and more dead bodies under the rubble. And still the number of dead and dying in the mountain villages in a region some 300 miles long and 120 miles wide could only be guessed at.

The fear continued. From time to time small earth tremors could be felt and when, a couple of days after the earthquake, the ground again trembled,

---

Avalanche destroys sanatorium

Seventy one people, most of them under 15 years of age, were killed when an earth slide triggered by an avalanche of melting snow sent hundreds of tons of debris crashing into a tuberculosis sanatorium at Plateau d'Assy, near Mont Blanc in the French Alps, in mid-April, 1970.

people rushed into the streets in their night-clothes, their hands sheltering their heads. Many preferred to sleep in the open; and the new 'houses', built on the rubble of the old, were made of harmless rushes. Some feared even to sleep, for they had heard that the mountain lakes could break their natural barriers, causing disastrous floods.

This particular horror, however, was spared the luckless population. Although many valley streams turned into torrents, there was comparatively little damage from water; nor did a tidal-wave follow upon the earthquake, the ocean level varying only by a few feet from its normal level.

Rock falls and avalanches, however, had caused major damage. Of these, the greatest and most catastrophic was that which destroyed Yungay and Ranrahirca and killed nearly 30,000 people in these and in neighbouring small towns and villages. On that day, 5,000 feet up in the heights of Huascaran, a party of Japanese mountain climbers visiting this famous mountain resort found themselves the horrified but fascinated spectators of this event. The avalanche began with an almost vertical fall of 10,000 feet of a vast mass of ice and rock, almost a third of a mile wide and nearly two miles long, from the western face of Mount Huascaran. Impelled by the tremendous height of its initial fall, this gigantic mass then poured down the valley at a speed estimated at nearly 250 miles an hour. The million cubic yards of ice that had become detached from the highest point of the glacier then set another 24 million cubic yards in motion.

In the path of this unimaginable terror lay small villages and the towns of Yungay on the west and Ranrahirca on the east of a mountain spur. Above Yungay, a 600-foot hill was swept up in the path of the avalanche and deposited on the other side of the valley. This and the unfortunate mountain towns absorbed the force of the huge landslide. Other rock- and earth-falls blocked roads, particularly in the coastal areas where the road-side slopes were steep, dammed the River Santa at Recuhat, and destroyed countless houses. Many of these slides took place in stages, giving the threatened population time to flee: but in Yungay and Ranrahirca there was small hope of escaping the roaring death . . . and only eight years after Ranrahirca and seven mountain villages had been the previous victims of the Nevado de Huascaran's monstrous ice-cap, when a part of it broke loose killing 3,000 people.

It took many weeks for the people of the devastated regions to recover from the effects of 'the giant's hand', as one Indian peasant called it, and the villages in the steep Andean valleys, tucked under the towering cliffs, suffered most severely through their sheer inaccessibility. Freezing rain made it even more difficult for troops and parachutists to reach the population.

Guns set off avalanche

Austrian troops stationed in the Alps during World War I began firing their cannon in practice one December morning in 1916. The reverberations set off an avalanche in which more than 2,000 people are believed to have died.

In the valleys life came back to normal more quickly. The 'uncomprehending silence', which one observer reported as brooding over shattered towns, turned to the noise and bustle of people trying to rebuild shattered lives. And when, on 2 June, Peru beat Bulgaria in a World Cup match, people even found the heart to cheer, and red-and-white Peruvian flags were planted to wave proudly over pathetic heaps of rubble that had once been homes.

Thousands of people without homes tried to organize new lives – and many realized they would be homeless for a long time. For many, too, there were no more jobs. Young people with knapsacks took to the roads, making for the sugar capital in the north, Trujillo. 'What is the point', one asked 'of rebuilding here?' And indeed with the trade of the towns disrupted and with little, poorly paid, work available on the *haciendas*, their reactions were reasonable. Once again it was the mountain peasants, who knew no other way of life, who suffered most harshly.

It seemed that the whole of Peru and half the world were anxious to help in the vast task of rehabilitation. Peruvian authorities encouraged visits from journalists and notable foreigners who would tell the rest of the world what had happened, and thus recruit much needed aid of all kinds.

Where any disaster is concerned the question that is always asked afterwards is: 'What could have been done to prevent it?' Where natural events are concerned, particularly in the case of one so overwhelming as the Peruvian earthquake, the answer must be 'Very little'. Most of man's protection must lie in warnings which are the result of constant vigilance. Hurricane, flood and avalanche warnings are now commonplace in many parts of the world; and even if they are sometimes too late, they help to save many lives. Predicting an earthquake is more difficult, but the steady series of major disasters to which the world is prone makes it apparent that research into both the prevention and warning of earthquakes is of vital importance.

The imminence of an earthquake can sometimes be detected by continuous monitoring of the fluctuations of the earth's magnetic field, its seismic activities and the strain and tilt of the earth's crust. Just as a threatened ice-fall can be safely triggered off, under controlled conditions, by the use of explosives, so explosives and drilling techniques could be used to provoke land movement and unlock dangerous faults under strain. So far, however, this is a science which has made few practical advances and 'the giant's hand' continues to crush and maim throughout the world.

Many lessons were learned from Peru's disaster. It became apparent that destruction would have been less if buildings had been better sited or better constructed. In the area affected by the worst of the earthquake, the damage was caused mainly to buildings which were of poor quality, unsuited to the type of soil on which they were constructed, and erected on badly laid foundations. The earthquake opened cracks in the saturated sand and clay soils and increased the level of underground water; while rock-sited foundations were not so seriously affected. In Huaraz, for example, the older parts of the town, built on the alluvium of the river, suffered the greatest damage; the new part, however, built on rock brought down by a landslide in 1941, was less damaged. Mud-brick buildings proved to be less equal to strain than brick or concrete, but in some cases concrete buildings collapsed because of the poor materials used in their construction.

These lessons are learnt at a fearful cost. In the final analysis, man's puny efforts are all useless when Nature decides to unleash the full fury of her powers.

Mass Poisoning in Iraq
(1971–1972)

Desperate measures to overcome a famine disaster led to an even
greater catastrophe in the Middle Eastern state of Iraq in the winter
of 1971–72. For, although the government took what it thought
were the correct measures to provide grain for its ten million people after
two years of severe drought, it failed to take account of human failings like
greed and impatience. The result was what is believed to be the greatest
mass poisoning in history, which left more than 5,000 victims dead and tens
of thousands more maimed for life.

In Old Testament times, and even before that, the people of what we now
call Iraq were among the most civilized on earth. The city of Babylon stands
on the edge of the area between the rivers Euphrates and Tigris christened
Mesopotamia by the Greeks. But time has stood still here over the centuries
while other nations and cultures have developed new lifestyles and more
prosperous ways of earning a living. It remains a largely agricultural area of
small towns and villages, its people ekeing a meagre existence from their
arid, sun-scorched fields. The summers of 1969 and 1970 were even drier
than usual. Grain crops were abysmal, and stockpiles had to be raided to
provide enough for the nation to eat. By 1971, what remained in granary
warehouses was at a perilously low level.

The ruling Ba'ath Party decided to buy foreign seed to make up the
deficiencies. The best available was Mexipak, a high-yield wheat strain
developed in Mexico by American Nobel Prize winner Dr Norman Borlaug.
The Iraqis ordered 73,000 tons of it, mainly from an American company,
and topped it up with a separate order for 22,000 tons of barley from U.S.
west coast suppliers. But Iraq insisted that all the grain be chemically treated
against plant disease. The most effective means of doing this was by
methylmercury dicyandiamide.

America, Canada and most of Europe banned the use of mercury-based
treatments after poison scares in Sweden, Pakistan and Guatamala in the
1950s, for though the silver-coloured liquid metal is useful in fighting
disease, it is also lethal to humans and animals, particularly when swallowed.
Iraq itself had suffered mercury-poisoning epidemics in both 1956 and
1960. But in a land where the grain yield was so vital, the authorities could
not afford to wait until an equally reliable seed treatment was discovered.

MASS POISONING IN IRAQ

On 16 September 1971, the freighter *Trade Carrier*, registered in Liberia, arrived at the southern Iraq port of Basra with the precious stocks of wheat and barley. The grain was a vivid pink colour after the mercury treatment, and each sack carried a poison warning. The wheat, mainly from Mexico, carried the Spanish words 'No usarla para alimento' while the barley had the same warning in English: 'Do not use for food'. There were also skull-and-crossbones logos, with the prominent words 'Poison Treated'.

Sadly, few Iraqis speak Spanish or English. And that ignorance was soon to prove fatal. So was the method adopted by the authorities to distribute the sorely-needed grain. Farmers were told they would not have to pay for it until it was harvested, in a year's time. Consequently, many decided to enjoy a prosperous year on credit by selling all the wheat they had been able to grow, despite the droughts, and filling their empty bins with the 'free' seed. Too many forgot to keep some grain back to make their own bread for the winter.

Lorry drivers were under strict instructions to drive straight from the docks to distribution warehouses. Yet some still arrived with part of their loads missing, claiming they had been robbed along the road. And some warehouses ignored the order to get a signed statement from customers, to the effect that they realised the new wheat and barley had been mercury-treated. As an additional warning, the Iraqi government had a plane drop half-a-million leaflets over agricultural areas. It was hardly a fool-proof method of alerting an increasingly hungry populace to the perils they faced if they used the seed for anything other than planting.

Soon wives and mothers all over Iraq were overcoming the qualms of their husbands and baking the grain into bread. Many of the survivors later told hospital authorities it was the best bread they had ever tasted. Families began stockpiling the seed for baking when special guests were expected. But within weeks the awful consequences of those tasty meals were seen everywhere. Children and adults were vomiting violently. Those who did not collapse found it impossible to keep their balance or co-ordinate their actions. Mercury attacks the brain and the nervous system.

The grain sacks contained information on what to do if treated seed was swallowed. They said: 'Give milk or white of eggs beaten with water, then a tablespoon of salt in a glass of warm water, and repeat until vomit fluid is clear. Repeat milk or white of eggs with water. Call a physician.' But they said it in English. And many of the victims were in no physical condition to call anybody. They lay helpless on their beds or where they fell, and were lucky if neighbours arrived in time to whisk them to hospital.

By Christmas, all the big city hospitals were crammed with poisoned peasants, and by January medical centres in all 14 Iraqi provinces were reporting hundreds of new arrivals every day. The government issued urgent warnings, ordering that all the contaminated seed be immediately returned to distribution warehouses. On no account should it be fed to humans or animals. The penalty for disobedience was death.

A month later the crisis took on another dimension. Poisoned beef was found in butchers' shops. Farmers who had fed their beasts the pink barley were now trying to get rid of their ailing animals before they lost too much weight. The government closed all abattoirs, and prescribed the eating of fresh or frozen meat for two months. Many Iraqis maintained a voluntary ban for much longer, and prices of alternative foods spiralled.

Official government figures put the total poisoned at 6,530, and listed 459 hospital deaths. But outside experts put the toll much higher. Edward Hughes, a Middle East writer for both the *Wall Street Journal* and *Time Magazine*, who wrote about the poison outbreak for the British *Sunday Times* in 1973, said: 'My investigations and private estimates of doctors and government officials on the scene suggest that as many as 6,000 died, and perhaps 100,000 were injured. Many of the ill never left their home villages; many of the dead were buried in unmarked graves.'

Hughes also wrote graphically of what he saw when he visited Iraq nearly two years after the poison grain disaster. 'I found hundreds of square miles of human devastation' he said. 'Hardly a village in the broad plain between the Tigris and Euphrates is without its victims. Entire families have been wiped out. I even saw one abandoned settlement where everyone had died or fled. I could not get its name, for there was no-one to ask, except a bent old crone on a nearby dirt trail; she uttered only a shrill "Doctor, doctor", pointing her stick feebly towards a larger town in the distance.'

Perhaps, though, the dead were the lucky ones. Hughes continued: 'As my car came to a crossroads, the driver gasped and braked. A dozen maimed youngsters aged 6 to 12 were trying to play football. Several of them lurched and reeled grotesquely, as if drunk, while others stood with vacant stares.

The Bermuda Triangle

A flight of five Grumman US Navy bombers took off from Fort Lauderdale, Florida, for a training flight on 5 December 1945. Two hours later, all contact with them was lost. A Martin bomber was dispatched to search for the missing planes. Twenty minutes later, it too disappeared. No trace of any of the planes or their crews of 27 men was ever found. The area in which they vanished later became famous as the 'Bermuda Triangle'.

'One lad of ten staggered uncertainly towards the ball, but as he kicked, his balance failed and he tumbled to the ground, writhing in frustration. Suddenly a small squealing boy ran across the courtyard, arms outstretched, to retrieve the ball for himself. Only when the boy fell headlong into a large bush did we realise with horror that he was almost totally blind.'

Science was the only winner from the disaster. After the last of the victims had stumbled home, the doctors unable to do anything more for the afflictions of feeling, sight, hearing and balance that would stay with the patients for life, the Baghdad authorites invited a team from Rochester University, New York State, to study the tragic effects of the catastrophe. The experts, led by Dr Thomas Clarkson, discovered, among other things, that mothers can pass mercury on to their unborn babies – one child was found to have three times the mercury concentration of the mother in his blood – and that certain resins can speed up the process of the body rejecting mercury.

But a failsafe antidote for mercury poisoning has yet to be found. And until seed sellers come up with an equally infallible fungicide treatment, until they label poisons in a language the users of their product can understand, and until human nature does not unwisely take advantage of situations it does not fully comprehend, the risk of an equally horrific outbreak of death and devastation in underdeveloped countries will always be with us.

Isle of Man Summerland Fire (1973)

Summerland was a dream come true for holidaymakers. It was 'Britain's first forget-the-weather family fun centre', according to the people who ran it. And Trust House Forte Leisure Ltd also proudly boasted that it was the largest indoor holiday resort in the world. On six brightly-lit floors beneath a pyramid-shaped solarium dome, trippers could while away grey days on slot machines in amusement arcades, play bingo, enjoy sauna baths, or relax in six bars and a restaurant. They could lounge on deck chairs amid potted palms, watching a live show, while their children enjoyed their own fun fair or the roller-skate disco in the basement.

The councillors of the island's capital, Douglas, were delighted with their £2 million investment. Some had been uneasy about waiving a local by-law to approve the building, but in the two years since it opened it had certainly helped amuse the tourists who were the lifeblood of many of the island's 56,000 residents. More than half a million had sampled its delights in the summer of 1972.

But on the evening of 2 August 1973, just 25 months after Summerland opened for business, the lucrative dream became a nightmare – and cost 50 people, ten of them children, their lives in a horrifying inferno.

Chilling drizzle had driven nearly 3,000 holidaymakers into the warmth of the fun centre, grafted into the cliff face at the northern end of the front. The 96 feet high building could hold more, but latecomers found most of the bars on the lower floors packed. In the vast Marquee Show bar, a three-man band was entertaining crowds beneath the transparent dome, above which the sky was darkening towards dusk.

Elsewhere, bingo players scanned their cards to the sound of laughter and chat from happy drinkers. In the basement, disc jockey Johnny Silver introduced a beat group who played the latest hits for energetic dancers. Then the voice of schoolteacher William Hefin Roberts, from Winsford, Cheshire, cut across the babble. It said: 'There's a fire out there.'

At first, Mr Roberts recalled, the man on duty at the main door seemed to take no notice. Then he spoke into a walkie-talkie radio. Mr Roberts ran towards the end wall of the complex to see if he could help fight the fire. The audience in the Marquee Show Bar also noticed the smoke. Eric Taylor, 51-year-old organist with the group entertaining the crowds, quipped: 'There appears to be a little fire – let's put it out with The Blue Danube.' But though the music went on, the people listening became uneasy. Some left their seats, only to return sheepishly when a Summerland employee joked about a chip-pan fire.

Ken Harding, the fun centre's technical services manager, was by this time leading the fire-fighters. Two staff were outside, trying to extinguish flames in a disused kiosk reached from the promenade by a concrete spiral staircase. The kiosk was attached to the wall of Summerland, and Harding, playing a hose on it from inside the building, urged his colleagues to pull the kiosk away with flagpoles. But it was already too late.

'The flames were shooting 20 to 30 feet high and licking the steel cladding of the main building,' Harding said later. 'I could see the steel was warping and opening with the heat, so I ran back and gave the alarm.'

On the upper floors, customers had already decided the billowing smoke was reason enough to leave. But as they made their way down the staircases, that smoke thickened. The kiosk fire had spread underneath the restaurant floor, bursting out again in an amusement arcade at the centre of the building. Acrid black fumes shot through with flames whirled up towards the acrylic dome of the building, forcing those descending to try to turn round in the crush. Suddenly, clothes and hair caught alight. Children and babies were dropped over the stair-rail to willing hands below. Other parents tried to battle against the tide of people, searching desperately for their families.

'The fire seemed to spread in seconds, it was terrible,' said one survivor. 'Mothers were screaming, tearing round looking for their children. It was absolute confusion.' Another said: 'There were children crying for their mummies and daddies, and there were daddies and mummies crying in anguish for their little ones with no idea where they were. It was more than the mind could bear.' A woman who ran a shop in the complex said: 'Everybody was dashing for the exits. I was knocked down in the rush. I was flat on my stomach and people were trampling over me. There was a kiddy under me. I managed to get her to safety.'

Wyn Price, manageress of the sauna baths on the top floor, said: 'Black smoke filled the building and then the flames came rushing up towards us. I dashed into the sauna and told everybody to get out. Then suddenly a sheet of flame shot across our floor level. I managed to get out through an emergency exit down some side stairs. I don't know if the people in the sauna got out. They were all in their underclothes.'

In the basement, children fled the dance floor. Two 14-year-olds, Sharon Walter and Sharon Smith, later told reporters: 'We tried to get out through a back door but we could not get it open. Burning plastic was dripping from the ceiling and someone put covers over us to keep it off us. Eventually we got out through a side door. We saw one person break a window to escape, and a man still wearing roller skates jump through another window.' Sharon Smith's parents were waiting in uncertainty outside. 'My wife flaked out two or three times,' Mr Smith recalled. 'I thought I was never going to see the girls alive again.'

Disc jockey Silver ushered 200 youngsters to safety, then went back into the fumes to try to save more people. He seriously injured his leg breaking the fall of a child thrown down from a higher floor. He was not the only hero. Entertainments manager Ted Oldham smashed a big window and handed children to willing helpers outside. And 6ft 5in Irish staff member Noel Quigley plucked youngsters off the floor and hurled them to safety through the front doors. 'He must have saved 50 or 60 like that,' a colleague said later. 'They were being trampled underfoot around him and even at his size he was knocked over several times.'

The understandable panic of those fleeing the flames was heightened when they found several escape routes locked. Staff smashed through doors into the adjacent Aquadrome swimming pool to lead some of those trapped to safety. And glass in two secured doors at the main entrance was smashed by holidaymakers. Alan Sandham, 17, from Salford, Lancashire, said: 'I tried three emergency doors that were chained or locked. I was told later it was to keep gate-crashers out. Lots of people panicked when they found doors chained. I saw people standing there tearing at the doors instead of running to find others that weren't locked. I can't help thinking the time that was wasted may have cost them their lives.'

Belfast holidaymaker Sam Farr said: 'A lot of people had to kick their way out through glass panels in the side of the building. Glass was melting in the heat. I saw one man with his hair on fire and his coat melted off his back, running with a youngster in his arms.' Mrs Elizabeth Arthurs, also from Belfast, who was drinking with her husband while their five children enjoyed the basement play area, said: 'We ran out of the Marquee Bar just before the floors collapsed in on other people. Some children with roller skates on were unable to run out.'

Her husband Peter said: 'About 100 people were lying on the ground where they had fallen, shouting and screaming. It was pandemonium. Emergency doors were locked and people started smashing glass. People were crawling over others lying near the doors. You could hear limbs cracking.'

Lorry driver Robert Bore, 46, from Skelmersdale, Lancashire, was on his way into Summerland with his wife when the fire began. He said: 'An inferno seemed to engulf the whole building. I removed one lady with face

The Summerland holiday centre in flames

injuries from the main entrance. I had just gone back for a second woman who had terrible leg burns when an explosion nearly blew us off our feet. I was within a few feet of the main entrance but it was impossible to get in to rescue anyone because of a solid sheet of flame. No-one could have got out through there.'

Those who reached fresh air stood sobbing on the promenade, staring at each stunned, shocked and scorched survivor who lurched out of the smoke. Was it a relative, a friend? The worst hurt were rushed to Douglas's Noble Hospital, in ambulances or holidaymakers' cars, volunteered or commandeered by police. As the walking wounded comforted each other, grisly visions of the less lucky ones appeared behind them, silhouettes against the raging flames, leaping screaming to the ground or motionless in the steel skeleton of the gutted building.

Holidaymakers and residents rushed to help the rescue services with first aid, paperwork and administration. The manager of the nearby Palace Hotel and Casino said: 'Almost everyone in the hotel left meals on tables to go and see what they could do. So did taxi drivers, hotel people, coach hire firms and people with private cars. We appealed through the hotel for volunteer blood donors and 20 people – all in their holiday clothes – came forward straight away. Food and holidays were forgotten. Everybody just wanted to help.'

The fire, fought by 93 of the island's 106 firemen on their total complement of 16 engines, was under control in just over an hour. In the blackened building, 12 bodies lay in a dark, narrow, windowless emergency staircase, all asphyxiated by the lethal fumes. On another narrow flight, 13 more tourists had been burned or trampled to death. But, almost miraculously, another survivor was discovered in the ruins. Barman Graham Harding, 19, had crawled under a storeroom sink and covered himself with a water-soaked jacket. He was unconscious but still alive.

Seven of his colleagues were not so lucky. Summerland held a staff roll call at 11 a.m. next day. It confirmed the worst fears of one girl among the 250 on the payroll. 'I have been up all night looking for two boys from our digs,' she said. 'Now they are not here.'

Identifying the horribly-burned corpses laid out in St George's church hall was an ordeal for relatives and a headache for the authorities. A policeman said: 'God help those who come to identify them – its worse than a bloody war.'

Frederick Allen, 60, and his wife Frances, 54, were also among the dead. They had come to Douglas to celebrate their silver wedding anniversary.

Mourning blanketed northern England and Ulster – it was peak season for Irish holidays on the Isle of Man. Manx people were devastated. The island

Girls die in factory

More than 145 workers, most of them teenage girls, died when a blaze in a fabric wastebin quickly spread through the premises of the Triangle Shirtwaist Company in New York's Manhattan on Saturday, 25 March 1911. The cramped factory was on the eighth and ninth floor of the ten-storey Asch building, on the corner of Washington Place and Greene Street. Only 12 girls reached the lift before acrid fumes made waiting for its return impossible. Ladders reached only the sixth floor, and firemen's hoses could reach only the seventh. Onlookers watched helplessly as terrified girls broke windows and leapt 85 feet to their deaths and the weight of other bodies brought down the flimsy fire escape stairs. The press of panic-stricken workers made it impossible to use inward-opening doors. In 18 minutes, the victims were all dead. More than 100,000 angry mourners attended a mass funeral.

had never suffered such a disaster. But the sorrow quickly turned to fury and frustration. How could such a catastrophe strike a supposedly-fireproof construction, the biggest new building on the island for a century?

It quickly became clear that Oroglas, a Perspex-like acrylic used in much of the construction, was partly responsible for the fire spreading so quickly and lethally. Summerland was the first big building to use it extensively, and construction chiefs in Britain were quick to point out that it would never have been allowed on the mainland, where strict building regulations limited the use of plastics and insisted on better means of escape.

London fire prevention officer Ronald Miller said: 'Plastic always causes problems. There is always very dense, toxic smoke and plastic melts and, still alight, drops all over the place, spreading fire more rapidly than ever. If I had been shown a description of this centre before it was built, I would have warned the planners they were creating a potential fire hazard.'

Lessons clearly had to be learned from the experience everyone had gained the tragic way. Manx Lieutenant-Governor Sir Peter Stallard appointed three outsiders – a judge, a Home Office inspector of fire services and a building professor, all from England – as a commission of inquiry. After hearing 91 witnesses over 49 days, they reported that the catastrophe was due to an amazing accumulation of human error and failure, but there were 'no villains'.

The commission said the fire was started, either accidentally or maliciously, by three boys playing in the ruined glass kiosk. The Galbestos coating caught fire six minutes later, and flames built up unnoticed in the concealed gap for 15 minutes before bursting through the Decalin the amusement arcade. Thirty tons of softwood flooring and wooden joists, plus the flame-hungry Oroglas of the roof and walls, turned the blaze into a holocaust. A sprinkler system, which would have cost £250,000, might have helped stem the flames, but the local authority had not insisted on one.

The commission's ruling that there had been 'no villains' stunned Manx islanders, who feared the catastrophe could ruin their tourist trade. 'If this is not villainy, what is?' screamed one local newspaper. Another reporter lamented that, as a layman, he had accepted the word of experts when he had a premonition of fire disaster while inspecting Summerland as it was built. Sadly, too many people who should have known better had done the same thing, and a seemingly-unrelated series of errors and omissions, each of which was not in itself fatal, had snowballed into a disaster. Fifty lives had been sacrificed to the lesson that well-intentioned progress should not be at the expense of the accepted wisdom of rules based on experience and common sense.

Ermenonville Forest Air Crash (1974)

Flags of 18 nations, topped with black crepe, fluttered over the scene. A thousand people, many still suffering the shock of their bereavement two months earlier, stood in silence. They were only a tiny fraction of those who had wanted to be there, at Thiais, near Orly airport. The others could only mourn in their native lands, hundreds, thousands, of miles away.

Few could understand more than a small part of the ceremony. It was opened in English by the Vicar of the Anglican Church in Paris. After him came Catholics, Jews, priests of the Armenian Christian Church, mullahs from Turkey, Morocco and Pakistan, Buddhist priests from Japan, and a holy man from India.

Perhaps the words of M. Achille-Fould, French Aviation Minister, were the most moving: 'The world-wide family of all in aviation is in mourning. May the earth of France lie easily on those we commit to it. France, too, looks on them as her own children.' It was France's epitaph on history's greatest air disaster.

Though a few bodies had been identified and handed over to relatives for burial, most of the staggering, tragic, total of 346 instantly killed men, women and children were being committed to a foreign grave on this spring Thursday of 9 May, 1974. The actual burial would not be public; that would take place in a few days' time, using heavy earth-moving machinery.

The worst air disaster in history had taken almost twice as many lives as any single accident before. At the time of writing, it still holds that unenviable record. It was what every airline had dreaded: an accident to a fully loaded, wide-body jet. As the mystery unfolded, grief gave way to bitterness. It *need* not have happened; it *should* not have happened. Who was to blame?

The DC10 of Turkish Airlines had flown in from Turkey and made a perfect landing at Orly Airport near Paris. Weather conditions were good on that early spring Sunday morning, 3 March, and the pilot taxied briskly up to the terminal buildings; almost immediately passengers started to embark and fill up his lightly-loaded aircraft, while those who had just landed were asked to stay on board. According to airline officials, 216 adult passengers and one infant embarked at Orly.

The need to get more than 200 people on a flight for which they had not booked meant that documentation was hasty. It seemed over the next harrowing hours that not all of the passengers had been listed; at least one man was travelling on a passport not his own, and some were using other people's tickets.

The plane re-started its three giant General Electric jets, and taxied along to the take-off runway at a few minutes past noon, carrying 335 passengers and 11 crew. In two minutes the DC10 was off, climbing powerfully into the bright sunny sky of France, the three engines – one under each wing, a third in the tail – belching vapour and exhaust. The time: 12.30 p.m.

The plane climbed fast on a wide eastern sweep to skirt Paris. Flight plans ordained that when eventually it turned to its north-west course for London it would be at 16,000 feet. Controllers of France's Northern Air Region watched it on their radar screens as it reached a height of 13,000 feet.

And then, quite simply, the plane vanished from all screens.

At 12.35 it crashed into a shallow depression within the Ermenonville State Forest north-east of Paris.

On that warm Sunday there were many people strolling along the numerous wooded pathways, but although the huge aircraft ploughed a thousand-yard furrow through the trees, shearing them off before kinetic energy was expended and the wreckage had come to rest, no-one on the ground was hurt.

It happened without any warning. Some claimed to have seen the aircraft explode in the sky; others had seen it under apparently perfect control, seeming to make an approach towards some not-too-distant airfield. Others, more expert, had seen it in difficulties at a low altitude, trying to drag its nose up from a shallow dive.

Thirty-five minutes after the crash, rescuers arrived by helicopter. One glance showed their journey had been in vain. Little fires, like those of an Indian village, were separated by hundreds of yards, indicating where parts of the engines and fuel system had ended. Bits of fuselage and the débris of human possessions were strewn over the ground; tatters of clothing festooned the branches of trees which had escaped destruction. No one could have survived for an instant.

Meanwhile, at London's Heathrow Airport, there was alarm as the DC10 became first late, then overdue. Anxious relatives awaiting the return of more than two hundred British passengers, demanded news. When it came, an elderly man collapsed, a young woman attacked the press with a stiletto-heel shoe and a man smashed press cameras. Mingled with the horror were elements of desperate hope, total incomprehension. Which of the London-bound passengers had transferred to the Turkish airliner? How could a plane, so fast, so safe and foolproof, just plunge to earth on a clear spring

Firemen carry away the remains of the DC10 passengers

The landing gear wheel amongst the strewn wreckage

day? But it had.

The 'black box', which had automatically recorded all the aircraft's movements, was recovered intact, but it merely stated that the plane had reached 13,000 feet and then dived to a lower altitude before crashing – a fact already well-established. Ground controllers reported having heard a few seconds of excited, unintelligible speech before total silence when the DC10 left their radar screens. This suggested a disaster at 13,000 feet, and not an incomprehensible exercise in hedge-hopping.

The most popular theory was a bomb, but aircraft authorities were adamant that all passengers and luggage had been screened.

A fortnight later: the probable truth. Bodies had been found, still strapped in their seats, a full seven miles from the rest of the wreckage. Then the aircraft's rear cargo door was found, nine miles away, and this seemed to be the missing clue.

Two years before, in Canada, the faulty latch on a DC10 cargo door had nearly caused a similar trajedy. The door had opened suddenly in flight and this, for a reason which was not at first clear to the highly skilled crew, seemed to jam a number of the controls. Somehow they nursed it back to base.

The United States Federal Aviation Administration gave instructions for doors to be modified so that it was impossible for them to open in flight. Further recommendations were made to the manufacturer, McDonnell-Douglas of California, that the floor of the passenger compartment, immediately above the hold, should be strengthened and air vents made in it. This expensive modification would have to be for subsequent aircraft: meanwhile, the doors must be corrected; and McDonnell-Douglas passed on these comparatively simple instructions to all its customers.

Comparison with the near-disaster over Canada proved that the Turkish plane's cargo door had opened at 13,000 feet. This, as over Canada, had caused instant depressurization of the lower, cargo compartment. As in every section of a modern airliner, the cargo compartment was kept at an air pressure approximating to that on the ground; and when this pressure dropped suddenly the light passenger deck immediately above it collapsed. In the more serious Turkish case it dragged seats down into the hold, sucking a number of them in which occupants were still strapped out of the open doorway.

At this point the pilot might have been able to dive safely to a lower altitude—but the control cables of a DC10, from flight deck to tail, run under the passenger deck, and in the Turkish aircraft these were instantly and completely jammed. Helpless, the aircraft fell into a shallow dive which no pilot could have righted.

The recovered door showed that a vital flange, part of the safety modification, was missing. There was no doubt that it had been fitted but no certainty as to when it had come adrift. A cargo handler at Orly was for a time under suspicion of not having closed the door before take-off and

Football stars killed

Eight star soccer players, including four top England internationals, were among 23 people killed when a British European Airways airliner crashed trying to take off from icy Munich airport, West Germany, on 6 February 1958. The players, all from Manchester United, were returning from a successful European Cup match in Belgrade, Yugoslavia.

furthermore of having been unable to read the instructions printed on it, but he and the airport authorities were able to dispel this suspicion.

Exactly a year later, a group of English people were taken to the scene by a French friend. The whole area had been enclosed by a high fence, and they had to be let in by the *Garde Forestière*. They looked around them in horror at the wreckage, the minutiae of human tragedy, the bits of clothing, luggage and the rest. It would take years to retrieve all this, and the French government had decided the job should not be done by souvenir hunters, hence the enclosure.

'Yes', said the *Garde Forestière*, 'he might have made it, you know, that pilot from Turkey, he might have saved many lives because the place where he came down was fairly clear. But, *hélas*, he hit this rocky eminence here. And the plane simply broke up, wings, everything, going everywhere. That is why the felled bit of Ermonenville Forest is so large, why the fence has to be so long . . .'

Almost two years after the tragedy the first of many claims from dependents and relatives of those who died was settled in an American court. Others, of course, would follow. The sum awarded was large; as much punitive, some said, as compensatory – in order, perhaps, to impress upon all concerned that something of this sort should never, could never, happen again.

American Mid-West Tornadoes (1974)

For the people of the Gulf and Mid-western states of the U.S.A. the word 'Twister' holds terror. Even the sound of an approaching tornado is awesome; anyone unlucky enough to be in the direct path of a tornado without any shelter available has little chance of surviving it.

In April 1974, in the worst tornado disaster since 1925 (when nearly 700 people were killed), a total of 324 people became victims of tornadoes in the space of eight hours, and hundreds more were injured, while damage ran into many millions of dollars. Although warnings had been given, a part of the area which was struck in 1974 was unfamiliar with tornadoes, and this contributed to the high death-toll.

Nothing can be done to prevent tornadoes and little is known about them, although no storm is more violent. Unlike hurricanes, which can be observed from within, tornadoes are so small that their study has not been practical. The conditions which give rise to them, however, are well-known and are present when warm moist air-masses meet cold dry air-masses.

Precipitating the events of 2 and 3 April 1974 was the swift eastward movement of an egg-shaped mass of cool dry air about one thousand miles across, while at the centre of the air-mass was a region of low pressure similar to that found in the calm eye of a hurricane.

This low pressure region moved very fast from central Kansas to Iowa and then on to the northern tip of Michigan. In the northern hemisphere air circulates counter-clockwise, round a centre of high or low pressure. Winds to the east of the cool air-mass were moving north, and by 2 April this northward flow was carrying moist air from the Gulf of Mexico which was rapidly warming up with the coming of spring and evaporating large masses of water.

Meanwhile about 200 miles to the landward, westward edge of the air-mass a cold front, flowing off the Rocky Mountains, developed, and a series of squall-lanes (instability lines) were formed. There the moist air welled upwards rapidly, spurring a compensating downward flow of cooler air from above and the series of squall-lines brought tornadoes over Alabama, like 'jabs from a boxer' as a meteorologist described it.

Research shows that tornadoes arise within small cyclones, a few miles across, which in turn arise within large thunderstorms. In the funnel of a tornado winds may swirl at 300 miles an hour or more – four times as fast as those in a hurricane. The movement of a tornado has been likened to a dancer, pirouetting on a rotating platform which is itself mounted on a truck, and this accounts for the terrifyingly erratic and unpredictable route many tornadoes take. At the edge of the tornado-funnel trees are uprooted; in the centre, buildings explode and railway carriages are blown over. The twister may be only 100 feet across, but it can leave a trail of damage half a mile wide.

On those two days in April 100 twisters struck in the space of eight hours in an area from Alabama to Windsor, Ontario, across the Canadian border. Two of the worst hit towns were Xenia, Ohio, and Brandenburg, Kentucky, and neither town had much experience of the killing twisters; there had been only seven tornadoes in the Xenia area in the last 24 years, and no deaths, and Brandenburg had never experienced a tornado before.

Since tornadoes strike more than a thousand times a year in the United States, people living in the affected regions have learnt to take shelter when warnings are given; to leave their cars if they cannot drive clear of the twister's path and find some hollow, if they can, in which to hide; to keep away from windows which can shatter; to take cover under large pieces of furniture. In the worst areas the houses are built with storm cellars in which the occupants can take refuge.

In the late afternoon, against a sky filled with blackness and flying débris, one particular twister roared its way through Xenia from the south-west, slashing a path of destruction three or four miles long and several hundred yards wide. New housing developments, old neighbourhoods, schools, churches, downtown businesses and a shopping centre, suffered equally. Within five minutes of sudden, shattering destruction 30 people died, nearly a hundred were injured, and thousands made homeless.

The people who had managed to take shelter emerged dazed, once the roaring inferno had passed, and took stock. They knew that the windows had shattered, for flying glass had rained upon them as they lay on the floors of the downstairs rooms, but out in the streets they discovered that almost every house had lost its roof and many their first floors. Some were virtually heaps of rubble and splinters. Dangling wires, loose signs, branches, traffic-lights – all were strewn higgledy-piggledy across once orderly streets.

Cars had been tossed along the roads; a train passing through the town with a load of new cars was safe, but all the cars were dented and their glass broken. Débris littered the streets blown from miles away and among it, untouched by the wind – such is the caprice of tornadoes – stood bizarre objects: a child's scooter, dressing-table ornaments, a pile of magazines, just as they had been left before the twister had reduced everything to chaos.

The town of Monticello lies in ruins

Tornado hits Chicago

Hailstones 'as big as pigeon's eggs' rained on Chicago on 28 March 1920, giving warning of the onslaught of a terrifying tornado. Cars were hurled through the air and houses shattered. One home was lifted up and turned upside down. Twenty eight people died and damage totalled $3 million.

At least half of Xenia had been destroyed and all the services disrupted. But by the next day the immense task of clearing up had already begun. Electricity was partly restored, and hundreds of volunteers came to help the population search for what remained of their possessions and to find some kind of shelter. A state of emergency was declared and national guardsmen — much of whose time was later spent in keeping sightseers away — were ordered out in Xenia, in Louisville, Kentucky, and in similarly stricken towns throughout the states of Alabama, Ohio, Indiana and Tennessee. In these states people sifted through the splinters that had been their homes, scraped the débris from the streets and sawed up fallen trees. There was a strange calm as with 'serene faces and certain hands' – as one reporter described it – the volunteers cleared up the rubbish against a background of persistent siren wails.

Throughout the affected areas stories abounded of individual incidents such as that at Windsor, where the roof was ripped off the local curling rink, killing and injuring those in its path, while the bodies of those who had been inside were found scattered over the neighbouring fields; and the metal frame warehouse of a construction company in Fountaintown, Indiana, which was lifted off the ground and carried a mile.

Perhaps one of the saddest results of the tornado's vicious attack was the effect it had upon the 1,600 people living in Brandenburg, Kentucky, 32 miles west of Louisville. This small farming community sat on the banks of the Ohio River, and most of its inhabitants had lived there all their lives. It was a small society, intimate, chatty and with an air of permanence. Its local paper was small and gossipy, and everybody knew everybody and all about each other. Modest houses, mostly of nineteenth-century architecture, stood on top of a pair of hills; the pace of life of Brandenburg was slow and restrained – it was 'a Mark Twain town'.

A few minutes of unleashed fury changed all this. Twenty-nine people died and scores were injured. Hundreds of people were made homeless as three-quarters of the buildings were damaged beyond repair. One 21-year-old girl and her 9-year-old brother were in a flat in an old two-storey house, clutching each other in terror as the tornado swept eastwards along the river's edge. Thirty seconds later they were trapped by wreckage while the neighbours in the flat downstairs – a woman and three young children – lay dead. The neighbour's infant daughter was found, in a field at the bottom of a hill 200 yards away, alive.

Later the river was dragged for bodies, as eye-witnesses spoke of houses, cars and bodies flying through the air. Such was the extent and importance of the destruction in this small community that many people decided to leave. It seemed pointless, they said, to try to rebuild: too much had gone for ever; the river town of Brandenburg had all but disappeared.

Months passed before the damage caused throughout the country could be repaired – it was estimated that damage to personal property alone had cost the country £1,000,000,000, and low-interest personal loans to home-owners and businessmen were immediately announced. Damage to property can be made good, but nothing can replace a way of life.

The Honduras Hurricane (1974)

Until September 1974 Honduras was to most people only the name of a country, somewhere in Central America. An unparalleled disaster was to change all that, for by press, radio and television, the almost unknown became suddenly and dramatically familiar.

Honduras lies on the Caribbean in the north and the Pacific in the south and south-west, with Nicaragua to the east, Guatemala to the west and El Salvador to the south. In extent it is slightly smaller than England, a country of mountains, deep valleys and fast-flowing rivers which flood down from the mountains to the coastal lowlands and thence to the sea. Essentially it is a very poor country. In 1870 vast sums of money were borrowed from London in order to build railways, but through incompetence and corruption most of the capital was dissipated and the country was left bankrupt and in a state of unrest. From 1883 until 1944 revolutions became a matter of course. No sooner had the Hondurans become familiar with one president than he was toppled from power and another, often very briefly, took his place.

Not that the majority of the country's some three million people have ever been interested in politics. For the most part they are of Indian stock, live in primitive conditions and are far too poor (£100 – or $250 – a year is considered a good wage) and far too busy trying to wring a meagre living from their small farms or farm-holdings to worry about what goes on in the Honduran capital of Tegucigalpa. Some breed cattle in the lowland pastures, but the country's chief product is bananas grown in large American-run plantations on the northern coastal plain and which, together with coffee, represents 50 per cent of the country's exports, the rest being made up of coconuts, timber and tobacco. It is a difficult country in which to travel because of a lack of good roads and railways and the deep valleys which cut through it like the troughs of waves (the Spanish word *honduras* may be translated as 'wavelike').

The country has two, or rather three, seasons – the wet from May to November, the dry from November to May, and September, the hurricane season. The terrible toll taken by hurricanes in the area (nearly 8,000 people lost their lives in Haiti when Hurricane Flora struck in 1963) has led countries on the Atlantic and Pacific seaboards – especially the U.S.A. – to

THE HONDURAS HURRICANE

develop meteorological services with a multiplicity of weather stations, fleets of aircraft, banks of computers and all the other trappings of modern technology to monitor the atmospheric conditions which give rise to the violent disturbances from which hurricanes are created. When one such build-up was spotted in 1974, an urgent warning went to Tegucigalpa informing the government of Honduras that it was likely to be assaulted by a hurricane within the next 48 hours. Following the obscure system then in force that bestows girls' names on hurricanes, this was given the somewhat frivolous name of 'Fifi'.

Unfortunately, communications being what they were, little could be done in the outlying districts of Honduras. Those who were informed of the danger could only wait; those who were not – and that was the bulk of the population – went about their back-breaking task of scratching a miserable living from the soil, quite oblivious to the approaching menace.

Hurricane Fifi arrived at dead of night on Wednesday, 18 September, with winds of 140 miles an hour, and torrential rain. Two feet of rain fell in 36 hours. Although the hurricane winds caused the initial damage, they soon passed and the subsequent fatalities were mainly the result of the flooding. The heavy rainfall caused the many rivers of Honduras to overflow from their sources high in the mountains right down to the plains. Dykes and banks disappeared into a maelström of swirling brown water, and almost everything that stood in the path of the floods as they roared down to the sea was swept away.

The poorly-built homes of the farmers and peasants – stone, wattle and clay for the most part – just disappeared. Even some of the sturdier houses were picked up and carried for several miles, and in some cases, when meeting an obstruction that even the roaring water could not move, would be piled one on top of another.

Worst hit was the district around the town of Choloma, standing on the banks of the river which gave it its name. Flood water poured through the town bearing trees, rocks and pathetic jumbles of wreckage that had once been homes, carrying away every standing thing along the river's bank. During the first two terrible days more than 3,000 died in the town, many of the bodies never being recovered. Those inhabitants who were left were faced with another great hazard – cholera. Bodies lay everywhere, many half-buried in the nine-feet layer of mud that the floods had left. Soon, under the hot, tropical sun, decay began to set in. Soldiers were rushed to the area and were soon collecting the bodies, piling them into heaps for mass cremation, contrary to the Roman Catholic practice of burial. Nothing, not even the deep religious beliefs of four centuries, could stand in the way of priorities.

THE HONDURAS HURRICANE

As they worked, scarves and handkerchiefs about their mouths to allay the dreadful odour of putrefaction, the pitiful survivors – about half the town's original population – stood and watched, helpless. Many, of course, had tragic stories to tell. 'People were very afraid to leave their homes,' said one survivor. 'I saw nine people from one family embrace each other; they were afraid to move. They died, holding each other in their arms.'

One old man who had lost his entire family in the flood went back to search the pile of wreckage that had been his home, and found the bodies of two dead people. He did not know them; they were not even people of Choloma. They were, as he remarked, 'just poor innocents who were swept down from the mountain and ended up here'. Another added that two separate floods had chased each other through the town early on the morning of Thursday, 19 September. 'The water poured across the street and between my home and my neighbour's like rapids.'

The second city of Honduras, San Pedro Sula, also took the full brunt of Hurricane Fifi and the floods which followed in her wake. With their homes wrecked or completely gone, some 400,000 people were suddenly homeless, without food and with the prospect of an epidemic very near.

The final death toll throughout the country was set at least at 8,000.

The first aircraft from neighbouring countries and the U.S.A. began to drone over the devastated areas, spotting thousands of terrified and desperately hungry survivors clinging to anything that protruded above the vast wastes of frothy, surging water. Some were soon saved, but the rescuers were unable to reach many of the rural areas of northern Honduras where thousands of peasants were marooned without food, fresh water or medical aid of any kind. To add to the difficulties, the only petrol refinery in the country had been isolated by the flooding of roads and the railway tracks, depriving the authorities of the fuel so vital for rescue work.

By 23 September helicopters from the U.S. base at the Panama Canal Zone were hovering wherever they could see signs of life, doubling their usual carrying capacity as they plucked wet, hungry and miserable survivors from roof-tops and trees. At first they were the only means of rescue, for bridges and railway tracks had been swept away and roads had disappeared beneath several feet of black, glutinous mud; electricity supplies were cut and telegraph-poles were down everywhere, while those that remained upright bore their pathetic bundles of squatting humanity whose upturned faces showed their mute appeal as the heavily-laden helicopters droned overhead.

As lines of communication were slowly restored, food and medical supplies began to arrive, Tocoa and San Pedro Sula becoming the main relief centres. Soon the stacks of supplies were beginning to grow, but the teams arriving from other countries ran into trouble. Corruption, always a major problem in any poor and under-developed country, became flagrant. Part of the Honduran army had been mustered to collect and distribute the food and other supplies; the rest was on guard along the Honduras/Salvador border and the government refused to bring them back and leave the border undefended. At the two main centres it was obvious that a large quantity of supplies was being diverted to a black market that had sprung into life within hours of the disaster.

Britain managed to bring some order out of the tension and even rioting at the centres. She had already sent in helicopters and troops with power-boats and medical teams from Belize in the then British Honduras, but realizing the problem was one of administration, co-ordinated all the endeavours of every assisting country through the newly-formed Whitehall Disaster Unit. This stamped out the corruption at source and helped the flow of rescue units, getting them with their supplies to the devastated areas where they were so urgently needed.

It was a prodigious task, for everywhere, it seemed, were thousands of starving people who had lost everything – corn, rice, beans and other subsistence crops having completely gone. For the country as a whole, things were even worse. With her economy utterly reliant on exports of bananas and coffee, and the plantations of these devastated, fresh crops had to be sown at once, with the prospect of at least two years wait before any return from the new plantings could be expected. Livestock had also perished in their thousands and these, too, would have to be replenished – although the country had no foreign currency available.

Only the generosity of other nations can enable Honduras to survive until she is able to return even to the near-starvation level that existed before Hurricane Fifi. Many peasants believe that the calamity was a punishment from God, but for what no-one is quite sure.

Seveso Chemical Disaster (1976)

Midway between Milan and the holiday resorts of Lake Como, the motorway cuts alongside the little Italian town of Seveso. It is a remarkably busy artery, stretching from city smog to blue skies and some of the world's most stunning scenery. During peak season, it carries tens of thousands of travellers each day.

At a passing glance, Seveso seems to be the ideal place to break the journey and stop for a meal or for petrol or simply to stretch the legs and explore. Indeed, the town first found fame for the high-class furniture produced there in workshops dotted among the picturesque homes of its friendly, generally well-to-do inhabitants.

After one curious glance, virtually all would-be sightseers do, however, pass on with a shudder and without hesitation. For Seveso, once proud of its trade and its tourism, is in the grip of a living nightmare which may never end . . .

On 10 July 1976, an explosion rocked the Icmesa chemical plant just outside town and spewed a bilious dust cloud into the air where it hung, spreading ominously above houses and farm land. Within 24 hours, vegetation downwind of the plant had begun to turn yellow. Leaves on plants and trees curled up and wilted and small animals, mysteriously, began to die. More alarmingly, young children started to develop sores on their arms and legs, red marks and rashes on their faces and high temperatures. The poison was just starting to take effect.

Doctors and officials of Icmesa, which was owned by a giant Swiss drug company, were totally baffled by the events which followed the blast at a small reactor in the factory, which produced agricultural herbicides. It was days before they realised that the explosion had produced a freak chemical 'cocktail' of Tetrachlorodibenzodioxin; more familiar to a horrified world as Agent Orange. It is the active ingredient of the defoliant used with such devastating effect by American forces in Vietnam. It was fully 10 days before the regional government declared the Seveso area polluted by dioxin. And by then it was too late.

For by then, scores of children and adults lay in hospital, their faces covered by gauze masks to hide terrible skin disorders which would leave many of them scarred for life. When the truth finally emerged, 11,000

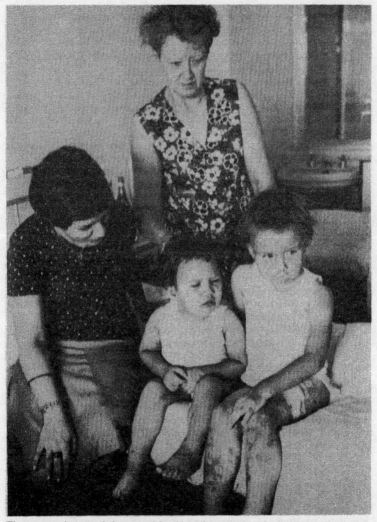

These young sisters are being treated for skin rashes caused by the poisonous gas

SEVESO CHEMICAL DISASTER

townspeople fled their homes, leaving 40,000 farm animals and domestic pets to die from the effects of the poison cloud or be slaughtered. In the eerie silence of what was later named Zone A – the very heart of Seveso – barely a living thing stirred.

Within months of the disaster, which is still known as 'Italy's Hiroshima', the number of children suffering from chloracne – a persistent, dioxin-caused eruption of sore, weeping boils all over the body – had risen to 417. Five decontamination workers contracted liver disease, despite working only four-hour shifts and wearing protective clothing. And, amid fears of abnormal births, at least 400 'high risk' expectant mothers underwent abortions. One leading doctor, Paulo Bruzzi, who today maintains a still-expanding file on the health of Seveso victims, says: 'Had those children been born . . . who knows?'

Several deformities were recorded in new-born babies within months of the Icmesa factory blast, but the full toll of horror will never be known because so many fled the town when the pollution danger was discovered. Attempts to elicit information from doctors all over Italy have met with failure. In an interview in August, 1981 – five years after the nightmare began – Dr Bruzzi declared: 'There is still a danger about which we can say nothing. That is cancer. We have seen many dead animals here . . . and I have to say that if dioxin affected man as it does rabbits, Seveso would have seen a very great disaster indeed. Yet cancer is something we cannot forget about for perhaps 10 years. We must go on watching Seveso with very great care for a very long time to come. It is too soon to ring bells of joy. The only bells to sound from Seveso must be alarms for the world.'

The Italian Government has declared that Zone A must remain closed for ever. It is a graveyard in which memories of a once-prosperous town are buried along with mounds of topsoil from less-contaminated areas – Zones B and R – and the rubble of 300 houses which were immediately demolished. A yellow fence, 10 feet high, with garish notices warning 'quarantine area' encircles the deadly core of Seveso, into which entry can only be gained with government permission for strictly limited periods, with the wearing of special protective clothing an equally strict regulation. The reason for such incredible caution is simple: no-one can be sure whether further tragedy is yet to come.

Recent tests revealed that poison levels in soil taken from the roadside in Seveso were ten times greater than was thought. The tests, carried out by a group of Padua University professors, were rejected by the authorities as 'mistaken'. Whatever dangers do still exist, one thing is certain: the £57 million paid out in compensation by the drug firm which owned Icmesa, Hoffman La Roche, is never going to make Seveso totally safe. In an interview, one government official said: 'It is true that no-one, as far as we know, has died as a result of the poison cloud. But the fact is that we know so little about what we are dealing with. We do not know yet if we have been lucky enough.'

Just as deep-rooted as the health horrors attached to the Seveso disaster are the psychological ones which linger on. Understandably, the birth rate among those who stayed or later returned to be re-housed in 'safe areas' has plummeted. Building contractor Ugo Basilico, 45, who has a son aged 10, declares: 'Before the cloud, I had thought it was about time we had another child. But now who knows? The doctor says it is better to wait. If you have a baby with a defect, it is there for life.'

Five years after the poison cloud spread its misery, at least 193 cases of chloracne had been recorded, leaving many children scarred for life or in need of drastic cosmetic surgery. It can only be guessed how far the tragedy has spread, for a little over four months after the chemical cocktail was, inexplicably, formed and released into the atmosphere, traces of dioxin were found in the mud . . . on a street in Milan. Years of squabbling, accusations and counter-accusations by the authorities and Icmesa officials have done little to help solve the mystery.

Those years of indecision have done nothing to dull the pain or encourage hope for youngsters like little Alicia Senno, who was just four years old when the cloud of doom first overshadowed Seveso. It was a scorching-hot summer, and Alicia had been happily playing outside for days, dressed in shorts and T-shirt with her sister Stefania, aged $2\frac{1}{2}$, and other friends from the neighbourhood.

They all heard the blast. They all saw the white cloud rise. And they all played on with their toys and games. With no alarm or word of warning, they continued to run around while unknowingly exposed to the horrific poison of dioxin, now said to be the most potent known to man.

It was five days after the explosion that Alicia first fell ill. The grotesque eruptions which began to sprout all over her pretty young face came as a terrible shock to her mother and father who, along with other townspeople, had still not been fully told the extent of the dangers which had been thrown

---

Coal dust explosion

The world's worst mining disaster happened on 26 April 1942, when 1,572 men died in a coal dust explosion in China's Honkeiko colliery.

SEVESO CHEMICAL DISASTER

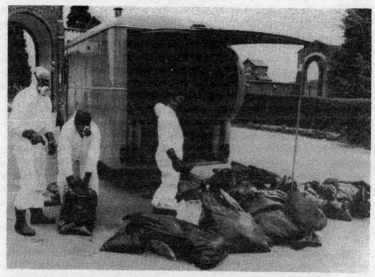

Public health department scientists gather up bags containing animal bodies

upon their community by a chemical mishap. It was only after the family was evacuated from its home that little Alicia, her sister and her mother were admitted to hospital while her father was temporarily put up at a hostel.

With a white gauze mask completely covering her face, save for slits for her eyes, nose and mouth, Alicia's condition rapidly worsened. The effects of chloracne ravaged her facial skin, leaving her in agony. As an early victim of the poison cloud, she became a human guinea-pig, being moved from hospital to hospital in Milan as doctors puzzled out how to try to deal with her appalling skin ailment.

Tissue samples were removed from her face for laboratory tests to see to what degree her skin could be regenerated. The horrendous boils did, eventually, clear up, only to re-appear again at regular intervals which is a common symptom of dioxin poisoning. At times, Alicia still has to wear that mask. It is a recurring ordeal which preys on her mind to such an extent that she is now terrified whenever a figure in white hospital uniform approaches.

Four-year-old Gianluca Bragiato was another early victim of the Seveso disaster. Months after leaving hospital, his mother still had to change the bandages which swathed his face twice a day. When visitors called at the family home, he would rush to bury his face in his father's lap to hide the shame of his disfigurement. He was terrified to show his face to jeering playmates at a nearby kindergarten and he was forced to keep well away from the sun, which made his pock-marked, scarred cheeks burn painfully. At the time of writing, young Gianluca's condition has improved considerably. Yet his doctor maintains: 'It is curable, we believe, though it may take years.'

In incredibly minute doses, measurable in parts per trillion, the chemical can kill mammals. After its widespread use as a 'forest-stripping' defoliant in Vietnam, where thousands of laid-to-waste acres are still heavily contaminated, experts came to the conclusion that in humans its effects – the extent of which are still unknown – can include, as well as chloracne and birth defects, tumours and possibly other serious disorders. Even, as is now feared, cancer.

For those who escaped the poison cloud, there was the grief of losing their homes and all their possessions. Many are adamant that no amount of compensation will ever be able to replace what they once had. Housewife Caterina Rivolta, aged 58, says: 'I would give anything to move back. All our lovely furniture is gone, as is the garden we so loved. My husband and I saved for 16 years to buy our home. Now all we can do is gaze through gaps in the fence, knowing that we cannot return. Nothing – not even any amount of money – will ever replace what we once proudly had.'

As well as the heartbreak which remains, there is still anger among the people of Seveso; anger not only over the bungles and delays which followed the explosion at Icmesa but also over the fact that nobody, not even workers at the plant, was ever warned about the potential dangers of the chemicals being handled there. Yet, who could have known that a freak reaction would result in the formation of deadly dioxin at searing temperatures of up to 158 degrees centigrade?

Still the debate rages on over what should be done to try to totally de-contaminate the area. Many experts believe that may never be possible. But others have proposed radical steps to rid the town of its nightmare. Professor Ghetti, Seveso's regional chief health officer, says: 'We should have burnt down the entire poisoned zone. What has happened here is on the same scale as Hiroshima. It is one of the most gruesome catastrophes in the world.'

Gold mine flooded

One hundred and fifty two men died when flood waters inundated the Witwatersrand gold mine in South Africa in 1909.

SEVESO CHEMICAL DISASTER

Professor Ghetti's 'solution' is, however, scoffed at by other experts, who claim that razing the contaminated areas would worsen the problem. They claim that at temperatures below 1,000 degrees centigrade, the dioxin would simply have been swept up into the air with the smoke and would, eventually, have come down somewhere else.

So the nightmare continues. Today, a crudely painted skull-and-crossbones has been daubed underneath the roadside sign which once proudly declared the name of the town Seveso. Looters and vandals, who moved in for rich and easy pickings despite exposing themselves to incredible danger shortly after the mass evacuations, have long since disappeared, as have the tourists and passing motorists whose trade once kept the town thriving. 'We used to do well from holidaymakers driving north' says the owner of a local petrol station, 'But no more. They won't even stop for gas unless they are about to run out. And as for eating here, well, would you?'

Meanwhile, in Zone A, amid the rubble-strewn poison dump which used to be the heart of Seveso, the only living things which stir are the protective-suited decontamination workers who occasionally foray into the area of devastation and desolation. No animal which ventures inside the high fence will survive for long. No bird ever sings in the town centre. For, while the human victims of Seveso are still, miraculously, alive, it is the town itself which has died.

The Tenerife Plane Crash (1977)

Tenerife is plagued by fog. Clouds bank up around the extinct volcano, Pico de Teide, and spread a sudden eerie mist across the Atlantic holiday island. On Sunday, 27 March 1977 it was very foggy.

A bomb, planted by terrorists of the Canary Islands liberation movement, had exploded in a shop at Las Palmas airport, on the neighbouring island of Gran Canaria, and aircraft were being diverted from Las Palmas to Santa Cruz. Among them were two Boeing 747 jumbo jets – Dutch KLM flight 4805 from Amsterdam and Pan Am flight 1736 from Los Angeles and New York.

The three air traffic controllers on duty in the control tower had eleven planes on the ground, all awaiting clearance for take-off. But their main concerns were the fast-thickening fog, which had reduced visibility to 500 yards, and the central runway lights, which were not working. To add to the confusion, two of the airport's three radio frequencies were out of action and the pilots had to talk to the controllers through the babble of the one remaining frequency. The scene was set for disaster.

The main east-west runway at Santa Cruz is two miles long and 2,000 feet above sea level. Parallel to it is a second runway which planes use to taxi to and from the terminal buildings. These two runways are joined at either end and are linked along their lengths by four access slipways. KLM flight 4805 and Pan Am flight 1736 were stuck in the queue on the second, 'taxi-ing' runway, the Dutch airliner just ahead of the American.

The waiting finally ended just before 5 p.m. KLM pilot Captain Jaap van Zanten announced to his 229 weary passengers that he had at last been given clearance to taxi forward in readiness for take-off to Las Palmas. Pan Am skipper Captain Victor Grubbs made a similar announcement to his 370 American passengers.

Because of the congestion on the taxi-ing runway, both pilots were ordered to move their planes on to the main runway and to taxi to the take-off starting point at the far end. The message went out from the control tower to KLM flight 4805: 'Taxi straight ahead to the end of the runway and make backtrack.'

Captain Van Zanten's mighty jet headed slowly up the long runway while

The wreckage of the Pan Am jumbo with the control tower looming behind

Captain Grubbs received his instructions from the tower – to follow the Dutch jet but to leave the runway by turning into a slipway on the left.

Captain Van Zanten completed his manoeuvre and pointed his airliner's nose into the fog that hid the two miles of main runway ahead of him. His co-pilot reported to the control tower: 'KLM 4805 is now ready for take-off. We are waiting for clearance.' The tower replied: 'OK, stand by for take-off. I will call you.'

THE TENERIFE PLANE CRASH

The reason for the horrific chain of events that occurred in the next few minutes may never be discovered. What *is* known is that while the control tower was checking on the position of the Pan Am jumbo, the Dutch airliner was readying itself for take-off. And while the American plane was still lumbering up the main runway before turning off onto one of the slipways, the KLM airliner released its brakes, increased thrust and began rolling down the two miles of runway . . . straight at Pan Am flight 1736, unseen through the fog.

The Dutch jet was already travelling at 150 miles an hour when Pan Am co-pilot Robert Bragg first spotted it. He said: 'I saw lights ahead of us through the fog. At first I thought it was the KLM standing at the end of the runway. Then I realised the lights were coming towards us.' Bragg screamed: 'Get off. Get off.' Captain Grubbs shouted: 'We're on the runway. We're on the runway.'

Agonisingly slowly, Grubbs slewed his jumbo through a 30-degree turn in a last desperate attempt to avoid disaster. But it was too late. The KLM plane was travelling too fast. It could not stop or swerve. The only option for Captain Van Zanten was to try to lift the nose of his jumbo in a bid to 'hop' over the plane blocking his path.

But Captain Van Zanten had passed the point of no return. Two seconds after lifting off, the Dutch plane smashed into the American jumbo at about 160 miles an hour. The nose of the KLM jet hit the top of the other plane, taking the roof off the cockpit and the first-class upper compartment. The giant engine pods hanging beneath the wings were next to hit the American plane. The port engines ploughed into the aft-cabin, killing most of the passengers instantly.

The KLM Boeing continued its terrible journey over the top of the Pan Am plane and along the runway, disintegrating and exploding into thousands of pieces. Not one person aboard the Dutch plane survived.

All the survivors on the Pan Am plane were sitting either up front or on the left-hand side, away from the impact. Part of the left of the plane was broken off by the crash, and the survivors either were hurled clear or leaped to safety.

The crash occurred at 5.07 p.m. but throughout the long seconds of disaster, the air-traffic controllers remained unaware of it. A Spanish airliner flying above Tenerife broke in to request landing permission. The control tower replied sharply: 'Radio silence, please. I will continue to call up KLM.' But KLM no longer existed. It was a litter of blazing, scattered débris.

It was not until a gust of wind blew a gap in the fog that the controllers realised they were witnesses to the ultimate horror everyone had dreaded – a crash between two jumbo jets, each weighing 240 tons, 231 feet long and with a tailplane the height of a seven-storey building. And both crowded with passengers.

Death was instant for all 229 passengers and 15 crew of the KLM jet. But among the survivors of the Pan Am jumbo, there were tales of panic, horror and heroism.

In the first-class compartment 'all hell broke loose' according to 37-year-old passenger Jim Naik, from California. He said: 'I was sitting with my wife Elsie when there was a sudden explosion. The plane went completely up in flames. I was struggling to get Elsie out with me but after the impact people just started tumbling down on top of us from the lounge above as the ceiling caved in. A piece of ceiling fell on my wife. Then a second explosion hurled me on to the runway. I was running back towards the plane to try to save Elsie when I saw a body falling out of the plane. It was my wife.'

Californian John Amador, aged 35, said: 'I looked out of a porthole and saw the KLM plane coming right at me. I ducked and, when I looked up, our own aircraft was split into three parts. I was afraid I was going to be roasted.' But he leaped to safety.

Mrs Teri Brusco, of Oregon, said 'The Dutch jet's wings took off the whole of the top of our plane. Everyone was screaming.' Her husband Roland pushed his wife through a jagged opening in the side of the plane and they then hauled out his mother. 'My mother was on fire. We started dragging her across the field to put the flames out.'

Briton John Cooper, a 53-year-old Pan Am mechanic, was travelling as a passenger on the flight deck when the plane was hit by the KLM jumbo. He was thrown clear and suffered only minor cuts. He said: 'There was a terrible crash. I just don't want to remember it. There were people screaming terribly, women and children enveloped in flames. I will never get the sound of that screaming out of my ears.'

Explosion in Halifax harbour

Two ships collided in Halifax harbour, Nova Scotia, on 6 December 1917, and destroyed half the town. The Belgian relief ship Imo rammed the French munitions ship Mont Blanc causing a mighty explosion that killed 1,600 people, injured another 8,000 and left 2,000 listed as 'missing'. The suburb of Richmond was destroyed, rail cars were hurled more than a mile and all 200 children in an orphanage were killed. One citizen of Halifax was more lucky . . . he was hurled a mile through the air but survived after landing in a tree.

THE TENERIFE PLANE CRASH

Dorothy Kelly, a 35-year-old Pan Am purser from New Hampshire, was heroine of the day. Later awarded a gallantry medal, this is what she remembered of the disaster: 'There was noise, things flying around. Nothing was recognizable. There was nothing around that looked like anything had looked before – just jagged metal and small pieces of débris. When everything settled, I realized that there was sky above me although I was still in what had been the aircraft. At first, I didn't see any people at all. There were explosions behind me and I realized that the only way out was up. The floor started giving way as I climbed out.'

Mrs Kelly leaped 20 feet to safety then looked back at the broken and blazing plane. There was a string of explosions and she heard people screaming from within the aircraft – so she ran back towards it.

'I saw the captain on his knees, not moving. I thought he had broken his legs. There were other people around with broken limbs. I grabbed the captain under the arms and pulled and kept encouraging him to keep going. I feared the fuselage would fall down on us. There was a huge explosion. I said: "We've got to move faster." I kept pushing and pulling and then dropped him on to the runway.'

Having saved the life of Captain Grubbs, Mrs Kelly dashed back and forth, dragging other dazed survivors clear of the wreckage until she was certain that there could be no one else left alive.

But explosions were ripping through the jumbo. A final series of blasts engulfed the plane in flames. There was no longer any hope of survival for anyone left aboard. Of the 370 passengers and 16 crew of the jumbo, more than 300 were dead within minutes of the crash and more than 60 were seriously injured. The final death toll on the day the two leviathans of the skies collided was a horrifying 582.

The Big Heat
(1980)

The Big Heat began in June, scoring out a vast, arid dust bowl across thousands of miles of land. Farmers faced ruin as their animals died and their crops were destroyed. Even the super-rich cattle ranchers of the mid-West saw fortunes wiped out. But the Big Heat came to cost more than dollars. It cost lives, on an incredible scale . . .

Summer 1980 saw a trail of disaster sweep across America as the highest temperatures ever recorded in the country turned life into a red-hot hell. Twenty states were hit hard by the killer heatwave and, within a month of the weather going wild on 22 June, at least 1,200 people had died. Old folk simply collapsed in the street. The crime rate soared as people were driven into a frenzy as the sun burned down. And, as youngsters were forced to stay indoors, cases of child abuse rocketed as family frustrations boiled over.

The mid-West and Southern states were worst affected. Dallas, Texas, bore the brunt of the Big Heat with an astonishing 23 consecutive days of temperatures in excess of 100 degrees farenheit. Carole Bowdry, the city's Director of a Child Abuse Prevention Program, had to admit: 'In the past few weeks, my caseload has been up substantially. It is becoming a terrible problem. If you're hot, you're going to get angry faster. If the parents are the type who are going to be abusive, this is the time when it will show up.' In Missouri, one tragic victim was a two-year-old boy, who died after two hours locked in a van parked in the street. He had been put there because his mother could not find a baby-sitter.

One of the most gruesome stories to emerge from the heatwave nightmare involved a band of illegal aliens from El Salvador, who had been smuggled across the border, en masse, from Mexico into Arizona. Of the 26 back-door immigrants who made what in normal circumstances would have been a hazardous journey, only 13 ever arrived. The rest died under a cruel, blazing sun.

The ages of victims in the worst-hit states ranged from six months to 90; no-one escaped the merciless melting-pot.

Raging brush fires, sparked on bone-dry, tinder-box land, swept Arizona. Part of a highway in Okemah, Oklahoma literally blew-up, scattering chunks of concrete as effectively as if it had been dynamited. In Macon, Georgia, the city's air-conditioned Coliseum had to be opened up as an emergency refuge for people in distress. By early July, the weathermen were predicting worse to come.

Extreme temperatures were accompanied by incredibly high humidity, picked up from the Gulf of Mexico, which made it almost impossible to stay out of doors for any length of time without contracting heatstroke. From state to state, governors were declaring emergency zones and setting up relief centres. In Washington, President Carter ordered the release of almost 7 million dollars in emergency federal funds to assist in 'heat relief' programmes. That cash aid brought little relief, however, to farmers whose losses by then had been conservatively estimated at a staggering 2,000 million dollars.

For the cattle men of Kansas the drought caused by the Big Heat was particularly ruinous. During one market day at the height of the freak weather in the small town of Hutchinson, 40 miles north-west of Wichita, Joe Thaxton, a part-owner of the market, stood in the shade of a tree, pushed his blue peak cap above his sweat-beaded forehead and told newsmen who had gathered to witness the death of a community: 'They're being forced to bring the cattle in one-and-a-half months early. They don't have no grass in the fields and they can't afford the price of cattle feed. So they have to sell; they don't have no choice. We're getting 30 per cent more to sell than we usually get at this time of the year and the prices are way down. If we don't get a good rain soon, 15 per cent of the farmers will go bankrupt. It will be a total disaster.'

Swiftly, the price of hay rocketed so high that farmers were unable to afford to feed their livestock. Ranchers were forced to make the agonizing choice of either borrowing heavily to afford foodstuffs which had more than doubled in price – or slaughter their cattle. Crops were decimated and in many areas the poultry industry was savagely hit. Corn, soya beans, green vegetables and fruit were all ruined. In Arkansas, America's main producer of chickens, the birds perished in the sizzling heat and many thousands had to be slaughtered.

The crippling, natural disaster could not have come at a worse time for the country's beleaguered farmers who were already facing deep financial trouble because of a combination of inflation, the recession and a Government ordered embargo on grain exports to the Soviet Union. According to one report in the British *Guardian* newspaper: 'Flying into Wichita provides a graphic overview of parched, brown fields shorn of grass or dotted with stunted crops. Each morning at dawn, the sun comes up as a bright red ball over the flat plain, signalling another day of unremitting heat.'

Bryce Owr, the county's agricultural agent, put the disaster into enlightening perspective when he told the newspaper: 'My father was a farmer. It hurt; but we had enough to get by on. In those days we were in the Depression and nobody had nothing, so your demands were not that great.

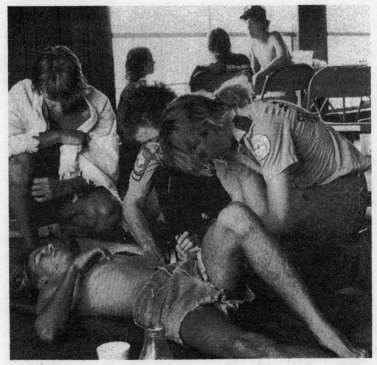

A young heat victim being treated in Houston

It can happen again. We have only been in the heat for a few weeks. But since it began, we have learned a lot about conservation. They have planted wind-breakers – trees and shrubs – and reservoirs have been made and a lot of land has been put back to grass. That binds it and stops it going to dust. We have learned a lot . . .'

The parallel with Depression-era America was especially poignant, for the scorching temperatures of summer 1980 topped even those of the worst previous heatwave of the mid-1930s, in which about 15,000 people are estimated to have died during three terrible years. Then, people took to sleeping on benches in public parks during the long, hot nights. In 1980, anyone who had dared to do that would have left themselves a sitting target

Horrific drought

Australia, facing rationing and hardship after years of war was, in 1944–45, hit by a disastrous drought. The harvest failed and the number of sheep in Australia fell by more than a third. It took 10 years for the sheep stocks to recover their original levels.

for the muggers and molesters whose trade in violence had been accelerated by the steam-bath conditions.

Across the sweltering states, night time temperatures often only dipped as far as the mid to high eighties. In towns across the country, where the Red Cross was busy distributing free fans and opening air-conditioned emergency centres, people were bringing their beds onto their porches or on to the strips of brown grass at the fronts and backs of their homes. Bars and restaurants did not report the expected sharp rise in demand for cold drinks – people just could not summon up the energy to leave their houses. One resident told journalists: 'The thought of food and cooking just repels me. I just want to sit at home in the cool. After a day's work you feel totally drained.' Needless to say, as the crime boom continued, there was a massive surge in the number of thefts of air-conditioning units. Demand for electricity also rose as millions of desperate inhabitants switched on all available air-conditioning in their search for at least a degree of relief.

For many, there was none. The death toll was highest in the poorer areas, where many people did not have air-conditioning. By 21 July, the people of Kansas were celebrating the fact that the mercury was registering a mere 93 degrees farenheit. It was only the second day in a month that it had not reached three figures, the peak of which was an almost unbelievably stifling 114 degrees. On one night in Washington, the temperature did not fall below 91 degrees, with a relative humidity of 85 per cent – the equivalent of a turkish bath.

Miners trapped

A coal mine disaster at Courrières, northern France, in 1906 killed more than 1,000 pitmen. The surviving miners, trapped far below ground, lost all sense of time. When rescued, they thought they had been incarcerated for four to five days. In fact, they had been underground for three weeks.

THE BIG HEAT

The Big Heat did bring to the simmering surface several stories of a rather more humanly quirky nature. In almost a double-take of the song about 'Mad dogs and Englishmen', hoteliers in Florida watched in utter amazement as thousands of British holidaymakers on cheap package tours went out to fry themselves on the beaches in the midday sun. One Palm Beach hotel owner declared incredulously: 'They are out there every day, lying on the beach or walking along the baking streets . . . even when the sun is at its height.' California, on the other hand, was in the grip of a new craze; people were spending a fortune visiting solariums for daily three-minute sessions under sun lamps to maintain their tans!

American industry suffered badly as the Big Heat continued to bite through July. Hundreds of companies were rocked by absenteeism as workers simply shut themselves indoors to escape the sun's piercing rays. Hospital staffs across the country were stretched to the limit treating sunstroke cases. One Dallas hospital alone treated thousands of sun-affected patients in little over a fortnight.

It seemed as if it would never end. Virtually every facet of private and public life took a blistering from the Big Heat. But the solar onslaught did subside and the rains did come. From the heatbowl of July, August began with cooler temperatures and almost as suddenly as it had all begun, nature seemed to return to normal . . . having left a trail of death and destruction in the wake of almost two months during which the sun went wild. The Big Heat was over.

North Sea Oil Rig Disaster (1980)

A mocking cheer of sympathy went echoing round the cinema as movie star Robert Redford appeared on screen, tugging a crude fur coat round his face to cover himself against the biting, snow-laden winds.

The all male audience in the private cinema were thoroughly enjoying Redford's performance as 'Jeremiah Johnson', a tough frontiersman fighting for his life in a desolate Rocky Mountain wilderness. The audience knew a thing or two about survival in the face of Nature's fury. They considered themselves experts.

On the flickering screen, a raging storm forced 'Jeremiah' to huddle deeper inside his makeshift shelter of branches and twigs. Outside the cinema a real-life gale, with winds of 70 miles an hour, battered against the double glazed windows, adding its own howling to the film's sound track.

The 100 seat cinema was at near capacity. Across a narrow corridor, on the same level, a staff of six were busy preparing the menu for an evening meal offering a choice of steak or fresh salmon. The adjoining restaurant already had a small group of customers starting on their first course of thick chicken broth and freshly baked rolls. In the accommodation block, one floor above the cinema, some men were lounging on their beds, watching television or writing letters to sweethearts, wives and children.

Slowly at first, the cinema began to shake and rock. It had happened before. There was no alarm, only some muttered curses from the audience as drinks began to spill over their tables and ashtrays tumbled to the floor. Gradually the cinema floor levelled itself again and a few of the men got to their feet, wiping cigarette ash and drinks from their trousers.

Then the floor began to tilt again, this time steeper and steeper. Tables began to slip towards the rear wall. Those men on their feet clutched unsteadily at the bar for support, until the counter wrenched itself slowly from the brackets holding it to the floor. There was a groaning sound of twisting metal as the angle of the floor increased, then a sudden explosive bang. The first fearful shouts came as the floor lurched at a crazy angle and men dropped to their knees, trying vainly to dig their fingernails into the thick carpet to prevent themselves sliding into the jumble of furniture and bodies piling up against the rear wall.

NORTH SEA OIL RIG DISASTER

A heavy trestle table tumbled end over end across the cinema, smashing through a window and allowing a sudden blast of bitterly cold wind into the room, blowing curtains, table cloths and cushions into a miniature whirlwind.

On the cinema screen, tilted at an angle of 25 degrees, actor Robert Redford huddled over a camp fire and prepared to skin and cook a deer. His image began to shake, the moving pictures slipping from the white screen. Redford's distorted face appeared briefly on the ceiling before the projector at the rear of the cinema broke free of its mountings and crashed into the wall.

One heavy chair slid along the wall and wedged itself in the emergency door as some of the men clawed their way along the carpet towards safety. For a few moments they tugged at the chair, then the emergency exit flew open. But the sudden movement of the door had not been the result of their frantic efforts, it had been struck on the outside by drums of oil tumbling down the corridor. Black waves of oil flooded into the cinema and the men who had almost reached freedom slid helplessly back into one sinking corner.

Ten seconds later, the cinema, the sleeping quarters, the restaurant and hospital and the whole complex of buildings on the deck of the Alexander Kielland oil platform accommodation rig, toppled 100 feet into the raging waters of the North Sea.

Two hundred and thirteen men – Norwegians, Americans and Britons, some of the toughest North Sea oil roustabouts, had been relaxing on board the supply rig that night, 27 March 1980. Their temporary home had been the 10,105 ton semi-submersible oil rig, once an active North Sea drilling and exploring platform, now converted into a floating hotel.

Even with surface waves of 30 or 40 feet, as they were that stormy March night, the rig should only have bobbed up and down by three or four feet, its steel legs half filled with water acting as stabilising ballast.

Although the Alexander Kielland's exploration days were over, the rig still supported a top heavy 200 ton drilling tower which her owners, the Stavanger Drilling Company of Norway, had not dismantled. But the rig had undergone other modifications. It had been adapted to carry a three storey accommodation block, providing a home, entertainment and medical facilities for 350 men.

The rig's new job was to move from site to site in the Norwegian sector of the North Sea oil fields, acting as a mobile depot providing a work force for other rigs which were in fixed production positions. The men of the Alexander Kielland would work for a few weeks at a time alongside new production rigs, and would then be towed to another site inside the Ekofisk

A crew accommodation platform

oilfield, halfway between the coasts of Norway and Scotland.

There was one other modification to the original design of the Alexander Kielland. Each of the rig's five legs was strengthened by tubular steel braces, hollow struts of one and a quarter inch steel. A ten-inch circular hole had been cut in one of the braces to install a hydrophone, an electronic listening device which would allow the Alexander Kielland to manoeuvre itself accurately into position above a beacon placed on the ocean bed. The hole, a mere pinprick in the awesome web of the rig's metalwork, had been casually sealed and then simply welded.

On the night of the disaster, the Alexander Kielland was on hire to the Phillips Petroleum Company and was stationed 150 miles off the Norwegian coast, rising and falling in the gathering storm alongside the production rig Edda. A 100-feet long flexible catwalk connected the Kielland and the Edda. While the Edda stood firmly with its own feet planted on the ocean bed, ten strong sea anchors, attached two at a time to each of the Alexander Kielland's legs, kept the 'floatel' in position beside the production rig.

As the wind and waves began to batter both platforms, senior oil technicians considered moving the Alexander Kielland further away from the Edda platform in case the floating rig dragged her anchors and scraped alongside the Edda. But the Alexander Kielland had ridden out bigger storms than the one blowing that night.

NORTH SEA OIL RIG DISASTER

The Alexander Kielland's anchors were holding fast. The 'floatel' was a rugged construction and her certificate of seaworthiness had been renewed only a month earlier by an insurance inspection agency whose engineers assured them that the four-year-old platform was in first class structural condition.

As night fell, no-one noticed the gaping cracks which began to spread along the 'pinprick' in the bracing strut as the waves pounded the Alexander Kielland. Shortly after 6.30 p.m., twisted and buckled by the forces of the ocean, the bracing strut gave way without warning and one of the giant supporting legs, immediately beneath the accommodation block, began to rip itself away from the platform.

Chief steward Thomas Greenwood of Keighley, West Yorkshire, was in the kitchen helping to prepare the evening meal, when the platform began to tilt wildly. He said later:

'The first thing I felt was a shudder, then the screeching of metal. I thought perhaps the derrick crane on the edge of the platform, used for lifting stores on board, was beginning to collapse. Then the whole kitchen began to tilt over. Pots and pans started to slide off the shelves and I heard pandemonium breaking out in the mess restaurant next door where plates were falling off tables and the furniture was beginning to topple over.

The men from the mess were dragging their way along the corridor as the platform went over at an angle of about 30 degrees and we all began pulling ourselves along the handrail towards the control room at the end of the corridor, the highest part of the rig. We had almost reached the control room when a river of oil from the busted drums on deck came gushing down the corridor and we all slipped back about 50 feet.

I found a way out halfway down the corridor and pulled myself on to the helicopter landing pad. I braced myself beside a window and helped to pull four or five people out and throw them towards the lifeboat. The last man was trying to climb up the gangway as the platform began to fall more steeply into the sea. He had almost made it when a blue gas cylinder broke loose from a shelf on the gangway and hit him. He just disappeared out of sight.'

On the sloping platform, now almost vertical, four men were killed when a 300-ton piece of machinery, a massive blow-out preventer valve, was ripped from its housing and smashed them into the sea. Greenwood, 37, found that the rig had tilted over so far that its lifeboats were entangled in the platform structure and he bravely managed to winch one of them down to the sea, 100 feet below. Then he set himself the task of trying to help the pathetic band of survivors closest to him.

Two men, numbed with cold, hung limply from metal railings on the platform, their lifejackets firmly caught. The steward cut one free with his penknife, watching the man drop into the waves and get carried towards the lifeboat. He tore the other man free and waited for a big wave to sweep towards them. Then he dropped him.

'He screamed all the way down to the water' Greenwood said. 'Then he was washed out behind the other man. I was hanging on to one edge of the platform, watching her going slowly over. At the far end I could see the accommodation unit, with the lads inside trying to smash the windows to get out. It was horrifying. When the rig became horizontal, the water and waves began to force their way into the accommodation and enormous pressure built up in the rooms and corridors. Then the windows started to blow out under the pressure. Lifejackets, quilts, mattresses and bodies were all blown out into the sea. I'll never forget that sight.'

When Greenwood finally threw himself into the water, he struck out for a lifeboat and spent the night afloat with 27 other survivors before a helicopter rescued them at dawn next day.

Oil company representative Ronald Jackson, 39, from Manchester, was one of the audience in the cinema when the rig began to tilt. 'All the chairs and bottles were just sliding along the floor' he recalled. 'They crashed into the movie screen and the water flooded through the windows and people just disappeared underneath. I panicked like mad when I saw electric cables burning and sparking outside the cinema just before the power failed. I made it to the deck but it was nearly impossible to climb in the dark. It was at 45 degrees by that time. Steel ropes were flying about, drums of oil were bursting open everywhere and the water level was rising. It was like a crazy nightmare.'

Jackson was thrown clear and struggled to a lifeboat.

Aboard the production platform Edda, only 30 yards away, the crew watched in stunned horror as the Alexander Kielland tipped most of the living souls aboard her into the surging waves. Many of the men on the Edda had been preparing to finish their working shift and getting ready to struggle back along the flexible catwalk to the Alexander Kielland for the hot meal,

Yachtsmen die

Fifteen yachtsmen died in August 1979, when appalling sea conditions hit the three-day race from Cowes, Isle of Wight, to the Fastnet Rock, off southern Eire. Twenty five of the competing boats sank and 19 more were abandoned in a Force 11 Atlantic gale. Only 90 of the 300 competing boats finished.

the comfort of the cinema and the safe luxury of a warm bed they believed awaited them.

As the first frantic Mayday radio messages filled the airwaves, the production crew of the Edda desperately lined the edge of their platform, ripping off their own lifejackets and throwing them to the drowning men in the water. The temperature in the North Sea that night was four degrees above freezing. No-one without a specially insulated survival suit could live more than 10 minutes before they died of exposure.

Only a pitiful few of the screaming men in the water managed to swim the short gap between the sinking 'floatel' and the production platform. The men of the Edda lowered ropes and baskets and winched down their own two lifeboats as they watched struggling survivors being dashed to their deaths in waves which slammed them into the twisted metalwork of the Alexander Kielland and the solid legs of the Edda.

Within minutes of the radio alert, the shore based rescue services had scrambled into action. As Sea King helicopters of the Royal Air Force at Boulmer, 180 miles away on the Northumberland coast, and the helicopters of the Royal Norwegian Air Force at Stavanger, roared into the air, a small flotilla of trawlers and supply ships were ordered to the scene of the disaster.

Two hours after take-off, Rescue 31, a Sea King of A Flight, 202 Squadron, Royal Air Force, hovered over the stricken platform, only 30 feet above the wave tops. Co-pilot Flight Lieutenant Michael Lakey was first to spot the bobbing liferaft with ten survivors aboard, men who had escaped the horror of the Alexander Kielland but who were already beginning to weaken and die of exposure in their liferaft.

Lakey reported: 'The sea was so rough that at first we thought it would be better to direct a surface rescue vessel to the liferaft rather than try to winch the survivors up ourselves. Then we realized this would take too long.'

Swooping down above the crashing seas, winchman Flight Sergeant Michael Yarwood lowered himself towards the life raft. Time after time he tried to get aboard the raft but the pounding waves smashed the raft against him, leaving his legs battered and bleeding. Yarwood realized he had only one chance to save the dying men. As one surging wave swept towards him out of the darkness, he unhooked his own safety lifeline and 'surfed' along the crest of the wave until he grabbed the edge of the raft. Then he guided the helicopter overhead and one by one the men were lifted to safety and dropped aboard the helicopter pad of the oil rig Edda.

A new danger for the flying rescue teams rolled in on the freezing night air – a thick sea mist enveloping and obscuring the wave tops. Frustrated by the fog and unable to see the surface of the water with their powerful searchlights, the crew of Rescue 31 reluctantly climbed to a safe height of

The enormous broken-off leg of the capsized platform is examined by experts

NORTH SEA OIL RIG DISASTER

2,000 feet to avoid the danger of ditching in the water or colliding with the Edda rig or other search aircraft. The enforced climb probably saved the lives of more than a score of Kielland survivors. At 2,000 feet Rescue 31 clearly picked up the bleeping signal of an automatic distress beacon. Homing in on the beacon in the misty blackness, they found a lifeboat with 26 exhausted and injured men aboard.

Again Flight Sergeant Yarwood was winched down into the ocean. He reported back that the lifeboat was not badly damaged and that none of the occupants were seriously injured. Unable to lift all the men off, the Sea King stayed hovering protectively above their frail lifeboat, radioing their precise position until a rescue tug reached the survivors. As the fog thickened around the Ekofisk oilfield, Rescue 31 flew 30 miles to an oil rig in the Auk field for re-fuelling and waited for dawn to resume the search.

First light brought an eerie calm to the North Sea. The distinctive silhouette of the Alexander Kielland had disappeared forever from the skyline. Clearly visible above the sea were four of the 'feet' of the platform. Half a mile away the swell was breaking over the drifting remains of the fifth leg, the main support which had been positioned below the corner of the platform holding the accommodation block.

The Alexander Kielland had turned completely upside down. Eighty-nine men had been rescued, fifty bodies had been recovered and seventy three were still missing.

The capsized platform was firmly tethered between the Norwegian tugs and salvage vessels and divers plunged into the icy water, hoping desperately to find men trapped among air pockets in the twisted wreckage. Trying to keep their own air supply hoses from becoming entangled, the divers began to feel their way down the hollow legs, hammering them furiously with metal bars, waiting for any feeble reply. They got no answers.

As major support ships arrived in the Ekofisk oilfield, more divers with powerful lights and underwater cutting equipment were sent 200 feet down into the silent upside-down world of the Alexander Kielland. They were confronted by a bizarre scene.

Peeping through the maze of corridors in the accommodation block, they reported overhead lighting below them and carpeted floors above. In the kitchen many of the ovens and sinks were still firmly secured to the 'ceiling'. The divers were ordered not to penetrate into the interior of the platform. They attached strong steel ropes to the Alexander Kielland to begin the long job of towing her back to the sheltered Norwegian fiords where a long detailed examination of the floating inverted wreck could be made.

Salvage experts knew that moving the upturned platform away from the scene would be a risky job. They feared that the superstructure of the platform might drag along the ocean bed and rupture one of the intricate network of North Sea oil and gas pipelines, causing a disastrous blowout. The divers and submarines were sent to the ocean floor to check if the Alexander Kielland and her overturned drilling derrick had enough clearance to tow her over the top of the Ekofisk pipelines.

The North Sea oilmen watched a grim underwater vista relayed to them from the ocean floor as they sat in the floating control rooms of their salvage ships, hunched before their television monitors. As the ocean bed came into focus they saw with some relief that the Alexander Kielland's 100 foot drilling derrick had sheared clean off and was lying on its side, no longer pointing straight down from the platform and no longer a threat to the triangle of pipelines just a few hundred yards away. The mass of ropes, cables and ladders hanging from the upturned platform made it extremely dangerous for any divers to approach too close.

The salvage controllers were ordering the cameras to give them close-up pictures of the drilling derrick when they caught the first glimpse of some of the men who had lost their lives. Even the hard-bitten oilmen were stunned and shocked by what they saw.

The bodies were entagled in the cables, some of them lay on the ocean floor, draped lifelessly across the oil pipeline they had worked so hard to lay and service. Some were clad only in jeans and t-shirts, lying still among the wreckage of the furniture from the Alexander Kielland's cinema. Others were in pyjamas and dressing gowns, trapped without warning and drowned in their bedrooms when their floating hotel had hit the waves and filled with water.

A day later the ocean-going tugs took up the slack on the steel hawsers attached to the Alexander Kielland and began the sombre journey towards the sheltered deep water of Stavenger Fiord. Over the next seven days, as the ghostly platform was towed underwater back to its homeland, 20 more bodies were recovered from the cold water of the Ekofisk oilfield.

In the North Sea, where death is never far away, the oil rig workers went about their daily business of capturing the riches under the ocean floor for an energy hungry world. Rewarded by salaries of up to £1,000 a week they suppressed their fears and waited for the engineers' reports to tell them why the Alexander Kielland had turned from a floating haven into a watery grave.

In London and Stavanger, committees of insurance brokers sat down to carve up the responsibility for footing the £30 million insurance loss for the Alexander Kielland and to choose a salvage contractor to try to coax more than 10,000 tons of steel, standing on its head, back on to its feet.

At R.A.F. Boulmer, gallantry awards were bestowed on the crew of Sea

NORTH SEA OIL RIG DISASTER

King helicopter Rescue 31. The Air Force Cross was awarded to pilot Flight Lieutenant Robert Edward Neville who displayed 'the highest standards of flying skill and leadership'. The Queen's Commendation went to Flight Lieutenant Michael Lakey and winch operator Flight Sergeant John Moody. Winchman Flight Sergeant Michael Yarwood was honoured with the Air Force Medal, praised for his 'outstanding courage, professional skill and pertinancity'.

A year after the disaster, the Norwegian Government inquiry concluded that modifications to the bracing strut of the Alexander Kielland had weakened the metal. They criticised the design and servicing of the platform, pointing out that the lifeboat launching mechanism had failed to operate and three of the Alexander Kielland's lifeboats had been smashed to pieces on the sides of the platform.

They described the emergency precautions as 'abysmal' and the safety checks as 'inadequate'. And they revealed that out of the 212 men on board only 76 of them had attended a safety course.

Perhaps this appalling tragedy, the worst of its kind, could have been avoided.

The Las Vegas MGM Fire (1980)

Las Vegas was the glittering gambling centre of the world, a neon-lit oasis in the Nevada desert that existed only for fun. First settled only in 1905, it was a mining community of just over 8,000 people until the 1950s, when favourable state gaming laws turned it, almost overnight, into a mecca for everyone chasing a get-rich-quick dream. Skyscraper hotels featuring lush casinos and floor shows studded with the top international stars mushroomed along the legendary Strip, luring gamblers from all over the globe to lose their money in fruit machines that offered a million dollar payout for a ten dollar stake. The rich and would-be rich flocked to the city without clocks to pursue their fortunes in a gaudy, unreal world.

But at 7.15 a.m. on the morning of 21 November 1980, cruel reality turned the tinsel dream into a nightmare. One of the worst hotel fires in America's history left 84 people dead, more than 600 others injured.

The Grand Hotel had been opened on the Strip by Hollywood film-makers MGM in 1973. It cost £50 million, had 2,100 bedrooms, and was named after the company's successful Thirties film starring Greta Garbo. Singing stars such as Tom Jones and Englebert Humperdinck earned up to £125,000 a week from cabaret sessions in the vast gambling saloon on the first of the hotel's 26 storeys. That saloon had shared in a bumper take for Nevada casinos in 1979 – an estimated $2,100,000,000. The odds were that 1980 would be even more profitable.

Then came the disaster of 21 November. It began when cooking fat in the basement kitchen which served the hotel's five restaurants overheated, and set fire to the ceiling. In seconds, a horrific fireball had built up and burst into the 140 feet long casino, one of the biggest in the world. Even at 7.15 a.m., it was still crowded with gamblers, be-jewelled and be-furred women playing the blackjack tables, dinner-suited men feeding dollars into the 1,000 slot machines. Ten of the gamblers died where they sat. Others seemed stunned, staring motionless at the roaring flames. 'Within 90 seconds, the entire casino had been engulfed', a card dealer recalled later.

Casino staff were among the first to react. Girl croupiers grabbed cash drawers and raced for the exits. Dealers dashed for the doors, cramming betting chips into their pockets as they ran. Security guards scooped up armfuls of dollar bills and dropped them into a fireproof vault before

THE LAS VEGAS MGM FIRE

Smoke pours from the MGM Grand Hotel at the height of the fire

escaping. Flames pursued the fleeing gamblers through the doors, blowing up two cars outside. Inside, a huge electronic Keno board, used for a bingo-style betting game, exploded and fuelled the fire, which fed hungrily on plastic fittings, flock wallpaper, plush carpets and synthetic furnishings. Gaping openings in the hotel walls, where construction work was in progress, created a convection effect, and breezes through windows broken by panicking gamblers also fanned the flames. But now an even more deadly menace emerged.

The burning furnishings and carpets gave off noxious gases, clouds of thick, choking, yellow-brown smoke which mushroomed up the staircases and lift shafts to the upper storeys of the building, where more than 1,000 guests were sleeping, unaware of the drama downstairs. None of the mirror-ceiling bedrooms had smoke detectors and, amazingly, no alarm was sounded. Fire chiefs said later that amplification systems burnt out before the sirens had a chance to blare. Some fire doors had been left open, which filled corridors with the creeping, suffocating blanket of fumes. Tragically, others had been left locked – a factor which was to cost several lives.

The first warning most sleepers had of their peril was the approaching din of fire-engines and ambulances as the Las Vegas emergency services swung into action. Then US Air Force helicopters arrived around the top floor of the skyscraper, urging people through loud-hailers to climb on to the roof to be rescued. A fleet of 12 choppers winched them up, landing them on the car park below. But some guests never made it. A rescue team led by Dr Phil Taylor later found 18 asphyxiated bodies on one staircase, huddled together in terror after finding themselves trapped between an impenetrable wall of smoke and a jammed door.

Panic and confusion set in, especially when those at the top of the building saw that the ladders of the 30 fire-engines ringing the hotel could reach only the ninth floor. Guests opened their room doors to be met with choking fumes. Many could not open their windows because of anti-suicide safety catches. They had to smash the glass to reach their balconies.

'People were screaming and throwing furniture through windows and begging to be saved,' said county fire chief Ralph Dinsman. The lucky ones scrambled down scaffolding hastily erected by workmen from a nearby building site, or were carried to safety on the hotel's exterior window-cleaning lift. Others could not wait for rescue. A desperate, half-choked woman flung herself to her death from a 17th floor balcony. Two men trying to climb from their sixth floor room also plunged to the ground and were killed.

Police with loud-hailers pleaded with guests at the upper windows not to try to clamber down the steep sides of the building. But many defied the warning – and lived to tell the tale. Donna Gleave, a survivor from the 20th floor, said: 'A man lowered his wife down from the 21st floor on a rope made from bed sheets, and I pulled her in at my window. Then we lowered ourselves to the 19th and were rescued.'

Two British businessmen escaped because their automatic alarm clock went off too early by mistake. Roy Taylor, events manager at the National Exhibition Centre in Birmingham, and David McAllister, from Aldershot, Hampshire, had a room on the sixth floor. Mr Taylor, 40, said: 'We'd forgotten to switch the clock off and it rang at 6.40. I turned it off and we were just going back to sleep when David mumbled about smelling something burning. We opened the bedroom door and were knocked back by a wall of smoke. We tried to open the window, but there were catches designed to stop people falling out. We hurled a coffee table through the glass then dropped mattresses and bedding on to a flat roof three floors 40 feet below. David hung by his hands from the sill, then dropped. I was about to do the same when he shouted, "Go back." I ducked as a shower of glass

A U.S. Air Force helicopter lifts a hotel guest to safety

cascaded down from above. It would have sliced my head off. Then I jumped. We were met by firemen who took us down smoke-filled stairs.'

British holidaymakers Russell and Lilian Ireland, from Ealing, West London, also battled their way out of the deathtrap. They were up early because they were due to check out and fly home. Then they heard sirens and smoke began pouring into their sixth floor room. 'There were no alarms, no sprinklers, and no directions to the fire escapes,' said Mr Ireland, 59. 'I grabbed Lilian and told two other women to follow us. The fire door was locked but we managed to tear the damn thing open. It was a hell of a difficult job.'

Up on the 22nd floor, James Mackey and his wife, from Michigan, learned what was happening from a radio newsflash. 'We put mattresses against the wall and stuffed towels under the door,' he said. 'We put a note on the door and prayed a lot.' Firemen rescued them.

Five floors below, Keith Breverton opened his door to find 'an impassable hell.' He said later: 'It was death, absolute death out there. People were screaming, "What shall we do?"'. Mr Breverton slammed the door shut, and lay on the floor to escape the worst of the smoke. Convinced he was about to die, he hastily scribbled notes on the only paper available – the backs of cheques. Firemen who found him unconscious revived him with oxygen before lowering him to safety.

As in the case of the 1974 Sao Paulo fire in Brazil, the horrific scenes resembled the Steve McQueen movie, *The Towering Inferno*. And following the example set in the film saved more than one Las Vegas guest. Greg Williams told reporters: 'I'd seen the film. I wrapped a wet towel round my head, got down on my hands and knees and crawled under the smoke to a fire exit.'

Outside, in the chill morning air, dazed guests wandered in the 43-acre grounds of the hotel, some barefoot and weeping, still in their nightclothes after a late night in the casino, some with fur coats draped over negligees. On the street a doctor pounded the heart of a man who had collapsed and a grim-faced priest moved among the injured waiting for an ambulance, absolving those least likely to make it. Again and again, rescue teams plunged into the blackened building after fresh alerts – people were trapped in the lifts, staff counting the multi-million takings in a locked room were unaccounted for.

After two hours, firemen had controlled the flames on the lower floors. Masked men edged upwards through the smoke to continue the grisly job of retrieving bodies. A construction worker stumbled over a huddled group in the pitch-dark casino. A waiter was found beside the tray on which he had been serving breakfast. Two guests were discovered, choked to death, in their rooms. Others were found where they had fallen in smoke-filled

Hurricane Camille

Holidaymakers at the luxurious Richelieu Apartments in Pass Christian, Mississippi, decided to hold a party and watch the storm after warnings that Hurricane Camille was heading for the American Gulf Coast on Sunday, 17 August 1969. Twenty six of them died when winds racing at 200 miles per hour smashed the apartments to pieces, and virtually wiped out the town. Camille, described by Dr Robert Simpson, director of Florida's National Hurricane Shelter as 'the greatest recorded storm ever to hit a populated area in the Western Hemisphere', spread devastation across a 70-mile swathe of Mississippi, Louisiana and Alabama. A total of more than 250 men, women and children died, 130 of them in the Mississippi town of Gulfport. Nearly 19,500 homes and 700 small businesses were demolished, and three large cargo ships were torn from their moorings and beached. The death toll might have been higher, had 150,000 people not had more sense than the Pass Christian revellers – they fled away from the coast before the hurricane arrived.

staircases. Amazingly, one guest was found alive in her room several hours after the fire was out. Firemen said she was 'just too afraid to come out'.

As the smouldering hotel was damped down and closed up, the questions began. Why was no alarm sounded? Why were there automatic sprinkler systems on only the bottom three floors? Why were there no smoke detectors in the bedrooms? Why were so many staircase doors locked, trapping many who might have escaped the disaster? Hotel president Bernard Rothkopf insisted that the building was not in breach of any building or fire safety codes, and he was backed by security expert Don Busser, who said: 'You cannot blame MGM management entirely, the state bears some responsibility.' He said the Grand had been completed to 1970 fire code standards. Though stringent new regulations had been introduced in 1979, they applied only to new buildings. Fire chief Dinsman admitted that no government agency had ever conducted a fire drill in any of the Las Vegas skyscrapers.

MGM Hotel Corporation stock slumped on the share markets as law suits on behalf of those killed or injured poured in. A total of 429 claims were filed, demanding almost two billion dollars in compensation and punitive damages. The tragedy also heralded a crisis for the whole of Las Vegas. It came just three months after thousands of gamblers were evacuated from a casino in nearby Lake Tahoe after a 1,000 lb bomb was planted. And it was followed, over the next five months, by three other hotel blazes in Vegas.

THE LAS VEGAS MGM FIRE

Sixteen people were hurt when fire broke out on the fifth floor of Caesar's Palace in April 1981, and in February, eight people died and 300 were hurt when four separate fires started at the Hilton. A waiter was later charged with starting the Hilton fires. He allegedly admitted igniting curtains accidentally with a marijuana cigarette and it was revealed that he had earlier worked at the Grand. But police ruled out arson as the cause of the MGM disaster.

Whatever the cause of the fires, public confidence in Las Vegas was undermined. Gambling revenues in the first three months of 1981 fell by more than $20 million as punters decided that the neon city was no longer such a safe bet. Many even questioned the whole idea of Las Vegas – brash, artificial and unashamedly money-oriented – and asked whether it had not become a faded monument to an earlier generation's vulgarity and bad taste.

But MGM had lost none of their enthusiasm for the Strip. On 30 July, 1981, the Grand re-opened after a $25 million rebuilding programme which included a $6 million computerised fire detection system. Each of the 2,900 rooms had four heat-activated sprinklers and a smoke detector, plus a ceiling speaker system to relay messages from the ground-floor emergency room, manned 24 hours a day. There a computer monitored 1,300 locations throughout the hotel, and could activate 1,000 different safety devices to halt the spread of fire and smoke, and guide guests to safety.

Corridors and stairways were all fitted with smoke detectors, plus an elaborate system of fans to isolate and remove fumes quickly. All doors could be opened automatically so no escape routes would be blocked. There were also manually triggered alarms on walls throughout the building. And guests booking in could put their minds at rest by watching a five-minute film, narrated by veteran Hollywood star Gene Kelly, on what to do in emergencies.

'People are very conscious of fire,' hotel president Rothkopf told newsmen. 'That is why we have spent all this money on equipment. This is now one of the safest high-rise hotels anywhere in the world.'

Mount St Helens Eruption (1980)

For years Mount St Helens volcano slumbered like a fairy-tale dragon, only occasionally rumbling and snorting. But at 8.32 a.m. on a sunny Sunday morning, 18 May 1980, its glistening snow-capped peak suddenly erupted with a cataclysmic blast that caused the mightiest volcanic landslide ever recorded.

The explosion which was equivalent to 500 Hiroshima atomic bombs was so powerful it was heard 200 miles away, and it was feared the climate of the entire world would be changed.

In the immediately surrounding area it turned 200 square miles of lush farmland, forests, streams and rivers near the Pacific coast of America's western state of Washington into an eerie grey, crater-strewn wilderness of death and devastation. Towns up to 100 miles away were paralysed by a blizzard of hot, choking gases and ash that plunged them into midnight blackness orchestrated with flashes of lightning and claps of thunder. Within days another massive ash cloud had circled the globe, miles high, causing hazy skies and strange sunsets all around the world.

Scientifically, the Mount St Helens disaster has been called the most spectacular and important geophysical event of 1980. In fact, it was probably the best-monitored and most vividly recorded major volcanic eruption in history – one that may well rival legendary Vesuvius in the telling in school classrooms for the rest of this century and beyond.

Incredibly, scientists had predicted for five years that the 9,677 feet volcano, called Fire Mountain in Red Indian language, was likely to erupt. But the U.S. Geological Survey team keeping watch could only estimate it would happen 'perhaps before the end of the century'. It had erupted only five times in 280 years. The last time had been 123 years earlier in 1857.

But on Thursday, 27 March 1980, the volcano, one of 15 in the Cascade range of mountains, suddenly started to boil up, sparking a series of events that amazed all the experts. They warned people that an explosion was now imminent and, but for that and the establishment of no-go areas for the public, the ultimate death toll of 60 would have been horrifically higher.

The volcano dominated a rugged landscape of peaks, fir forests and valleys with streams and rivers overflowing with salmon, trout, wild animals and birds, so it was a favourite haunt for thousands of campers, hitch-hikers and hunters. Around it were dotted logging camps, weekend homes and small towns and hamlets.

The authorities thought they had done all they could to minimise the risk of death and injury. The mountain itself was peppered with monitoring devices to give the earliest possible warning of the 'Big Bang'.

The area immediately around it was declared a red zone barred to everyone. And circling that was a larger blue zone supposed to be open only to people with special permits, such as geologists, official photographers, lawmen and approved officials.

So, with the time bomb already ticking, the scene was set. For seven weeks, throughout the rest of March and April to the middle of May, the volcano simmered, shuddered and hiccuped. It was as if the great, craggy monster was just turning over in its sleep, belching acrid fumes from its mouth.

Then came the first danger signs. A fracure nearly three miles long snaked across the summit and the north face began to bulge as thousands of tons of molten rock started to move inside the volcano. It swelled at a rate of about five feet a day until it stood out 320 feet like a grotesque boil on the beauty-spot mountain's neck.

Still, the watching scientists did not quite know what to expect. But by this time, as publicity had mounted nationwide, the public were throwing all caution to the wind and letting curiosity get the better of them. They flocked to the area from all over the country in the hope of seeing the eruption. And many were to pay for it with their lives. Sheriff Les Nelson, of nearby Cowlitz County, who helped police the blue no-go zone, said later: 'Loggers, tourists, property owners, newsmen and mountain climbers violated the rules constantly. They went over, under, around and through our blockades. Nobody would listen to us.'

Then, as breakfast sizzled in frying pans on that sun-kissed Sunday morning in May, the unbelievable happened. Geologist David Johnston, 30, was manning an observation post five miles north of St Helens sending reports back to the Government Geological Survey base. At 8.32 a.m. he radioed: 'Vancouver! Vancouver! This is it. The mountain's going.' And at that moment he died – blasted to eternity. His body was never found.

In split-second sequence there was first an earthquake reading magnitude five on the Richter scale, followed by an earth shattering explosion that caused the catastrophic avalanche. More than a mile of the north face, consisting of earth, snow and boulders of ice and rock, rocketed downwards. The intense heat of the blast melted the ice into an estimated 46 billion gallons of water.

That, in turn, created a 30-mile wide maelström of mudflow and flood that

MOUNT ST HELENS ERUPTION

Mount St Helens erupts, sending smoke, ash and ice chunks high into the air

cascaded 15 miles down the nearby North Toutle River and valley at speeds up to 80 miles an hour, obliterating everything in its path and burying it to depths of up to 150 feet. The avalanche was quickly overtaken by a 200 miles an hour, 20-mile wide horizontal hurricane of scalding ash, suffocating gasses and boulder-size débris that scythed down all that stood in its way for miles around.

More than 20 idyllic lakes and 150 miles of trout and salmon streams were destroyed. Thousands of fish were boiled alive in the sizzling waters. Others leapt spectacularly ashore to die on land. An estimated two million birds and animals were wiped out, including deer, elk, bears and goats.

Huge logging trucks and bulldozers were swept up and tossed about like confetti and about a million fir trees were flattened as the avalanche and blast clogged up the landscape with débris. Bridges snapped like twigs. Roads, railway lines and abandoned trains, buses and cars were all consumed. Hundreds of homes were either destroyed or badly damaged.

More than 2,000 people fled from the advancing morass. People in towns as far as 10 miles away had been thrown from their beds by the blast. Police ordered residents up to 35 miles away to get out – quick. Soon more than 5,000 terrified people were huddled in temporary shelters as police closed all roads within 50 miles and planes were banned from flying anywhere near the area.

Static electricity from the eruption sparked a huge forest fire that rapidly engulfed a timber forest three miles from St Helens, hampering rescue workers and fleeing survivors.

And, as all this was happening, there was a third phenomenon. A gigantic gush of sulphurous ash, stony fragments and molten rock, blasted vertically 13 miles high from the mountain. Blast after blast ripped the guts out of the volcano for nine hours, sending an estimated 400 million tons of débris into the earth's atmosphere and outer space.

The colossal cloud, blown east and south by strong winds, quickly brought towns in Idaho and Montana to a stop as tons of grey ash descended on them and clogged them up. That day it piled up four inches deep throughout Washington State and neighbouring Oregon.

Washington State police spokesman William Richards said: 'It's totally dark here. You can't see anywhere.' James Lanterman, a 60-year-old radio ham, broadcast dramatically from his mobile home 20 miles north-east of St Helens: 'The air is so full of smoke and pumice stone that a person wouldn't live outside. The falling dust is inches thick and the eruptions from the mountain are causing a terrific lightning storm.' The ash blanket was so enormous that some towns even sent out snowploughs to clear routes for emergency services. Hospitals filled up with people complaining of breathing problems. In Montana Governor Thomas Judge ordered all State offices, schools and businesses to close and urged people to stay indoors and breathe through gauze masks.

All road and rail services in Washington State were halted for hundreds of miles, and planes were cancelled and grounded as far away as Denver because of hazards to visibility and also to engines, posed by the dust. In fact, the mountain spewed more ash and rock than Vesuvius in A.D. 79.

Just two days after the blast the massive ash cloud had cast a shadow nearly 2,500 miles long and 1,000 miles wide across the U.S. It took only three days to cross the whole of America and only 17 to go right round the world. It shaded the sun and Dr. William Donn, of Columbia University's Geological Observatory, said he feared it would throw a shroud around the earth and cause average temperatures everywhere to drop by one degree.

As the dust settled on the disaster area, incredible tales of death, survival and heroism began to emerge. One victim was the pilot of a crop-dusting plane 100 miles from Mount St Helens who was killed when he flew into a power line – either because he was blinded by volcanic ash or because it got into his engine.

Fred Rollins, 58, and his wife, Margery, 52, tourists from California who had talked their way through the blue no-go zone blockade early on the fateful Sunday morning, were found dead in their car, buried by molten mud.

Rescue pilot Captain Robert J. Wead, one of the team of helicopter aces who, amazingly, managed to pluck 198 people from the jaws of the disaster, said: 'People were fried in the heat.'

Other dead included campers – a young father found with his arms around his two small sons, and a young couple in a tent, crushed by toppled trees.

But the most astonishing victim was 84-year-old Harry Truman. He had lived for 50 years in the shadow of Mount St Helens and had built himself a

Vesuvius erupts, again

Vesuvius, the Italian volcano that buried Pompeii and two other towns in AD 79, killing 2,000 people, gave the twentieth century a grim reminder of its power on 18 March 1944. She exploded in her most violent eruption for 40 years, and by the time she went quiet again eight days later, 26 people were dead, two villages were under lava 30 feet deep, 5,000 people were homeless, and 60 Allied planes were unable to take off to fight the Nazis because of falling stones.

Crocodile allies

More than 1,000 Japanese soldiers were trapped in swampland on an island in the Bay of Bengal and bombarded by British artillery through the night of 19 February 1945. But the British had an unlikely band of 'allies'. As darkness fell, an army of huge crocodiles, attracted by blood in the water, moved in, attacking both the living and the dead. No one knows how many Japanese fell victim to the crocodiles, but by morning only 20 of the original 1,000 troops were still alive.

guest house beside lovely Spirit Lake, just five miles from the peak. Before the disaster, he was urged repeatedly to move out just in case there was a major eruption. But he stubbornly refused, saying: 'I am part of the mountain, the mountain is part of me.'

His brave stand made him a national hero overnight. Fan mail poured into his home from all over the world. He stood his ground – and died in the first seconds of the catastrophe, buried by the avalanche. Since then he has become a folk hero with books and songs written about him.

Other courageous men died, too, including official geologists and photographers monitoring the mountain from the fringe of the red total exclusion zone.

And there were the survivors. Like two loggers who walked out of the devastated area with more than two-thirds of their bodies burned.

Perhaps most remarkable of all were the family who had been camping out in a tent when it was buried by ash. Michael and Lu Moore and their two children, including a three-month-old baby, scrambled clear, then hiked across the disaster area for a day and a night before they were spotted and rescued by a helicopter crew.

Mrs Moore, 31, said later: 'It was horrible. We had to climb over trees that had been felled by the shockwaves. The acid stench of the ash was everywhere and it was hard to breathe.'

After it was all over – with damage estimated at £1 billion – scientists went back to the top of the volcano and found it had literally blown its top. The eruption, which made it the most active explosive volcano on mainland America for 4,500 years, had lopped 1,313 feet of the mountain's height and left a yawning, fiery hole measuring about one mile by two miles where the lava cone had been. It continued to smoulder and have minor eruptions for months afterwards.

U.S. President Carter went to the scene four days after the disaster and

MOUNT ST HELENS ERUPTION

saw the devastation from a helicopter. He said: 'There is no way to describe it. It's a horrible sight. I don't think there is anything like it in the world. The moon looks like a golf course compared to here. It will take decades to clean up the damage and volcanic ash that has covered thousands of square miles.' He immediately declared a Federal emergency to clear the way for Government aid.

Eleven days after the disaster, rescue worker Robert Wead said: 'The area looks like a nuclear wasteland. Trees and vegetation are laid out flat – singed, burned, steaming, sizzling.'

But nature and mankind eventually stepped in to bring new life to the ravaged region. The débris flow and floods created new lakes and streams. By the end of 1981, volcanic lilies, ferns and berries were starting to grow across the bleak, grey landscape. Work started on salvaging the millions of tons of torn-up trees scattered across the area like giant toothpicks – enough timber to build up to 100,000 new homes and plans were finalized to plant millions of new trees. Meanwhile, the dragon mountain that flashed its fiery breath around the world resumed its restless sleep – until the next time.

St Valentine's Day Fire (1981)

It was 2 a.m. and time for the last dance for disco-goers celebrating St Valentine's Day at the Stardust. The club was packed with 841 young people, mostly under 21, enjoying themselves at Dublin's most popular night-spot.

Top prizes in a disco-dance competition had just been carried off by elated winners, the bar was about to close and the disc-jockey was introducing one of the last hit records that would be played. From the corner of his eye, the DJ noticed two club stewards carrying fire extinguishers towards what appeared to be a smouldering curtain. He gave the matter little attention thinking perhaps that someone's tossed-away cigarette had started a minor fire. Seconds later, the cries of the dying filled the air . . .

Within moments, the entire hall in the heart of Dublin's Artane working-class suburb, was ablaze. The vast ceiling began to simply melt in the intense heat, raining white-hot droplets onto panic-stricken teenagers. The lights went out and youngsters were trampled underfoot in the blind stampede to escape the fireball which enveloped the Stardust.

Forty six were killed and 130 injured, some of them terribly; in the early hours of 14 February 1981, in the worst single disaster the shocked city of Dublin had ever seen. The inferno, which may have been the work of an arsonist, had shot out of control so quickly because the hall was, literally, a plastic palace. The chairs overlooking the dance floor were covered in red plastic and stuffed with polyurethane foam which gives off a lethal black smoke when lit and can raise room temperatures in a fire to 1,500 degrees farenheit in under half a minute. The ceiling, reduced to a molten mass, was covered by tiles, which seemed to 'explode' according to witnesses. Inflammable curtains were draped around the walls and all the tables were made of plywood with plastic tops.

The Stardust was a tinder-box, waiting for the fuse to be lit. Yet, only four months previously, it had been inspected for fire safety – and approved. A judicial inquiry followed the holocaust and experts are now looking towards much more stringent safety standards. That, of course, is scant consolation to the families of those who died or the ones still bearing the terrible scars from the nightmare that marked St Valentine's Day.

None of those who survived will ever forget the scenes as fire took hold of the Stardust. 'It was complete pandemonium' said Eamonn Quinn, 24. 'There were flames everywhere and the whole place seemed to go up in a matter of minutes. The only way out was through the exit doors. The toilet windows were barred because vandals kept breaking the glass.'

As a scrum of screaming youths pushed through the main doors and five fire exits, DJ Colin O'Brien witnessed the horror. He said: 'There was just total panic. People grabbed on to me when I was on the stage. The fire spread in a matter of a couple of minutes. People were grabbing me and asking me the way out. I was being pushed and pulled in every direction. I ended up behind the stage and was pushed into a ladies' loo. I found there was fresh air there and not much smoke. I stayed there for a couple of minutes. Eventually smoke came in and I tried to get out through the roof of the loo – but it was made of concrete. I went out of the door and felt my way by the walls until I reached the exit. I couldn't see where I was going.'

Artane's parish priest, Father McMahon, was called from his bed as firemen fought a desperate battle to contain the flames, often being hampered by blocked exits and a crowd of morbid sightseers which had gathered. Said Father McMahon: 'The first thing I saw was people trapped in the front part of the building where the flames had cornered them in a toilet. The firemen outside were trying to break through the window, but were having a terrible time getting through.'

Bravely, Father McMahon dashed inside the blazing, dark and smoke-filled Stardust to see if he could help those still trapped. 'The ceiling was gone,' he said, 'and just the girders were left. There were bodies lying all over the place. The people who were dead were in God's hands immediately. The people who really needed help were those outside who were going frantic trying to rescue their sisters or girlfriends. That was really gruelling.' Father McMahon administered the last rites to those who were dying and then helped carry other victims, some of whom were appallingly injured, to a fleet of waiting ambulances. Later, he visited survivors in hospital and said: 'Some were so shocked that they did not know who they were.'

Secretary Maureen Ashe, 22, said: 'The noise and the screams were awful. I will live with that sound for the rest of my life.' Another survivor, 18-year-old Pauline Brady added: 'I saw three girls with their hair ablaze. They were so shocked they did not know what they were doing. I doubt very much if any of them got out alive.' Doorman Michael Cavanagh, who at one stage tried to combat the raging flames with a fire extinguisher, recalled: 'It was pointless. The place was a sheer inferno. There was panic everywhere. It was terrible.'

On the morning of 15 February, a cold, miserable Sunday, the grim task of identifying the bodies began. Grief-stricken mothers and fathers were led

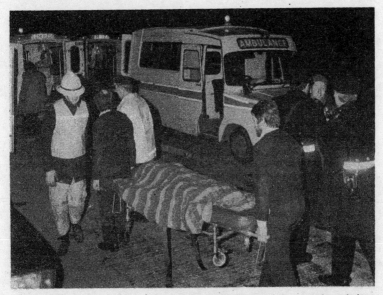

The dead and the injured are taken away by ambulance

around a makeshift morgue as officials and rescue workers started to piece together exactly who had died. In many cases, though, it was useless. So many bodies were burned beyond recognition that they were, eventually, only identified with the help of medical and dental records.

For the relatives of those who survived there was blessed relief. Yet in one heartbreaking and ironical case, a 46-year-old mother, Mrs Mary Coyne collapsed and died in the street after hearing that her son and two teenage daughters who had been at the disco were safe. For others, the scars of memory will remain for the rest of their lives.

A life, in John Keegan's case, without the two cherished daughters who perished in the fire. A third daughter, Antoinette, aged 20, survived. Mr Keegan found her after a frantic search of the city's hospitals and morgues. Her body was so badly charred that it seemed to be as black as coal. All remaining members of the Keegan family, including Antoinette, needed psychiatric help for many months after the blaze. The mental wounds of the 237 families affected were taking much, much longer to heal than any physical ones.

ST VALENTINE'S DAY FIRE

The day after the inferno, Irish premier Charles Haughey visited the charred shell of the Stardust and immediately announced an official day of mourning. He was told that some senior fire officers had been warning the Irish authorities 'for years' that there could be a major disaster at a discotheque. One, Mr Brian McMahon, a former chairman of Ireland's Chief Fire Officers' Association, told newsmen at the scene: 'I am not surprised that this terrible tragedy has occurred. I have given repeated warnings about the fire dangers in discotheques over the years. It is vital to have an inquiry into the whole area of fire inspection. Something is terribly wrong.' Prime Minister Haughey simply declared, on ordering a full public inquiry: 'Words cannot adequately express my sense of shock and anguish at this appalling disaster.'

He did, however, hear one heart-warming story to emerge from the tragedy – that of the courage of soldier Thomas Dowdall, who rescued at least four terrified teenage girls from the Stardust hall when the fire was raging at its peak. Seeing a barrel-shaped trolley full of empty bottles, which was apparently blocking an escape route, he dragged the screaming youngsters onto it and literally wheeled them to safety. One, 18-year-old Shirley McGregor, said later: 'He told me "I don't care if I break every bone in your body – you are going over the barrel." Without doubt he saved my life.'

Indeed, there were several acts of valour, although firemen later said that in some cases their own rescue efforts had been hampered. One senior fireman declared: 'It came almost to a fighting match to get people out of the way so we could go in to rescue those inside. I believe that some who were burned had gone back in to try to help their friends.'

In the aftermath of the Stardust disaster, a 200-page report prepared by the British Fire Research Centre at Borehamwood in Hertfordshire revealed that there was no single cause for the inferno, but a combination of several factors. All the material in the club, except for the ceiling tiles, was inflammable . . . something that building regulations in Britain and many other countries would never allow. Many of those who perished died from the poisonous fumes given off by these materials. Regulations to ban the use of such materials in Ireland had been under discussion in the country for a staggering four years. Ironically, they did come into effect . . . ten days after the Stardust disaster.

Allegations were made during the public inquiry that emergency exits at the Stardust had been locked – an accusation the management strenuously denied. Head doorman Thomas Keenan did say, however, that during certain periods on a disco-dance evening, exit doors were locked for up to 90 minutes at the start of the night in an effort to deter gatecrashers from slipping in without paying. Martin Donaghue, an electrical inspector, told the tribunal that he made 30 visits to the Stardust in 18 months to check instances of faulty lights.

Despite the assertions of one teenage girl witness that she saw two youths using a cigarette lighter to set fire to cloth-covered seats behind a curtained-off area of the dance hall, and the massive police hunt which followed, it has never been established whether there really was a mystery arsonist or arsonists.

However, there have been lessons learned from the Stardust disaster. Fire safety standards have been tightened and dance hall licences are closely scrutinized by city authorities, following the formation of a committee by members of the families of victims.

The parents are trying to persuade Dublin Corporation to build its own very first leisure centre in the city so that surviving children will have an alternative to other Stardusts. Ann Byrne, 22, who lost her 21-year-old brother Brian, in the blaze says: 'I've two children – and I don't want to watch them as teenagers walk into similar death traps.'

For the very real fear which still lingers, despite the political promises and the public inquiries, is that which Ann expresses along with so many other grieving relatives: it could so easily happen again.

The Potomac Airliner
Crash (1982)

T he storm had formed over New Orleans, swirling out of a trough of
low pressure over the Gulf of Mexico. It swept north-east overnight, leaving the southern states under an unusually thick blanket
of snow. In Alabama, a man died when the frozen branches of a tree fell on
him. Atlanta, Georgia, and Chicago both recorded their lowest temperatures of the century. By the morning of Wednesday, 13 January 1982, the
blizzards had reached the capital, Washington DC. At 1 p.m., the Federal
Aviation Authority closed National Airport, a mile from the White House,
for 73 minutes so ploughs could clear runways of a five-inch covering of
snow.

In government offices all over the city, civil service chiefs anxiously
scanned the cloud-laden skies, and soon after lunch, agreed to let all staff
head for home early to beat the expected drifts. Soon all roads out of the
capital were choked with cars inching their way cautiously through the
blinding snow. A vast snake of traffic edged across the frozen River Potomac
on the dual-carriageway 14th Street Bridge, part of Jefferson Davis
Highway, the busiest route between Washington and the suburbs of
Virginia. Then, at exactly 4 p.m., terror roared out of the sky in a disaster
that was to claim 78 lives, and stun a nation.

Air Florida Flight 90 had been due to leave National Airport for Fort
Lauderdale and Tampa at 2.15 p.m. But it was 3 p.m. before the 71
passengers – three of them carrying babies – left the departure lounge and
filed into 21 rows of seats in their Boeing 737 twin-engined jet. Forty one
seats were left empty. Captain Larry Wheaton, 35, and co-pilot Roger Pettit
checked their instrument panels and apologised for yet more delays while
airport workers de-iced the wings with glycol fluid. Though visibility was
still restricted to less than half a mile, the airport had re-opened, and the two
men watched an arriving plane taxi to the terminal, noting the huge icicles
hanging from its wings.

'I'm certainly glad there's people taxiing on the same place I want to go'
said Wheaton. 'I can't see the runway without these flags. Maybe further
up . . .' Head stewardess Donna Adams looked out at the white landscape
and said: 'I love it out here, look at all the tyre tracks in the snow.' Pettit was
more concerned with practicalities. 'Boy, this is a losing battle, trying to de-

ice those things,' he murmured, watching men at work on the wings. 'It gives you a false feeling of security, that's all it does.'

At 3.58 p.m. the Boeing finally taxied out for take-off from runway 36, at 6,870 feet the longest at the National. Passengers were relieved that their long wait was finally ending. The sun of Florida seemed even more inviting in this Arctic weather. The two pilots viewed the slushy runway through the still-falling snow, and elected to lift the nose wheel earlier than usual to help take-off. Just after 3.59 p.m. the plane left the ground.

Inside 30 seconds, the crew knew something was terribly wrong. 'God, look at that thing . . . that doesn't seem right,' said Pettit. 'Easy, vee-two, forward, forward,' urged Wheaton. 'Come on, forward . . . forward . . . just barely climb . . .' he continued. The plane was shuddering and shaking badly. A crewman yelled: 'Falling, we're falling.' Pettit turned to his captain: 'Larry, we're going down, Larry . . .' Wheaton replied coldly: 'I know it.' At 4.01 p.m. Flight 90 crashed.

On 14th Street Bridge, less than a mile from National Airport, drivers trapped in the crawling traffic jam heard the plummeting jet before they saw it. 'I heard a roar but I couldn't see anything for the snow,' said Justice Department clerk Lloyd Creger. 'The engines were so loud, they had to be going at full blast. I couldn't hear myself scream. Then I saw the plane coming out of the sky. It was just falling, but there didn't seem anything wrong with it. The nose was up, and the tail was down. Then there seemed to be no sound at all.' Another driver sobbed: 'I heard the noise of the jet getting louder and louder. I threw open my door and ran for my life. I didn't stop to turn round, I just heard a massive bang as the plane hit the bridge.'

The stricken plane only just cleared a railway bridge to the south of the two choked road spans. As it roared low over the helpless commuters, a wheel struck a truck on the southern carriageway, and the plane tumbled over the parapet into the Potomac between the road bridges. It ripped the tops off five cars, and swept others into the icy water.

Bridge collapses

Thirty five workers were killed on 15 October 1970, when a 400-foot span of a box-girder bridge being built over the River Yarra at Melbourne, Australia, buckled, twisted, and plunged on to a pier below, sparking oil blazes and oxy-acetylene explosions. The West Gate Bridge was to have been an eight-lane highway, two-and-a-quarter times as long as the Sydney Harbour Bridge. The Royal Commission of Inquiry into the disaster blamed: 'Mistakes, miscalculations, errors of judgement and sheer inefficiency.'

THE POTOMAC RIVER AIRLINER CRASH

The ice on the river shattered like a windshield hit by a rock, and débris bounced into the air. Stunned witnesses slowly realised the enormity of what had happened. 'There was twisted metal from crushed cars everywhere,' said reporter Al Rossiter. 'Some of the vehicles started burning, and the truck that had been hit was hanging over the edge at a 45 degree angle.' Vito Maggiolo said: 'There were bodies lying all over the bridge, and bodies on the ice in the river.' U.S. Air Force Sergeant Jerome Lancaster said: 'I counted about six or seven people in the water who were alive, but they were messed up. We threw a rope out to one passenger.'

The tail section of the Air Florida jet

Plane catches fire

All 301 people aboard died when a Saudi Arabian Tristar plane caught fire at Riyadh airport on 20 August 1980.

The Boeing had broken into three sections on impact. The nose plunged straight under the surface, killing everyone inside. The main fuselage belly-flopped and settled briefly, and horrified onlookers could see people inside, strapped to their seats, as the jagged wreckage slowly sank. But the tail miraculously floated for twenty minutes, and most of the survivors came from there. Five emerged, battered and shaken, and scuttled across the ice to safety. Others were spilled like dolls into the icy water, and desperately clung to pieces of wreckage or ice floes, screaming for help. People on the bridge threw every available cable out to them, and yelled: 'Hold on, help will be here soon.'

But the nightmare conditions – a city clogged by snow and traffic – made it impossible for the emergency services to react at full speed. Some staff were among those sent home early. Ambulances, fire-engines and police cars were trapped in the jams, having to swing on to the wide pavements in front of the White House to get through.

Incredibly, a second accident within minutes added to the chaos of the capital. A subway train packed with 1,000 commuters was derailed less than a mile and a quarter from the bridge, leaving three people dead, and many hurt. Emergency services had to be diverted to cope there, too.

The first rescue vehicles to reach 14th Street Bridge arrived on the Virginia side of the Potomac, at the same time as the first of a dozen police and Armed Forces helicopters arrived overhead, hovering dangerously close to the bridges to try to winch survivors to safety. And now the disaster took on almost bizarre proportions. TV crews alerted by the call-up of the emergency services arrived with their cameras, and began to send live coverage of the drama to a multi-million, coast-to-coast audience. Ameri-

Train plummets into river

A crowded train travelling between Samastipur and Banmukhi in the North India state of Bihar plunged off a bridge into the swollen River Bagmati on 6 June 1981, killing nearly 800 people in the world's worst-ever rail disaster.

Patricia Felch is rescued by a paramedic with the National Park Police

Inset: A U.S. Park Police helicopter hovers over a female passenger floating in the Potomac River

THE POTOMAC RIVER AIRLINER CRASH

cans hardened by Hollywood disaster movies now watched with guilty fascination as real death and real heroism unfolded before their very eyes.

People were drowning and freezing to death less than 50 feet from the shore, in water where they could survive for only ten minutes. They feebly splashed around until the numbing cold paralysed muscles, making swimming impossible. They reached despairingly for lifelines hanging from helicopters, then slumped back beneath the surface, their hands too cold to keep a grip. A rescue official said: 'It was heartbreaking to see them so close and not be able to help. No one would live more than a few minutes in that water.'

Stewardess Kelly Duncan, 23, dressed only in her thin short-sleeved blouse and uniform skirt, failed repeatedly to grasp the rescue rings. It seemed she was doomed. Then helicopter pilot Donald Usher risked the lives of himself and crewman Gene Windsor by settling his craft almost on the water, while Windsor clambered out on to the landing skids, and snatched the helpless girl to safety. She was rushed to hospital with a broken leg and hypothermia – her temperature had fallen to 90F – but she survived, the only one of the five-strong crew to do so.

Priscilla Tirado was also in the water. She lunged at a cable but could not reach it. Her fading strength sent her under the surface, but she bobbed up again, and the helicopter crew threw her a lifebelt attached to a line. She pushed her arm through it, and seemed secure as the helicopter began to tow her to shore. But again she lost her grip, and plunged back into the water. Hundreds on the bridge and millions of telly-viewers watched her agony in despair. But one man reacted more positively.

Lennie Skutnik, a 38-year-old desk worker on his way home from the Congressional Budget Office, tore off his jacket and boots, and waded into the water, regardless of his own safety. Mrs Tirado, 23, was almost unconscious, but Skutnik managed to push, pull and even kick her to the bank, where willing hands dragged them ashore. They shared an ambulance to hospital, he suffering from hypothermia, she critically ill – and unaware that her husband Jose and two-month-old son Jason had both drowned.

Hero Skutnik, later praised by President Ronald Reagan, was modest about his part in the rescue. 'She just gave out,' he told reporters. 'Her eyes rolled back and she had just started to go under when I grabbed her. You could tell just by looking at her that she didn't have an ounce of energy left in her. She seemed to be losing the will to live. I didn't notice the cold at all while I was in the water. The only time I felt it was in the ambulance going to hospital afterwards. I noticed my toes were cold, that was all. I don't think I was any kind of hero. It was just an automatic reaction.'

Another hero did not live to tell his tale. Five times he grabbed lifelines thrown down by helicopters, but on every occasion he handed the rope to others who were dragged or lifted to shore. 'He could have gone first,' said pilot Donald Usher. 'We threw the ring to him but he passed it to a man who was bleeding badly from a head injury. We went back four times, and each time he kept passing the ring to someone else, including three ladies hanging on to the tail section. The last time we went back, he had gone. The ice had formed over where he had been. We stayed there ten minutes, just in the hopes he had crawled into the fuselage and found an air pocket, but it became obvious he had gone. He's the real hero of this whole thing. If you were in his situation, a hundred yards from shore and knowing that every minute you were closer to freezing to death, could you do it? I really don't think I could.'

Co-pilot Gene Windsor said: 'The guy was amazing, I've never seen such guts. It seemed to me he decided that the women and the injured man needed to get out of there before him, and even as he was going under he stuck to that decision. Afterwards we looked everywhere for him, but he was gone.' Only when all the bodies had been recovered was the identity of the bald man with the black moustache established. Arland Williams, 46, a federal government employee, was the only one who had died from drowning alone. All the rest had broken limbs.

Mercifully, most of the plane's passengers died instantly on impact. But some of the 78 victims died horrifyingly slowly. One elderly man's story was told by Salvation Army major Harold Anderson: 'He was alive when police saw him under the ice, and he watched rescuers trying to get to him to get him out of the water. He was trying frantically to get out, but by the time they got the ice broken he was gone. They couldn't revive him.'

The first survivors were admitted to the George Washington Medical Center 45 minutes after the crash. Three-and-a-half hours after the disaster hospitals were officially told to expect no more patients. Only five people aboard the plane had survived. Four drivers on the bridge had been killed. Sixteen people were in hospital.

The grisly search for bodies went on long after dark. Floodlights and the flashing lights of rescue vehicles lit up an eerie scene as men with boathooks

---

Death in Egypt

The world's worst single-vehicle death crash happened in Egypt on 9 August 1973. A bus crashed into an irrigation canal, killing 127 people.

THE POTOMAC RIVER AIRLINER CRASH

fished from a tug and rubber dinghies between the ice floes near the wreckage of the white and blue Air Florida jet. Helicopters switched their attention from the river to the bank, airlifting the less seriously hurt away from the tragic scene. Bodies were laid out in the snow, and a makeshift mortuary set up in a tent. Army ice-breakers arrived, and divers in specially thick wetsuits tried to batter their way into the fuselage, to reach bodies still strapped into seats. At dawn, rescue teams were greeted by the heartbreaking sight of a woman and a baby floating, frozen stiff on the icy surface.

Two people are hauled away from the jetliner wreckage

The world's worst famine

More than 20,000,000 died from famine in northern China between 1969 and 1971, it was revealed in May 1981. One hundred years earlier, 9,500,000 peasants had died in a famine in the same area.

Diving operations continued over the next week, but it was a slow process. Visibility under water was reduced to 18 inches, and the jagged wreckage was surrounded by treacherous currents and submerged ice. Spilled aviation fuel made the wreckage slippery, and the Arctic weather never let up. One diver had to be rescued when his breathing valve froze up, and a barge carrying a crane was holed by ice. Divers were restricted to 30 minutes at a time in the 25 feet deep water, despite maximum protective clothing. It took them seven days to recover the 'black box' flight recorders, vital to the subsequent inquiry into why the crash happened.

Because of the snow, no-one, not even the control tower staff at National Airport, had seen Flight 90 leave the ground. The Federal Aviation Authority investigators had to rely on the automatic tapes of the pilots, quoted earlier, and the evidence of the few survivors.

Both stewardess Kelly Duncan and passenger Burt Hamilton, 40, spoke of the plane shuddering badly soon after lift-off. Mr Hamilton, whose seat was by the galley at the back of the jet, said: 'I knew something was wrong as it took off. The plane seemed to take an awful long time to pick up speed. It really started vibrating – a strong shaking, so bad that I tightened my seat belt and started to pray a lot.'

Businessman Joseph Stiley, 42, a private pilot, also claimed he knew that all was not well. Thumbing through his papers with his secretary Patricia

Mysterious meteorite

At precisely 7.17 a.m. on 30 June 1908, a mighty meteorite or some other mysterious object exploded over the Tunguska River valley in northern Siberia causing the most terrible devastation. Two thousand square miles of forest were laid bare. Herds of reindeer were incinerated. Nomads 45 miles away were hurled to the ground and their tents torn away. The explosion was heard 600 miles away. Yet even today no one knows the cause nor the death toll of a blast equivalent to that of a 30-megaton nuclear bomb.

THE POTOMAC RIVER AIRLINER CRASH

Felch, he turned to her as the engines roared and said: 'We're not going to make it, we're going down.' Later, in hospital with two fractured legs, he said: 'Things were not going right soon after we started down the runway. We didn't have the speed. It seemed like the pilot tried to abort, but ran out of runway. He had to make the decision to go, so we took off. We got up a little bit, but it didn't climb like a normal 737. We got a fairly decent angle, then stalled and we went down. We were in the air only 20 or 30 seconds before impact, when I passed out.'

The disaster was the first major crash since President Reagan had fired 11,500 striking air traffic controllers the previous August. The controllers' union had warned then that pilots flying blind in winter would miss the help from the ground they usually relied on, but Federal Aviation chiefs dismissed air traffic control error as a possible cause of the accident.

The crash also raised questions about the safety of National, rated by pilots as one of the trickiest airports in America. Though accident-free since 1949, the airport – maintained by the government mainly for the convenience of Congressmen and civil servants – is set in the heart of a heavily built-up urban area, and can be used only by smaller jets. Larger aircraft have to fly out of Dulles Airport, 30 miles west of the capital. The short runways at National leave no room for second thoughts by pilots, and flight-paths are awkward, partly because of minimum noise requirements, partly because planes taking off have to make a sharp left-hand turn to avoid the 555-foot high Washington Monument.

But investigators were concerned not with the National's shortcomings, but with why Flight 90 hit 14th Street Bridge when it should have been at least 500 feet above it. They concentrated on three possibilities: fuel contamination causing loss of power, pilot error, and the most likely cause of the crash, ice.

Since man first took to the air, ice on the wings, restricting their power to lift, or ice in the engine, distorting air intake and reducing power, have

---

Ships collide

Fifty lives and £2,500,000 worth of ships were lost because of fog in the English Channel on the night of 11 January 1971. The Panamanian tanker *Texaco Caribbean* collided with a freighter nine miles off Folkestone, split in two and sank with eight crew. Next night 21 more sailors died when the German freighter *Brandenberg* struck the wreckage. And a month later the Greek freighter *Niki* went down with 21 hands after also hitting wreckage.

always been a danger. And within days of the Potomac disaster, it was revealed that, just one week before the crash, the British Civil Aviation Authority had warned their American counterparts that the Boeing 737, normally one of the world's safest aircraft, was particularly vulnerable to icy conditions. The British Airline Pilots' Association had reported that the jets tended to pitch up or roll unaccountably when ice was on the wings. And BALPA's technical secretary, Terence Staples, said: 'There does not have to be a large deposit. Even a small amount, which might not be easy to see, can cause difficulties.'

Boeing immediately instructed all airlines to ensure that the wings of 737 jets were inspected before take-off, and any ice removed. And the British authorities ordered 737 pilots to increase take-off speeds by up to five knots, and to slow the rate at which they allowed the nose to rise.

The Australian Bushfires (1983)

Even by the dusky, throat parching standards of Southern Australia
it had been a scorcher of a summer. In the big cities of Adelaide and
Melbourne everyone who could headed for the Great Ocean Road
and resorts like Airey's Inlet in the hope of a cool dip and a brief respite from
the sweltering heat.

For weeks now fire chiefs had been repeating their warnings of a tinderbox
death trap. In some parts of the Outback there had been no rain for three
years or more. But it was the Bush – the scrub and grassland lying between
the major towns and cities and the actual Outback – that was threatened by a
single spark. For the thousands of Bush dwellers, many of them third and
fourth generation families, it was a risk they were prepared to live with. The
true Bush townships of 200 and 300 inhabitants live a tranquil existence,
their arid soil turned into rich pasture by irrigation, time and toil.

From the moment they enter school children learn firefighting techniques
and by their teens are willing recruits to their local 'Bush Brigade', carrying
water packs with powerful hand pumps on them to deal with any sudden
outbreaks. The moment a fire breaks out the village fire truck, klaxon
sounding, rounds up a platoon of volunteers. Dozens more 'beaters', the
name given to huge spade-like mops, are deployed in the damping down
operation.

Huge fines, and even jail, are the penalty for careless tourists who throw a
match from a car window or dump a bottle that could magnify the sun's rays
to ignition point.

The dangers were well enough broadcast, well enough understood. But
awareness was not enough to prevent the Travelling Inferno that swept
across Victoria and South Australia faster than an express train. Shortly
after 3.30 p.m. on 16 February 1983, ironically Ash Wednesday in the
ecclesiastical calendar, the first alarm was raised.

The first fires started in the Dandenong Ranges where temperatures had
nudged past the 110 degrees mark on the hottest February day on record.
There were to be conflicting theories as to the cause. Arson was suspected in
several instances, and there was the possibility of overhead power cables
snapping in the unusually strong 50 mph winds and setting light to the
eucalyptus trees. But one fact could not be disputed. When the fires began
there was simply no controlling them.

Anyone who has ever suffered from a bad cough will have reached for the menthol and eucalyptus medicine resting on many a medicine cabinet shelf. Without the menthol, eucalyptus is a killer not a cure. The oil filled leaves of the eucalyptus tree are highly inflammable. The bark burns with the speed of paper, the foilage erupting in a fireball. As if bowled along the ground by a mighty hand the fireballs gather speed, moving at speeds of more than 70 mph. Ash Wednesday's blazes began simultaneously in no less than seven places, three outside Adelaide in South Australia, four within 50 miles of Melbourne in the state of Victoria. Soon they were moving along fronts of up to 100 miles with murderous intent. Death and destruction followed.

Cockatoo, a tiny town east of Melbourne was the first township to be engulfed in the holocaust. By now the 40 foot high fireballs, fed by the occasional wood-framed house, were capable of leaping 50 feet into the air and vaulting a six lane highway. A survivor was to describe later how he watched from his verandah the evil golden globes sweeping across a ridge 500 yards away and five minutes later engulfing the home from which he and his family managed to escape.

A university expert was later to describe the bush fire that swept through Cockatoo as '30 times more intense' than normal. The County Fire

---

Fire at the Club Cinq-Sept

On Saturday, 1 November 1970, the popular Club Cinq-Sept was packed with young French people not only from the small town of St Laurent de Pont, but also Grenoble, Aix-les-Bains and Chambery. The interior of the club was trendily decorated with plastic psychedelic structures creating a grotto-like effect. To prevent gatecrashers, all exits, apart from the main turnstile, were locked on this particular night. At around 1.40am a boy dropped a match onto a cushion. Within one minute the entire psychedelic interior of the club was a fury of flames, fumes and dripping plastics. Only 30 people managed to escape through the main turnstile before it was jammed with bodies. The fact that there was not even a telephone on the club's premises meant a considerable delay until the fire brigade arrived, by which time nothing could be done. One hundred and forty six youngsters died in France's worst ever fire.

Obviously, safety and building regulations had been ignored, and the Mayor, two building contractors and the surviving owner were given suspended sentences, although many parents felt these were too lenient.

Two of the
8500 homeless
survivors of
Australia's Ash
Wednesday
bush-fires.

THE AUSTRALIAN BUSH FIRES

> ## Aberfan Landslide
> On 21 October, 1966 a rain-sodden, 800-foot-high tower of waste coal slag slipped, tumbling half a mile before slowing down. In its path it engulfed a school, a row of cottages and a farm. In the school the children were attending morning service on the final morning before their half-term holidays. The death toll was 116 children and 28 adults; hardly any family in the small community did not suffer a bereavement. Worst of all, the question of the tip's safety had been raised many times, and the danger signs had been totally ignored.

Authority had not time to muster sufficient water tankers to fight the fireballs. There was a call to evacuate. And then the flames hit Cockatoo.

With one road in and one road out there was nowhere to run. People hid in their homes, under their homes. They tried to escape by car, but in more than one case the Travelling Inferno, now moving at speeds of up to 100 mph overtook them and engulfed them. In the hills outside Cockatoo a terrified family of eight hid inside a water tank for 10 hours as the fire raged outside and the water inside almost boiled. But the greatest act of survival was to be inside the village school whose brick walls at least withstood the flames. There 120 children cowered under wet blankets as their parents played hosepipes on the roof. By daybreak on Thursday 29 people had lost their lives and more than half the town's houses were just blackened stumps. As relief helicopters hovered overhead Cockatoo resembled a war zone. But the death toll was to increase as the angry flames turned their attentions elsewhere.

At Mount Gambier in South Australia a family of five died in another car horror as they tried to race the flames to safety. Twelve firemen found their two water tankers as much use as covered wagons against the Sioux nation. They, too, died.

To the West of Melbourne the holiday hamlet of Aireys Inlet was wiped off the face of the seared earth. Holidaymakers wept openly on the beach as kangaroos jumped from clifftops into the sea and drowned as they too tried to escape.

Trapped between the Bush and the Ocean people staying in their beach homes at Lorne and Angleseay had spent a bizarre and horrifying Wednesday night vigil on the sands as the fire ravaged their homes on the clifftops above.

In the heart of Melbourne startled residents could now see the smoke on ridges less than 20 miles away. They could taste the ash on their tongues and the rank, acrid smell that follows a firestorm filled their nostrils. They could taste something else too; the fear that they might be next.

Ever since the first raising of the alarm on the Wednesday afternoon the Victoria County Fire Authority, swelled by hundreds of volunteers, had worked tirelessly round the clock. In one forest blaze alone, near Warburton 700 fire-fighters with 50 water tankers, stood their ground. Nearer Melbourne bulldozers and excavators stood ready to dig huge fire troughs in which, hopefully, the flames would simply die away.

Spotter planes with infra-red equipment added a technological touch to the grim scenario. By Friday morning the fires were largely under control. But the dangers of further outbreaks were said by the Victoria County Fire Chief to be 'perilously high'.

Acrimony and recrimnation entered the arena. The Prime Minister Malcolm Fraser abandoned his general election campaign to deal with the disaster. He ordered massive federal aid to help the homeless and ordered a weekend of national mourning. Forty eight hours of holocaust horror had seen Australia's worst ever bush fire claim the lives of more than 70 people.

It had rendered more than 8,500 people homeless, had devastated some 150,000 acres of farm and forest land, crippling the dairy industry and bankrupting the fruit growers.

More than 200,000 sheep and cattle had perished. No one could count the

Fire in Sao Paulo

On 1 February, 1974 fire broke out on the eleventh floor of an office skyscraper called the Joelma Building in Sao Paulo, Brazil. Probably ignited in an overheated air-conditioning vent, the fire spread with horrifying speed because the interior of the building was constructed in highly-inflammable materials. Within minutes 650 people were cut off by the flames. Several people were trampled to death in the initial panic, as they fled to the upper floors. However, the flames quickly spread upwards and the only escape was to jump to almost certain death. Despite heroic efforts by the fire services, their ladders were not long enough. Ropes were thrown from helicopters to haul people from the roof before the heat died down enough for them to land. The fire was brought under control after four hours, by which time 220 people had died, indirectly because of Sao Paulo's inadequate building regulations and undermanned fire-fighting services.

THE AUSTRALIAN BUSH FIRES

> The Black Hills of Dakota were in mourning in 1972 after 14 inches of rain, the normal average for a year, fell in just one night. The disaster began late on Friday, 9 June. The downpour ran off the hills in a torrential flood, funneled through narrow canyons, until it washed over an earth dam and sent a five-foot high wall of debris-filled water through the heart of Rapid City, the second largest town in South Dakota. By the time the flood subsided on Saturday morning, 237 people were dead, five were missing and 5,000 were homeless in a 30-mile long, half-mile wide path of sudden destruction.

numbers of dead among the protected species of kangaroo and koala bear. An early estimate of the damage put the figure at £500 million.

The soul searchers asked themselves: 'What went wrong? Where did the fire-fighting system break down?' But there was no simple answer, except to blame the weather. In 1939 71 people had died in bush fires in Victoria on a day known nationally as 'Black Friday'. Now February 16th 1983 has taken its place in the calendar of catastrophes. For the people of Southern Australia, Ash Wednesday is a day they will never forget.

THE WORLD'S
GREATEST
MISTAKES

Acknowledgements

With a book such as this, covering such a wide variety of true stories, the author must draw much of his inspiration from earlier works. It would be impossible to mention even a major proportion of them, but the author wishes in particular to acknowledge the following writers.

Stephen E. Ambrose: *Crazy Horse and Custer* (Macdonald and Jane's 1976); Charles Bateson: *The War With Japan* (Cresset Press 1968); Dee Brown: *Bury My Heart At Wounded Knee, An Indian History of the American West* (Barrie and Jenkins 1970); Basil Collier: *The War in the Far East* (Heinemann 1969); Rupert Furneaux: *The Two Stranglers of Rillington Place* (1961) and *Great Clashes of the Twentieth Century* (Oldhams 1970); James Gilbert: *The World's Worst Aircraft* (M. & J. Hobbs and Hodder and Stoughton 1975); Robert Gray: *A History of London* (Hutchinson 1978); Royal B. Hassrick: *The Colourful Story of the North American Indians* (Octopus 1974); James Leasor: *Singapore* (Hodder and Stoughton 1968); Walter Lord: *A Night To Remember* (Longman and Holt, Rinehart & Wilson) and *Day of Infamy* (Longmans, Green & Co 1957); Sir Crompton Mackenzie: *Gallipoli Memories* (Cassell 1929); John Michell and Robert J. M. Rickard: *Phenomena, A Book of Wonders* (Thames and Hudson 1977); Alan Moorehead: *Gallipoli* (Hamish Hamilton 1956); Piers Paul Read: *The Train Robbers* (W. H. Allen, the Alison Press and Secker and Warbug 1978); John Selby: *The Thin Red Line of Balaclava* (Hamish Hamilton 1970); Nevil Shute: *Slide Rule* (Heinemann 1954); Time Magazine: *Special report on the Mafia* (May 16, 1977); Philipp Vandenburg: *The Curse of the Pharaohs* (Hodder and Stoughton 1976).

The publishers would like to thank the following organizations and individuals for their kind permission to reproduce the photographs in this book.

Associated Newspapers Ltd., 65; Aston Martin, 29; The British Tourist Authority, 162 left; Daily Mirror Library, 21, 41; Mary Evans Picture Library, 53; Illustrated London News, 113; Keystone Press Agency, 25, 27, 32, 36 below right, 95, 97 above and below, 109, 111 below, 119, 120 above, 126, 128, 133, 138, 144, 145, 147, 162 right, 185, 186 left, 213 below right, 219, 221; Mansell Collection, 11, 15, 35, 54, 71 above and below right, 74, 114, 120 below, 173, 213; National Army Museum, 202, 205, 209; Popperfoto, 36, 43, 50, 68, 71 left, 73, 76, 83, 85, 86, 93, 101, 131, 141 above left and right below, 154, 161, 178, 180, 182, 186 right, 187, 196, 199; Radio Times, Hulton Picture Library, 176, 206.

Contents

Introduction

For every success in the history of the world, there has also been a mistake. For every breakthrough, there has been a setback. For every genius, there has been a blunderer.

The successes, of course, are well recorded for posterity. The names of the geniuses are carved on monuments and written large in history books. But what of the people who got it all wrong . . . those who, often because of one tiny slip-up, changed the course of events?

This book sets out to put the record straight. Gathered together within these covers is the greatest galaxy of mistakes, mishaps and misfortunes ever assembled.

Some are simple, humorous cases of ordinary people whose errors of judgement would otherwise be forgotten—like the priest who married the bride to the best man. Others are remarkable instances of mismanagement—like the town that alone waged war against the Soviet Union for half a century.

There are also hoaxes (like the joker who fooled the British navy) and gullibilities (like the con-man who sold off the White House and the Statue of Liberty).

Add to these the touching tales of errors that are, quite simply, human and very understandable. Like the man who lost £32 million of his firm's money, and the speck of fluff that revealed a secret royal romance.

There is also a more serious side to this book. For told here are the stories of mistakes so monumental that they have irrevocably altered the course of history. They are mistakes that have cost dearly in money, honour and human life. They include the sinking of the Titanic, the crash of the R101 airship, the assault on Gallipoli, the defence of Singapore, Custer's Last Stand and the rise of the Mafia.

Take all these incidents and a whole lot more—slip-ups, follies, mistimings and incomprehensible idiocies. What you end up with is the most astonishing miscellany of mistakes ever assembled. Some are laughable. Some are sad. But we believe that they will all prove utterly fascinating.

7

Chapter
One

People and Places

American president, English baker, African tribeswoman, Italian explorer, the British Navy, Australian, Brazilian and Canadian planners – the list of those who have made monumental mistakes is as wide ranging as it is endless. And it takes no more account of status than it does of nationality – as the following pages show.

The baker who burned down London

He left an oven alight – and sparked off the Great Fire of 1666

For a humble tradesman, John Farynor had attained a special honour and reputation. He was baker to King Charles II, recently restored to the English throne after his exile in France.

Farynor had been the royal baker for five years when, one evening in 1666, after another long and weary day, he climbed the stairs to bed above his bakery in Pudding Lane. He snuffed out his candle and settled down for a peaceful night's sleep. But as he slept, a flame still flickered in the bakery beneath. He had failed to damp down his bread ovens.

The flame grew. And at two o'clock that morning, on September 2, 1666, the fire in the bakery sparked off one of the worst conflagrations in history, the Great Fire of London.

Sparks rising from Farynor's establishment set fire to a pile of hay stacked in the courtyard of the nearby Star Inn and lit up the sky. Pudding Lane lay at the centre of an overcrowded area of old London, and thousands of the local inhabitants were soon out in the streets watching the blaze. They were not unduly alarmed. Fires were common in this city of pitch-soaked timbers and lathe-and-plaster constructions. Only the year before, King Charles had written to the Lord Mayor urging him to enforce more stringent fire regulations. But previous fires had fizzled out, and there was no reason to think that this one would be any different.

Pudding Lane was a dumping ground for offal from nearby Eastcheap Market, and no one of any note lived there. But it was close to the main road running down to London Bridge, so in the early hours of the morning the mayor was informed. When he arrived at the scene he was singularly unimpressed. 'Pish!' he said. 'A woman might piss it out.'

Diarist Samuel Pepys was no more impressed. He was awoken by his maid at 3 a.m. at his house about three-quarters of a mile to the east near Tower Hill. He wrote of the fire in his diary: 'I rose and slipped on my nightgown and went to her window and thought it to be at the backside of Mark Lane at the farthest, and so to bed again and asleep.'

Pepys carried the news of the fire to the court, and thereby to the king, when he arrived at his office in Whitehall shortly before midday. No one had

bothered to tell the king before then. It was Sunday, after all.

But any idea that the fire would fizzle out was soon dispelled. On Sunday afternoon the blaze reached the River Thames, and warehouses loaded with timber, oil, brandy and coal exploded like bombs, one after another.

A steady dry wind blew continuously from the east, so that, although the fire barely reached Pepys's house a short distance away, it spread uncontrollably to the west. There was one stage on the Sunday when the blaze might have been halted. But the fire-fighters smashed up the water pipes to fill their buckets more quickly and cut off the area's water supply.

The inferno swept on unabated from Sunday to Wednesday. By then, 13,000 houses had been destroyed, 87 parish churches burned down and 300 acres blackened. The shops built on London Bridge caught fire. Sparks carried across to the opposite bank of the Thames and started small fires in Southwark. The Guildhall and the Royal Exchange – the city's financial centre – were reduced to ashes.

The greatest conflagration was at St. Paul's Cathedral, where the heat caused the stonework to explode and ancient tombs to burst open, revealing mummified remains. The cathedral's roof melted, and molten lead flooded down neighbouring streets.

Remarkably, only eight people died in the Great Fire of London. Most citizens had plenty of time to flee. The roads were crammed with handcarts piled with belongings, and the surrounding countryside was one vast refugee camp.

Pepys was among those who left the city. He wrote, 'With one's face in the wind, you were almost burned with a shower of fire drops [from this] most horrid, malicious, bloody flame . . . [above it all was] a smoke so great as darkened the sun at midday. If at any time the sun peeped forth it looked red like blood.'

By Wednesday night the fire had been virtually contained, largely due to the personal intervention of the king, who organised the fire-fighters in knocking down buildings to clear a fire-break. But London smouldered for weeks afterwards. Cellars were still burning six months later.

Baker Farynor's blunder did result in some good, however. The shameful slums of central London were wiped out in a single week. And the fire purged the last vestiges of London's previous disaster, the Great Plague of 1665, which had claimed 100,000 victims.

Files of documents on pending trials were found stacked in a public lavatory in Rome Law Courts when lawyers invited newsmen to see the Italian legal system in action.

> A woman was pronounced dead by a doctor after she was found frozen stiff in her unheated caravan in 15 degrees of frost. Porters were wheeling her into the morgue at a hospital in Ontario, Canada, when they heard a faint gasp. It was the 'dead' woman, who later recovered with no ill-effects.

40 years in bed – with 'flu

A doctor taking over a local practice visited a 74-year-old woman who had been bedridden for 40 years. He could find nothing wrong with her. He discovered that one of his predecessors had ordered the woman to bed because she had influenza and had told her not to get up again until he returned. He forgot to return.

Within a few days, the 34-year-old single woman had recovered. But she remained in her sickroom awaiting the doctor's visit. Several weeks elapsed and he still did not call. By then the patient had discovered that she enjoyed being waited on hand and foot – and she refused to budge.

At first, she was nursed by her mother. But when the old woman died, a brother-in-law took over. Finally, a new doctor to the area paid a routine call to the patient's home in Taunton, Devon, and examined the woman, now aged 74 and still keeping resolutely to her bed. He referred her case to a geriatrics specialist.

The specialist, Dr. Peter Rowe, said: 'By the time I saw her, she couldn't have got up if she had wanted to. She was decidedly plump and far from keen to leave her bed.'

Dr. Rowe reported the case to British medical journals in 1978, but, because of medical ethics, the woman's name was never revealed. The doctor told how it took seven months of sympathetic encouragement before the old lady was persuaded to leave her bed; and how, happily, she took to her feet again for three 'fairly active' years before her death at 77.

> STERILITY MAY BE INHERITED.
> – *Pacific Rural Press*

13

East is West

Columbus died without knowing he had discovered America

A light breeze filled the sails of the three tiny wooden-hulled ships and gently wafted them out of the bustling port of Palos, on Spain's southern coast. The date was Friday, August 3, 1492.

There was more than a little apprehension among the 87 men on board. This was to be a voyage of discovery – beyond the horizon of the known world. Ahead lay the Atlantic Ocean, mighty and mysterious.

But for one man watching the coast slipping slowly out of sight from the 70-foot-long flagship *Santa Maria*, the thought of sailing into the unknown held no terror.

Captain Christopher Columbus – born in about 1445 Cristoforo Columbo, the son of a Genoese clothmaker – was a proud, stubborn, ambitious mariner who dreamed of opening up a new sea route from Spain to the rich spice isles of the East Indies. For years, while sailing the shipping lanes around Portugal and Spain and down the coast of Africa to the Canary Islands, he had been planning an Atlantic crossing.

Columbus was convinced the world was round, an unpopular theory in his day, but one that was gaining support. He believed the eastern coast of Asia and the gold-rich lands of the Orient lay west of Europe, within easy sailing distance.

Now at last he was on his way, under the patronage of Spain's King Ferdinand and Queen Isabella. (His first projected attempt had been turned down eight years before by Portugal's John II.) He was about to make perhaps the biggest blunder of any explorer – but, in doing so, he was also to make the greatest discovery.

He headed his ships for San Sebastian in the Canaries, then, on September 6, eager not to miss the prevailing easterly winds, he turned the small fleet west into the open Atlantic. The square-rigged ships made good progress in the following wind. But by the middle of the month, with land still not in sight, his men became worried. They feared they might never be able to return to Spain.

Columbus, too, must have begun to doubt his estimate of the distance to the Indies. On September 19, he began to keep a false log, in which he sought to allay the fears of his crew by underestimating the miles he was sailing.

Together the *Santa Maria*, with her attendant vessels, the *Pinta* and *Nina*,

rode out the perils of the Sargasso Sea, sometimes battered by high seas, at other times becalmed for days. Columbus, desperate for his expedition to succeed and mindful of the rewards that would be heaped on him by a grateful king and queen, clutched at any evidence that they were nearing land. Hopes were often raised and dashed.

Then, at two o'clock on the morning of October 2, just 37 days after they had left the Canaries, a seaman on board the *Pinta* raised the cry: 'Land!' Later that day, the small fleet hove to off an island which Columbus named San Salvador.

Columbus wrote in his log that day: 'There we soon saw naked natives ... A landscape was revealed to our eyes with lush green trees, many streams and fruits of various types.' The next day he wrote: 'I saw that some of the men had pierced their noses and had put a piece of gold through it ... By signs, I could understand that we had to go to the south to meet a king who had great vessels of gold.'

On October 17 he noted: 'On all these days I have been in India it has rained more or less ...' He still firmly believed that he had made his landfall on the eastern coast of Asia.

Columbus set about exploring, and sailed among the Caribbean islands to the north coast of Cuba, and on to Hispaniola. He was much impressed by what he saw and in his log of October 28, while off the Cuban coast, he wrote: 'I dare to suppose that the mighty ships of the Grand Khan come here and that from here to the mainland is a journey of only ten days.'

After eight months at sea, Columbus returned in triumph to Spain where he was made 'Admiral of the ocean sea and governor of the islands newly discovered in the Indies'. He made four voyages of discovery to Central America in the next ten years, and only towards the end of his explorations did he begin to doubt whether he had in fact found the eastern coast of Asia.

It was on his third voyage to the New World, in 1498, that he began to reflect on the possibility that he had found a new continent. A more southerly course across the Atlantic had led him to the island of Trinidad, and, while exploring in the nearby Gulf of Paria, he came to the place where the mighty Orinoco River of South America flows into the sea. In his log of August 14,

---

In reference A, the cover letter at Reference B is an error. The additions at Annex B to Reference B are already incorporated in Annex A to Reference B, and are those additional items per pack that will be required if the complete schedule at Annex A to Reference B are approved.
– British Defence Ministry publication

1498, he wrote: 'I believe that this is a very large continent which until now has remained unknown.'

In the next few years, Italian adventurer Amerigo Vespucci and others were to confirm his suspicions. Vespucci explored much of Brazil's coastline, and it was the accounts of his discoveries that eventually won him the honour of having the great new continent named after him.

But in 1502, when Columbus set out on his fourth voyage, he still believed that the islands he had discovered on his first two voyages were off the eastern coast of Asia. He reasoned that a passage through to Asia must exist between these islands and the great new land to the south. So he set out to find it. And for the second time he stumbled across America without really knowing it.

For nine months, in gruelling weather, he explored along the coasts of Honduras, Costa Rica and Panama. Then, in May 1503, with his storm-battered ships worm-eaten, leaking and in danger of sinking, he struck north in a desperate bid to reach the new Spanish settlement of Santo Domingo, on the island of Hispaniola. He failed, and spent 12 months as a castaway on Jamaica before being rescued with his crew and taken back to Spain.

Columbus died on May 20, 1506. He was never to know that the land he had discovered was in fact the vast continent of America.

The prophetess who led her tribe to death

Nongqawuse had a fatal charisma. She was so smooth-tongued that she led an entire South African tribe to obliteration. And she was just 14 years old.

One hot, still day in 1856 she sat on a rock overlooking a pool in the Gxara River and, as she stared at the placid water, she imagined she saw faces reflected there.

She ran back to her village and told the elders of her tribe, the Gcaleka Xhosas, that she had seen the faces of her ancestors and that they had spoken to her. They had told her that they were ready to be resurrected to lead a holy war against the Europeans who were taking over their country.

But, said, Nongqawuse, the ancestors would only return to earth at a price. The tribe would first have to prove their faith by destroying all their worldly wealth. They would have to burn their crops and slaughter all their

> **The evening of clairvoyance on Tuesday December 4 at 7 p.m. has been cancelled owing to unforeseen circumstances.**
> – *East Kent Times*

cattle – otherwise they would be turned into reptiles and insects and destroyed in a tempest.

February 18, 1857, was the appointed day on which the ancestral dead would be reborn to fight again. The Gcaleka Xhosas met the deadline. They spent almost a year taking part in a prolonged orgy of ceremonial massacre and destruction.

Eventually the great day arrived. The hungry tribesfolk rose early for fear of missing the promised miracle. Nongqawuse told them to watch the sun rise and to chart its progress across the sky. It would, she predicted, halt in the heavens – then retrace its course to set for the first time in the east.

Throughout the day, the sun continued on its inevitable course. Tribespeople, half blinded through staring at it, wailed in despair. And, as the sun died in the west, their despair turned to anger. Even hungrier than they had been at dawn, they peered around for the young prophetess – but she had fled.

Nongqawuse sought sanctuary with the British in King William's Town. They placed her, for her own protection, on Robben Island. Later she moved secretly to Eastern Province, where she lived on a farm until her death in 1898.

The tribe she had led to ruin were not so lucky. They had no food, nor the means of providing themselves with any. Though many were helped by neighbouring tribes and European charity, 25,000 died of starvation.

Just one of those days

Joe Ramirez, 19 years of age, drove to the court house in a New York suburb to face a traffic charge. As his case was about to be called he realised that his parking meter was running out, so he asked the judge for time to feed it. His request was granted.

Joe raced out and was starting across the street when a policeman grabbed him for jay-walking. He gave Joe a ticket – and a long lecture. So long a lecture that a traffic warden got to his car first and gave him a ticket.

When he got back to court, the judge had gone to lunch. Joe had to feed the meter until he returned. He was duly fined $5, as he had expected, but when he took out his wallet to pay, he found that his parking fees had left him with only $2. The court clerk accepted the money on a promise that the remainder would be forthcoming and Joe, now broke, walked two miles home.

When he arrived at his house, he found a letter on the mat. It read: 'Please report for induction in the U.S. Army. . . .'

The golf club that sold its own course

The Royal Melbourne is one of the most exclusive golf courses in the world. Australia's rich and famous, as well as many international stars, have played there. But for one disastrous week, it was uncertain whether there would ever again be a Royal Melbourne to play on.

The crisis occurred at the start of the 1978 Australian PGA Championship. Stars like Johnny Miller and Severiano Ballesteros were competing on the immaculately manicured 18 holes when the club committee made the greatest golfing blunder of all time. They sold almost a third of the course from under the golfers' feet.

The club had planned to make extra cash for improvements by selling one acre of wasteland to a local house-builder. Instead, they got their plans mixed up and sold him the 8th, 9th, 10th and 11th fairways.

The builder, Mike Warson, discovered the mistake only when he was refused planning permission to subdivide the acre he thought he had bought. 'My surveyor checked up and found that the club had signed away 60 acres,' he said.

The land that the club had inadvertently sold was worth almost $20 million – a hundred times more than Warson had paid for it. He said: 'It's quite a bargain, even if you don't know what a five-iron looks like. We all had a good laugh at the club's expense.'

But as the championship continued, Warson decided to help the club out of the bunker it had landed itself in. He returned the land.

A golfer at Livermore, California, sent a ball through the window of an aircraft landing at the local airport. It struck the pilot on the head but the plane landed safely.

The cowboy yarn written by computer

Computer expert Gilbert Bohuslav was so proud of his brainiest 'baby', a computer named DEC 11/70, that he thought he could teach it to write a Western story.

DEC 11/70 is the most advanced computer in its class at Brazosport College, Houston, Texas. It had already proved itself a master at playing chess with Bohuslav, so the young computer engineer fed into it some new information – all the most-used words in every Western movie he had ever seen.

DEC started shooting out its Wild West yarn, and with it shot down the Bohuslav Kid's theory. For this is the story that DEC told:

'Tex Doe, the marshal of Harry City, rode into town. He sat hungrily in the saddle, ready for trouble. He knew that his sexy enemy, Alphonse the Kid, was in town.

'The Kid was in love with Texas Horse Marion. Suddenly the Kid came out of the upended Nugget Saloon. "Draw, Tex," he yelled madly. Tex reached for his girl, but before he could get it out of his car, the Kid fired, hitting Tex in the elephant and the tundra.

'As Tex fell, he pulled out his own chess board and shot the Kid 35 times in the King. The Kid dropped in a pool of whisky. "Aha," Tex said, "I hated to do it but he was on the wrong side of the Queen." '

Bohuslav gave up his experiment and went back to playing chess.

Politician Horatio Bottomley backed the wrong horse when he attempted to clean up on a race in Belgium. In fact, he backed several wrong horses.

Bottomley, who owned an English racing stable, tried to beat the bookies by entering his six best horses for one minor race at Blankenberg. He then bet varying amounts on every horse and ordered his jockeys to race home in a particular order.

Unfortunately for Bottomley, a thick sea mist blew in over the lengthy coastal racecourse, causing the leading jockeys to lose touch with one another. The plotting politician watched horrified as his horses straggled past the finishing post in a hopelessly unplanned order – losing him a small fortune.

Through the roof

Opera house costs soared by £55 million

Australia's Sydney Opera House is awe-inspiring – a beautiful, soaring, shell-like edifice standing on a peninsula that juts into the city's magnificent harbour.

Sydneysiders agree that it is worth every penny of the £5 million it was estimated that it would cost. Unfortunately, the estimate was a bit out – £55 million out, give or take a million or so.

For not only is the Sydney Opera House the biggest modern building in the world, but it also turned out to be the most expensive, the most difficult to construct and the longest to complete.

The design of the Opera House began as rough drawings made in the early 1950s by Danish architect Jorn Utzon, who conceived the idea while gazing at Elsinore Castle, the setting of Shakespeare's *Hamlet*. Utzon submitted his ideas when the New South Wales government ran an international competition for the best plans for their prestigious cultural showpiece. He won and moved to Australia to launch the project, which eventually got under way in March 1959.

It did not take long for Utzon to discover that his original concept, grandiose as it was, did not work. For a start, the architect had planned the ten massive shells of the roof as thin skins of self-supporting concrete, but, since they were up to 200 feet high, the shells had to be supported by hefty arches. The redesigning of the roof made it the heaviest in the world – 26,000 tons, not including the million white tiles needed to face it.

As costs zoomed, so did the blood pressure of the New South Wales leaders. They launched lotteries with enormous prizes to help pay the bills for their white elephant. Plans were trimmed back so that, in size and seating, the auditoriums did not match those of opera houses already existing. There were

21

stories of walls being built, then pulled down again so that workmen could move their equipment from one part of the building to another.

A tough Minister of Works, David Hughes, was ordered to devote himself virtually full-time to the Opera House project. He and the architect clashed bitterly and publicly. Utzon resisted alterations pushed through by Hughes and claimed that the minister was spoiling the work already done. He said Hughes had wasted more than £15 million and lost over two or three years' work by pulling down and rebuilding parts of the structure. Hughes replied that Utzon had described the Opera House as a symphony – 'and if he had had his way it would remain an unfinished symphony'.

In 1966, Utzon left Australia. He complained that he had not been responsible for any of the original estimates on which the project had been given the go-ahead and said that they had always been unrealistic.

The project continued under a consortium of Australian architects who got to grips with the problems of the interior, which in four-and-a-half acres had to accommodate an opera and ballet theatre, a concert hall, a recording theatre, a cinema, and numerous restaurants and public rooms.

The fate of the operatic auditorium was sealed when the Australian Broadcasting Commission won the right to run the biggest hall, which had originally been earmarked for opera. So operatic and ballet performances were banished to the smaller theatre, which holds only 1,500 people – 1,300 fewer than the theatre from which the resident Sydney company were waiting to move.

As opening date approached, more problems cropped up. No car parks were considered until it was too late to fit them in. Plans for an underground car area beneath a nearby public park had to be dropped when construction workers refused to pull down two ancient trees on the historic site where Aborigines had performed the first native dance for British settlers in 1811. Because they had nowhere to park, members of the Sydney Symphony Orchestra threatened not to play. They said they did not fancy hauling their

> Lew Grade, later to become international film and TV magnate Lord Grade, once visited a London theatre and saw a double-act which he considered a winner. He rushed backstage after the show, congratulated the performers and promised to make them big stars if they would sign up with him as their agent. He promised to double the money they were then getting.
>
> The two performers were most enthusiastic about the offer, so Grade asked them: 'Who's your agent at the moment?' They replied: 'Lew Grade.'

Danish architect, Jorn Utzon, and the Sydney Opera House.

instruments through the streets of the city in full evening dress. They also inquired how they could be expected to get their 75 players into an orchestra pit that had been designed to seat only 60.

The ballet company complained that off-stage facilities were a joke. The lack of space at the side of the opera stage meant that if a ballet dancer took a flying leap he would flatten himself against a brick wall.

Front-of-house managers expressed doubts about the performances ever starting on time. They said that, since access roads had not been completed, theatregoers who had the foresight to journey by taxi instead of their own car would never get through the roadworks and would arrive spattered with mud after tramping through potholes.

Many artists complained about the lack of facilities for rehearsals and the absence of changing rooms. They even complained about the toilets, which they said either did not work or collapsed underneath them. But last-minute repairs were made and eventually a local newspaper reported: 'It's all cisterns go'.

The Sydney Opera House was opened by the Queen in October 1973. Opera lovers and concertgoers from all parts of Australia, along with dignitaries and guests invited from around the world, all left the amazing building later that night with praise for the awe-inspiring concept that, despite all the odds, had at last been proved a success – for the building had impressed almost everyone who had seen it.

But on that balmy, glittering night in 1973, one voice was not heard. As a final gesture of goodwill by the New South Wales government, the VIP invitation list had included Jorn Utzon. He did not attend.

When the bride married the best man

One day in the early 1920s, in Ireland, best man Albert Muldoon walked up to the altar with the bridegroom in the tiny church at Kileter, County Tyrone. But instead of standing to the right of the groom, Albert stood on his left.

The bride arrived and the ceremony began. The priest, seeing Albert standing on the left, put all his questions to him – and Albert answered them. The priest continued to the end of the ceremony and then invited the happy couple to sign the register. The slip-up only came to light when the true bride-groom insisted on signing after the priest had asked Albert to do so.

A second ceremony was immediately held – this time with Albert standing on the right.

Albert said afterwards: 'My pal Christopher, the bridegroom, was so nervous that he didn't seem able to speak, so I thought I had better answer for him.'

————————

The mile-an-hour 'super-car'

The world's press was lined up to witness the delivery of the first of a new range of supercars. The £32,000, 140-mile-an-hour Aston Martin Lagonda was about to be handed over to the Marchioness of Tavistock at her home, Woburn Abbey. The Marchioness had bought the car with her Diners Club credit card as a seventeenth-wedding anniversary present for her husband, the Marquess, son of the Duke of Bedford, owner of the Abbey; and she had invited press and television to record the handing-over ceremony.

But the Lagonda, which had taken London's 1976 Motor Show by storm, failed to arrive with the awaited throaty roar and screech of tyres. Three months earlier, the mini-computer which was to have revolutionised the car's controls had blown up ('Someone misconnected a black wire to a red one,' said

American director Peter Sprague) and now, by the time of the ceremony, the Aston Martin technicians had failed to fix the trouble. And so the fastest speed that the 140-mph supercar achieved was when four embarrassed helpers pushed it down the driveway of Woburn Abbey at approximately one mile per hour. . . .

Victor Grant was saving up for a new car. It was to be a surprise, and he did not tell his wife that he had already amassed £500 and hidden it in a bundle of old clothes. Grant was out when the dustmen called at his home in Wrexham, North Wales – and his wife gave them the bundle to put on the dustcart. When he arrived home, Grant discovered the mistake and hired a mechanical digger to excavate the rubbish dump. After two days' searching, he gave up and started saving again. This time, he put his money in the bank.

Operatic white elephant

White elephants do not come much bigger than the opera house at Manaus, in Brazil. It stands as a monument to the grandiose but impracticable dreams that made the city one of the most expensive in the world.

During the Brazilian rubber boom of 1890 to 1911, Manaus, sited near the junction of the Rivers Negro and Amazon, blossomed from a jumble of shacks to become the capital of the rubber industry and one of the most beautiful cities on earth. It boasted castles, châteaux, mosques, pallazos and Tudor-style mansions.

Almost all the materials, including the stone, were imported from Europe and paid for from the vast rubber fortunes then being amassed. Once the newly-rich tycoons had provided Manaus with street lighting, a sewage system, a floating dock, ornamental gardens and South America's first electric tramway, they looked around and wondered what else they could build.

That is when the most expensive materials of all were brought in to construct an opera house to be called the Teatro Amazonas. The beautiful building, with its elaborate murals and its dome of green, blue and gold tiles, was completed in 1896.

But, while the local authorities had spared no expense in building the opera house, they had overlooked one vital factor. There were too few customers. The auditorium seated 2,000, but the population of Manaus was less than 40,000. And the vast majority of the rough Amazon rubber men had no interest whatever in opera or the theatre.

Shortly after its opening, the opera house, on its imposing site overlooking the River Negro and the surrounding forest, was closed down and left to rot. The termites and humidity took over. Even when the giant chandelier crashed from its rotting supports, nobody did anything about it.

The building – and Manaus itself – slipped into obscurity and decay as the rubber industry declined. By 1930, the boom was no more than a memory.

In recent years, however, new industries have been introduced to the city, and the magnificent opera house, with its ornamental gardens, has been restored. The sound of music now rings out once more from its plush and pretentious interior. But this time it is not opera singers who fill the Teatro Amazonas with their music, but a local school choir who use the building for rehearsals about six times a year.

The Montreal Olympics fiasco
The Games raced away with a billion dollars

Montreal played proud host to the 1976 Olympic Games – and then faced a bill of $1 billion. That was the city's incredible debt after staging the Games – more than eight times the amount originally budgeted for.

Estimates of the cost of the billion-dollar Olympics had been so far out that, when they ended, Montreal property owners faced a Special Olympic Tax (levied in an effort to pay off the debt) for the next 20 years. The Province of Quebec shouldered the rest of the deficit and set about paying it off with extra tobacco taxes and a lottery.

When the Games finished, the main Olympic stadium and two Olympic hotels had still not been completed. Union troubles, bad weather, bad planning and bad money management were blamed.

It was thought that the spectacular facilities would pay for their own upkeep after the international athletes had all gone home. But the 10,000-seat Velo-

> **East German swimmer Sylvia Ester set a world 100–metres record of 57.9 seconds in 1967 – but officials refused to recognise it because she swam in the nude.**

drome (built at a cost of $50 million – $1 million for each registered track cyclist in Canada) could attract only 300 paying customers to its first national championships.

Other examples of extravagance were the $1½ million spent on walkie-talkie sets for security forces, $1 million rent for 33 cranes (more than the cost of buying them outright), and $½ million paid to the Montreal Symphony Orchestra and Chorus for miming to pre-recorded tapes played over the loudspeakers.

As soon as the Games ended, more than 3,700 tons of second-hand materials, ranging from boxers' bootlaces to 10,000 television sets, went on the market at knockdown prices. The unwanted debris filled warehouses the size of three football pitches, and only the Canadian Army had enough trucks to shift it all.

Quebec Sports Minister Claude Charron estimated the post-Olympic cost of running the complex at $5½ million a year, with income of only $2 million. He said: 'It is a monstrous heritage, born of outrageous expense, socially unjustified and economically unrealistic.'

The last word

Epitaph on a gravestone in a cemetery in Woolwich, London:

> **Sacred to the memory of**
>
> **MAJOR JAMES BRUSH**
>
> **who was killed by the accidental discharge of a pistol by his orderly 14th of April 1831**
>
> **Well done good and faithful servant**

Epitaph on a gravestone in a churchyard in Sheldon, Vermont, USA, to an unknown burglar shot while robbing a store in 1905:

> **HERE LIES
> A BURGLAR**
>
> **This stone
> was bought
> with money
> found
> on him**

The world's first driver – and crash victim

Nicholas Cugnot, French artillery officer, has three major world 'firsts' to his name. He became the first motorist when he invented and built a three-wheeled steam car in 1769. Within a few minutes of starting up, Cugnot became the world's first car-crash victim. He drove into a brick wall.

The intrepid inventor was not badly hurt and not at all disheartened. He improved the steering and the braking system on his car until it was capable of carrying four people at two miles an hour. He won a contract from the French War Ministry to build a much larger vehicle as a military carrier.

But Cugnot's road tests of his vehicles proved so dangerous to life and limb that, after several further crashes, he notched up yet another 'first' – he became the first man to be jailed for dangerous driving.

His military carrier was never put into service, and in 1804 he died in obscurity.

> Within the space of 20 minutes on the afternoon of October 15, 1966, a 75-year-old driver in McKinney, Texas, perpetrated four hit-and-run offences, drove on the wrong side of the road four times, caused six accidents, collected 10 traffic tickets and earned himself the label 'world's worst driver' in the *Guinness Book of Records*.

Hell hath no fury . . .

An airline pilot installed his mistress, a pretty stewardess, in a London flat. All was well in the love nest for a year, until the pilot, a married man, tired of his girlfriend and ordered her out.

The mistress pleaded with him to be allowed a few days to move, and he agreed. It proved a costly mistake.

The pilot went on a round-the-world flight. When he returned to the flat the girl had gone, leaving the apartment immaculately tidy. Only one thing was amiss – the telephone was off the hook.

He picked up the receiver and heard an American voice endlessly repeating the time. Before departing, the mistress had dialled the speaking clock in Washington D.C.

The cost of his broken love affair was a telephone bill for £1,200.

The princes who never were
How a hoaxer fooled the British navy

The first anyone heard about the royal visit was a telegram from the Foreign Office in London to the Home and Atlantic Fleets lying at anchor off Weymouth, Dorset.

It was 1910, and Britain's naval might was unmatched. The greatest ship of the fleet was HMS *Dreadnought*, flagship of the Royal Navy. And it was to the *Dreadnought* that the message from the Foreign Office came. The telegram, signed by Foreign Under-Secretary Sir Charles Hardinge, ordered the ship to prepare for a visit by a group of Abyssinian princes. The

William de Vere Cole on his wedding day. *Inset* Virginia Woolf.

navy should fête them, make them feel important, and generally impress them with the invincibility of imperial power.

The officers of the *Dreadnought* set to, never suspecting that the telegram might be anything but genuine.

Meanwhile, at London's Paddington Station, an elegant man in top hat and morning suit was laying down the law to the stationmaster. He said he was Herbert Cholmondesly of the Foreign Office and he wanted a special train laid on to convey a party of Abyssinian princes to Weymouth. He wanted that train right away.

The stationmaster rushed off to prepare a VIP coach – never suspecting that Cholmondesly might be an impostor.

The 'man from the F.O.' was William Horace de Vere Cole, a wealthy young society man, practical joker extraordinary. It was he who had sent the telegram. And the four 'princes' who stepped aboard the special train at Paddington were his friends – famous novelist Virginia Woolf, judge's son Guy Ridley, sportsman Anthony Buxton and artist Duncan Grant. All had been heavily made up, bearded and robed by theatrical make-up expert Willy Clarkson. They were accompanied on their journey by an 'interpreter', Virginia Woolf's brother Adrian, and by joker Cole himself.

The group arrived at Weymouth to be greeted by a red carpet and a guard of honour. They were piped aboard the *Dreadnought*, which had been bedecked with bunting for the royal visit. Nowhere in the fleet could an Abyssinian flag be found, nor the music for the Abyssinian national anthem. Instead, worried officers ordered the hoisting of the flag of Zanzibar, and the band played that country's national anthem. No one need have worried – the 'princes' did not know the difference.

As the group inspected the fleet, they handed out visiting cards printed in Swahili and spoke in Latin with an unrecognisable accent. Everything they were shown was greeted with delighted cries of 'Bunga-bunga'.

They were shown every hospitality. In return, they tried to bestow Abyssinian military honours on some of the high-ranking officers. They asked for prayer mats at sunset. But they refused all offers of food and drink 'for religious reasons' – they had been warned by make-up man Clarkson that if they tried to eat anything their false lips would fall off.

The ruse was almost uncovered on two occasions. Firstly, when Anthony Buxton sneezed and half his moustache flew off (he stuck it back on before anyone noticed), and secondly, when the group were introduced to an officer who was related to Virginia Woolf and who also knew Cole quite well. But the officer did not see through Virginia's disguise and, extraordinarily, he showed no sign of recognition when he looked at Cole.

The royal party hastily ended their visit and, after posing for photographs, returned to London, where they revealed their outrageous hoax. The whole operation had cost Cole £4,000 – a princely sum in those days.

But Cole would pay almost any sum and go to almost any lengths for the sake of a practical joke. He once dressed as a workman and dug a huge hole in the middle of London's bustling Piccadilly. He kept an eye on his hole in the road for several days, watching the visits of numerous puzzled council officials. It was a week later before they realised they had been hoaxed and filled it in.

On another occasion, Cole was walking through Westminster with a Member of Parliament when the arch-joker bet the MP that he could beat him to the next corner, even after giving him a ten-yard start. The MP agreed, not realising that Cole had slipped his gold watch into his acquaintance's pocket. As the MP began running, Cole shouted: 'Stop thief!', and called over a policeman to search the 'fugitive's' pockets. The watch was found and the MP was whisked off to the nearest police station, where he had the unenviable task of persuading the police that they had all been taken for a ride.

But Cole's favourite practical jokes involved disguises. While an undergraduate at Cambridge University, he dressed up as the Sultan of Zanzibar and paid an 'official visit' to his own college. He was even conducted around his own quarters.

Another of his outlandish impersonations was when he arrived at a meeting of leading trade unionists and marched on to the platform to address them. The audience was expecting a speech by Britain's first Labour Prime Minister, Ramsay MacDonald, and indeed Cole, after spending hours making up before a mirror, did look exceedingly like him.

The real MacDonald, however, was 'lost' somewhere in London in a taxi driven by one of Cole's accomplices. Cole meanwhile was telling the union leaders that they should all work much harder for less pay. The speech did not go down well.

Canadian photographer Peter Duffy, assigned to cover the unveiling of a plaque at City Hall in Prince George, British Columbia, decided to liven up an otherwise dull afternoon by taping a large coloured nude photograph over the plaque, but under the covering drape. Then he stood back, camera at the ready, as the mayor performed the unveiling.

Duffy said: 'The mayor didn't see the picture at first, but when he did his mouth just hung open. Instead of the usual ripple of applause, there was absolute silence. Then I was sacked.'

The law really can be an ass

The law is a ass – a idiot.' That was the verdict of Mr. Bumble the beadle in the Charles Dickens classic, *Oliver Twist*. If Mr. Bumble had ever visited the young states of North America, he would have found his prejudices particularly well founded. For there, the legislators were busy drafting a whole new range of asinine laws.

These laws have been added to over the years. And, because of bureaucratic forgetfulness, they remain in force (although not often enforced) to this day.

Woe betide the citizen at Greene, New York, who eats peanuts and walks backwards during a concert – he faces the risk of prosecution.

Carrying fishing tackle in a cemetery is illegal at Muncie, Indiana. Slurping soup in a New Jersey restaurant is against the law. In Memphis, Tennessee, a local law demands that a woman must not drive a car unless a man walks in front with a red flag.

The good people of Milwaukee must keep their pet elephants on a leash while walking them on the public streets. In Oklahoma it is illegal to get a fish drunk or to attempt to catch whales in the state's inland waters.

Even insects have not escaped the attention of the law-makers. In Kirkland, Illinois, a law forbids bees to fly over the town.

Cafés are not supposed to sell ring-doughnuts in Lehigh, Pennsylvania. It is unlawful in Lexington, Kentucky, to carry an ice-cream cornet in your pocket.

The law-makers of yester-year really had a field day at Corvallis, Oregon. Spare a thought for a young girl wanting to buy a cup of coffee there after 6 p.m. Local laws say she must do without. Over at Lynn, Massachusetts, it is forbidden to serve coffee to babies in restaurants. And at Waterloo, Nebraska, barbers are barred from eating onions between 7 a.m. and 7 p.m.

But the prize for law-making gone mad must go to Thurston County, Washington. Officials there wanted to ensure that police and firemen who worked on Sundays did not have to be paid overtime rates. The legal experts were set to work and came up with the following solution: for the purposes of assessing pay rates, Sundays were henceforth abolished.

No person shall walk, run, stand, sit or lie on the grass in this pleasure ground.
— Byelaw of Newquay Urban Council, Cornwall

35

A canal goes down the drain

It was a tough job for Jack Rothwell and his workmates – dredging a busy stretch of the Chesterfield Canal, near Retford in Nottinghamshire. It had proved quite a problem, what with all the mud and rusting bicycles, prams and refrigerators. Now they were finding it impossible to shift a heavy iron chain lying on the bottom of the canal.

Finally, Jack, foreman of the gang, ordered the chain to be hooked to their dredger. Driver Kevin Bowskill started up and, with one sharp tug, the obstruction was freed. The workmen hauled in the chain, along with a large block of wood that was attached to the end of it, and knocked off for a tea-break.

While they were away, a passing policeman noticed an extraordinary whirlpool in the normally placid canal. He also noticed that the water level was falling. He rushed off to find the dredging gang. By the time they all returned, the canal had disappeared.

It was then that realisation dawned. Jack and his men had pulled out the plug of the canal. One-and-a-half miles of waterway had gone down the drain.

The plug, put there by James Brindley when he built the waterway 200 years earlier, had remained undisturbed until Jack's gang came along in the summer of 1978. Now, the millions of gallons of water that had filled the canal were all draining into the nearby River Idle. All that was left were a number of forlornly grounded holiday cruisers, complete with angry owners, the dredger itself, which was stuck firmly on the muddy bottom . . . and a plughole.

The town that stayed at war for 110 years

A simple slip-up put a British town at war with one of the mightiest nations on earth for more than a century. The long but peaceful war was between Russia and the border town of Berwick-upon-Tweed.

Over the centuries, Berwick had changed hands 13 times between Scotland and England. In 1482, it finally became part of England. But because of its special place in history, the town was traditionally referred to as a separate entity in all State documents.

At the outbreak of the Crimean War, England declared war on Czarist Russia in the name of Victoria, Queen of Great Britain, Ireland, Berwick-upon-Tweed and all British Dominions. The war ended in 1856, but, by an oversight, the Paris Peace Treaty of that year made no mention of Berwick.

And so the town remained officially at war with Russia for a further 110 years – until, in 1966, a Soviet official made a special goodwill visit to Berwick to declare peace.

The town's mayor, Councillor Robert Knox, replied: 'Please tell the Russian people that at last they can sleep peacefully in their beds.'

The Martians have landed!

Orson Welles' radio play threw America into a panic

Orson Welles directs *War of the Worlds*.

A few minutes after eight o'clock on the night of Sunday, October 30, 1938, a sombre voice interrupted a radio broadcast to warn Americans: 'Ladies and gentlemen, I have a grave announcement to make . . .'

The words that followed, beamed out in a programme networked across the United States, caused remarkable scenes of panic. For the grave announcement was that Martians had landed in North America and were sweeping all resistance before them in a series of bloody battles. The USA was being taken over by men from outer space.

THE WORLD'S GREATEST MISTAKES

The announcement was part of an off-beat radio play – but one so realistic and produced by such a genius of the theatre that most people who heard it took it for fact.

The programme had started undramatically enough. At 8 p.m. listeners heard: 'The Columbia Broadcasting System and affiliated stations present Orson Welles and his Mercury Theatre Of The Air in *War of the Worlds* by H. G. Wells.'

Then came the booming voice of Orson Welles: 'We know now that in the early years of the 20th century, this world was being watched closely by intelligences greater than man's.'

He was interrupted by a news announcer apparently reading a routine bulletin: 'Tonight's weather . . . For the next 24 hours there will not be much change in temperature. A slight atmospheric disturbance of undetermined origin is reported over Nova Scotia, causing a low-pressure area to move down rather rapidly over the north-eastern states, bringing a forecast of rain, accompanied by winds of light-gale force. Maximum temperature: 66. Minimum: 48. This weather report comes to you from the Government Weather Bureau.

'We now take you to the Meridian Room at the Hotel Park Plaza in downtown New York where you will be entertained by the music of Ramon Raquello and his orchestra.'

Nothing to cause alarm at that stage. But the atmosphere was being cleverly built up. Listeners who had tuned in from the start were already lulled into forgetfulness that what they were listening to was really a radio play.

Not that there were many listeners. After 16 Mercury Theatre shows, CBS bosses readily admitted that their dramatic series was not proving to be a major hit. Mercury Theatre had only 3 per cent of the listening audience. Most people were tuned on Sunday nights to The Charlie McCarthy Show on a rival network.

That was why Welles, worried by the ratings, was throwing everything into

---

Norway's King Haakon visited the BBC's London studios in order to record a broadcast to his people. The title of the programme was 'This is London', and it was to begin with a royal fanfare.

Unfortunately, the BBC Sound Library misunderstood its instructions and, instead of supplying a recording of a fanfare, produced one of a funfair.

The King's introduction went out over the air as: 'Roll up, roll up . . . all the fun of the fair . . .'

THE WORLD'S GREATEST MISTAKES

War of the Worlds. He knew that CBS would ditch his show if it did not find a big-money sponsor. And it would not get a sponsor if it did not gain more listeners.

Welles and his Mercury Theatre associates, Paul Stewart and John Houseman, had been working on the play for five days. They had rehearsed it, rewritten the script, and rehearsed again. On the Thursday night before it went on the air, the three men had listened to a tape of their work so far. They were not happy.

Welles, who had been rehearsing for another play in New York at the same time and who was almost asleep on his feet, was as glum as anyone had ever seen him. He said: 'Our only chance is to make it as realistic as possible. We'll have to throw in as many stunts as we can think of.' The team stayed up all night adding newsy-sounding snippets to the script. The next day Stewart worked on suitable sound effects – the noise of panicking crowds, gunfire and screams.

By Sunday night, the studio was littered with paper cups and food bags after a nervous eight-hour rehearsal. But at 7.59 p.m., as Welles gulped a bottle of pineapple juice before going on the air, everyone agreed that this show had a chance . . . that it would pinch listeners from Charlie McCarthy . . . that it would get the Mercury Theatre talked about.

What followed over the next 24 hours certainly got the Mercury Theatre – and Welles in particular – talked about. It also won listeners from the McCarthy show, and sooner than Welles had thought.

By chance, the McCarthy variety show had a new singer featured that Sunday night. He was an unknown. He came on at ten minutes past eight, and bored listeners began twiddling their dials to find out whether there was anything better on CBS. They joined *War of the Worlds* after all the preliminary announcements had been made. They had no inkling that a play was in progress. All they knew was that strange things were happening along the eastern seaboard. The CBS announcer was telling them so. . . .

'Ladies and gentlemen, I have a grave announcement to make. The strange object which fell at Grovers Mill, New Jersey, earlier this evening was not a meteorite. Incredible as it seems, it contained strange beings who are believed to be the vanguard of an army from the planet Mars.'

Soft music followed. A subtle touch to get people anxious, unsettled, edgy. What was going on?

The announcer broke in again. There was a nervous, panicky tone to his voice. The Martians, hideous leathery-skinned creatures, were spreading out. New Jersey police were racing to intercept them.

There was more music, more feverish announcements, chilling silences. People were glued to their sets. Neighbours had been called in to listen, too.

Relatives had been telephoned and warned. Across the whole of America, people were beginning to panic.

Then the announcer spluttered on to the air again: 'We take you now to Washington for a special broadcast on the national emergency by the Secretary of the Interior.' A solemn voice was heard urging people not to panic – but in the same breath telling them that the Martian landing was not restricted to New Jersey. Space vehicles were falling to earth all across the States. Thousands of troops and civilians had already been slaughtered by death-ray guns.

There were interviews with eye-witnesses, many parts being played by brilliant actor Joseph Cotten. The witnesses told how they had seen fiery objects land and foul creatures emerge from them, how death-rays had wiped out thousands, how the aliens were unstoppable.

One of Welles' actors impersonated the President of the United States and warned the American people against the dangers of panic. The show ended with an announcer screaming from the top of the CBS skyscraper that Manhattan was being overrun. His feverish commentary trailed off in a strangled scream.

By that time, many listeners had already left their radio sets. Those who stayed with the show to the end realised that it was all just a play. Those who did not were in a blind panic.

In New Jersey, where the Martians were first reported to have landed, the roads were jammed with cars racing for the hills. Families fled from their homes with wet towels over their heads, believing this would save them from the nauseous space gases they had been told about. Furniture and valuables were being piled into trucks and cars. The stampede had started.

The panic spread outwards. In New York, restaurants emptied. Bus terminals and taxi ranks bulged as people tried to get home to comfort their families. Wives rang around the bars trying to find husbands. And the word spread.

Sailors in the U.S. Navy were recalled to their ships in New York harbour to be ready to defend America against the Martians. From Los Angeles to

> **Czech housewife Vera Czermak was heartbroken when she learned of her husband's unfaithfulness. In a fit of depression, she hurled herself out of the window of her third-floor Prague apartment. Three floors below, Mr. Czermak was walking along the street. Mrs. Czermak landed on Mr. Czermak. Mr. Czermak died and Mrs. Czermak survived.**

THE WORLD'S GREATEST MISTAKES

Boston there were reports of 'meteors'. Some impressionable people actually claimed to have seen Martians.

State reserve troopers called their HQs to volunteer for the defence of the world. In the Deep South, weeping, hysterical women prayed in the streets. Church services across the land were interrupted as people burst in to break the news to congregations. There was even one case of an attempted suicide.

The switchboards of newspapers and radio stations were jammed. But, surprisingly, there was no inkling of the panic in the CBS studios, where, with screams and announcements of martial law, Welles was bringing his production to a gruesome close. Welles and Cotten were told about the incoming phone calls, but Cotten said: 'They're just cranks.' Towards the end of the play, two policemen turned up at the back of the studio but, realising it was all just a play, they did not mention the panic to anyone and, instead, stayed to listen to the finale.

The first Welles knew of the result of his over-enthusiastic endeavours was when he left his apartment the following morning and saw his name in flickering lights on the neon newsboard of the *New York Times* building: 'Orson Welles Causes Panic.' He bought the newspapers and read the main headlines in the *New York Herald Tribune* – 'Attack from Mars in Radio Play Puts Thousands in Fear' – and in the *New York Times* – 'Radio Listeners in Panic: Many Flee Homes to Escape Gas Raid from Mars.'

Welles, already a well-known actor at the age of 24, was fiercely criticised for the unthinking action that had thrown half the USA into terror. Newspapers lambasted him for irresponsibility. There was talk of criminal action.

Dozens of people brought lawsuits against CBS; the total claim was $750,000. But all the suits were withdrawn and, far from taking Welles' show off the air, CBS bosses patted themselves on the back for having hired the most talked-about actor in America. The Mercury Theatre's ratings soared. It even found a sponsor.

Radio's biggest blunder had paid off.

Fairground customers queued up to see the amazing 'King Kong' – 23-year-old Mike Towell in an ape costume. Mike's act had been a big success in fairs around Britain. But his biggest hit came when he visited Huddersfield, Yorkshire. As he climaxed his act by bending back the bars of his cage and leaping into the audience, one frightened man picked up an iron bar and whacked him over the head. The man fled in panic and 'King Kong' was rushed to hospital to have six stitches put in his scalp.

Captain Cook speared to death by natives in Hawaii, 1777.

How paradise was lost

The travellers who destroyed the Island of Love

Try to imagine the nearest thing to paradise on earth and you might well think of Tahiti. For this tiny dot in the vast emptiness of the Pacific has been praised by travellers through the ages as the most beautiful place in the world.

Approach Tahiti on the deck of a ship and the island appears out of the ocean like a vision from fairyland. It is only 35 miles long yet it is capped by a 7,000-ft mountain with majestic pinnacles soaring into a ring of cloud. The slopes of the mountain glitter with streams that rush through the tropical forests clinging to its sides.

Surrounding the mountain is a flat shoreline encompassed by coral rocks, grey volcanic sand and crashing surf. Beside the island's single bumpy road are dotted huts whose woven palm walls shift noiselessly in the light breeze.

43

Captain Bligh's *Bounty*.

PEOPLE AND PLACES

Today there is also the port of Papeete, with pretty white yachts, and white holidaymakers strolling around the harbour. But 200 years ago there was no port, no white people – only what early navigators described as 'the second Garden of Eden'.

The Tahitians lived an idyllic life. They were bronzed and beautiful and sensual. Love was unhidden, natural and shared. Diarists among the first explorers have recorded that the men were tall with shining teeth and perfect skins, except for the tattoos with which they adorned themselves. And the women were perfect, especially to the eyes of the sailors who had been months at sea without seeing a female form. These women wore brightly coloured, loosely fitting dresses which displayed their charms almost completely. They often went bare-breasted and generally wore flowers in their long dark hair.

Flowers – hibiscus, frangipani and jasmine – adorned the island generously. There was fruit in abundance, too, particularly coconuts and breadfruit. And in the sea there was fish for the taking. The 40,000 islanders who lived on Tahiti two centuries ago did not have to work hard for a living. Food and fresh water was provided by nature. The climate was constant. There was little sickness. No danger. Love was what life was all about. By any standards, Tahiti was indeed paradise.

Then came the white man. On April 13, 1769, Captain James Cook sailed his ship *Endeavour* into Matavai Bay, near Papeete, and dropped anchor.

His crew were not the first white men to visit Tahiti. Louis Antoine de Bougainville, in *La Boudeuse*, had put in for provisions the year before, and the Royal Navy's Captain Wallis, commanding the *Dolphin*, had called in 1767. But Bougainville had barely set foot ashore and Wallis stayed hardly a month, most of the time confined to his sickbed. Cook's longer stay, and his return to the island, were to change Tahiti for ever.

Cook was an adventurer of thirty-nine, a tough Yorkshireman from a poor background who had begun his sea career as Able Seaman Cook in the Royal Navy. He made his name as a navigator by charting Newfoundland and, against all expectations, was given a commission and put in charge of the *Endeavour* with orders to carry out astronomical surveys on Tahiti and then head south to seek the fabled 'Southern Continent'.

He arrived in Matavai Bay with ninety men, most notable of whom was a wealthy young amateur botanist, Joseph Banks, who had contributed largely to the cost of the expedition. On his return to England, he was to be lauded by society, lionised to a greater degree than Captain Cook, and eventually become president of the Royal Society, an honour he held until his death.

When the *Endeavour* dropped anchor, she must have seemed a mighty vessel to the Tahitians, used only to their outrigger canoes. But by Royal Navy standards, she was not so impressive – a 350-ton converted collier, just a hundred feet long and carrying twelve guns. The *Endeavour* had sailed from Plymouth eight months previously and the men aboard were ravenous – for fresh food, excitement and women. They had heard of the legendary beauty of the Tahitian girls and they peered expectantly shorewards as the islanders' canoes came out of Matavai Bay to inspect them. They were happy to heed Cook's final instructions before anchoring: 'Endeavour by all fair means to cultivate a friendship with the natives and treat them with all imaginable humanity.'

The Tahitians were shy at first and meekly offered palm fronds as a sign of peace. But they soon became more confident and invited the strangers to visit their homes. Joseph Banks was awed by the beauty of the place. He wrote: 'The scene we saw was the truest picture of Arcadia, of which we were going to be kings, that the imagination can form.'

Cook's first job was to set up a camp ashore, where he could prepare his instruments for the astronomical observations, most importantly the transit of Venus across the Sun due to occur on June 3. But arrangements were hampered by the islanders' petty pilfering. A constant guard had to be kept on the ship; otherwise the Tahitians would clamber aboard from canoes and steal virtually anything not fastened down. While dining ashore with a chieftain and his family, Banks had a telescope and a snuff box stolen. And Cook lost a valuable quadrant, later recovered. But most serious of all, a band of Tahitians seized a musket from one of the camp guards, who opened fire on them.

In his log, Cook glossed over the incident. But Sydney Parkinson, an artist brought along by Banks to draw the plants of the island, later put the incident in its true perspective. He wrote of the guards' reaction to the order to fire: 'They obeyed with the greatest glee imaginable, as if they had been shooting at wild ducks. They killed one man and wounded many others.' And he added: 'What a pity that such brutality should be exercised by civilised people against unarmed ignorant Indians. The natives fled into the woods like frightened fawns. They were terrified to the last degree.'

The first cracks had appeared in paradise.

The second blow fell a week later. A chieftain who had become particularly friendly with the Englishmen complained that the *Endeavour*'s butcher had threatened his wife. Cook had the butcher lashed to the rigging and invited the chief and his family on board to witness the culprit's punishment – a thrashing with the cat o'nine tails. The Tahitians wept openly and pleaded with the captain to free the man. But Cook refused, and the punishment went ahead – to the accompaniment of wails from the chief and his family. The islanders were learning the meaning of white man's justice.

What particularly bewildered the Tahitians, however, was the visitors' attitude to love-making. Among the islanders, the act was as natural as eating and was often carried out in the open, particularly among the young, who might be only 11 or 12. The Tahitians could never understand why the English sailors wanted to creep away with the women into the woods. What were they ashamed of?

At first, love on the island was offered to the white men absolutely free. Native girls would make their intentions very obvious, even to the guards on duty around the camp. The sailors and marines from the *Endeavour* availed themselves of the maidens' charms at every opportunity. So too, it is believed, did most of the officers and scientists aboard, with the exception of Cook.

But the recent visits by the ships of Wallis and Bougainville had left on the islanders the first stain of the civilised world – venereal disease. By the time the *Endeavour* left Tahiti – three months after its arrival – half the ship's company were afflicted. Also, by that time love on Tahiti was no longer free. At first, the price was an iron nail. Then two nails. Then a handful. Eventually, crewmen had to be punished for using up the ship's badly needed store of this item.

Just before the ship was due to sail, two men deserted and headed for the hills with native girls. They were recaptured and given the lash.

The *Endeavour* sailed south for Australia and Antarctica on July 13, the slow old collier being accompanied out to sea by canoes filled with waving and weeping natives. Waving back from the ship were a Tahitian chief and his servant who had begged Cook to take them with him. But they were not to survive the two-year voyage. Neither were 32 of the crew, who died of white man's diseases the *Endeavour* had carried around the world.

Cook made two further voyages to the Pacific. In August 1773 he sailed into Matavai Bay in command of another converted collier, the *Resolution*, with a crew of 117. He was accompanied by the slightly smaller *Adventurer*, with 83 men, commanded by Lieutenant Tobias Furneaux, who had sailed on the original Tahitian expedition with Wallis. Cook and Furneaux stayed only 16 days before heading south again to explore Antarctica and New Zealand. They returned to Tahiti in April 1774 and this time remained for six weeks.

Relaxing after the rigours of Antarctica and with no vital duties to perform

> He said: 'I was playing my recording of the *Messiah* when Mrs. X said that this was not the time for music. She then made overtures to me.'
>
> – *News of the World*

on the island, Cook and his men had time to take stock of the changes that had been wrought by the islanders' contact with the white man. They found that a Spanish ship had called at Tahiti and that influenza and venereal diseases had taken their toll of the natives. The favours of the island girls were again enjoyed by Cook's men, but nails were no longer the payment. The beautiful girls who had once innocently revelled in their own nakedness now demanded Western clothing from the sailors.

Cook's conscience was disturbed. He wrote: 'We debauch their morals and introduce among them wants and diseases which they never before knew, and which disturb the happy tranquillity which they enjoyed.'

When the *Resolution* and the *Adventurer* left Tahiti, they took with them a handsome young islander called Omai, who, on his arrival in England, was paraded like a circus monkey around London society and was even introduced to George III.

Cook remained at home with his wife and six children for less than a year before setting sail once again. With him on his final journey to Tahiti went Omai.

In August 1777 the *Resolution* dropped anchor in Matavai Bay for the last time. Omai, who was returning to his people as an ambassador of the civilised world, stepped ashore laden with fine cloth and gifts for the Tahitians. The islanders readily accepted them, then roundly snubbed Omai. Perhaps not surprisingly, the Tahitians, particularly those of noble birth, were intensely jealous of their kinsman, who had suddenly gained all the status symbols of that civilised society which they now valued so highly.

Omai had to be put by Cook on to a nearby island, Huahine, where he lived in a small house built by the crew and surrounded himself with the useless trappings of a European gentleman. Cook also had to give him firearms to protect himself from his own people.

During this visit by the English there was a new exchange of customs. Cook was introduced to a Tahitian rite which shook even this worldly-wise traveller – the human sacrifice of a prisoner, who was clubbed to death as part of a

---

Viennese authorities decided to build up a women's section in the city's police force, and recruited 60 girl constables. They gave them quarters in the city's biggest police barracks, with male police trainees in the same building but on different floors. The target of a 60-strong female force had to be scrapped, however, after it was found that 36 of the girls, all unmarried and aged between 19 and 25, were pregnant.

---

religious ceremony. And the Tahitians witnessed a European punishment which appalled them – a man caught stealing had his ears cut off.

Cook learned that two Spanish ships had called at the island during his absence. Their purpose had been to set up a missionary station, but they had been unable to convert the islanders and had departed after less than a year, leaving behind an abandoned makeshift church. (But the missionaries would be back – and next time their influence would be more permanent.)

Cook left the island for the last time in September 1777. He sailed for Hawaii where, at the age of 50, he was speared to death by natives.

Though Cook was an adventurer with a toughness born of the hard age in which he lived, he showed a surprising sensitivity to and understanding of the Pacific islanders. He wrote in his journal: 'It is my real opinion that it would have been far better for these poor people never to have known our superiority in the accommodations and arts that make life comfortable than, after once knowing it, to be left abandoned in their original incapacity. They can never be restored to that happy mediocrity in which they lived before we discovered them.'

The white men who followed Cook showed no such understanding of – and precious little mercy for – the 'noble savages' of Tahiti.

In 1778 Captain Bligh's *Bounty* stayed at the island for six months, during which several of the crew entered into permanent liaisons with Tahitian girls. After the *Bounty* sailed from Tahiti, the crew, led by Fletcher Christian, mutinied. Bligh was cast adrift (but survived), and the rebel *Bounty* returned to Tahiti. Some of the mutineers stayed there, others went on to the Pitcairn Isles.

In 1791 the Admiralty sent the *Pandora* to Tahiti to seek out the mutineers, who had by now been assimilated into the island life. The *Pandora*'s crew discovered that hundreds of American whaling ships had been using Tahiti as a base and that their influence on the island had been disastrous. The Tahitians were now unwashed drunkards, wearing white men's rags, their ancient customs and lifestyle forgotten.

In 1792 Bligh returned to Tahiti and reported that smallpox, dysentery and venereal disease were rife.

The final blow against this island paradise was struck in 1797 when the ship *The Duff* landed four clergymen and 34 other Britons, led by the fiercely Protestant Henry Nott. Their mission was to convert the natives to Christianity. It was a Christianity which made up in fanaticism what it lacked in mercy.

The missionaries built a church and won the islanders to it by first concentrating their influence on the chieftains. The missionaries succeeded to such an extent that within 20 years of their landing the Christian religion was obligatory in many parts of the island and 'pagans' were put to death by their own people, love outside marriage was banned, and dancing, music and even the wearing of flowers were forbidden. Guilt, the one sense the Tahitians never seemed to have known, had at last been introduced to the island.

The missionaries had brought the promise of eternal life, but nothing to lengthen the existence of the Tahitians on earth. When Captain Cook first visited Tahiti in 1769 he estimated the population at 40,000. By the turn of the century it was down to 13,000. In 1843, when the island was annexed by the French, it had dropped to less than 9,000. And the ravages of disease were to reduce yet further what had once been a proud and thriving race.

When, a century after Cook, the painter Paul Gauguin arrived on Tahiti to paint paradise, he found that he was too late. He wrote: 'Day by day, the race vanishes, decimated by the European diseases. The natives have nothing – nothing to do and nothing to think of except drinking. Many strange and picturesque things existed here once but there are no traces of them left today. Everything has gone.'

Paradise had been lost for ever.

Man-ape made monkeys out of the archaeologists

The archaeological world's greatest blunder was its long acceptance of the Piltdown Man as the missing link in man's evolution from the ape.

In 1912 Charles Dawson, a lawyer and amateur geologist, collected the remains of a skull from a gravel pit near Piltdown, Sussex, and sent them to one of the world's leading experts on the history of man, Dr. Arthur Woodward of the British Museum. Together, the two men continued excavations of the pit until they had collected an amazing array of teeth, bones and prehistoric tools.

Woodward pieced together their finds – and announced that what they had unearthed was the skull of a creature, half-man, half-ape, which had lived 500,000 years ago. Although the skull was that of a woman, the find was officially named *Eoanthropus dawsoni* – Dawson's Early Man. The discovery was heralded as the first firm proof of Charles Darwin's controversial theory of evolution, and it made Dawson famous throughout the world.

Dawson continued his excavations in the Piltdown area and, over the next few years, pieced together a second skull. The finds ended upon his death in 1916, at the age of 52; others continued the search but found nothing. This was later realised not to have been so strange. For the Piltdown Man was a fake.

The skull was indeed that of a human, but the jaw and teeth were those of an orang-utan. The teeth had been filed down to look like human teeth, then the complete skull had been skilfully stained and aged before being broken up and buried in the gravel pit.

It was not until 1953 that the hoax was revealed by newly developed techniques of age-testing. And although no one has fully solved the mystery, Hoax Suspect Number One has always been Dawson. He was ambitious for academic distinction. And once, a visitor walked into his laboratory uninvited to find Dawson busy over a bubbling crucible – staining bones.

Two business ladies require a sleeping partner for beauty salon.

                                 – London evening newspaper

Diamonds – or ostrich droppings?

Experts refused to believe the evidence of the world's richest gem-fields

The rich and famous refused to believe the evidence before their eyes when diamonds were first discovered in Hopetown, South Africa – and so chances of becoming even richer and more famous were lost.

One leading authority asserted that diamonds could not possibly exist naturally in the region. They must have been eaten elsewhere by wandering ostriches, he insisted, then dispersed throughout Hopetown in the ostriches' droppings.

He was wrong. The 'ostrich droppings' had been present for untold centuries. And they were diamonds of unsurpassed quality.

Stories had abounded of 'pretty pebbles' having been found in the area. Across an ancient map of the territory was scrawled: 'Here be diamonds'.

THE WORLD'S GREATEST MISTAKES

A couple took a taxi home after Christmas shopping in the
busy West End of London in 1932. But after unloading their
parcels into their house, they discovered that they had one
package too many. They unwrapped it and found a leather
jewel case packed with diamonds, emeralds and rubies. The
honest couple took the treasure to the police who valued it
at £300,000 – more than £2 million by today's values. After
it had remained unclaimed for three days, the police
managed to track down the owner, who still had not
realised that she had mislaid the jewels. The owner was the
Grand Duchess Zenia, who had escaped from Russia during
the Revolution. Her treasure was part of the Russian Crown
Jewels.

Yet, reminded of such stories, locals would simply smile knowingly . . . and
dismiss them.

Farmer Schalk van Niekerk was less sceptical about the stories than most.
Towards Christmas of 1866 he found children of Hopetown playing klip-klip,
a game known elsewhere as fivestones, or jacks. They were using pebbles, and
Van Niekerk quickly recognised one stone as being different from the others –
excitingly different.

He stopped and picked it out of the handful of pebbles. He offered money
for it to the wife of the owner of the land on which the children were playing.
She laughed. Who would want to pay money for a pebble? Have it, she said.
The stone, she added, had been found by one of the children in a hollow dug
by a Bushman. There were lots, lots more to be found, she was sure.

Van Niekerk, astonishingly, seems to have taken no action about his discovery until the following year, when he discussed the stone with a passing
trader, John O'Reilly. This itinerant, who was later to claim that he
recognised the true value of the stone on sight, promised 'to find out what it
really was'.

In Hopetown, O'Reilly began to boast of having found a diamond and was
ragged unmercifully. Traders laughed at him and one of them bet him 'a dozen
of beer' against the likelihood of such a find. A disheartened O'Reilly was prepared to throw the stone in the river. Instead, he journeyed to Colesberg,
where he met further derision. Then he showed the stone to the acting civil
commissioner of Colesberg, Lorenzo Boyes. At last, O'Reilly had found someone to take him seriously.

'I believe it to be a diamond,' the official declared. But others remained
unconvinced. The local chemist was consulted and offered to top the wager of

a dozen beers with a new hat for Boyes if the stone proved to be anything but a topaz. 'I'll take the bet,' said Boyes.

Further identification of the 'pretty pebble' could only come from an expert. Fortunately, less than 200 miles away lived the foremost geologist of the Cape Colony. He was a doctor named William Guybon Atherstone.

Boyes sent the stone to Atherstone. It was placed in an ordinary envelope, with a covering letter, and travelled on the post cart to Grahamstown, where the doctor was in practice.

The mail arrived while Atherstone sat in his garden. He opened the envelope and read the letter. He looked in the envelope, but there was no stone. He assumed it must have fallen to the ground when he opened the envelope and called his daughter to help search for it. In a wild scramble they found what appeared to be 'a dull, rounded, apparently water-worn river stone'.

Despite his experience, Atherstone had not seen an uncut diamond before, but he subjected it to several tests – and became certain that the stone which had been sent to him was a diamond. He sought confirmation from his neighbour, Father James Ricards, later the first Roman Catholic Bishop of Grahamstown. The priest tested the stone in the one way he knew would prove its identity – by cutting his initials on a pane of glass in his study (the window is now in Grahamstown Cathedral).

Atherstone wrote to Boyes: 'I congratulate you on the stone you have sent me. It is a veritable diamond, weighs 21¼ carats, and is worth £500. Where that came from there must be lots more.'

The diamond was sent to Capetown, then sent by ship to London. It was to be three months before the famous jewellers Garrards reported that it was indeed worth £500. But far from reviving enthusiasm in the Cape and South Africa as a potential source of wealth, the diamond created suspicions about its origins.

At the time, the Exposition Universelle was being held in Paris. John Blades Curry was responsible for the Cape's stand, and on hearing Garrards' findings on the diamond he tried to build up enthusiasm for this momentous discovery. He met with the same kind of ridicule and scepticism that had confronted O'Reilly. The *Illustrated London News* refused to publish a picture of it. Then Garrards refused to have anything further to do with the stone, suggesting that they had been unconsciously part of a swindle. 'If you should find diamonds in such quantities as to affect the market,' Garrards told Curry with marked sarcasm, 'we may be sorry. But with our present information we must decline to move.'

Curry then tried Sir Roderick Murchison, rated the highest geological authority in Britain, in his attempts to prove that the diamond had been found in the Cape. 'My dear sir,' Murchison replied, 'if you tell me that this

53

diamond was picked up at the Cape of Good Hope I am bound to believe you and I do, but if you ask me to say on the strength of such an isolated fact that the Cape is a diamond-producing country I must decline. Indeed I will go further, I will stake my professional reputation on it that you have not got the matrix of the diamond in South Africa.'

Then along came O'Reilly with his second diamond, weighing nine carats. The French consul in Capetown, Ernest Heritté, reported: 'I never saw a rough diamond of greater beauty, either in respect of its crystallization or of its natural brilliancy.'

Though the rest of the world thought little of the Hopetown discoveries, the Governor of the Cape, Sir Philip Wodehouse, quickly snapped up both of O'Reilly's finds for £500 and £200 apiece.

The news again reached London. In the winter of 1868, diamond merchant Harry Emmanuel, of London's Hatton Garden, sent out mineralogist Professor James Gregory to investigate.

Gregory journeyed to the Vaal and Orange Rivers and gravely asserted that any diamonds in the district must have been carried in the gizzards of ostriches from some far-distant region. 'The whole story of the Cape diamond discoveries is false, and is simply one of many schemes for trying to promote the employment and expenditure of capital in searching for this precious substance in the colony.'

At the height of the controversy, experts pronounced on one of the diamonds that Professor Gregory had chosen to dismiss. It was a magnificent white diamond weighing 83½ carats. It was to be known as the Star of Africa and amply denied Gregory's arguments.

Professor Gregory's findings were quickly forgotten. But not the learned expert's name. For years afterwards, a mis-statement or a lie about diamonds was laughingly dismissed as a 'Gregory' – in contempt for the professor who thought the world's largest diamond strike was just so much ostrich dung.

The driver of a road roller on the M5 was proud of the walkie-talkie set he kept in his cab.

One afternoon, in a storm, he signalled to his construction HQ: 'Mayday . . . weather terrible . . . am ditching for tonight.'

That night, a full-scale air-sea-rescue operation was launched in the Bristol Channel for the survivors of an air crash. All shipping was alerted, coastguards put on special watch, lifeboat crews ordered to stand by and an RAF plane put on readiness.

We've captured the Loch Ness Monster

Sightings of the famous Loch Ness Monster have been reported for more than 1,000 years. But in 1972 experts believed they had at last captured the 'beastie'.

What they did not know was that, some weeks earlier, the crew of a British cargo vessel taking live elephant seals from the Falkland Islands to a zoo in England had found one of the seals dead. They threw the body overboard. It was picked up in the nets of a fishing boat and, for a prank, the fishermen dumped the body in Loch Ness.

It was found there by zoologists organising a search for the monster. The experts packed the half-ton, 15-foot giant in ice, loaded it into a van and headed south for England to announce their news to the world.

However, locals alerted the police to the monster-snatchers' activities and the order was flashed to all cars: 'Nessie must not leave Scotland – she belongs to us.' Roadblocks were set up, the van was stopped on the Forth Road Bridge, and 'Nessie' was impounded by the police.

It was only after a blaze of publicity that the true identity of the creature was revealed.

55

Chapter
Two

Sea and Air

When man tackles the elements, his fallibility is only too clearly displayed. It wasn't an iceberg that sank the *Titanic* – it was human error. It wasn't a storm that caused the R101 airship to crash – it was one man's pride. The following pages contain some of the greatest disasters the world has ever known, plus a few of the sillier mistakes that men have made when they have taken to the sea and the sky.

The Curse of the Pharaohs

Death awaited the discoverers of Tutankhamun's tomb

Death will come to those who disturb the sleep of the Pharaohs . . .' That was the warning found inscribed in the tomb of the Egyptian boy king Tutankhamun at Luxor when it was opened in February 1923 – for the first time in 3,000 years.

The man who led the expedition to Egypt to excavate the ancient tomb was an Englishman, 57-year-old Lord Carnarvon. And the Curse of the Pharaohs was well known to him. He knew what had happened to the man who, in the late 19th century, had brought another Pharaoh's coffin back to England. Arthur Weigall, one of the men in Lord Carnarvon's team, had told him all about the owner of that coffin: 'No sooner had he obtained the coffin than he lost his arm when his gun exploded. The ship in which the coffin was sent home was wrecked. The house in which it was kept was burnt down. The photographer who took a picture of it shot himself. A lady friend of whom the owner was very fond was lost at sea. The list of accidents and misfortunes charged to the spirit connected with the coffin is now of enormous length.'

But before the expedition went down into the tomb of Tutankhamun, Weigall heard Carnarvon make light of the Curse. Weigall warned : 'If he goes down in that spirit, I give him two months to live.'

Carnarvon's scorn of the Curse was perhaps only bravado. For two months earlier, he had received a letter from a well-known mystic of the day, Count Hamon. The cryptic message read: 'Lord Carnarvon not to enter tomb. Disobey at peril. If ignored will suffer sickness. Not recover. Death will claim him in Egypt.'

The English nobleman was so concerned about this warning that he twice consulted a fortune-teller – who twice forecast Carnarvon's early death in mysterious circumstances.

And within two months of breaking into Tutankhamun's tomb, Carnarvon *was* dead. Moreover, within six years, 12 more of those who had been present when the funerary chamber had been breached had also died prematurely. And over the years that followed, the Curse of the Pharaohs claimed several more victims among those who had been associated with the fateful expedition. One of them was the man who had twice warned Carnarvon of disaster – Weigall.

The sinister saga began in April of 1923 when one morning Carnarvon awoke in his Cairo hotel room and said: 'I feel like hell.' By the time his son arrived at the hotel, Carnarvon was unconscious. That night he died. His death was attributed to a mosquito bite – which was noted to be in the same place as a blemish on the mummified body of King Tutankhamun.

Carnarvon's son was resting in an adjoining room at the moment his father died. He said: 'The lights suddenly went out all over Cairo. We lit candles and prayed.'

Shortly afterwards there was another death at the hotel. American archaeologist Arthur Mace, who had been one of the leading members of the expedition, complained of tiredness, suddenly went into a coma and died before doctors could even diagnose what was wrong with him.

Deaths followed one upon another. A close friend of Carnarvon, George Gould, rushed to Egypt as soon as he heard of the earl's death. Gould visited the Pharaoh's tomb. The next day he had a high fever. He died within 12 hours. Radiologist Archibald Reid, who X-rayed Tutankhamun's body, complained of exhaustion. He went home to England and died shortly afterwards. Carnarvon's personal secretary on the expedition, Richard Bethell, was found dead in bed from apparent heart failure. British industrialist Joel Wool was one of the first visitors to the tomb. He died soon afterwards from a mysterious fever. By 1930, only two of the original team of excavators who had broken into the tomb were still alive.

The Curse of the Pharaohs was still taking its toll half a century later. In 1970, the sole survivor of the Tutankhamun expedition, 70-year-old Richard Adamson, gave a television interview to 'explode the myth' of the death curse.

Mourners at a funeral in Moinesti, Rumania, were astonished to see a face peering down on them from the open coffin as it was being carried shoulder-high across a road outside the cemetery.

The 'body' – a woman – then leaped out of the coffin and ran off down the road.

She ran straight into the path of a car, was knocked down and killed.

THE WORLD'S GREATEST MISTAKES

He told viewers: 'I don't believe in the myth for one moment.' Afterwards, as he left the Norwich television studios, his taxi collided with a tractor, throwing him out on to the road. A passing lorry missed his head by inches.

It was the third time that Adamson, who had been security guard to Lord Carnarvon's expedition, had tried to put paid to the legend. The first time he spoke against it, his wife died within 48 hours. The second time, his son broke his back in a plane crash. After the third occasion, Adamson, recovering in hospital from head injuries, said: 'Until now, I refused to believe that there was any connection between the Curse and what happened to my family. But now I am having second thoughts.'

A year later, the Curse of the Pharaohs struck again, but this time Tutankhamun had no hand in it. British Egyptologist Professor Walter Emery was digging for the tomb of the god of medicine, Imhotep, at Sakkara, near the Pyramids, when he uncovered a statue of Osiris, the god of death. The professor was handling the statue when he fell dead from a cerebral thrombosis.

Fears of the Curse of the Pharaohs were revived in 1972 when the golden mask of Tutankhamun was crated for shipment to Britain for an exhibition at London's British Museum to mark the 50th anniversary of the tomb's discovery.

In charge of the operation was Dr. Gamal Mehrez, director-general of the antiquities department of the Cairo Museum, where he was responsible for the safe keeping of 20 ancient mummies. Dr. Mehrez did not believe in the Curse – not even after his predecessor had suddenly died within hours of signing an agreement to send the treasures of Tutankhamun to Paris. Mehrez said: 'I, more than anyone else in the world, have been involved with the tombs and mummies of the Pharaohs. Yet I am still alive. I'm the living proof that all the tragedies associated with the Pharaohs are just coincidence. I don't believe in the Curse for one moment.'

On February 3, 1972, the shippers arrived at the Cairo Museum to remove the crated golden mask of Tutankhamun and prepare it for its journey to London. That day, Dr. Mehrez died. He was 52. The cause of his death was given as circulatory collapse.

Unperturbed, the organisers of the exhibition continued with the arrangements. A Royal Air Force Transport Command aircraft was loaned for the job of transporting the priceless relics to Britain. But within five years of the flight, six members of the plane's crew were to be struck by death or ill fortune.

During the flight, Chief Technical Officer Ian Lansdowne jokingly kicked a box containing Tutankhamun's death mask. He said: 'I've just kicked the most expensive thing in the world.' That leg was later in plaster for five months, badly broken after a ladder inexplicably collapsed under Lansdowne.

The aircraft's navigator, Lieutenant Jim Webb, lost all his possessions after

Above The mummy of Tutankhamun.

Above right Lord Carnarvon (left)
entering the tomb of Tutankhamun.

Right The Earl of Carnarvon.

THE WORLD'S GREATEST MISTAKES

his home was destroyed by fire. A girl aboard the plane quit the RAF after a head operation left her bald.

A steward, Sergeant Brian Rounsfall, said: 'On the flight back, we played cards on the coffin case. Then we all took it in turns to sit on the case containing the death mask and we laughed and joked about it. We were not being disrespectful – it was just a bit of fun.' Sergeant Rounsfall was 35 at the time. In the following four years, he suffered two heart attacks, but survived, a worried man.

Less lucky were Lieutenant Rick Laurie, chief pilot aboard the Britannia aircraft, and Engineer Ken Parkinson. Both were perfectly fit men; both died of heart attacks.

Parkinson's wife said: 'My husband suffered a heart attack every year at about the same time as the flight.' The last attack, in 1978, killed him. He was 45.

Chief pilot Laurie died two years before him. At the time, his wife said: 'It's the Curse of Tutankhamun – the Curse has killed him.' He was just 40.

Is there any logical explanation for the mysterious deaths of so many people? Journalist Phillip Vandenberg studied the legend of the Curse of the Pharaohs for years. He came up with a fascinating suggestion. In his book, *The Curse of the Pharaohs*, he says that the tombs within the Pyramids were perfect breeding grounds for bacteria which could develop new and unknown strains over the centuries and could maintain their potency until the present day.

He also points out that the ancient Egyptians were experts in poison. Some poisons do not have to be swallowed to kill – they can prove lethal by penetrating the skin. Poisonous substances were used in wall paintings within the tombs, which were then sealed and made airtight. Grave-robbers who in ancient days raided the tombs always first bored a small hole through the chamber wall to allow fresh air to circulate before they broke in to plunder the Pharaohs' riches.

But the most extraordinary explanation of all for the Curse was put forward in 1949. It came from the atomic scientist Professor Louis Bulgarini. He said: 'It is definitely possible that the ancient Egyptians used atomic radiation to protect their holy places. The floors of the tombs could have been covered with uranium. Or the graves could have been finished with radio-active rock.

Mr. Sid Rawle, aged 29, a former gravedigger, is now the editor of an underground newspaper.
– Manchester newspaper

Rock containing both gold and uranium was mined in Egypt 3,000 years ago. Such radiation could kill a man today.'

If there is any truth in the belief that the ancient Pharaohs can be held responsible for 20th-century deaths, then there is one case which overshadows all others. In 1912, a liner was crossing the Atlantic with a valuable cargo – an Egyptian mummy. It was the body of a prophetess who lived during the reign of Tutankhamun's father-in-law, Akhenaton. An ornament found with the mummy bore a spell: 'Awake from the dream in which you sleep and you will triumph over all that is done against you.' Because of its value, the mummy was not carried in the liner's hold, but in a compartment behind the bridge on which stood the captain, whose errors of judgment played a part in causing his ship to sink. The story of the sinking of that ship, and of the death of 1,513 passengers aboard her, is told elsewhere in this book. Her name was the *Titanic*.

The 'Unsinkable' Titanic

The first SOS signal in history failed to save 1,513 men, women and children

The sea was as smooth as a millpond and the sky brilliant with stars when Frederick Fleet, the look-out in the crow's nest, spotted the towering grey mountain of ice.

'Iceberg right ahead,' he shouted down his telephone to the bridge. And so began two hours and 40 minutes of incredulity, fear, and finally horror for the 2,300 passengers of the White Star liner – the 'unsinkable' *Titanic*. For that was all the time that it took, from the moment the iceberg was sighted, for the biggest and supposedly safest liner in the world to sink beneath the icy waters of the North Atlantic.

It was 11.40 p.m. on April 14, 1912, when the warning call came from the crow's nest. Immediately, the huge vessel swung to port – but not soon enough. The *Titanic* scraped along the jagged side of the iceberg.

On the bridge, officers congratulated themselves on a near-miss. But below the water line, the Atlantic Ocean poured in through a 300-foot gash in the ship's plates.

George Rowe was one of the quartermasters on the *Titanic*. This is how he described the crash: 'The first I knew of the disaster was when I felt a peculiar shiver run through the vessel. It became icy cold and my breath froze in the air. Then I saw the iceberg – and I shall never forget it.

'At first I thought we had hit a windjammer as I caught a glimpse of something sliding past the ship on the starboard side. In the glare from the light of thousands of portholes, the smooth surface looked just like wet canvas.

'I ran over to the side and realised that I was looking at an iceberg. It was so big that it seemed to fill the sky. It was a giant among icebergs and towered menacingly even above the bridge.

'For a few seconds I gazed at it unbelievingly. It was just a few feet away and I felt I could have touched it. Then it was gone – swallowed up in the blackness.'

Even when the ship's master, Captain Ernest Smith, Commodore of the White Star fleet, realised that the hull of the world's wondership had been breached, he showed no signs of alarm. After all, the *Titanic* was 'unsinkable'. That had been the proud boast when the liner had left Southampton for New York four days earlier, at the start of her maiden voyage.

The ship's 850-foot-long hull had been made up of 14 watertight compartments. And the ship had a double bottom. It was the safest in the world. In fact, the *Titanic* could have remained afloat with all of her first four watertight compartments flooded. But the iceberg had torn through the first five – and, because of some strange quirk in the ship's design, Bulkhead Number Five did not stretch up as high into the ship as the others. With the first four compartments flooded, the liner's bows would dip, the water would flow over Bulkhead Number Five into the sixth compartment . . . then into the seventh

---

The Meteorological Office at Bracknell, Berkshire, was asked by a governmental committee for the official ruling on when winter begins and when it ends. The committee expected an answer that would pin down the times to precise seconds. The answer given, however, was: 'Winter begins when all the leaves have fallen off the trees and ends when the bulbs start coming up again.'

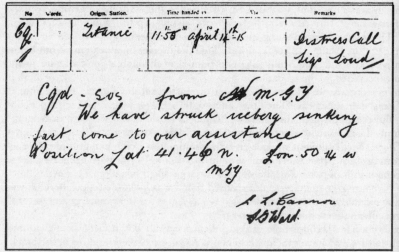

No	Words.	Origin. Station.	Time handed in	Via	Remarks
69. 1	7	Titanic	11·55ᵖᵐ april 14 ᵗʰ-15		Distress Call Sigs Loud

Cqd - sos from M.G.Y
We have struck iceberg sinking
fast come to our assistance
Position Lat 41·46 n. Lon 50 14 w
MGY

L. L. Gammon
JG Ward.

The *Titanic*'s distress call.

. . . and the eighth. . . . And it would then simply be a matter of time. . . .

The myth of the *Titanic*'s unsinkability was only one of an incredible combination of human errors, without which neither the liner nor the 1,513 lives need have been lost.

Why was the *Titanic* travelling so fast – 22 knots – when a mass of icebergs had been reported in the area? Just before the crash, the liner was at 'full ahead', despite the fact that during that evening wireless signals had been received from other vessels including the *Baltic*, containing the information that she was heading straight into an icefield.

The *Baltic*'s message had been handed to George Ismay, the line's managing director, who showed it to some of the passengers before it was posted in the chart room at 7.15 p.m.

Why was the *Titanic*'s radio out of contact with other shipping? A final ice-warning message was sent to the liner by the *Messaba* at 9.40 p.m. It is known that the message was received by the *Titanic*. But it was never acknowledged, and it is doubtful whether it ever reached the bridge.

If that message had got through and been heeded by Captain Smith, 1,513 lives would certainly have been saved. For, less than an hour earlier, Smith had been heard discussing the danger of icebergs with his officer of the watch. Smith gave orders for a strict look-out to be kept, but he did not feel that the situation was serious enough to warrant a cut in speed.

Why, also, did the *Titanic* have only 16 lifeboats – with just 1,250 seats for he 2,300 people on board? The liner had sufficient fittings to handle 48 feboats.

The White Star Line was perfectly within its legal rights to provide such an adequate number of boats. British Board of Trade regulations covering the nip had been drawn up in 1894 and were now ridiculously out of date. The ules specified the number of lifeboats to be carried by passenger ships of more han 10,000 tons. Liners had grown in size dramatically since then – the *Titanic* was 46,328 tons – yet the regulations had never been amended.

But the biggest question mark of all hangs over the role of another passenger hip – the *Californian*, one of the vessels that had earlier sent ice warnings to the *Titanic*. Because of the ice danger, it had stopped only about eight miles away rom the spot where the *Titanic* was slowly sinking. Yet it did not arrive on the cene until after the *Titanic* had slipped beneath the surface of the Atlantic.

Aboard the 6,000-ton *Californian* it had been an uneventful night. Earlier n the evening, the wireless operator had tried to break in on messages being ent out by the *Titanic* in order to warn of the ice danger. No one knows the xact nature of the warning that he eventually sent. What is known is that he elt snubbed by its ungracious reception. At the end of his duty, he went down o his bunk after switching off his wireless set. The time was 11.30 – just ten ninutes before the *Titanic* hit the iceberg.

On the bridge of the *Californian*, the third officer watched the lights of the *Titanic* speeding towards them. He reported to the ship's master, Captain tanley Lord, who suggested that they try to contact the liner by morse light. They tried over and over again. But there was no response whatever from the *Titanic*, which sped by into the icefield.

Aboard the *Titanic*, the passengers were at first puzzled rather than frighten- d by the slight listing of the ship. As they walked up the stairways on to the leck to find out what had happened, there was no sign of panic. They firmly elieved the boasts about the liner's invincibility.

Although the *Titanic* struck the iceberg at 11.40 p.m., it was not until five ninutes after midnight that the order was given: 'Uncover the lifeboats.' As rewmen pulled off the boats' canvas covers, the ship's band struck up a rag- ime tune – and kept on playing.

Later there was a bang and a flash as the first distress rocket went off. The assengers at last began to realise that they were in danger. Until then, people ad been reluctant to get into the lifeboats. Wives had pleaded with crewmen o be allowed to stay with their husbands. Husbands had urged them to get nto the boats. Now, officers called out: 'Women and children first,' and no ne argued.

One of the first-class passengers, Lady Duff Gordon, had refused to get into everal boats. Then she and her husband found themselves standing beside

one of the officers who was in charge of a small lifeboat and who had bee
having little success in persuading passengers to get into it. The officer said
'Do get into the boat, madam. I shall be so pleased if you would.' Lady Du
Gordon stepped into the lifeboat.

American millionaire Benjamin Guggenheim had been wrapped in warr
clothing by his steward. He appeared on deck, sought out his valet and re
appeared later wearing full evening dress, 'so that I will go down like
gentleman.'

Others who were to go down with the ship that night were its captain; i
designer, Thomas Andrews; millionaire Isadore Strauss; Colonel John Jaco
Astor, who was returning from honeymoon with his bride; and famed journal
ist William Stead.

Stead would never have died if he had heeded his own warning. For in 189
he had written a short story describing his vision of a mighty liner sinking i
northern waters with the loss of hundreds of lives. Stead, who was a spiritualist
had foreseen his own death.

Death indeed was now not far away for most of the passengers of the *Titanic*

In the wireless room, operator John Phillips tapped out 'CQD' . . . 'CQD' . .
over and over again. CQD was the traditional maritime distress call of th
period. But an international convention had just decided to recommend th
use of the signal SOS instead. So halfway through the night, Phillips decide
to change signals – and sent out the first SOS in history.

Half a dozen ships began racing to the scene. But the two ships closest t
the *Titanic* did not hear the desperate calls for help. Aboard the stationar
Californian, the wireless operator was fast asleep. And 60 miles away the Cunar
liner *Carpathia* was steaming southwards with its wireless operator away from
his set, on the ship's bridge. When he did return to the wireless room, the tim
was almost half past midnight. He decided to put through a courtesy call t
the great new liner he knew to be in the vicinity. Unbelievingly, he heard th
reply: 'SOS. We have struck an iceberg. Come at once.'

At two o'clock the *Titanic*'s wireless operator received the order: 'Abando
ship. It's every man for himself.' He ignored it and continued tapping ou
'SOS . . . SOS' until the very last moment.

British publishers Ladybird Books were surprised to
receive an order from the Ministry of Defence for a set of
books for its staff explaining how computers work. The
firm wrote back pointing out that the books were designed
for children aged nine and upwards. The Defence Ministry
replied confirming the order.

In one of the last overcrowded lifeboats to leave the *Titanic* stood Mrs. Emily Richards, then 24, and off to join her husband in the USA. She had her 10-month-old baby, George, in her arms. She said later: 'We pulled away from the liner. The sea was full of wreckage and bodies. Some people had jumped overboard and were screaming for help. The sea was very icy. We wanted to pick them up but our boat was overloaded already.'

As the lifeboats drifted away from the doomed liner, the passengers who had escaped looked back helplessly on a scene that they thought could only have been dreamed up in hell.

The *Titanic* lay with rows and rows of lights still blazing on a millpond sea dotted with icebergs. The ship was still not far from the monstrous grey mass of the giant iceberg that it had struck.

The liner's four funnels, towering 175 feet above its keel, stood out against the starry sky. They leaned forward at a crazy angle. And at 2.20 a.m. the *Titanic* began to slip beneath the surface. The band was still playing, its music carrying eerily across the still expanse of sea. But now the ragtime had ended, and a hymn was struck up. Some survivors remember it as the old hymn *Autumn*; others say it was *Nearer My God To Thee*. The ship's lights illuminated hundreds of spider-like figures clinging to the decks and to the sides of the liner as its propellers were lifted above the water line. One by one, they fell or jumped into the sea to certain, freezing death.

'There was a long, rumbling boom, like distant thunder,' said Emily Richards. 'The lights went out, flashed on again, then went out for good. The stern rose until it was pointing almost straight up in the air. Then the *Titanic* slipped swiftly and smoothly out of sight.'

The lifeboats packed with shivering survivors drifted until dawn, when the liner *Carpathia* arrived on the scene and picked up 705 of them.

Most of the survivors were first- and second-class ticket holders. These had been given priority in the lifeboats, and all their children were saved. Of the steerage children only a third survived.

The officers on the bridge of the *Californian* had kept occasional watch on the *Titanic* through binoculars. They had noted how, like their own ship, it had stopped amid the ice. They had watched the flickering lights in the distance. They had again tried to contact the *Titanic* by morse light, but had received no response and given up. Then, at 12.45 a.m., they had seen rockets bursting into the air over the *Titanic*. They had thought that such a display of fireworks was most curious, but did not investigate. At 2.20 a.m. the men on the *Californian* noticed that the lights in the distance had disappeared. They took no action.

Courts of inquiry in Britain and America later severely censured Captain Lord of the *Californian* for failing to appreciate the nature of the rocket signals reported to him. Lord contested the findings right up to his death in 1962.

The inquiries also found that Captain Smith had made a mistake in not turning south or reducing speed. But no blame was attached to his course of action, because it was common practice at the time.

The British inquiry also made some important recommendations. It advised that the number of lifeboats on a ship should be based on the number of people carried and not on tonnage, that ship's wirelesses should be manned night and day, and it warned that any captain running his ship full speed into an icefield in future would lay himself open to the charge of negligence.

All of which came too late to save those who perished.

It was a disaster that, strangely, had been foreshadowed not only by William Stead's short story but, in uncanny detail, in a novel published 14 years earlier.

The book, written by Morgan Robertson, told the story of the biggest and most luxurious liner ever built . . . of how it set out from Southampton to New York on its maiden voyage . . . of how it hit an iceberg in the North Atlantic . . . of how its hull was torn open beneath the waterline . . . and of how it sank with an appalling loss of life because it failed to carry enough lifeboats.

The name of the ship was the *Titan*.

———————

Terror of the aircraft stowaways

No one saw their dash to the plane. The two young men who had been hiding behind a ramp at Havana Airport sprinted across the blazing hot runway until they were in the shade of one of the giant wings of a DC8 airliner. The aircraft was halted at the end of the main runway, waiting for clearance for take-off. The two men clambered on to the wheels and climbed up the landing gear. Then they huddled in the wheel bay – the space inside the wing which houses the undercarriage in flight.

Within minutes Armando Ramirez and George Blanco were airborne. The DC8 of Iberian Airways thundered down the runway and soared into the blue Caribbean sky to start its transatlantic journey to Madrid. The undercarriage was retracted and the two men squeezed themselves against the sides of the wheel bay so that they would not be squashed by the landing gear. The wheel bay door closed beneath them and all was darkness, roaring engines and whistling wind.

Ramirez and Blanco relaxed for the first time since putting into action their daring plan to escape from Fidel Castro's communist regime in Cuba. They had fled their homeland with no possessions whatsoever – nothing that could possibly have slowed that vital dash across the runway at Havana. They were also dressed lightly, in thin trousers and short-sleeved shirts.

As the airport fell away behind the DC8, Ramirez huddled tighter in his corner. He realised now that this was going to be a long, cold journey. Blanco edged himself around the retracted undercarriage seeking a more comfortable position in which to spend his first flight. He ended up crouched over the wheels.

At that moment a warning light flashed on the flight deck instrument panel. Something was wrong with the undercarriage. It had not locked home. The first officer flicked a switch and the landing gear began descending again. Blanco was taken by surprise as the wheels jolted downwards. With a scream that was muffled by the slipstream, he lost his grip and fell out of the wheel bay to his death.

The undercarriage retracted once more, and this time no red light flashed on the controls. The pilot was satisfied. For Ramirez, however, the journey was becoming a nightmare. He had been able to do nothing to save his friend, and now that the plane was heading for its cruising altitude of 30,000 feet the cold in the wheel bay was becoming intolerable. It was increasingly difficult to breathe, too. Ramirez passed out.

During the Spanish airliner's 4,500-mile flight, the temperature in the wheel bay fell to − 40˚ Centigrade and the rarefied atmosphere became almost devoid of oxygen. But the young Cuban was tough. As the DC8 landed at Madrid he regained consciousness briefly, and astonished ground staff watched him fall out of the wheel bay on to the tarmac.

Ramirez recovered in hospital to begin his self-imposed exile.

Space scientist Dr. Hubert Strughold wanted to disprove the old and unscientific adage: 'A pilot flies by the seat of his pants.'

He injected his buttocks with the anaesthetic novocaine until his posterior was completely numb. Then Dr. Strughold, who in the 1960s was head of America's Space Medicine Programme, took off as passenger in a jet plane.

The pilot looped, rolled and went through every acrobatic trick in the book. Dr. Strughold, who had flown without upset many times before, returned to earth feeling very ill. He announced: 'The pants are one of the pilot's most valuable flight instruments.'

Hang on, we're about to land!

It was a long and boring flight for 20-year-old Harry Griffiths, from Toronto. It was December, 1942, and the Boston bomber of which he was co-pilot was being ferried from one airfield to another. It was now droning along at 7,000 feet over Lake St. Louis, Quebec. The only people aboard were Griffiths and the American pilot.

At this stage of the flight, Griffiths was due to check the bomb-bay. He scrambled into the cramped compartment, but, failing to notice that the bomb-bay doors had not fully closed, he dropped out of the plane. As he did so, he grabbed the edge of one of the bomb doors and hung on for his life, screaming for help.

The pilot, 29-year-old Sid Gerow, from Minnesota, heard him but could not leave the controls to haul him aboard. Instead, he brought his plane down until it was skimming the ice of frozen Lake St. Louis at 100 miles an hour – as low a speed as he dared fly for fear of stalling. Griffiths then let go his hold, dropped 20 feet and skidded over ice and through snow for 1,000 yards.

The bomber's pilot flew off, radioing for a rescue team. But it was a local farmer who found the young flyer. Griffiths was sitting in the snow, cold and shaken but smiling. He had suffered only cuts and bruises.

Equally lucky was the steward aboard an Eastern Airlines Dakota who was sucked out of the plane when the cabin door flew open at 2,500 feet above Tulsa, Oklahoma, in 1949. As he was swept into the slipstream, his left foot became wedged between the door and one of the hinges.

The pilot made an emergency landing at Tulsa. Ambulancemen, ground staff and passengers rushed to see if anything was left of the steward. They found him lying on the tarmac, unconscious but unhurt. He had fainted as soon as the plane landed.

A dealer in Connecticut advertised a car for '1,395 bananas' – meaning $1,395.

A woman turned up and offered him 25 bananas deposit and, when he refused to accept them, sued the dealer for false advertising.

She won her case, produced the other 1,370 bananas and drove off in the car.

The R101 inferno

One man's pride destroyed the airship dream

I t was the most unnecessary fiasco in the history of flying. The tragedy of the R101 airship is not just the story of a disaster which claimed 48 lives. It is an unbelievable catalogue of inefficiency, incompetence, pride, prestige and petty politics.

It all began when the Vickers aircraft and engineering firm, the most experienced builders of airships in Britain, proposed to the Conservative government of 1923 that giant airships be used for passenger services to different parts of the Empire. The government would commission them – and Vickers would, of course, build them.

Before a decision could be made, the Conservatives fell, and in 1924 the first Labour Parliament came to power on promises of nationalisation and State control. A new success for robustly capitalist Vickers did not fit into their scheme of things. So Ramsay MacDonald's men made the most astonishing decision. They decided to commission not one, but two airships to exactly the same specification. The R100, a capitalist airship, and the R101, a socialist airship. One to be made by Vickers and one by the Air Ministry. The government would then decide which of the two was the better craft.

73

THE WORLD'S GREATEST MISTAKES

The capitalist team's chief calculator was a man called Nevil Shute Norway – now better known as novelist Nevil Shute. Many years after the disaster, he wrote: 'The controversy between capitalism and State enterprise had been argued, tested and fought in many ways, but the airship venture in Britain was the most curious of them all.'

Through the mid-1920s the two ships were designed and slowly took shape. The R100 was built in a leaky World War One airship hangar at Howden, Yorkshire. Local labour was recruited for much of the manual work – and that presented the capitalist team with their most unexpected problem. According to Shute, the local women were 'filthy in appearance and habits, and incredibly foul-mouthed. Promiscuous intercourse was going on merrily in every dark corner.'

Lord Thomson of Cardington, Labour's air minister, was responsible for the R101, and it was at Cardington, near Bedford, that the airship was built. The problems there were technical. And when they appeared they tended to be swept under the carpet.

Extraordinarily, the Air Ministry decided that petrol engines would be unsafe for their airship and chose diesel engines instead. The Cardington design team argued against the decision but were ignored. So eight-cylinder diesel units were ordered – engines originally designed for railway locomotives. They weighed twice as much as the R100's petrol-power units, vibrated alarmingly and were far less efficient.

Indeed, so little check was kept on the weight of all the gadgetry that was being built into the R101 that it was not until the airship was first inflated and tested that it was discovered that its lifting power was about half of that which it should have been. The team immediately began taking out of the craft all the extra equipment which they had confidently built into it.

The effect was disastrous. The airship was unbalanced. The bags of hydrogen rolled around inside the craft. It bucked alarmingly in flight. The outer casing split time and time again and had to be covered with patches. The fins were beautifully streamlined but tended to stall. The gas valves were so sensitive that they leaked perpetually. The propellers broke when put into reverse, and a heavy backward-facing engine had to be fitted in order that the airship could manoeuvre when docking.

Many such problems were also encountered – and surmounted – by the Vickers team, led by designer Barnes Wallis, who was to become famous in World War Two for his dam-busting bouncing bomb. But such was the rivalry between Wallis and R101 chief designer Lieutenant-Colonel Victor Richmond that, throughout the five years of construction, neither man visited or even wrote to the other to discuss common problems.

The R101 was finished first. A large VIP crowd was invited to Cardington

R101 airship moored to its mast, seen from the surrounding countryside.

The unveiling of the R101 memorial at Allone, near Beauvais.

to marvel at the enormous airship's graceful lines as it swung gently on its mooring tower. Two hundred yards long and filled with 5 million cubic feet of hydrogen, it was the largest airship in the world.

The R100 lacked the beauty of its sister ship, but had one rather important advantage over it. It could fly safely. In growing desperation, the Cardington team cut their airship in two, stuffed an extra gas tank in the middle, put the craft together again and once more hauled it to its mooring tower. Within minutes, the whole skin of the airship began rippling in the wind, and a 90-foot gash opened up along its side.

The public were never told of these snags, and on June 28, 1930, the R101, a victim of its own over-inflated publicity, was flown to Hendon to take part in an air display. The crowds gasped as the airship suddenly dipped its nose and dived spectacularly before pulling up sharply. They were in even greater awe when the craft, already too low for comfort, repeated the manoeuvre and pulled out of its dive just 500 feet above the 100,000-strong crowd.

What the spectators did not know was that the spectacle was unplanned – and that the sweating coxswain had been struggling at the controls to avert disaster.

Neither were they told that when the R101 was examined afterwards, more than 60 holes were found in the hydrogen bags. The highly inflammable gas was pouring out everywhere.

A brave Air Ministry inspector reported: 'Until this matter is seriously taken in hand and remedied I cannot recommend the extension of the present permit-to-fly or the issue of any further permit or certificate.'

His report was ignored by his superiors.

Now the Cardington team were frantic. They saw the whole enterprise as a battle between capitalism and socialism, a battle that the socialists were losing. And the big test was approaching – the R100 was to fly to Canada and back, the R101 to India and back. The Cardington team suggested a postponement of both trips. The Howden team, revelling in their rivals' problems, refused to call off the R100's journey.

On July 29, 1930, seven years after Vickers first proposed the giant airship project, the R100 set off for Canada. It completed the round-trip successfully and without fuss.

As the date of the R101's planned trip to India approached, the Cardington

Cordon Bleu cook required for directors' dining room. Good salary plus luncheon vouchers.
– Times

team became more alarmed. There was dissension among the designers. The Air Ministry was recommended to delay the great publicity stunt.

It was then that folly and ambition were compounded into disaster by Air Minister Lord Thomson. During the construction and testing of the R101, he had been persistently pushing behind the scenes to promote the project. Thomson, an army general before he turned socialist, was a charming man, a 55-year-old bachelor, sophisticated and much sought after by women; but he was also proud, ambitious and unswervingly stubborn.

He wanted the R101 to fly him to India without any further delays. He wanted to make a magnificent impression when the airship arrived at Karachi. His ambition was to become Viceroy of India and he hoped that the spectacle would help him achieve that aim.

Nevil Shute wrote: 'To us, watching helplessly on the sidelines, the decision to fly the R101 to India that autumn of 1930 appeared to be sheer midsummer madness.' He said of Thomson: 'He was the man primarily responsible for the organisation which produced the disaster. Under his control, practically every principle of safety in the air was abandoned.'

A final conference about the trip was held at the Air Ministry on October 2. Thomson said he wanted to start for India the next day. His staff protested. Thomson insisted. Eventually, take-off was agreed for the evening of October 4.

Thomson told the conference: 'You must not allow my natural impatience or anxiety to influence you in any way.' But no one believed that the caution was sincere. After all, he had already issued an official directive to everyone concerned in the project: 'I must insist on the programme for the Indian flight being adhered to, as I have made my plans accordingly.' He had also announced: 'The R101 is as safe as a house – at least, to the millionth chance.'

Test flying was far from complete by October 4. The R101 had not been issued with an airworthiness certificate, so the Air Ministry wrote one out for themselves. Poor-weather tests had not even been embarked on. The airship had not flown at full power.

Major G. H. Scott, who had successfully captained the R100 across the Atlantic to Canada and back, was to be the senior crew member of the R101. He had heard most of the warnings about the R101. He knew it was underpowered and unstable. But he decided to go along 'for the ride'.

Another VIP passenger was to be Air Vice-Marshal Sir Sefton Brancker, the tall, monocled director of civil aviation. He was extremely sceptical – and said so. He had seen reports on the R101's trials. He had learned that when the airship dived at Hendon it had virtually broken its back. He knew that hydrogen constantly poured from holes caused by the gas bags chafing against each other and the superstructure.

Thomson told him: 'If you are afraid to go, then don't.' Sir Sefton went.

> 'Intersection Six is still being planned,' said a spokesman for the Department of the Environment. Asked where it was going to be, the spokesman replied: 'We aren't quite sure but I imagine it would be between Intersection Five and Intersection Seven.'
>
> – *Manchester Evening News*

At 6.30 on the evening of October 4, Thomson and his valet stepped aboard the R101. There were four other passengers, plus 48 crew. It was a wet, miserable evening. The leaky airship was already grossly overweight and had to drop four tons of water-ballast to get away.

At 8 p.m., while the airship was over London, it received a new weather forecast by radio. It predicted a 40 m.p.h. headwind over northern France, with low cloud and driving rain. Major Scott had the perfect excuse for listening to his own fears and turning back. After all, the R101 had never flown in any but good weather conditions. Scott discussed the report with Thomson. The airship continued on its journey. . . .

At 2 p.m., the R101 was over Beauvais, in northern France. It had travelled only 200 miles in more than seven hours and was flying dangerously low, as well as rolling and pitching a great deal. But in the control room, slung under the hull, the watch changed normally.

Inside the vast hull itself, other crewmen and passengers slept. The cabins were twin-berthed and formed the upper deck of a two-floor module sealed off from the roar of the engines and the beating of the weather. On the lower deck was the vast lounge – 60 feet long and more than 30 feet wide, with wicker settees, chairs and tables, and potted plants disguising the supporting pillars. Outside the lounge ran promenade decks with huge observation windows. Also on the lower deck were the ornate dining room, a smoking room, kitchens, and stairs leading down to the control room.

At about five minutes past two, the nose of the R101 dipped. Foreman engineer Henry Leech, alone in the smoking room, slid off the settee. His glass and soda syphon clattered from the table.

Radio operator Arthur Disley was roused from sleep. He had only just turned in after tapping out a message back to Britain. It had said: 'After an excellent supper, our distinguished passengers smoked a final cigar and have now gone to rest after the excitement of their leave-taking.' Now, Disley realised, something was wrong.

In the control car, the navigator saw that, although the altimeter recorded 1,000 feet above sea level, the airship was ominously close to the ground. He had not realised that the seemingly slight hills around Beauvais were so high.

79

THE WORLD'S GREATEST MISTAKES

Engineers John Binks and Albert Bell were chatting in one of the gangways. Both fell with a bump when the ship dived.

Rigger Alf Church was walking to the crew area at the end of his term of duty when he heard an officer shout: 'Release emergency ballast.' Church ran back to his post and jettisoned half a ton of water from the nose.

The R101 righted itself and again roared forward against the wind and rain. In the smoking room, Leech picked up the glasses and the soda syphon. They were unbroken. He replaced them on the table and lounged back again on the settee.

In Beauvais, the town clock had not long struck two, and several citizens were leaning out of their windows watching the strange airship sail by. It passed over the centre of the town, about 200 yards above the ground. It was rolling and dipping as it vanished beyond a wood.

On the edge of the wood, 56-year-old Alfred Roubaille was out poaching, hoping to bag a couple of rabbits for his family's Sunday lunch. He plodded across the sodden ground, stopping every now and then to lay his snares.

Roubaille heard a roaring of engines above. He looked up – and fled to the shelter of the trees. From there, he – and he alone – saw from start to finish a catastrophe which shook the world.

The R101 was flying straight and level, but very low. Suddenly the nose of the airship dipped for the second time. The airship's telegraph rang. Coxswain Oughton wrestled with the controls. The elevators did not respond. The nose of the ship, somewhere forward of the huge lettering R101, had been bared. The frail fabric had split. The wind was gusting in and the hydrogen was pouring out.

Alfred Roubaille said later: 'The airship started to sink towards the ground. She was moving slowly forward and pointing her nose downwards.'

The first officer, Lieutenant-Commander Atherstone, peered at the looming earth through the window of the control room. He realised the airship was doomed. He ordered Chief Coxswain Hunt to race through the hull and alert everyone that the ship was about to crash.

Radio operator Disley heard Hunt scream: 'We're down, lads.' Disley swung his legs from his bunk. Leech leapt from the smoking room settee. In the engine-gondolas suspended beneath the hull, engineers Cook, Bell, Binks and Savory watched horrified as the ground came up to meet them.

Roubaille said: 'Just as the airship was nearing the ground, a strong gust of wind blew her down hard.'

The R101 pancaked into the moist earth of a flat field no more than a hundred yards from the poacher. For a moment, the only sound was the gush of escaping gas. Then came the explosions.

A blinding flash lit the sky. Two further explosions quickly followed, and an unbelievable white inferno engulfed the once-majestic airship.

Engineer Victor Savory was blinded by the flash of flame that seared in through the open door of his gondola. He leapt for the opening, landed on the soft soil and fled.

His colleague, Albert Cook, tried to get out of his gondola door but found it blocked by a girder, dripping with blazing cellulose from the hull.

'I lay down and gave up,' he said. 'But only for a moment.'

Then Cook dragged away the girder with his bare hands and, pitifully burned, hurled himself into some undergrowth.

Engineers Binks and Bell believed they were lost when their gondola became engulfed in flame. Then came the miracle . . . a ballast tank of water above the gondola burst. The water cascaded on to the gondola and put out the flames. They fled.

Leech was still in the smoking room. He had just got up from the settee when the blazing metal ceiling crashed down on it. He flattened himself on to the floor, then crawled on all fours towards a hole that had opened in the wall. He leapt through the flaming envelope of the airship.

Leech was out, safe. But then he heard the cries of Disley, who was inside the blazing hull, clawing at it and even trying to bite an opening in it with his teeth. Leech ran back into the inferno to help him, but suddenly a fiery hole opened up in the hull and Disley flung himself through it. Leech and Disley raced away across the field together.

Savory, Cook, Binks, Bell, Leech and Disley. Of the 54 people aboard the R101, they were the only survivors.

Poacher Roubaille said: 'I heard people in the wreckage crying for help. I was a hundred yards away and the heat was awful. I ran as hard as I could away from that place.'

For the dying victims of a ship that had been built by stubborn pride, for the man who had been the most stubborn and proud of them all, there was no hope on earth of escape from the hungry flames.

Irish railway officials made a mistake when they wrote an offhand reply to fiery playwright Brendan Behan in a dispute over a fare refund. They signed their letter 'for N. H. Briant'. Behan wrote back: 'Dear for N. H. Briant, If you don't want to give me back my 12 quid, say so. I've more to do than to be answering your silly letters. I'm usually paid more than 12 quid for writing as much as this. For Brendan Behan, Brendan Behan.'

Saga of the 'battleship-submarines'

During World War One, Britain decided to build a new type of giant submarine – a sort of underwater battleship that would give the Allies command below the waves as well as above them. The new submarines were labelled K-boats.

The first two flotillas of K-boats were ready for action by the end of 1917. But when they were put to the test, these 325-foot steam-powered monsters of the deep proved to be unmanoeuvrable on the surface, slow and clumsy when diving and, once underwater, very difficult to bring to the surface again. This was their lamentable track record:

Fire broke out aboard the K-2 on its first test dive. K-3 inexplicably dived to the sea bed on its first test – with the Prince of Wales, later to become George VI, aboard. The boat eventually resurfaced and its illustrious passenger was saved.

Later, on exercise, K-3 was rammed and sunk by K-6. K-4 ran aground. K-5 sank and its crew died. K-6 got stuck on the sea bed. K-7 ran down K-17 on exercise, putting itself out of action for good.

K-14 sprang a leak before it had even got out of port on its first trials. And later, on exercises in the North Sea, it was run down and sunk by K-22. K-17, on the same exercise, went out of control and sank after colliding with both an escorting cruiser and with K-7. Finally, K-22 was damaged beyond repair after getting in the way of yet another cruiser.

The K-boats operation was scrapped in 1918 after it had claimed 250 British lives but not one German sailor was killed.

A business man, fed up with the foul smell from a sausage skin factory near his home in Welwyn Garden City, Hertfordshire, bought the entire plant.

He was then told by the local authority that the factory's use must still be confined to trades within the category of 'existing rights'.

Apart from sausage skin manufacture, these included the boiling of blood, the breeding of maggots and the preparation of glue and manure.

The Torrey Canyon disaster

Captain is blamed for the world's worst oil pollution

On the morning of Saturday, March 18, 1967, Captain Pastrengo Rugiati was asleep in his cabin when the message came down from the bridge: 'Bishop Rock 25 miles dead ahead.' It was around dawn and the rocky landmark west of the Scilly Isles was still out of sight. But it showed up on the radar.

On the bridge was First Officer Silvano Bonfiglia, who had been in charge of the ship and its Italian crew since Captain Rugiati had gone to his bunk at 2.30 a.m. During the night, as the ship had headed north towards England, it had been on automatic pilot. The route was supposed to be to the west of Bishop Rock. But when First Officer Bonfiglia checked the bearings at 6.30

a.m., he found that the ship was off-course. It was heading, not to the west of the Scillies, but to the east. The ship's bow was aimed straight for the treacherous 20-mile-wide channel that separates the Scillies from Land's End, Cornwall.

In good weather, most ships could pass through that narrow channel without danger. But not this ship – an oil tanker en route from Kuwait to Milford Haven, South Wales, with 120,000 tons of crude oil aboard. Nearly 1,000 feet long and with a 50-foot draught, this was one of the biggest ships in the world – the *Torrey Canyon*.

As soon as Bonfiglia realised the error, he took the tanker off automatic pilot and steered towards Bishop Rock. His plan was that the tanker should head for the rock for another hour, then change course to pass safely around it.

Having completed the manoeuvre, Bonfiglia telephoned the captain with the news. But, to his astonishment, Captain Rugiati countermanded the plan. Without coming to the bridge, he ordered Bonfiglia to alter course back again to the route through the channel. Bonfiglia did so, and put the *Torrey Canyon* back on automatic pilot.

Within half an hour, Rugiati had dressed and was on the bridge. After a conversation with another officer, Bonfiglia went off duty. At 8 o'clock, with the ship still 14 miles off the channel, the skipper adjusted his course once again so as to pass about six miles from the Scilly Isles. He was well aware of the danger of his action. For slap in the middle of the channel between the Scillies and Land's End are the Seven Stones, a group of rocks which through the centuries have been the graveyard of hundreds of ships. The Seven Stones are usually visible, but at high tide they are submerged. At mid-morning on March 18, 1967, the weather was fine, visibility good, the sea calm – and the tide high. If Captain Rugiati were as little as two miles out on his course, he could find himself right on top of the Seven Stones.

Shortly after 9 a.m. the crew of the lightship which guards the Seven Stones saw the *Torrey Canyon* approaching, heading straight for the mile-wide line of rocks. The lightship's warning flag was raised and rockets were fired. There was no response from the tanker.

Captain Rugiati may or may not have realised that he was heading for the rocks. It was his plan to veer to port as he entered the channel, and this he did. Still on the bridge, he took the tanker off automatic pilot, swung the bows round west until they were pointing due north, then switched back on to automatic. He was prevented from swinging further to the west by the presence of two fishing boats ahead of him.

The *Torrey Canyon* was still heading for the rocks – at its full speed of 16 knots. At the last minute, Rugiati realised that disaster was staring him in the face. He ordered his helmsman to go to the wheel and turn hard to port. The

helmsman swung the wheel round . . . but nothing happened. He called the captain and Rugiati realised that the wheel was ineffective because the steering was still on automatic. Rugiati switched to manual, and the tanker's bows began to swing around. But vital seconds had been lost. At 8.50, the *Torrey Canyon* hit the submerged Pollard Rock – the first of the Seven Stones – and stuck fast.

For a moment, Rugiati remained speechless. He realised that he had captained his giant oil tanker – difficult to manoeuvre at the best of times – at top speed and with no hand on the wheel straight on to a group of well-charted rocks. The captain sombrely demanded damage reports. The information he received was as bad as he could possibly have imagined. He knew that he had blundered – with disastrous consequences.

Worse was to come. . . .

0900 hours: The *Torrey Canyon* is fractured along half the length of its hull. Oil is pouring into the sea at 6,000 tons an hour from the ship's 23 full oil tanks. Rugiati orders an attempt to be made to regain buoyancy by jettisoning oil. He hopes that the tanker can be lightened to float itself off the rocks. The pumps start up and thousands more tons of oil flood into the sea.

1100 hours: A Royal Navy helicopter hovers over the *Torrey Canyon*. It is immediately clear to the helicopter crew that the oil pollution is on a scale unprecedented anywhere in the world.

1200 hours: The Dutch salvage tug *Utrecht* arrives on the scene. Salvage experts board the *Torrey Canyon* and estimate that the tanker is aground over three-quarters of its length.

1500 hours: Three further tugs and two ships of the Royal Navy arrive on the scene. The navy begin spraying the edges of the ever-growing oil slick with detergent. Meanwhile, in London, Ministry of Defence chiefs are ordered to Plymouth to set up emergency headquarters in the battle to combat the oil heading for West Country beaches.

2100 hours: 30–40,000 tons of crude oil have been pumped into the sea since 0900 hours. Now the pumps fail as the ship's boilers are flooded.

March 19: More Royal Navy vessels ring the *Torrey Canyon*, pouring detergent on to the growing oil slick.

March 20: The Royal Navy's chief salvage officer arrives on board, along

---

Amateur fire-eater Christopher Dawson swallowed too much turpentine and paraffin during his act. While driving home that night, he was stopped by police. Dawson, of Taunton, Somerset, failed a breathalyser test and was fined £100.

THE WORLD'S GREATEST MISTAKES

with agents of the American owners, the Union Oil Company of Los Angeles. The salvage men reckon that there is a reasonable chance of saving the ship, provided that the weather stays fine and the tanker does not break its back.

March 21: An explosion rips through the aft-superstructure of the tanker, killing the chief salvage officer of the Dutch team. There is a danger of further blasts, but work carries on. By now, all the original crew of the *Torrey Canyon*, except for Captain Rugiati and three officers, have been taken off by the life-boat from St. Mary's, on the Scilly Isles.

March 22: Prime Minister Harold Wilson, who has a summer retreat on the Scilly Isles, orders a team of government advisers and scientists to go into emergency session to investigate all possible means of saving the coastline, its beaches and its wildlife from the drifting oil mass. Things look grim. A heavy swell has built up and it is now extremely dangerous to manoeuvre salvage craft alongside the *Torrey Canyon*.

March 23: The wind, which since the crash has remained north-westerly, increases in force to 20 knots. Twenty-four ships are now spraying detergent on the oil. Final preparations are made for attempting to refloat the *Torrey Canyon* on the high spring tides of March 26 and 27.

March 24: The wind changes to south-westerly – pushing the vast oil slicks straight towards the Cornish coast. Since the crash an estimated 50,000 tons of oil has been spewed into the sea. Aboard the *Torrey Canyon* there remain a further 70,000 tons.

March 25: The first oil hits the coast – thick, black and clinging. It builds up in layer upon layer on beaches, harbour walls, cliffsides and on the hulls of pleasure boats. And with the oil comes a pathetic flotsam – thousands of blackened seabirds, either dead or dying. Sixteen miles from the befouled coastline, three tugs attach lines to the *Torrey Canyon* in readiness for a trial pull. Air is pumped into the empty tanks to increase buoyancy, but the tugs only succeed in pivoting the vessel round on the rocks by about eight degrees.

March 26: It is Sunday, the first day of the high spring tides. Salvage men curse as a gale blows up, but by mid-afternoon the wind has abated slightly and four tugs strain to haul the giant tanker off the rocks. With a crack, and a frightening whiplash, the main cable linking two of the tugs to the tanker snaps. Minutes later, the tanker breaks its back on the rocks ... spilling another

---

It is small wonder that morale is so low. Dentists, inadequately paid for their work, are pulling out in droves.
– *Freedom* (Scientology journal)

0,000 tons of oil into the sea. All attempts at salvaging the ship are abandoned. The disaster is complete.

March 27: The coastline from Land's End to Newquay, Cornwall, is black with crude oil. And it is only the beginning. Vast slicks are heading up the English coast – and equally enormous patches of oil are heading for the French coast. To make matters worse, the oil is drifting on to the beaches on the highest spring tides for 50 years.

March 28: The weather worsens, but an attempt is made to ignite the oil floating around the tanker. It fails. Captain Rugiati, his remaining crew and the salvage experts decide finally to abandon the tanker. The twisted hulk, washed by heavy seas, is breaking up. From the Defence Ministry in London, the order goes out: BOMB THE TORREY CANYON.

For the three days that followed, Buccaneer fighter-bombers of the Royal Navy rained bombs on to the oil tanker, which by now had broken into three parts. The pilots had to carry out their task with pinpoint accuracy. The decks of the ship had first to be opened up by the Buccaneers' 1,000-pounders, then the remaining oil below-decks had to be ignited.

The navy flyers did their job well: after the first four hits, the flames and smoke of the burning oil made it difficult, from a height of 2,500 feet, to aim further bombs on to the wreck, yet, of the 40 bombs dropped, 30 scored direct hits. To help keep the oil burning, Royal Air Force Hunter fighters flew over the wreck, jettisoning their wing-tip fuel tanks on to the inferno.

The following day, oil was still seen to be pouring from the wreck, so the Buccaneers and Hunters returned, firing rockets and dropping napalm and high-explosive bombs. Bombing continued on the third day, but no new fires were seen – the remaining oil had been burnt up.

There was plenty of oil still around, though – on the sea and on the beaches. On April 6 oil from the *Torrey Canyon* reached the Channel Islands. On April 9 it reached the shores of Brittany, and sixty miles of it, up to 12 inches thick, fouled the French coast. About 5,000 tons of oil had to be removed by an army of workmen. The last slicks were finally 'sunk' by the French Navy, using detergents in the Bay of Biscay in June – three months after the disaster.

In the meantime, a board of inquiry was held in Liberia, where the tanker was registered. Its conclusions were:

'The master alone was responsible for this casualty. It was his decision to pass to the east of the Scilly Isles. It was his decision to pass between the Scilly Isles and the Seven Stones. He made these decisions without consulting his officers and without any prior advice to them of his intentions. The board concludes that the master did not exercise sound judgement or exercise the practice of good seamanship. Nor can it be considered that he took proper action under the circumstances.

'The board considers that the master was imprudent in his decision to pass to the east of the Scilly Isles, instead of the west as originally intended. Considering the facts that the master's experience in the waters to the east of the islands was very limited and that the *Torrey Canyon* was an extremely large and deeply loaded tanker, his decision exposed his vessel to an unnecessary risk which could easily have been avoided.'

The board of inquiry criticised Captain Rugiati for failing to go directly to the bridge upon being told that the ship was off its original course. It also censured him for 'failing to reduce speed at any time prior to stranding' and for 'permitting his vessel to continue on automatic steering while nearing the Scilly Isles.'

Finally, the board reported: 'This casualty was one of the most serious nature. Apart from the loss of a fine ship and its cargo, the resulting oil pollution inflicted untold hardship and damage. It was one of the worst disasters in maritime history. The cause was entirely the negligence of the ship's master and the degree of that negligence we consider to be of a very high order. A master charged with the responsibility for navigating one of the largest vessels in the world must exercise the care and caution which that responsibility demands. In this case, the master utterly failed to adhere to these standards. We recommend therefore that the licence issued to the master of the *Torrey Canyon* be revoked.'

Rugiati, a broken man, returned home to Genoa, where he went into hospital, seriously ill with pleurisy and suffering from depression. He would see no one but his wife and two sons. But soon, as the extent of his personal suffering became known, letters began pouring into the hospital at the rate of 200 a day. Most were letters of sympathy from people in Britain.

Rugiati eventually agreed to talk about the disaster. Friends were shocked when they met him. A shattered man, bent, grey, dazed, unshaven and trembling, he said: 'Those letters from England have given me back a little faith in myself. I am responsible for what happened and I have been suffering nightmares of guilt over it.

'The worst thing is knowing that I could have saved the ship if only I had had another 30 seconds to manoeuvre. As the ship was about to hit the rocks I tried to throw the helm. But it was on automatic and it would not respond. Nothing could be done.

'If only I had had another 30 seconds.'

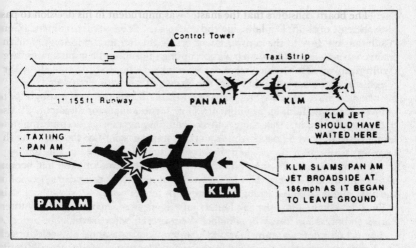

Control Tower

Taxi Strip

1' 155 ft Runway

PAN AM

KLM

KLM JET SHOULD HAVE WAITED HERE

TAXIING PAN AM

KLM SLAMS PAN AM JET BROADSIDE AT 186 mph AS IT BEGAN TO LEAVE GROUND

PAN AM

KLM

The world's worst plane crash

Two jumbo jets collided, and 582 lives were lost

It was the ultimate horror that everyone had dreaded – a crash between two jumbo jets loaded with passengers. It happened on March 27, 1977, on the Atlantic holiday island of Tenerife, in the Spanish-administered Canary Islands. And it claimed 582 lives.

The crash occurred on a Sunday, always the busiest day of the week at Santa Cruz. As many as 180 planes take off or land with their cargoes of holiday-makers. This particular Sunday was foggy – not unusual for Tenerife, where clouds bank up around the extinct volcano, Pico de Teide. There was also a great deal of confusion and extra traffic at Santa Cruz airport that day. A bomb, planted by terrorists of the Canary Islands liberation movement, had exploded in a shop at Las Palmas airport, on the neighbouring island of Gran Canaria, and aircraft were being diverted from Las Palmas to Santa Cruz. Among them were two Boeing 747 jumbo jets – Dutch KLM flight 4805 from Amsterdam and Pan Am flight 1736 from Los Angeles and New York.

By early afternoon, Santa Cruz airport was overcrowded even by its own hectic standards. Eleven planes were on the ground, most of them waiting for clearance for take-off. Dealing with the unexpected flood were three air-traffic controllers on duty in the control tower beside the terminal buildings. Their main concern was the fog, which was becoming thicker by the minute, and the central runway lights, which were not working.

A further problem was that two of the airport's three radio frequencies were out of action and all the waiting pilots had to talk to the controllers through the babble of the one remaining frequency. The scene was set for disaster.

On Pan Am flight 1736, the 370 American passengers were becoming restless. They had paid $2,000 each for a cruise starting from Las Palmas. Their liner was waiting for them when the news of the bomb explosion was passed to the aircraft and it was diverted to Santa Cruz. The holidaymakers had been sitting impatiently aboard their jet for two hours, unable to disembark because the airport did not have enough landing steps to go round.

On KLM flight 4805, the 229 Dutch passengers were also restless. They too had been bound for Las Palmas before their aircraft was diverted.

The KLM pilot, Captain Jaap van Zanten, was something of a celebrity. His handsome face had appeared in the airline's advertisements to underline the expertise of their staff and the safety record of their planes. Van Zanten was certainly experienced; he had been flying with KLM for 27 years and was one of its three most senior pilots. It was because of his experience that Van Zanten decided that he would not join the expected queue for fuel at Las Palmas airport when his and all the other craft were finally allowed into it, but instead would order his jumbo jet to be loaded now with the fuel that it would need – fuel that was later to incinerate the entire aircraft. . . .

Van Zanten's counterpart on the Pan Am jumbo was Captain Victor Grubbs, a 56-year-old veteran of World War Two. Unable to taxi around the refuelling Dutch aircraft to get ahead of it in the line of planes waiting on the runway, he tried to alleviate the boredom of his passengers by inviting them up to inspect the cockpit in groups.

By now, visibility was down to 500 yards – low, but still within the permitted limit for take-offs. The fog was thickening fast, however, and since no one

---

A big-selling vodka firm decided to drop its advertising line, which went: 'I thought the Karma Sutra was an Indian restaurant until I discovered Smirnoff.' An executive of the firm said: 'We conducted a survey and discovered that 60 per cent of people did think it was an Indian restaurant.'

elished the idea of being stranded at Santa Cruz overnight, the crews of the
wo jumbo jets were anxious to get clearance for their flights to Las Palmas.

The main runway at Santa Cruz is two miles long and 2,000 feet above sea
evel. It runs east to west. Parallel to it is a second runway which planes use to
axi to and from the terminal buildings. These two runways are joined at
ither end, and are linked along their lengths by four access slipways.

At a few minutes before 5 p.m., Van Zanten and Grubbs breathed sighs of
elief when word came from the control tower that they should prepare their
ircraft for take-off. Because of the congestion on the taxi-ing runway, both
ilots were ordered to move their planes on to the main runway. The KLM
nd Pan Am jumbos arrived together at the eastern end of the main runway.
.he control tower then ordered the two jets to taxi westwards up the runway
o the take-off starting point at the far end. They did so, with the KLM jet
eading.

These manoeuvres went on largely out of sight of the three air-traffic con-
rollers. Swirling sea fog blanketed the airport, and, because Santa Cruza
ad no ground radar, the controllers could not follow the pattern of slow-
oving aircraft on the ground. They had to rely on that single busy radio
hannel.

The control tower radioed KLM flight 4805: 'Taxi straight ahead to the
nd of the runway and make backtrack.' Captain Van Zanten's mighty jet
eaded slowly up the long runway.

Captain Grubbs then received his instructions from the tower – to taxi
orward and to leave the runway by turning into a slipway on the left.

The third turning to the left off the main runway at Santa Cruz airport is
esignated Slipway C3. It involves a 130-degree turn and leads straight back
o the terminal buildings. It would have been a slow and awkward manoeuvre
or the Pan Am jumbo. The fourth turning off the runway – Slipway C4 – leads
1 a circle to the top of the runway, where the KLM jumbo was now swinging
round in readiness for take-off.

Captain Van Zanten completed his manoeuvre and pointed his airliner's
ose into the darkening fog that hung over the two miles of main runway
head of him – and over the Pan Am jumbo which, hidden from view, was
ill lumbering towards him.

The Pan Am jet passed the turn-off to Slipway C3 and headed on for Slip-
ay C4. At about the same time, Captain Van Zanten's co-pilot was relaying
is message to the control tower: 'KLM 4805 is now ready for take-off. We
re waiting for clearance.'

Tower: 'OK. Stand by for take-off. I will call you.'

The tower then asked the Pan Am jumbo if it had yet cleared the runway.
Vhen told that it had not yet done so, the tower then asked the American co-

93

pilot to report immediately the runway was clear. But moments later, th
KLM plane began rolling. . . .

A jumbo jet weighs 240 tons, its wingspan is 195 feet, it is 231 feet lon an
its tailplane is the height of a seven-story building. At 5.07 p.m. on that fatef
Sunday, two such planes were heading towards each other – one at a craw
the other at 150 miles an hour.

Pan Am co-pilot Robert Bragg was the first crewman to spot the approach
ing Dutch jumbo. He said: 'I saw lights ahead of us through the fog. At first
thought it was the KLM standing at the end of the runway. Then I realise
the lights were coming towards us.'

Bragg screamed: 'Get off. Get off.' Captain Grubbs shouted: 'We're o
the runway. We're on the runway.'

Grubbs slewed his jumbo into a 30-degree turn to try to get out of the pat
of the oncoming airliner. But it was too late. The KLM plane was travellin
too fast. It could not stop or swerve. It had passed the point of no return.

Captain Van Zanten lifted the nose of his jumbo at the last minute. A chann
was gouged out of the runway by the Dutch plane's tail as the captain tried t
leap his giant machine over the Pan Am jet. His effort was in vain. Tw
seconds after lifting off, the Dutch plane smashed into the American jumbo
about 160 miles an hour. The nose of the KLM jet hit the top of the other plan
taking the roof off the cockpit and the first-class upper compartment. Th
giant engine pods hanging beneath the wings were next to hit the America
plane. The port engines ploughed into the aft-cabin, killing most of the passe
gers instantly.

The KLM Boeing continued its terrible journey over the top of the Pan A
plane and along the runway, disintegrating and exploding into thousands
pieces. Not one person aboard the Dutch plane survived.

All the survivors on the Pan Am plane were sitting either up front or on th
left-hand side, away from the impact. Part of the left of the plane was broke
off by the crash, and the survivors either were hurled clear or leaped to safet

Throughout the long seconds of disaster, the air-traffic controllers remaine
unaware of it. A Spanish airliner flying above Tenerife broke in to reque
landing permission. The control tower replied sharply: 'Radio silence, pleas
I will continue to call up KLM.' But KLM no longer existed.

Suddenly, a gust of wind blew a gap in the fog. And those in the contro
tower had a momentary vision of horror as a blazing jumbo showed throug
the mists. A few seconds later another gap appeared . . and the controllers sa
what remained of a second Boeing.

The radio waves became filled with a babble of voices. 'There's a jumbo o
fire.' 'No, there are two of them.' 'Can you contact Pan Am 1736?' 'Contro
tower, have you seen fire on the runway?' 'Fire tenders, fire tenders.'

The small rescue team on duty at the airport was quickly at the scene. But there was little it could do. The KLM jumbo was an unrecognisable litter of scattered debris. The Pan Am jumbo was a blazing mass. Everyone who had escaped had done so within the first couple of minutes.

Heroine of the crash was Dorothy Kelly, a 35-year-old Pan Am purser from New Hampshire. This is what she remembered of the disaster: 'There was noise, things flying around. Nothing was recognisable. There was nothing around that looked like anything had looked before – just jagged metal and small pieces of debris. When everything settled, I realised that there was sky above me although I was still in what had been the aircraft. At first, I didn't see any people at all. There were explosions behind me and I realised that the only way out was up. The floor started giving way as I climbed out.'

Mrs. Kelly leaped 20 feet to safety then looked back at the broken and blazing plane. There was a string of explosions and she heard people screaming from within the aircraft – so she ran back towards it.

'I saw the captain on his knees, not moving. I thought he had broken his legs. There were other people around with broken limbs. I grabbed the captain under the arms and pulled and kept encouraging him to keep going. I feared the fuselage would fall down on us. There was a huge explosion. I said: "We've got to go now – faster." I kept pushing and pulling and then dropped him on to the runway.'

Mrs. Kelly had saved the life of Captain Grubbs. As explosions ripped the jumbo, she dashed back and forth, dragging other dazed survivors clear of the wreckage until she was certain that there could be no one else left alive. Later, Mrs. Kelly, her face scarred, her eyes blackened and with one arm in plaster, said: 'I feel as if I have just gone 20 rounds with Muhammad Ali.' She was subsequently awarded a medal for gallantry.

Pan Am passenger Jim Naik, a 37-year-old Californian, was in the first-

---

Ad-men reckon that half the battle of launching a new car can be won by presenting the right image. But they do not always get it right . . .

Ford introduced a glamorous new model in Mexico and, after much name-searching, came up with the title: Caliente. But they quickly changed it to the unromantic S-22 when dealers pointed out that Caliente in Mexican means 'street-walker'.

General Motors did not have any greater success when they introduced their Chevrolet Nova to Mexico. Sales were slow – and so was the name of the car . . . In Mexico, No-va means 'won't go'.

THE WORLD'S GREATEST MISTAKES

AUDIENCE TRIED TO SPOIL PLAY BUT PLAYERS SUCCEEDED

– Sunderland Echo

---

class compartment when 'all hell broke loose – just as if we were in a movie.'

This was Naik's story: 'I was sitting with my wife Elsie when there was a sudden explosion. The plane went completely up in flames. I was struggling to get Elsie out with me but after the impact people just started tumbling down on top of us from the lounge above as the ceiling caved in. A piece of ceiling fell on my wife. Then a second explosion hurled me on to the runway. I was running back towards the plane to try to save Elsie when I saw a body falling out of the plane. It was my wife.'

Briton John Cooper, a 53-year-old Pan Am mechanic, was travelling as a passenger on the flight deck when the plane was hit by the KLM jumbo. He was thrown clear and suffered only minor cuts. He said: 'There was a terrible crash. I just don't want to remember it. There were people screaming terribly – women and children enveloped in flames. I will never get the sounds of that screaming out of my ears.'

Californian John Amador, aged 35, said: 'I looked out of a porthole and saw the KLM plane coming right at me. I ducked and, when I looked up, our own aircraft was split into three parts. I was afraid I was going to be roasted.' But he leaped to safety.

So did Mrs. Teri Brusco, of Oregon. She said: 'The Dutch jet's wings took off the whole of the top of our plane. Everyone was screaming.' Her husband Roland pushed his wife through a jagged opening in the side of the plane and they then hauled out his mother. 'My mother was on fire. We started dragging her across the field to put the flames out.'

Several passengers remained strapped in their seats after the crash. They appeared numbed and did not try to save themselves. Then came the series of explosions that engulfed the plane in flames. Of the Pan Am jumbo's 370 passengers and 16 crew, more than 300 were dead within minutes of the crash and more than 60 were seriously injured.

But at least there were some survivors from the American jet. On the KLM jumbo, all 229 passengers and the crew of 15 were wiped out, including a Dutch wife who had boarded the flight at Amsterdam after telling her husband she was going on holiday with friends in Spain. Instead she flew off to her death – with one of her husband's best friends.

One further tragic lie came to light after the crash. A Dutch businessman told his wife that he was flying off to a company meeting in Switzerland. Instead, he boarded KLM flight 4805 for Las Palmas to spend an illicit holiday with an attractive woman neighbour. Before setting out, he had written a card to his wife and given it to a colleague to post from Zurich. The card, complete with loving greetings, arrived two days after his death.

And what of the man who set in motion the terrible chain of events of March 27, 1977? Antonio Cubillo, leader of the Canary Islands separatist movement, the man who ordered the bomb to be planted, said from his exile in Algiers: 'The Spaniards did not want holidaymakers to see the damage at Las Palmas. So it is their fault that the planes crashed. I do not have 582 deaths on my conscience.'

The shipwreck survivor who sacrificed his life in vain

The tiny liferaft was just a dot on the surface of the vast Pacific. Aboard it were Bill Quinlan, aged 48, and his 18-year-old nephew, David Lucas. David was reasonably hopeful that they would soon be spotted by a passing ship, but his uncle was despondent and morose. He blamed himself for the predicament they were both in.

Quinlan, a married man with two children, had set sail with his nephew from San Diego, California, on a 4,000-mile voyage to the Galapagos Islands. But after 1,000 miles their trimaran ran into a hurricane. A giant wave lifted the 40-foot yacht and smashed it upside down with the two occupants underneath it. They struggled to the surface, gasping for air, but Quinlan was soon back under the yacht again – trying to free the liferaft which was roped to the deck. It took him an hour, but he made it.

The next task was to rescue fresh water and rations from the cabin. Quinlan was beneath the yacht again and Lucas was holding the end of a rope attached to his uncle's waist, when the young man saw a giant black fin slicing through the water. Blood from a cut on Quinlan's leg had attracted a shark.

Lucas hauled on the rope and dragged his uncle back on board the liferaft. The raft began drifting away from the trimaran as the shark circled them. The two survivors knew that they would have to make do with the meagre rations they already had.

The storm receded, and the blazing summer sun – it was July, 1978 – beat down on the little raft. It was well away from the main shipping routes, and the men aboard it lay drifting for five days without once sighting another vessel.

Quinlan took stock of the emergency supplies. There was one can of water and two cans of food. He spoke softly to his nephew: 'God alone knows how long it will be before someone spots us. There is enough food and water here to keep one man going for two weeks. You are only 18. You have a full life ahead of you.'

And with those words, Quinlan slid over the side of the raft.

Lucas grabbed his uncle and tried to haul him back but Quinlan, the stronger of the two, struggled free and began, with steady strokes, to swim away from the raft. He never once looked back.

'I shouted for him to return,' Lucas said later. 'I cried but he never looked round. I didn't know what to do. I cannot swim and I could only watch him vanish out of sight. I saw sharks in the water and I knew he was as good as dead. I'm sure I will never again meet anyone as brave as my uncle.'

But Quinlan's heroism was in vain. The very next day, a Mexican fishing boat picked up Lucas. His rations were untouched.

When he was put ashore, Lucas travelled north to Arcata, California, to the home of his uncle's wife, Vicki. There he handed over the only two possessions left by Quinlan – a gold ring and a tin on which was the scratched message: 'I love you. I'm sorry.'

Hydrogen bombs rain on Spain

Bomber crash threatened nuclear catastrophe

A giant U.S. Air Force B-52 bomber kept its rendezvous with a flying tanker over the Mediterranean coast of Spain at 10.20 a.m. on January 16, 1966. The cargo of the B-52 was four 1.5-megaton hydrogen bombs, and the plan had been circling over the eastern Mediterranean for 12 hours. Now, the bomber had to take on fuel in mid-air from the tanker before flying back to the United States.

Aboard the B-52, the captain took up position 20 miles behind the tanker at 30,000 feet. It had been a long and boring mission, no different from the

American soldiers and Spanish police guard the wreckage of bomber and tanker.

100 bomber flights made by U.S. Strategic Air Command along the Iron Curtain borders every day of the year.

Aboard the K-135 tanker ahead, Major Emila Chapla kept a steady course as he watched the bomber manoeuvre into position behind him. Earlier, Chapla had taken off from the U.S. airbase near Seville, Spain, with more than 30,000 gallons of aviation fuel aboard. It was just a routine, everyday job.

The B-52 closed the distance, ready to fit its nosepipe into the fuel boom that trailed from the underbelly of the tanker plane. Chapla watched the B-52 drift closer. He thought it was approaching too high and too fast. He gave a radio warning to the B-52, but his urgent words had only just been uttered when the two huge aircraft collided. The B-52 came up under the tanker and hit its belly.

Major Chapla fought to control his severely damaged plane and to return it, blazing, to base. In the B-52, the captain knew that his aircraft was doomed. The superstructure and the cabin were crushed, and the plane began to break up. The captain and two of his crew baled out – just before a tremendous explosion, which set the giant bomber spinning earthwards, shedding thousands of fragments on its way.

Amidst the debris that rained down on the Spanish coast that morning were four 20-foot-long hydrogen bombs.

The bombs fell in the vicinity of the village of Palomares. None of them exploded. That would have been impossible without their having first been primed aboard the B-52. But it was feared that their casings might have been split open by their TNT detonators exploding on impact, and no one knew for sure what effect leaking radio-active plutonium and uranium would have on the unsuspecting civilian population of Palomares.

99

THE WORLD'S GREATEST MISTAKES

As soon as the crash occurred, a military disaster team was assembled and flown from the United States to Spain. Meanwhile, American military advisers in Spain broke the news to the Madrid authorities, and a stream of top brass and politicians poured into Palomares.

A bald statement was issued to the press to the effect that an American plane had crashed but that there had been no civilian casualties. No mention was made of the nuclear weapons. The peasantry of Palomares were unaware of the dangers that surrounded them. But, with the arrival of the American disaster team and the unprecedented security clamp on the area, newspapermen began putting the clues together. They discovered that the crashed plane was a B-52. They guessed that it had been carrying nuclear bombs, and that those bombs were now scattered over rural Spain.

Piece by piece, the newsmen put together the jigsaw of the disaster, even though they were barred from the area. The outside world was told in huge headlines what was going on around Palomares. But in the village itself the peasants were told nothing. They were barred from harvesting their crops and were ordered to remain in the village. As troops and search planes swarmed over their farmlands, the 2,500 people of the Palomares district became increasingly alarmed.

If they had known what danger they were in, they would have been even more inclined to panic. For the three bombs which had fallen near their village had all been split open by their detonators, spilling plutonium and uranium into the atmosphere. The slight breeze blowing that day was wafting an invisible poison across the dusty Spanish countryside.

The first bomb to be recovered was spotted in open fields by aerial searchers. The TNT explosion had blown out a small crater, and the shattered casing was partly buried in the earth. There had been little leakage. Another splintered bomb was found in hilly countryside about three miles out of Palomares.

A third bomb was found by a villager close to his home on the outskirts of Palomares. It was in a small crater and smoke was coming from it. Not only smoke but, unknown to the villager, radio-active dust. The puzzled Spaniard examined the shattered bomb, stood on top of it and gave it a kick. He went off to look for someone who might know what the mystery object was, and it was only after some hours that word got to the Americans that a bomb had been found.

Three bombs accounted for . . . but where was the fourth?

Fisherman Simo Orts provided the answer. He had been out in his boat when the air crash occurred 30,000 feet above him. Some minutes later he watched a long metal object sink slowly out of the sky beneath two parachutes. It fell into the sea only yards from his boat and quickly sank. Orts circled the spot but all traces of the mysterious object had disappeared. He continued

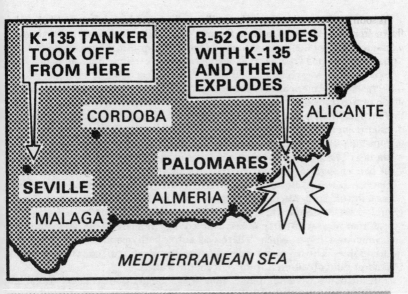

K-135 TANKER TOOK OFF FROM HERE

B-52 COLLIDES WITH K-135 AND THEN EXPLODES

CORDOBA

ALICANTE

PALOMARES

SEVILLE

ALMERIA

MALAGA

MEDITERRANEAN SEA

A villager washing clothes in Palomares.

his fishing, then set sail for home. When he arrived back in port, he told his friends about the strange occurrence. They decided to inform the local police. But, because of the cloak of secrecy thrown by the Americans over what they had code-named Operation Broken Arrow, not even the Spanish police knew exactly what was going on.

When the Americans eventually heard of the fisherman's tale, they sent out experts to track down and interrogate the puzzled Orts. His description fitted. The bomb had fallen into the sea suspended beneath a parachute designed to hold it over a target area. The second parachute had been the safety 'chute. Orts took a team out in his boat to show them exactly where the bomb had hit the sea. The trouble was that, once out in the Mediterranean, he could not be sure enough to pinpoint the spot exactly. All the searchers knew was that the bomb was likely to be somewhere within a ten-square-mile area about six miles offshore, where the craggy seabed ranged in depth from between 100 and 5,000 feet. Somewhere down there was the fourth bomb.

A marine search party was assembled off Palomares, with 20 ships, 2,000 seamen and 125 frogmen. There was also a bathyscaph and two miniature submarines. The team was ordered to find the bomb at all costs before drifting sand or mud obscured it from view on the seabed.

If the bomb were not found, there was a danger that its safety equipment might in time rust away, allowing the radio-active contents to pollute the Mediterranean – or even causing an explosion that would create a deadly nuclear cloud over the coast of Spain. There was also the possibility that, if the bomb were abandoned, the Russians might try to find it and unravel its secrets. The bomb *had* to be found.

And found it was. On March 15, two months after the air crash, the crew of the mini-submarine Alvin spotted an indentation in the mud at 2,500 feet. They investigated more closely, resurfaced – then, agonisingly, failed to find it again. A day later they picked up the trail and discovered a parachute on the seabed. They followed the ropes of the 'chute ... and there, on a narrow ledge overhanging a 500-foot precipice, lay the bomb.

It took a further three weeks to secure the bomb without dislodging it from the ledge. But on April 7, 1966, after several near-disasters, the hydrogen bomb was raised undamaged to the surface. Meanwhile, the people of Palomares had been largely cleared of the danger of contamination, and compensation was being agreed for the loss of crops.

A nuclear tragedy on an unthinkable scale had been averted.

Deep-freeze meat: Best Scotch beef from Wales.
— *Glasgow Herald*

GREATEST MISTAKES

Death of the Red Baron

German air ace tempted fate, and flew to his death

In the heat of the battle for the air during World War One, at a time when a pilot's life expectancy was three weeks, young flyers on both sides guarded themselves with lucky charms and surrounded themselves with superstition. Among the German pilots of the string-and-canvas flying machines, one superstition was held to be more important than all others: not to be photographed

efore a mission. Only afterwards, would they allow a camera to record their
ictories.

On the morning of April 21, 1918, Baron Manfred von Richthofen, the
eadliest ace that air warfare has ever known, laughed at the superstition. He
aused to play with a puppy at the door of the hangar which housed his bright
ed Fokker triplane, and he smiled into the lens of a camera held by a visitor
⊃ the airfield.

Baron von Richthofen could afford to laugh at superstition. After all, at the
ge of 25, he was the most famous flyer in the world. He was considered almost
nvincible. The day before, he had shot down his 80th aircraft. He was a
ational hero, known as the Red Knight of Germany and the Red Baron,
ecause of the 'flying circus' of blood-red planes that he led twice a day into
ne skies over war-torn France and Belgium to wreak havoc among British,
rench, Australian and Canadian aircraft.

Richthofen stepped into the cockpit of his Fokker at 10.15 that morning as
military band played in honour of his victories. He took off from the airfield
t Cappy with two dozen other planes and flew towards the village of Sailly-
-Sec, in the Somme valley, where they were to assemble.

At about the same time as Richthofen was bumping down the take-off strip,
nother pilot was preparing for take-off 25 miles away, at Bertangles. He was
Loy Brown, a 24-year-old Canadian who flew a Sopwith Camel with 209
quadron of the newly formed Royal Air Force. Brown, a volunteer flyer from
oronto, was very unlike the flamboyant Red Baron, whom he was shortly to
neet in combat. Retiring and modest, he had notched up 12 official German
ills' – certainly less than his actual tally, because he seldom bothered to claim
is victories. Brown had recently been promoted to captain and had been
warded a Distinguished Flying Cross. He was flying two long and dangerous
nissions every day of the week and was keeping his tired body going by regular
fusions of brandy and milk.

Brown had heard much about Baron von Richthofen and had learned to
spect the pilots of his amazing 'flying circus'. Richthofen, on the other hand,

---

It can be a mistake to cross swords with the great wits of
the age. In Georgian days a Member of Parliament
indignantly broke off from his speech in the House of
Commons and said: 'The Prime Minister is asleep.' Lord
North opened one eye and said: 'I wish to God I was.'

Lady Astor once told Sir Winston Churchill: 'If I were
your wife, I'd put poison in your coffee.' Churchill replied:
'And if I were your husband, I'd drink it.'

had never heard of Captain Brown, the man who, at 11.15, was flying 10,0⊘
feet above him, one of a flight of 15 RAF planes, over Sailly-le-Sec.

Below him, Brown saw the mighty circus attacking two slow RE8 reco⊘
naissance planes which were wheeling, twisting and turning in an attempt ⊘
escape the onslaught. Brown flipped his Camel into a steep dive and, ⊘
arrangement, seven of his colleagues followed suit. Eight was about the mo⊘
of their battle-scarred squadron that they could risk committing to the fra⊘
As they roared down towards the dogfight being enacted at 3,000 feet, th⊘
knew that they were heavily outnumbered by the Germans and that one ⊘
the eight who were joining battle was really only along for the ride. He w⊘
Lieutenant William May, an Australian who had just arrived in France an⊘
had been ordered to keep on the edge of any dogfight until he had gained mo⊘
experience. May circled the mêlée and watched as the seven other Came⊘
engaged the German planes – allowing the two beleaguered RE8s to flee in⊘
a bank of cloud.

The outnumbered RAF pilots were amazingly successful. Within a matt⊘
of minutes they had downed four of the German planes, one being shot dow⊘
by new boy May. But no sooner had May sent the enemy aircraft to the groun⊘
than Baron von Richthofen himself swooped down to line the Australian up ⊘
his sights. The Fokker's twin Spandau machine-guns raked the fuselage ⊘
May's plane. The Australian received only a minor injury but he was in serio⊘
trouble. Try as he might, he could not shake the Red Baron from his tai⊘
He spun and wheeled, but he was too inexperienced to outmanoeuvre th⊘
German ace.

Brown saw what was happening and disengaged from the dogfight. Ma⊘
was now making a determined run for home, his plane low to the ground, th⊘
Baron only 25 yards behind him. With the advantage of height, Brown swoope⊘
down until he had caught up with the German. An Australian battery open⊘
fire on Richthofen's plane, but the Baron kept determinedly on.

So intent was he on his prey that the victor of 80 air battles forgot the ver⊘
first rule in the book of aerial warfare: always look behind. Brown was rig⊘
there on his tail, his right thumb hovering over the trigger button of his Vicke⊘
machine-gun. The Red Baron came into his sights and Brown opened fire⊘

Pilot Douglas Corrigan took off from New York in dense
fog in 1938, planning to fly west to California.
Unfortunately he got his bearings wrong and flew due east
for 28 hours. He landed in Ireland and gained the nickname
'Wrong-Way Corrigan'.

---

one long burst which sent a neat line of bullets along the Fokker's fuselage, starting at the tail and running up to the cockpit.

The nose of the Fokker dipped and the plane glided earthwards. It hit the ground and rolled neatly to rest near the British lines on the outskirts of Sailly-le-Sec. A British soldier looked into the cockpit and found Baron Manfred von Richthofen sitting bolt upright, dead. An officer took a snapshot of the scene, to be dropped over the German lines the next day.

Meanwhile, back at Cappy airfield, a German photographer was watching the sky. He was awaiting the return of the 'flying circus', so that he could take his second photograph that day of the ever-victorious Red Baron.

The mutineers who sailed away to death

The three new recruits to the crew of the sailing ship *Leicester Castle* were a surly bunch. They had joined the British cargo ship at San Francisco, though whether by choice is not known. For this was 1902, and, although press gangs no longer roamed the streets of the world's major ports, there were other devious methods of obtaining crew members for long and hazardous voyages – such as getting them roaring drunk and leading them aboard the ship just before it sailed.

Not that Captain John Peattie, master of the *Leicester Castle*, would personally have had anything to do with such deception. The tough Scotsman would have left all that to his first mate. All Peattie knew was that there were three new crew members for the voyage back to London, and that was that. The three were James Turner from Oregon, Jack Hobbs from Illinois and Ernest Sears from Idaho – all ordinary seamen who had served previously on ocean-going vessels.

The three Americans kept their own company. But they did ask a lot of questions about the ship's route. And when on August 12 they were told that the ship was passing to the north of the Pitcairn Islands, in the middle of the Pacific, the reason for their questions was made plain.

Turner, Hobbs and Sears had decided to desert. They had lashed together some timber to make a rough raft, which they had hidden in the hold. And just before midnight, they put their plan into action.

Sears knocked on Captain Peattie's cabin door and asked the master to come to the saloon immediately to help tend a crewman who had been injured on deck. Peattie followed Sears down the passageway and entered the saloon - to be confronted with Hobbs armed with a revolver. The Scot made a dive for the gunman but Sears smashed a length of wood down on his head. As Peattie lay on the floor, Hobbs fired four bullets into him.

The only man on watch that night was another Scot, the young second mate, Iain Nixon. Hearing the shots, he rushed down to the saloon and was shot through the heart with a single bullet. He fell dead in the doorway.

The captain, however, was still alive. One bullet had missed his heart by inches, the others had hit him in the arm and shoulder. The whole of the ship was awake now and, while some of the men tended the captain's wounds, the others dashed up on deck to find the attackers.

They were too late. Sears and Hobbs, along with their friend Turner, were crouched on their makeshift raft drifting away into the darkness of the Pacific.

The mutineers had taken with them only a few days' supply of food and water. They were obviously heading for the Pitcairn Islands – there was no other landfall that they could have contemplated.

The three men were clever enough to have worked out that the faint breeze then blowing would move their raft slowly towards the islands. But it did them no good. For when the other crewmen had told them that the *Leicester Castle* was passing the islands, they had been only partly right. No one aboard except the captain and the first and second mates knew that the lack of wind had caused them to sail 300 miles to the north of the Pitcairns.

The three mutineers were swallowed up by the endless Pacific. They were never seen again.

Nobody believed the Subbay family, of Cherbourg, France, when they claimed that their clock was jinxed. The old grandfather clock sometimes struck 13 instead of 12 – and when it did, the unlucky number was always accompanied by an accident. When the head of the household first heard the 13th chime, he fell downstairs. On another occasion his wife scalded herself and, like her husband, had to be rushed to hospital. A sceptical relative moved into the house so that he could disprove the jinx. At the 13th stroke of midnight a heavy lamp standard fell on his head and he too was rushed to hospital.

The £12 million air giant that ended in a scrapyard

In 1942 the aircraft factories of Britain were turning out bombers as fast as they could build them. But despite the pressures of war, there were still dreamers around. And most of them seemed to have been gathered in one oom in London's Whitehall, where a committee headed by air pioneer Lord Brabazon was deciding the future of the British aircraft industry.

What these wise men proposed was that work should start on a giant airliner that could fly halfway around the world – one that could carry passengers from London to New York non-stop. It would cost a lot of money to build, and here was no spare money during the war effort. It would use valuable factory pace, and there was none of that spare either. Nevertheless, in March 1943, he decision to build two prototypes of this giant plane – called the Bristol Brabazon – was announced in Parliament. It was to be the prestige aircraft of the century. And the word went out: money no object.

The planemakers at Filton, near Bristol, needed no prompting. They designed a plane that was to be the biggest in the world – a fantastic 70 tons

Above The Bristol Brabazon on its first trial flight. *Right* Lord Brabazon.

empty and 140 tons laden, with a 230-foot wing span, 50 feet high and with engines developing 20,000 horse-power.

They built a brand-new hangar in which to assemble the prototypes. They extended the runway at Filton by demolishing most of the village and by concreting over a new main road. They built a ridiculously lavish full-scale mock-up of the aircraft, complete in every detail, even down to the soap dish in the women's powder room. Passengers? Well, they could fit about 75 of them in, with sleeping berths, bars and promenades – this at a time when the Americans were already building 150-seat aircraft.

At the end of 1949, seven-and-a-half years after Lord Brabazon's report, the first Bristol Brabazon made its maiden flight at Filton, watched by the world's press. The flight was a success. But six months later it was discovered that the flying giant was suffering from metal fatigue. It was cracking up. Its operational life would be about two years.

In September 1952, the House of Commons was told that the Bristol Brabazon was being scrapped. The cost of the project had been £12½ million. Only one plane had ever been completed. The biggest airliner in the world was sold for scrap for £10,000.

Chapter
Three

Victims and Villains

For every man with money, there is another scheming to relieve him of it. For every man with a trusting nature, there is another ready to make him a little wiser. When the gullible discover that they have blundered, it is usually too late. In the pages that follow you will meet people who have paid dearly for one simple mistake.

The Great Train Robbery

How the perfect crime became the great foul-up

**AUGUST
3
1963**

It was high summer in the heart of the English countryside. The date was August 3, 1963, the place Bridego Bridge at Sears Crossing, Buckinghamshire – the setting for a crime that was to capture the world's imagination and to become known as the Great Train Robbery.

It was shortly after three o'clock in the morning on that August day that 15 men loaded 120 mailbags into a lorry after robbing the Glasgow-to-London night mail train. The mailbags contained £2½ million.

The Great Train Robbery was almost the perfect crime. Almost. For due to a monumental blunder, it turned into a disaster that made the villains who pulled off the robbery the most notorious criminals in the world.

The plan for the raid was hatched in January 1963. It all began with a meeting between a London solicitor's clerk and Gordon Goody, one of the leading lights of a South London 'firm' of criminals. The rendezvous, cheekily enough, was the most famous court in the land, the Old Bailey. There, the clerk boastfully confided to Goody that someone he knew had information about where a vast sum of money could be 'lifted'.

Goody was interested. He called in his friend, Ronald 'Buster' Edwards. And through a string of contacts and secret meetings over the next few days, the incredible project was outlined to them.

Every night, according to the informants, old banknotes from all the banks in Scotland were sent by train to London to be destroyed. The money was always in what was called the High Value Packages Coach which formed part of the night mail train from Glasgow to Euston. There were usually five Post Office workers in this coach, which was always next-but-one to the diesel engine. The other coaches further down the train were manned by dozens of mail sorters. But the coach next to the engine contained only parcels. It was unmanned. The amount of money being carried in the High Value Packages Coach varied from day to day but always rose dramatically after a bank holiday. On August 6, for instance, it might be as much as £4 million. The problem was how were they to rob the train?

However the job was to be tackled, Goody and Edwards realised that it was going to be too big a task for them alone. Through the spring of 1963, the gang grew as more and more tough and specialised criminals were recruited. The team even included members of a rival 'firm' then operating in London.

The gang contained a colourful bunch of villains. Principal among them were: Goody, a tough 32-year-old loner with a sharp taste in clothes and girls: Edwards, aged 30, an overweight but likeable club owner who was a devoted family man: Bruce Reynolds, also 30, married but fond of high living: Charlie Wilson, 32, a resourceful criminal friend of Reynolds: Jimmy White, a quiet, 42-year-old ex-paratrooper: Bob Welch, 34, a South London club owner and one of the top men in the second 'firm': his friend Tommy Wisbey, a 32-year-bookmaker: and Jim Hussey, aged 30, who ran a restaurant in London's Soho.

The gang also brought in three specialists: 'wheel man' Roy James, 23, a silversmith and racing driver, winner of several major races: Roger Cordrey, a 38-year-old florist who was an expert at adjusting' railway signalling equipment: plus a retired train driver. At the last minute, they also recruited a small-time thief and decorator, with a pretty wife, an engaging smile and a yearning for the luxury life he could never afford. His name was Ronald Biggs.

Bridego Bridge carries the main Scottish railway line over a winding back road through Buckinghamshire farmland. It was at this spot that the gang had decided to rob the train. By August 2, they had all assembled at a large and lonely farmhouse, Leatherslade Farm, 26 miles from the bridge. They were dressed in an assortment of commando gear. They decided that it would be a good cover if they looked like soldiers out on a night exercise. To complete the picture, they had two Land-Rovers and a lorry painted army green.

At around midnight, these motley 'soldiers' of fortune set out from the farm

> **The career of outlaw Jesse James ended in a shoot-out at Northfield, Minnesota, in 1876. The gunfight began when a bank cashier refused to open a safe. One of the James gang fired at the cashier, alerting the townsfolk who put the bandits to flight. It was later discovered that the safe had not been locked.**

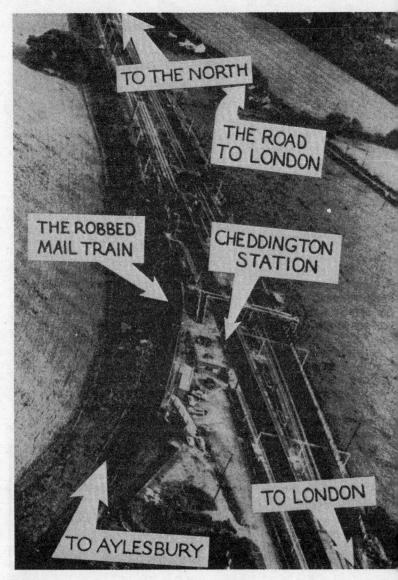

TO THE NORTH

THE ROAD TO LONDON

THE ROBBED MAIL TRAIN

CHEDDINGTON STATION

TO AYLESBURY

TO LONDON

in convoy and drove to Bridego Bridge to prepare the amazing ambush. They were armed with pickaxe handles, coshes and an axe to break down the door of the coach. Cordrey, the diminutive rail-equipment fixer, organised the switching of the two warning lights – one several hundred yards up the track and another closer to the bridge. The first warning light, sited beside the track, would cause any train to slam on its brakes. The second, on a gantry above the line, would bring the train to a full stop. The gang also cut the lines to trackside emergency telephones and to nearby farms and cottages. Then they waited.

The train was due to come into view from the bridge at 3 a.m. The timing had been checked night after night on dummy runs by the gang. On the morning of August 3 it was right on schedule. The look-out man alerted the rest of the gang by walkie-talkie, and they all took up positions on the embankments beside the line.

On the train, driver Jack Mills looked out for the usual green trackside light. But tonight it was amber. He put on the brakes and throttled back the mighty diesel. The overhead signal gantry came into sight. It was showing a red light. Mills stopped the train directly under it and asked his fireman, David Whitby, to use the emergency telephone beside the gantry to find out what was going on.

Whitby vanished into the darkness. Mills heard him ask someone: 'What's up, mate?' Then nothing. Whitby had encountered Buster Edwards walking down the track, had asked his innocent question – and found himself bundled down the embankment and pinioned to the ground by some of the burliest, most villainous-looking thugs he had ever seen.

Back in the cab of the train, driver Mills was being attacked from both sides. He kicked out at the men trying to climb up into the cab but he was overpowered from behind and hit twice across the head. Blood poured down his face, and the next thing he remembered was being handcuffed to fireman Whitby.

The gang had got their train but they still had not got at the money. The next step was to separate the engine and the two front coaches from the rest of the train and drive the engine forward from the gantry to Bridego Bridge, where the cargo was to be unloaded.

The 'heavies' in the gang then launched themselves against the High Value Packages Coach. With axe, crowbar and coshes, the door and windows were smashed in, and the five petrified Post Office workers inside were suddenly faced with what must have seemed like the advance force of an army. The postal workers were made to lie down on the floor while the gang unloaded the mailbags through the shattered coach door and along a human chain which led down the embankment and into the back of their lorry.

THE WORLD'S GREATEST MISTAKES

Then, sweating but jubilant, the gang drove back in their military convoy to Leatherslade Farm. The operation had gone exactly according to plan, but for the knock on the head received by driver Mills. In time, it proved to be a big 'but' – for the violence used against him weighed heavily at the robbers' trial, and his death some years later brought claims from his family that his health had deteriorated dramatically after the raid.

But, for the moment, as the mailbags were piled up in the living room of Leatherslade Farm, the future for the gang looked rosy. They spent the rest of the night counting out the money. They set aside sums for major bribes and backhanders, and shared out the rest. In all there was £2½ million.

Years later, in a remarkable book about the robbery*, Goody related how he had sat with a bottle of whisky in his hand listening to the police wavebands on his VHF radio. He heard one policeman tell a colleague: 'You're not going to believe this, but someone's just stolen a train.'

The gang members had all concocted their alibis and made arrangements to salt away their shares of the loot until the hue and cry was over. They left the

* *The Train Robbers* by Piers Paul Read (W. H. Allen, the Alison Press and Secker & Warburg, 1978)

The mail train at Bridego Bridge, the pick-up point for the lorry.

farm and went their separate ways brimming with confidence. It was short-lived. . . .

Most of the gang had left damning evidence behind them at Leatherslade Farm. There were fingerprints, clothing and vehicles. But the robbers had not been over-worried. They had arranged for an associate to stay at the farm after they had moved out and to clean it from top to bottom so that not even a hair from their heads would be found if the police ever searched the place.

The job was never done. The contract was bungled. The 'perfect crime' became the ultimate criminal foul-up.

When the police found the farmhouse hideout, most of the robbers went on the run. Detectives knew who they were from the fingerprints and palm prints they had left. One single Monopoly board was a mine of information to forensic scientists. Soon the faces of the robbers were on posters all over Britain.

Within a year of the robbery, most of the gang were in jail. The 30-year sentences which were meted out for 'a crime against society' shook the thieves – and even created a measure of public sympathy for them. Goody, Welch, James, Wisbey and Hussey all got 30 years, although they were eventually released after serving 12 of them. Cordrey got 14 years and was freed after seven. But the robbers who gave police the most trouble were Reynolds, Buster Edwards, Wilson, White and Biggs.

With his paratrooper's training, White went on the run in England, taking with him his wife and baby son. He evaded capture for three years but, with his money stolen or blackmailed from him by 'friends', he was almost glad to be caught. He was captured while working as an odd-job man on the Kent coast, and in 1965 was jailed for 18 years. He eventually served only nine of them.

Reynolds and Edwards also evaded arrest, even though their names and faces were known to every policeman in Britain. They hid out in London for almost a year, then fled with their wives and children to Mexico City. Edwards even underwent plastic surgery to alter his appearance. But their money was being spent at a frightening rate and their life as exiles began to pall.

Both eventually returned to Britain. At the end of 1966 Edwards gave himself up to police. He was given a 15-year sentence and served nine years. Reynolds was arrested in Torquay, Devon, in 1968 – five years after the robbery. Chief Superintendent Tommy Butler of the Flying Squad knocked on the door of the Reynolds' home at 6 o'clock on a November morning and said: 'Hello, Bruce – it's been a long time.' Two months later Reynolds appeared in court and was sentenced to 25 years in jail. He was released in 1978.

Life in prison was never easy for any of the train robbers. They were all kept under the closest security because of two sensational escapes. Wilson was sentenced, along with the rest of the gang, to 30 years' imprisonment in 1964.

He remained in jail for just one year. He escaped, with outside help, from Winson Green Prison, Birmingham, and joined Reynolds and Edwards in Mexico City. But, like his friends, he tired of the place and settled down under a false name with his wife and three daughters in a smart suburban home near Montreal, Canada. But early in the morning of January 25, 1968, Chief Superintendent Tommy Butler arrived at the front door. Behind him, and surrounding the house, were 50 men of the Royal Canadian Mounted Police. Wilson was flown back to England to continue his 30-year sentence. He was also released in 1978.

Apart from the few members of the gang who had never been caught and convicted, the arrest of Wilson and Reynolds and the surrender of Edwards left only one man still wanted by the police – Biggs, the small-time crook who had been lured by the glittering promise of the crime of the century was sentenced to 30 years' jail along with Goody and the rest. In July 1965 he was out of prison again – 'sprung' by an armed gang who broke into London's Wandsworth Prison. He fled to Australia with his wife and children. But later, with the police not far behind him, he moved on to Brazil, leaving his family in Melbourne.

Early in 1974 a reporter of a London newspaper tracked down Biggs and set about writing his story. Unbeknown to the reporter, however, the newspaper's executives had tipped off Scotland Yard about the scoop they were about to break. As a result, on February 1, 1974, Chief Superintendent Jack Slipper and another police officer arrived in Rio de Janeiro to arrest Biggs.

The former Train Robbery Squad officer was soon given a new title by the British press: Chief Superintendent Slip-up. For Brazil had no extradition agreement with Britain, and the Rio police refused to hand over Biggs. Then Biggs's young Brazilian girlfriend announced that she was pregnant. The father of a Brazilian child could not be deported. After his much-publicised swoop, Slipper flew home empty-handed. And the last – though probably the least – of the Great Train Robbers went free.

Police in Venezuela issued a warrant for the arrest of a known criminal. Unfortunately for them, the man's house was built slap across the Venezuela-Colombia border.

When they called to arrest him, he ran into his bedroom, locked the door and phoned his lawyer. The bedroom was in Colombian territory, and the offence with which he was to be charged was not punishable in that country.

The Venezuelan police gave up.

Hans van Meegeren.

Kings of the art forgers

Fake 'Old Masters' have fooled dealers and even museums

Brimming with confidence, David Stein walked into the shop of a well-established New York art dealer one afternoon with three water-colours under his arm.

The dealer stood back and admired them. He carefully studied the certificates of authentication and was impressed by the signatures on them – 'Marc Chagall'. There was some discussion over money, and a cheque for $10,000 was handed over.

Both men parted happily – the dealer because he had bought the paintings so cheaply, Stein because he had got rid of three more fakes.

Those three 'Chagalls' had not even existed seven hours before. Stein had awoken in his New York apartment at six o'clock that morning and remembered that he had an appointment with the dealer at one in the afternoon. So he had decided to get down to a bit of quick forging.

He had 'aged' three sheets of paper with cold tea. Then, after dreaming up suitable subjects, he had polished off the three paintings without a break. He had rushed out to have the paintings framed and, while waiting, had written himself three certificates of authentication. Then he had gone off to keep his appointment with the dealer.

That day's forgeries had been in the style of Chagall, but they could equally have been based on the work of a dozen artists from Renoir to Gauguin. Stein could turn his hand to them all. And that is where he went wrong.

'If only I had stuck to dead men,' he lamented later. For at the very time that he was selling his three fake water-colours, Chagall was in New York. The Russian-born artist had arrived to see two of his enormous murals erected in the Metropolitan Opera House. The dealer had an appointment to visit him, and he took along the three paintings to show the old artist. Chagall took one look at them and declared: 'Diabolical.'

The police came for Stein that same night. 'They arrived at the front door, and I left through the back with a glass of scotch in my hand,' he said. Stein fled to California, where he was arrested and decided to confess all.

The four-year reign of Stein, king of the art forgers, was at an end. The suave, sophisticated, 31-year-old man-about-town spent 16 months in a New York jail after being indicted on 97 counts of counterfeiting and grand larceny. While inside, he helped the police to form an art-forgery squad.

When he came out of jail in 1968, Stein, who was half-British, half-French, decided to put all such risky ventures behind him. He said goodbye to his three American galleries, his New York apartment and his art earnings of up to $500,000 a year, and returned to Europe. Unfortunately, he did not realise that further charges were awaiting him, and he was sentenced to two-and-a-half years in a French prison.

By the time he came out again, Stein was famous throughout the art world. His bogus Old Masters were much sought after. But he decided to paint and

Railway staff at Wolverhampton station picked up from the platform a note which had been thrown from the window of a passing train.

It read: 'Mr. Russell, of 32 Vale Road, Bloxwich, Staffs, has left the kettle on the stove. Please inform the police.'

The police, duly informed, called at Number 32 to find the kettle on the stove but the gas unlit.

David Stein signing one of his paintings with others in the background.

THE WORLD'S GREATEST MISTAKES

sell his own works in his own style. He was instantly successful, and set up homes and businesses in Paris and London.

Stein remained bitter about the people he saw as the real fakers – the pretentious phoneys of the art world.

'People who buy a painting and find out that they have made a mistake are angry because they have displayed their own ignorance,' he said. 'About two or three hundred of my works are still on the market as originals. I see them in dealers' catalogues, in salerooms and even in museums. A lot of the art world is fake.'

Just how much of the contents of museums and art galleries is fake, and just how much is genuine, we shall never know. The art forgers are just too clever for most experts.

America's Cleveland Museum of Art had to remove from display one of its most prized possessions, a wooden Madonna and Child, supposedly carved in Italy in the 13th century. In fact, it was carved around 1920 by an Italian art restorer, Alceo Dossena. His fake was only discovered in 1928 when the sculpture was X-rayed and modern nails were found to be imbedded in the wood.

The museum put the Madonna and Child in its basement and looked around for other works to replace it. Three weeks later it bought a marble statue of Athena for $120,000. It too was a Dossena fake.

In 1918 the New York Metropolitan Museum of Art paid $40,000 for a seven-foot statue of an Etruscan warrior which had supposedly been buried since pre-Roman days. One arm of the warrior was missing, as was the thumb of his other hand.

In 1960 Alfredo Fioravanti confessed to the museum that he was one of six men who had created the statue between them 50 years earlier. He produced the warrior's missing thumb to prove it. The thumb fitted perfectly.

In 1975 the same museum had to withdraw from display a beautiful 'Greek' bronze horse when it was shown to be a fake. The horse had been one of the museum's most popular attractions.

Among the most renowned art forgers of this century was the hard-drinking Dutchman, Hans van Meegeren. His exploits came to light after World War Two, when he was put on trial for helping the Nazis. He had sold to Hermann Goering for $150,000 an exquisite painting purporting to be by the Dutch master Vermeer.

Van Meegeren's answer to the charges of complicity made against him was that he had not sold a Vermeer but a Van Meegeren. The painting was a fake – and it was only one of dozens that he had sold for vast sums around the world.

At first, the judge did not believe him. But he gave the painter a chance to prove his boast. Van Meegeren was placed under guard in his Amsterdam studio and told to paint another Vermeer that could fool the experts. He did so, and was freed.

The master forger's freedom was short-lived, however. As more and more Van Meegerens came to light he was brought to trial again – this time on a charge of deception. He was jailed for 12 months, but died before he could complete his sentence.

Even the grand old master Michelangelo is reputed to have raised much-needed funds as a struggling young man by selling to a Rome cardinal a statue of Cupid which the artist had first stained and buried to age it into an 'antique'.

Perhaps the most prolific forger of sculptures was Giovanni Bastianini, who, before his death in 1868, turned out terracotta busts by the dozen under contract to an art dealer. They were considered to be perfect examples of Renaissance sculpture, and the Florentine faker's works appeared in museums around the world. There are still two in London's Victoria and Albert Museum.

In 1977 a beautiful wooden carving of a kneeling stag was given pride of place in the antiques department of Harrods, the department store in London. It was reputed to have come from a French château and to have been carved around 1580. The price tag was £9,800.

Then Frank Sedgwick, a 47-year-old ex-fitter whose hobby was woodwork, walked into the store and said: 'That's mine.'

What was claimed to be a fine example of 16th-century craftsmanship had been knocked up by Sedgwick in a fortnight. He had carved it five years earlier at his home in the Kent village of Petham and had sold it for £165. It had changed hands several times since, and each time its antiquity and its price had grown – until Harrods accepted it for sale. After Sedgwick's visit, they removed it.

Famous faker Clifford Irving (see page 144), the American author jailed for his forged biography of Howard Hughes, once wrote another biography, entitled *Fake*. It was about the exploits of a stateless Hungarian, Elmyr de Hory, whose paintings have hung in dozens of galleries around the world.

The book reported that De Hory's paintings were among millions of dollars'

In 1928, Liberian President Charles King put himself up for re-election. He was returned with an officially stated majority of 600,000 votes. King's opponent in the poll, Thomas Faulkner, later claimed that the election had been rigged. When asked to substantiate his allegations, Faulkner pointed out that it was difficult to win a 600,000 majority with an electorate of less than 15,000.

THE WORLD'S GREATEST MISTAKES

> The Reverend Edgar Dodson, of Camden, Arkansas, chose
> for a sermon the theme 'Thou shalt not steal'. While he was
> preaching, someone stole his car.

worth of fakes sold to a Texan millionaire. The ensuing scandal made De Hory
famous, although he says firmly that he had never tried to pass his work off
as someone else's: that is, he has never put a famous signature to one of his
own paintings, even when that painting has been in the precise style of a
sought-after artist.

In 1974, at the age of 60, De Hory was taken from his home on the island of
Ibiza and put into jail in Majorca. There was no formal charge, and he was
out again after four months.

Like so many with his talents, he never disguised his contempt for the
international art pundits who 'know more about fine words than fine art'.
He claimed he could paint a portrait in 45 minutes, draw a 'Modigliani' in
ten, and then immediately produce a 'Matisse'.

'The dealers, the experts and the critics resent my talents,' he said, 'because
they don't want it shown how easily they can be fooled. I have tarnished the
infallible image they rely upon for their fortunes.'

Even distinguished experts of the most famous art gallery in the world, the
Louvre, in Paris, have been taken for a costly ride. The gallery's worst blunder
was revealed in 1903 when a Parisian painter claimed that he was the creator
of one of its most treasured possessions – a beautifully intricate golden headdress called the Tiara of Saitaphernes.

The claim was untrue. The tiara was a fake, sure enough. But the man who
had made it was not the Parisian painter. Its creator was a Russian goldsmith,
Israel Rouchomowsky – and he did not want the false claimant to take credit
for his work. So Rouchomowsky travelled to Paris to put the record straight.
The administrators of the Louvre continued to deny that the tiara was a fake,
until the old Russian produced the original designs he had drawn for the
headdress eight years earlier – and, to rub salt into open wounds, began
working on a new tiara, as intricate in every detail as that in the Louvre.

In the Louvre today hangs what must be the best-known and best-loved
painting in the world. It is also one of the most copied. It is the Mona Lisa.
In 1911, the famous smiling lady was stolen. Three thieves, dressed as workmen, had walked casually into the gallery before it shut one evening and had
hidden in a basement room. The next day, the Louvre was closed for cleaning.
The 'workmen' wandered into the hall where the painting was hung, took it
off the wall and walked out of the gallery carrying it, frame and all.

Of the three men, only one had been in this line of business before. He was Vincenzo Perugia, an Italian burglar. The other two were art forgers Yves Chaudron and Eduardo de Valfierno, who had developed their forgery techniques in South America. There, they would interest a crooked dealer or collector in a particular painting at a gallery and promise to obtain it for him, at the right price. The two would then present themselves at the gallery as art experts and take the painting down in order to study it. They would then produce an exact copy, attach it to the back of the genuine painting, and invite their prospective buyer to the gallery to put his mark surreptitiously on the back of the canvas. Later they would remove the fake from the original and take it to the client. There, on the back of the canvas, the buyer would see the mark he had made – the 'proof' that he was getting the genuine article.

In each case, the gallery experts were none the wiser – they still had their original – and the buyer, when he discovered he had been tricked, could hardly complain to the police.

Chaudron and Valfierno switched their operations to the world's art capital, Paris. There, they went one stage further with their elaborate deceptions. They printed phoney pages of newspapers, which included stories about valuable paintings having been stolen. They would show the stories to gullible collectors and then sell them forgeries of the 'stolen' works.

Finally, the tricksters decided that they were ready for their biggest coup. They would forge the Mona Lisa. But this time they would make sure that the buyers would never later be confronted by the genuine article and discover they had been tricked. For this time Chaudron and Valfierno would steal the original.

They recruited Perugia into their gang and, within months of pulling off their amazing robbery, they had forged six Mona Lisas and sold them to gullible Americans for $300,000 each.

Chaudron and Valfierno still had the genuine treasure hidden, but whether they planned to destroy it, sell it, or even return it, will never be known. Their accomplice, Perugia, stole it from them and fled to Italy, where he clumsily tried to sell it himself.

The gang were uncovered and the Mona Lisa was returned to the Louvre, where, under heavy guard, behind a thick glass panel, and surrounded by electronic alarms, it remains today.

STRIP CLUBS SHOCK.
MAGISTRATES MAY ACT ON INDECENT SHOWS.
– Daily Mirror

Multi-millionaire Howard Hughes.

The Howard Hughes hoax

Publishers paid a fortune for an autobiography that never was

Hey, listen to this ... I've just had a wild idea.' The words were spoken by author Clifford Irving as he drove to a bar near his home on the Mediterranean island of Ibiza. Irving, crouched behind the wheel of his battered grey Simca, excitedly outlined to his friend Richard Susskind the idea for the publishing coup of the decade – the autobiography of the richest eccentric in the world, the legendary Howard Hughes.

If only they could get Hughes to talk, however briefly, they would have done what no one else had dared to try, and make themselves rich and famous into the bargain.

In fact, they failed to speak to the multi-millionaire. And the only coup that Irving pulled off was something quite different from the publishing coup of

'Biographer' Clifford Irving.

> **Pauline Jenkins had a 'hell of a shock' on her wedding night
> when she discovered that her husband was a woman. 'I
> threatened to leave there and then,' she said. 'But I went
> downstairs and made a cup of tea instead.'**
>
> *– News of the World*

the decade – it was the publishing hoax of the century.

Because Hughes would not speak to him, Irving did the next best thing he could think of. He wrote Hughes's autobiography himself, inventing most of it and lifting the rest from published material on Hughes.

Irving's logic was simple. Hughes was ageing, sick, possibly drug-addicted and, most important of all, a fanatical recluse who would allow no one near him apart from the small bodyguard of Mormon male nurses who cared for and protected him in a succession of hotel-suite hideaways around the world. If Hughes wished to challenge anything anyone wrote about him, he would have to appear in a courtroom. And Hughes would never break his long years of hermit-like existence to do that.

So what was there to stop Irving from making up his own Hughes 'autobiography', with reams of 'quotes' from the multi-millionaire, and selling it for a fortune?

Irving had always been a romantic, his imagination outrunning his moral scruples. Born in New York in 1930, he went to art college, where he displayed a slight talent – a talent that, many years later, was to equip him for the role of forger. He graduated from Cornell University in 1951 and announced that he was off to see the world. An incurable adventurer, he sailed the Atlantic, lived with California's beatniks and Kashmir's drop-outs, and ended up with his slim, blonde wife Edith living and writing on the fashionable Spanish island of Ibiza.

The publishers of Irving's books were McGraw-Hill of New York, and they looked after him well. They advanced him money when he ran short and they gave him help and encouragement when his efforts seemed to be flagging. It was to McGraw-Hill that Irving turned when he came up with his 'coup'.

Irving wrote to the publishers telling them that he had sent a copy of one of his earlier books to Hughes for his comments. The recluse had replied – and the author had quickly followed up with an offer to 'ghost' his autobiography. Surprisingly, Hughes had agreed. Would McGraw-Hill be interested?

McGraw-Hill certainly were interested, and the deal was struck. Hughes was to get a payment for allowing a series of tape-recorded interviews. In addition, hefty advance payments were to be made to Irving.

The whole lot – money for Hughes and advances and expenses for Irving – added up to about $1½ million. And it went straight into the author's pocket. It was frittered away by Irving and his friend Susskind on lavish holidays and junketing in Europe, the Caribbean and Central America. Wherever Irving went, he claimed to be fixing secret meetings with Hughes or his associates. In reality, he was staying at the best hotels, eating the best food, dining with the most beautiful women – and spending money as if it were going out of fashion.

Over the months, he countered inquiries from McGraw-Hill by pointing out Hughes's pathetic insistence on secrecy. And he cleverly kept his publishers interested – and quiet – by sending them sample manuscripts, letters apparently signed by Hughes, and tantalising details of the recluse's private life.

The manuscripts contained, quite simply, lies – quotations supposedly transcribed from fictional tape-recordings made by Irving in conversation with Hughes. But cleverly intertwined with these outright lies were half-truths and rumours embroidered from newspaper cuttings.

The letters signed by Hughes were really written by Irving to himself. But so clever were the forgeries that, when McGraw-Hill showed them to New York's leading handwriting analysts, they endorsed them as Hughes's.

The details Irving gave in memos about the recluse's private life were the only elements of fact in this otherwise great work of fiction. But these hitherto unpublished revelations did not come from Hughes's own tongue, or even from Irving's own researches. They were lifted from the memoirs of a former Hughes aide, Noah Dietrich. These memoirs, which Dietrich had been

Edith Sommer-Irving, wife and accomplice of Clifford Irving.

planning to turn into a book of his own, were secretly borrowed' by Irving, who milked them of some of their more interesting anecdotes.

The picture that Irving and Susskind had so far built up of Hughes was a dramatic one. According to Irving's information, the recluse was a far more glamorous character than the self-tortured misanthrope everyone imagined him to be in the last few years of his life. For instance, according to Irving, Hughes had flown secret missions from Britain during World War Two, had had a long and close friendship with novelist Ernest Hemingway, with whom he shared adventures and reminiscences, and, even during his silent years, was globe-trotting the sun-spots of the world having fun and games. All nonsense, of course, but just the material to make the book sell. McGraw-Hill were eager to publish.

The publishers kept pouring the money into Irving's pockets. The cheques that they made out to Hughes were quickly soaked up from the Swiss account in which they were deposited. The account, in the name of H. R. Hughes, had in fact been opened by Edith Irving using a passport forged for her by Clifford.

The goldmine suddenly ran out in 1971. By the most phenomenal coincidence, someone else had been dreaming up the same plot as Irving, and a rival publishing house announced that an official autobiography of Hughes was on its way.

Panic reigned at McGraw-Hill, as it did at the offices of the Time-Life organisation, who had agreed to buy the serialisation rights of the Irving book for a vast sum. Irving tried to confuse the issue by producing a new forged letter from Hughes demanding extra money for the final tapes and denouncing the rival book as a fake. McGraw-Hill once again fell for Irving's bland assurances of his sincerity – but they themselves had to announce the existence of their own Hughes autobiography for the first time.

The fat was in the fire. The Hughes organisation arranged a press conference at which reporters who had followed the saga of the billionaire recluse over the years were invited to put questions to Hughes himself over a direct telephone link. At the same time, Swiss banking authorities were investigating Edith Irving, alias 'Helga Hughes', who had drawn so much money out of the H. Hughes account in Zurich.

A man who had been deaf in one ear from the age of three was eventually cured when he changed his doctor. The man, a factory worker from Bridgwater, Somerset, was being examined by his new doctor when a cork popped out of his right ear. He said: 'I must have put it there when I was a child.'

Irving held out for as long as he could. But his lies and denials were finally seen for what they were when beautiful Danish singer Nina, once famous as part of the husband-and-wife folk duo Nina and Frederick, revealed that at a time when Irving claimed he had been meeting Hughes, the author had really been with her.

Irving confessed. Susskind, the man who had helped him set up the literary hoax of all time, was jailed in New York for six months. Irving was fined £4,000 and sentenced to two-and-a-half years in prison. His wife was sentenced to two years and a similar fine.

Clifford Irving maintained his remarkable sense of romantic melodrama right to the end. After hearing Edith sentenced, he sobbed: 'I have put my wife in jeopardy. She has suffered terribly. I have heard her cry herself to sleep at night.' Then he began planning yet another money-making project – a book about his $1½ million super-hoax.

And the man whose fabulous wealth made all these dreams of avarice possible? Hughes died on a jet between Mexico and Texas in 1976, with the full story of his mysterious life still untold.

The man they couldn't hang

A series of blunders allowed John Lee to cheat the hangman and live out his life in peace. For Lee has gone down in history as the man they could not hang. Three times, murderer Lee stood on the newly built scaffold at Exeter Jail on February 23, 1885 – and three times the trap-door failed to open. Each time, Lee, 19, was taken back to his cell, engineers inspected the trap-door, the executioner pulled the handle, and, without Lee on the scaffold, the mechanism worked perfectly.

Lee had his death sentence commuted to life imprisonment. He was released after 22 years and later emigrated to America, where he died.

The theory for Lee's amazing good fortune is that when prisoners were helping to build the new scaffold they nailed a warped board underneath the planking. This board was beneath the spot where the chaplain stood while the prisoner was on the scaffold. The chaplain's weight would press out the board so that its end would cover the end of the trap-door and prevent it from opening.

Each time the engineers tested the trap-door they blundered in not having someone on the warped board where the chaplain had stood.

The £32 million 'mouse'

Lowly clerk gambled away a giant bank's assets

Few people in the world of high finance had heard of Marc Colombo. There was no reason why they should have done. He was just one of 59,000 names on the payroll of Lloyds Bank, a lowly foreign-exchange dealer in the Swiss backwater of Lugano.

But in September 1974, Colombo hit the headlines all over the world in a way that left hard-headed money experts open-mouthed in amazement. Lloyds Bank International announced that 'irregularities' at Lugano, the smallest of their 170 overseas branches, had forced them to suspend both Colombo and branch manager Egidio Mombelli – and had cost the bank a staggering £32 million.

It was the biggest loss ever announced by a bank in Switzerland, and a loss unprecedented in the history of British banking. The news wiped £20 million from Lloyds' London shares and left their top officials in despair over the loophole that had allowed it to happen.

What had the handsome 28-year-old wheeler-dealer been up to? And how had he got away with it?

Colombo was a little man with big ideas. He watched as the world's leading currencies daily changed their values on the foreign-exchange market, offering enticing opportunities for men shrewd and brave enough to buy when the price was right and sell at a profit. He decided to grab a piece of the action for his bank.

The 1973 Middle East War and the subsequent Arab oil embargo had sent exchange rates haywire, and Colombo was convinced that the dollar would lose value against the strong, stable Swiss franc. So, in November 1973, he plugged into the international phone network of money dealers and struck what is known as a forward deal.

He contracted to buy 34 million U.S. dollars with Swiss francs in three months' time. If, as he expected, the dollar was worth less when the time came to settle, he could buy back his francs with cheap dollars. But the dollar's value did not tumble. It went up. And Colombo lost seven million francs on the deal – about £1 million. A lot of money to a £9,000-a-year clerk, but not a lot, he reasoned, to a bank which had just announced half-year profits of £78 million.

Colombo, who had worked at the branch for less than a year, knew that reporting the loss to his boss, Mombelli, would probably get him the sack.

So he decided to increase his stake, and go for double or nothing.

So he began an amazing gambling spree. Without Lloyds suspecting a thing, he used their name and risked their money to set up transactions totalling £4,580 million in just nine months. At first, he was betting that the dollar would lose value. It did not. So he switched to gambling that it would go on rising. It did not.

In most offices, a checking system would soon have put a stop to Colombo's antics. Because most foreign-exchange deals are by phone, they are difficult to monitor, so confirmation in writing is usually sent to a third party at the contracting dealer's office. This ensures that holdings of different currencies can be balanced and risks minimised.

But Lugano had a staff of only 16, and no one, including Signor Mombelli, suspected that Colombo was anything other than a diligent, honest employee.

Colombo continued making deals he was not authorised to make with banks he should not have been dealing with. He was blatantly ignoring the £700,000 daily limit on debts or holdings laid down by head office. He was not covering his gambles on buying with counter-balancing orders to sell. He was using inter-bank swap arrangements to borrow cash to cover up losses. And instead of declaring his transactions in records sent to head office and the Swiss authorities, he was logging them in his diary.

Such madness could not go on forever, and the day of reckoning came in August 1974. A senior French banker mentioned casually to a Lloyds man in London that Lugano 'has reached its limit with us'. Alarm bells began ringing at Lloyds' offices in Queen Victoria Street. A phone check with a German bank revealed that it, too, had had massive unauthorised deals with Lugano.

Top executives left London secretly next morning. Unannounced, they confronted Colombo, Mombelli and Karl Senft, the man in charge of all three of Lloyds' Swiss branches. They seized all the papers they could find and flew back to London with the three Swiss employees.

Painstakingly, officials worked all weekend, unravelling the intricate and costly web Colombo had woven. To their horror, they found that he had contracted speculative forward deals worth £235 million which were still unpaid. And he had not hedged his bets. He had committed the bank to

---

A Louisiana firm was given an old mattress to renovate. The workers had already thrown away and burned a lot of the old stuffing when they came across $20,000 hidden in the remainder. They returned this money to its forgetful owner; the other $6,000 he had hidden they had burned.

risking a sum 'largely in excess of the combined capital and reserves of all three banks in Switzerland'. Yet the official ledgers showed deals worth only £36,000.

With special permission from the Governor of the Bank of England, Lloyds transferred huge sums of money to Lugano to cover the promises Colombo had made. Then the bank's international money market director, Robert Gras, spent three weeks trying to minimise the damage – secretly, for any leak would have made the delicate operation more difficult and expensive. It was a mammoth task. When at last the books were in order, and all debts had been settled, Lloyds had lost £32 million.

When the bombshell news was announced by chairman Sir Eric Faulkner, Colombo and his wife had fled their luxury villa on a mountainside above Lake Lugano. Mombelli too had disappeared on an 'extensive holiday'.

But a year later they were both in court in Lugano, facing charges of criminal mis-management, falsification of documents and violations of the Swiss banking code. Colombo admitted exceeding his authorised dealing limits and conducting transactions with unauthorised banks, but denied accepting illegal commissions and criminal intent.

The prosecution described Colombo as the mouse that made Lloyds tremble, and accused him of gambling wildly like a man at a casino. He replied: 'Being a foreign-exchange dealer is always a hazardous operation. It is a gambler's profession.'

When questioned about how his losses had snowballed, he said: 'There was the pride of the foreign-exchange dealer who will not admit failure. I was at all times convinced that I could recoup my losses, but it only takes a little unforeseen something to upset the market. I was a prisoner of events.'

Mombelli, 41, made no secret of the fact that, all along, he had not really understood what was happening. He had initialled papers without realising their significance. The judge described him as 'a disaster, a bank manager without brains'. But Mombelli said after the trial: 'It's a foreign-exchange Mafia. For every dealer you need at least four administrators to check what he is doing. They do things that no ordinary banker understands.'

Lloyds in London were astonished when the two men walked free from the

---

In accordance with his usual custom, an unknown benefactor walked into the Church Army offices, handed over a cheque for £500 and left without waiting for thanks.

As large numbers of these parasites are around at this season, it may be useful to give some hints as how to exterminate them.

– *Western Daily Press*

---

court. Colombo was given an 18-month suspended sentence and Mombelli one of six months, and they were fined only £300 each, because the judge accepted that they were not lining their own pockets.

Colombo's only motive seems to have been to boost his own ego. Even if his wheeler-dealering had ended in profit, he would still have faced dismissal for unauthorised use of the bank's money. And a profit, after all, had not been an impossible dream for the young Colombo. . . . He later claimed that if his deals had been allowed to stand they would, through later developments on the foreign-exchange market, have netted Lloyds Bank £11 million profit.

Dirty works afoot

Sexually explicit literature fills the bookstores of Australia, as it does those of most major nations of the world. But it is not so long ago that a severe literary censorship operated in the country.

Within the present era, for instance, even posters simply portraying Michelangelo's classic nude statue of David were seized in a police raid on an Australian bookstore. And there have been as many as 5,000 books at a time on the country's 'banned' list, among them Aldous Huxley's *Brave New World*, Ernest Hemingway's *A Farewell To Arms* and Daniel Defoe's *Moll Flanders*.

But the petty purges on 'licentious' literature were on one occasion shown up for what they were. The law was made to look an ass by blundering into an elaborately laid hoax.

It happened in 1944 at a time when censorship was at its most oppressive. Arousing police suspicion in that year was an extremely progressive literary journal called *Angry Penguins*, published in Adelaide. One day its two editors, Max Harris and John Reed, received at their office a remarkable cultural scoop. It came in the form of a package from one Ethel Malley and contained a mass of avant-garde poetry written by her brother Ern before his death in obscure poverty at the age of 25.

Harris and Reed were so impressed with their new find that they published a special edition of their journal 'to commemorate the Australian poet Ern Malley'. When the journal was issued, two young Sydney poets laughed themselves hoarse. For they were the real authors of the 'poems', which had been composed by stringing together meaningless words and phrases at random.

The two hoaxers planned to keep their secret for a while, to prolong exposure of the experts who were so quick to praise such gibberish. But events overtook them. For South Australian police seized copies of the journal and accused Harris, as editor of the poems, of publishing indecent matter.

In court, the detective who had impounded this volume of nonsense interpreted one of the poems as being about a man who went around at night with a torch. 'I think there is a suggestion of indecency about this poem,' he said. 'I have found that people who go around parks at night do so for immoral purposes. In fact, the whole thing is indecent.'

Of another poem the detective said: 'The word incestuous is used. I don't know what it means but I regard it as being indecent.'

Harris was convicted and the detective was commended for his 'zealousness and competency'.

Brotherhood of fear

Compensation of $30,000 launched the multi-billion-dollar Mafia

No one knows for certain where the word comes from. It may be derived from a Sicilian dialect term for boldness, bluster, swank or swagger, or from the Arabic 'mehia', which means boastful. But wherever it originated, the word Mafia now means only one thing: fear.

The Mafia is the largest, most successful criminal organisation in the world. And it spells fear not only for its victims and its unwilling customers, but also for its members.

The autocratic society of the Mafia began as a resistance movement in 13th-century Sicily. It flourished over the centuries as a secret brotherhood which protected Sicilians against a succession of invaders. To the foreigners' despotism the islanders preferred even the Mafia's perverted system of justice.

By the 1940s the Mafia was so powerful that it could 'fix' the Italian Army and hand over the whole of Western Sicily to the Allies without a shot being fired.

But it is in the USA that the Mafia's grip is now the most frightening, powerful and insidious. And its reign of terror in that country dates back to two sad but well-meant blunders made by U.S. governments half a century apart.

The first was made in New Orleans in 1890 when 11 immigrant Mafiosi were lynched. Naively, the U.S. government paid $30,000 compensation to the widows of the hanged men. But the money was seized by the criminal brotherhood to launch their first organised operation of extortion.

The second blunder was Prohibition in the 1920s. In unison, the fragmented Mafia families leaped at the opportunity of supplying bootleg liquor to help 'dry' America drown its sorrows during the Depression. By the time the law was repealed in 1933, the Mafia had branched out into other criminal activities like vice, gambling and 'protection'. And when there was no longer a market in illicit liquor, the brotherhood put their amassed fortunes into seemingly respectable businesses.

The Mafia families rule by fear – often fear of each other. The gang warfare of the 1930s alerted Americans to the size of the problem in their midst. The biggest gang killing was in September 1931 when Salvatore Maranzano, head of the senior Mafia family, was murdered along with 40 of his men. But such killings also alerted the Mafiosi themselves to the dangers of advertising their power in blood.

Leaders of Mafia groups from the Atlantic to the Pacific got together to form 'The Commission', a loose-knit group of about a dozen members who respresent the nation's 24 Mafia 'families'. Always at their head is 'Il Capo di Tutti Capi', the Boss of Bosses, whose job it is to keep the younger and more fiery members in line.

The role of Il Capo di Tutti Capi was glamorised in the book and film *The Godfather*, which used as their inspiration for the title role the story of a frail old man, Carlo Gambino. Under Gambino's severe but diplomatic guidance,

> **Police at Southend, Essex, raced for their patrol cars after a woman phoned their station to report that she had seen a saloon car driving by with a body protruding from the boot.**
> **The police eventually caught up with and flagged down the car, which had two legs sticking out of its boot.**
> **Their owner turned out to be a helpful garage mechanic who was trying to trace a rattle for the car's driver.**

> **WE DISPENSE WITH ACCURACY.**
>   – sign in London chemist's shop window

the Mafia flourished. He frowned on public killings, and he excluded from the families hot-headed young bloods. During his reign, there were few ritual oaths: scraps of paper burning in a new member's hand while he recites, 'This is the way I will burn if I betray the secrets of this family.'

In 1976 Carlo Gambino died peacefully in his bed at the age of 73 – and new and less respected members of the fraternity fought to become his successor. Fifty new members were immediately invited to take the oath of allegiance. And the killings began again, although more quietly and never on the scale of the 1930s gang wars.

U.S. police and government agencies have sought consolation from the Mafia's low-key approach of recent years, and they have noted with satisfaction the following facts. More than 800 members were jailed during the 1970s. In Chicago, warring families almost wiped each other out – 22 died between 1974 and 1978. In New York, the Mafia lost control of vast areas of crime, and throughout the States, its grip seemed to be slackening.

But this victory is largely illusory. The brotherhood is still so powerful that the bill for keeping Mafiosi hit-men away from the 2,000 'squealers' prepared to give evidence to the government is a staggering $20 million a year.

Moreover, the Mafia can accept the loss of a few dozen members a year to the police and FBI, since it has 3,000–5,000 criminals working for it across the country. And it can write off the loss of some of its vice and drug activities because it owns as many as 10,000 legitimate firms, producing profits estimated at $12 billion a year. That fantastic sum is five times the profits of America's largest industrial corporation, Exxon.

In the United States today, people may start their lives wrapped in a Mafia-produced nappy, listen to rock music from a Mafia record company, dine out on a Mafia steak, drive a car bought from a Mafia dealer, holiday at a Mafia hotel, buy a house on a Mafia-financed development and be buried by a Mafia funeral parlour.

Even the $12 billion a year raised from these activities is small-fry compared to the brotherhood's profits from crime. In an exhaustive survey, *Time* magazine reckoned that the Mafia takes in at least $48 billion, of which $25 billion is untaxed profit; and that, because of the mob's grip on the market, the average citizen has to pay an extra two per cent for almost everything he buys.

That is the price of a problem which a naive government tried to buy off for $30,000 in 1890.

Psst! Want to buy the Eiffel Tower?

Con-man sold Paris's most famous landmark - twice

I f there is indeed a fool born every minute, for every fool there seems to be a con-man ready to make him a little wiser.

Two of the most extraordinary confidence tricksters of all time were Count Victor Lustig, an Austrian who worked in the French Ministry of Works, and Daniel Collins, a small-time American crook. Together they managed to sell the Eiffel Tower – not once, but twice.

The count set about pulling off the deal by booking a suite in a Paris hotel in the spring of 1925 and inviting five businessmen to meet him there. When they arrived he made them take vows of secrecy, then told them that the Eiffel Tower was in a dangerous condition and would have to be pulled down. He asked for tenders for the scrap metal contained in the famous landmark. The count explained the hotel meeting and the secrecy vow by saying that his ministry wanted to avoid any public outcry over the demolition of such a well-loved national monument.

Within the week, all bids were in and the count accepted that of scrap merchant André Poisson. The deal was struck, and a banker's draft was handed over at a final meeting at which the count introduced his 'secretary', Collins.

141

THE WORLD'S GREATEST MISTAKES

Then the con-men played their master-stroke. They asked Poisson for a bribe to help the deal go smoothly through official channels. The duped dealer agreed willingly, and gave the back-hander in cash. If he had ever had any suspicions, they were now wholly allayed. After all, a demand for a bribe meant that the two men must be from the ministry.

Lustig and Collins were out of the country within 24 hours. But they stayed abroad only long enough to realise that the outcry they had expected to follow their fraud had not happened. Poisson was so ashamed at being taken for a ride that he never reported the hoax to the police.

The count and his partner returned to Paris and repeated the trick. They sold the Eiffel Tower all over again to another gullible scrap merchant. This time the man did go to the police, and the con-men fled. They were never brought to justice, and they never revealed just how much money they had got away with.

Lustig's exploits may well have been inspired by a Scot, Arthur Furguson. Within a couple of months, in 1923, he sold three London landmarks to different American tourists. Buckingham Palace went for £2,000 deposit, Big Ben for £1,000 and Nelson's Column for £6,000.

He emigrated to the United States in 1925. In Washington, he found a Texas cattleman admiring the White House and, pretending to be a government agent, spun a slender yarn about how the administration was looking for

ways of cutting costs. Now, if the Texan would care to rent the White House at a knockdown rate of $100,000 a year . . .? Furguson was in business again.

The Scotsman moved to New York where he explained to an Australian visitor that, because of a widening scheme for New York Harbour, the Statue of Liberty would have to be dismantled and sold. A great loss to the USA, but would it not look grand in Sydney Harbour . . .?

The Australian immediately began to raise the $100,000 that the con-man asked for the statue. But his bankers advised him to make a few further inquiries, and the police were tipped off.

Furguson was arrested, and a court sentenced him to five years in jail. When he came out, the master-hoaxer retired from the ancient-monuments business and, until his death in 1938, he lived in California – languishing in luxury on his ill-gotten gains.

All that glittered was not gold

Greed over-rode commercial commonsense among the backers who queued to pour cash into the pockets of two German tricksters – Franz Tausend and Heinrich Kurschaldgen. For the pair claimed that they could manufacture gold.

Tausend and Kurschalden never worked together, but they both used similar methods to prise cash out of the wallets of the gullible.

Tausend was a former travelling tinker who had briefly studied chemistry in Zurich. His claim that he could make gold by mixing lead and solder was so convincing that level-headed businessmen and even aristocrats contributed to his Chemical Research Society.

One of the original backers was influential Rhineland industrialist Alfred Mannesmann, who paid £5,000 into the society. Another was Erich Ludendorff, the famous World War One general, who saw Tausend's discovery as a way of easing Germany's war debts.

For a short time, Tausend paid dividends on investors' cash so that none of them would realise they were being led up the garden path. But then the double-talking tinker became greedy. With the £125,000 he had collected, he bought two magnificent castles near Bolzano, Italy, and fitted them out

143

THE WORLD'S GREATEST MISTAKES

with the best that money could buy. His ex-waitress wife even assumed the title of baroness.

Reports of the lavish hospitality offered at the castles made investors suspicious and they began to investigate. They had Tausend arrested and brought back to Germany. In 1931, he was convicted of fraud and jailed for three years and eight months.

While Tausend was living in style in Italy, Kurschaldgen was also enjoying the good life by claiming that he could make gold and even radium. Kurschaldgen, who had not studied chemistry since his schooldays, relied on his eloquence and impressive laboratory equipment to dupe the wealthy of north-west Germany and beyond into financing his work.

He had a simple method of convincing hard-headed businessmen that he could manufacture gold. In demonstrations at his laboratory, investors saw him mix flasks of sand and water. The mixture was turned into gold by an electric current. Only later was it discovered that tiny grains of gold had secretly been added to the water.

Kurschaldgen was reputed to have made about £10,000 from his regular investors. A British consortium was hoodwinked into paying him £50 a month, and an American millionaire offered him £50,000 for the secret of his discovery.

But, like Tausend, Kurschaldgen became greedy. He began to live the high life – and to give the game away. He was brought before a court at Dusseldorf in 1930 and jailed for 18 months.

Chapter
Four

Victors
and Vanquished

The Japanese attacked Pearl Harbor and found the defenders sadly unprepared. The U.S. 7th Cavalry attacked Sitting Bull's camp at Little Bighorn and found the defenders surprisingly well prepared. The story of war is full of mistakes – mistakes that have cost dearly in wasted lives.

The rise and fall of General Custer

Vanity led him to death in the ill-fated 'Last Stand'

General George Armstrong Custer was known by the Indians as Pahuska, the 'Long-Haired One', because of the flowing straw-coloured locks of which he was so proud. He was also known as 'Hard Backsides' because of the long chases he made without leaving the saddle. But he was best known to the Indians of the North American Plains as a callous mass-killer – an annihilator of entire tribes.

Custer, who was in command of the famous U.S. 7th Cavalry, gained his bloody reputation when, in 1868, he was sent by General Philip Sheridan, the 'Angry Bear' of the frontier forts, to subjugate the Plains Indians who refused to be herded into the reservations set by for them. Why Custer should have been picked for this important task is a matter for conjecture. For his career as a soldier had been extremely patchy.

He was born on December 5, 1839, in New Rumley, Ohio. He graduated from the U.S. Military Academy, West Point, and, thanks to the Civil War – in which he distinguished himself by his pursuit of the Confederate Commander-in-Chief, General Robert E. Lee – he soared to the rank of brigadier-general at the age of only 23.

Success went to Custer's head. He became a vain, flamboyant glory-seeker. He grew his blond hair shoulder-length and covered the walls of his

148

room with pictures of himself. When the Civil War ended in 1865, Brigadier-General Custer's ego was severely deflated when he was returned to the rank of captain. He became something of a laughing stock among his men, but within a year had fought his way back to the rank of lieutenant-colonel.

It was then that his self-esteem almost became his undoing. Without consulting senior officers, he decided to take a vacation – and left his camp to visit his wife, Libbie. Custer was court-martialled and suspended for a year without pay. He used the time to write about his own adventures in the most heroic terms. He also ran up bills which, as he later moved from fort to fort, never quite seemed to catch up with him.

In 1868 he was reinstated and given a special mission – one that required tact, diplomacy and compassion. Newly promoted General George Armstrong Custer, aged 28, had none of these virtues, yet he was sent off to solve once and for all the problems of the Plains Indians.

The Indians, mainly Cheyennes and Sioux, had been slowly pushed westwards by land-hungry white men for decades. But in the 1860s, the process was speeded up. This was because roaming bands of Indian buffalo-hunters were becoming an embarrassment to the authorities – despite the fact that land treaties had allowed the Indians this freedom of movement. Now the authorities wanted the land on which the buffalo roamed. It was decided that those Indians who had not so far settled down in reservations to subsist on meagre government handouts must at last be made to toe the line.

Custer was reckoned to be just the man to get the message across.

In the autumn of 1868, a peaceable old chief called Black Kettle, leader of the Southern Cheyennes, settled down with his tribe for the winter on the bank of the Washita River, about 100 miles from the nearest white military outpost, Fort Cobb. He asked that the 200 families within his branch of the tribe be allowed to move to the protection of the fort for the winter, but he was refused. General William Hazen, the fort's commander, told Black Kettle and his deputation to return to the Washita, where they would be allowed to remain until after the snows had melted.

President Lincoln said of General Ambrose Burnside: 'Only he could wring spectacular defeat out of the jaws of victory.' At the Battle of Antietam, during the American Civil War in 1862, Burnside ordered his troops to advance across a narrow bridge over a river. They could hardly cross more than two abreast, and were mown down by Confederate gunners. What Burnside had not considered was that the river was less than three feet deep and his army could have walked across unhindered.

THE WORLD'S GREATEST MISTAKES

The assurance meant nothing. For, in December 1868, Custer was sent in to make an example of Black Kettle's people. Before dawn one foggy morning, Pahuska, the Long-Haired One, ordered his men to surround the Cheyenne camp. When the soldiers appeared through the mist, Black Kettle had his horse saddled and set out alone to parley with them. He did not know that Custer's mission was 'to proceed to Washita River, the winter seat of the hostile tribes, and there to destroy their villages and ponies, kill or hang all warriors and bring back all women and children'.

Black Kettle had hardly left the perimeter of the camp on his mission of peace when the cavalry charged. According to Indian legend, he was shot dead as he raised his hand to halt the approaching soldiers. Custer organised the massacre that followed. His orders were to kill the warriors, but the executions were indiscriminate. More than 100 Cheyennes were shot dead, only about a tenth of them warriors. The rest were women, children and old men. Hundreds of ponies were also slaughtered so that the survivors would have no means of flight. And 50 women and children were taken prisoner.

Fear and hatred of Custer spread among the tribes and was nurtured over the following months as he launched pitiless campaigns against all other Indians in the area.

This then was Custer, the man chosen by Washington to make the West safe for civilised Christians, the man who by treachery and butchery forced the surrender of one tribal chief after another – until he met his match in Sitting Bull.

Tatanka Yotanka, or Sitting Bull, was a leader of the Hunkpapa, the fiercest and most independent branch of the Sioux nation. Sioux means Dakota, and it was there and in neighbouring Montana that Custer discovered he was not invincible.

In 1868, the Black Hills of Dakota had been given for all time to the Indians who lived there. Many tribes considered the hills, the 'Paha Sapa', to be holy places and the centre of the spirit world. The treaty suited the white man in 1868 because he considered them valueless. But it did not suit him six years later when Custer led an expedition into the hills and reported: 'They are full of gold from the grass roots down.' The treaty was immediately disregarded and Custer pushed a trail through to open up the wealth of the Black Hills. The Indians called it the 'Thieves' Road'.

A commission was sent out from Washington to negotiate with the Sioux, Arapahos and Cheyennes who had claims to the Black Hills. But the tribes were not willing to sell their holy ground or to swop it for other territory. Sitting Bull told the commissioners: 'We want to sell none of our land – not even a pinch of dust. The Black Hills belong to us. We want no white men here. If the white man tries to take the hills, we will fight.'

Unable to get the precious Black Hills by fair means, the white man tried foul. The war department issued an ultimatum that any Indians not on their official reservations by the end of January 1876 would be considered hostile and that 'military force will be sent to compel them'. Sitting Bull received news of the ultimatum only three weeks before the deadline and he protested that his tribe could not contemplate moving camp in mid-winter. On February 7 General Sheridan – the man who had once announced that 'the only good Indian is a dead one' – was ordered to attack. And the man he chose to deal the major blow against his most formidable enemy, Sitting Bull, was his faithful executioner, Custer.

Throughout the early months of 1876, roving troops of horse soldiers drove tribes of peaceful Indians out of the Powder River and Tongue River Basins near the Montana-Wyoming border. With their tepees burned, their horses killed and with little warm clothing, the straggling groups of survivors, led by Sitting Bull, gathered in a ragged but proud band in the 'Valley Of The Greasy Grass' – the Little Bighorn valley.

As the army's aims became increasingly obvious, every Indian who was not part of the Little Bighorn camp felt isolated and threatened. Members of tribes who would previously have chosen to remain well apart joined Sitting Bull's settlement. Even Indians who had long since resigned themselves to life on the reservations deserted them in their thousands to flock to the Little Bighorn valley.

According to a white scout, Lewis Dewitt: 'Sitting Bull had a great power over the Sioux. He knew how to lead them. He told the Sioux many times that he was not made to be a reservation Indian. The Great Spirit had made him free to go wherever he wished, to hunt buffalo and to be a leader of his tribe.'

By June of 1876, there were gathered together in the valley Sitting Bull's Hunkpapas, the Oglalas of his ally Crazy Horse, Blackfoot Sioux, Arapahos, Sans Arcs, Brules, Minneconjous and Cheyennes – in a forest of tepees and makeshift tents stretching three miles along the west bank of the Little Bighorn River. There were at least 10,000 Indians, of whom some 3,000 or 4,000 were warriors.

Mrs. Mary Wilson was entertaining friends at No. 10 Downing Street while her husband, Harold, then prime minister, was working upstairs. The discussion turned to theology and one of the guests said: 'Fortunately, there is the one above who knows all the answers.'

'Yes,' replied Mrs. Wilson, not realising the significance of the remark, 'Harold will be down in a few moments.'

THE WORLD'S GREATEST MISTAKES

They all knew that the big battle was coming. It would be the last chance for the Sioux to hold on to the land of their ancestors and their gods. So they held a sun dance.

The dance was the greatest celebration the Sioux nation had ever known. The spring grass was by now lush and the buffalo plentiful, so they filled their bellies, danced and tested their courage. Sitting Bull, his body already marked with the numerous scars of previous sun dances, had 50 pieces of flesh cut from each arm for this occasion. He then danced non-stop around the sacred pole, staring constantly at the sun. When dusk fell, he continued dancing – through the night and into the next day. After 18 hours, he fainted. When he was revived, he told the tribe that he had seen a wonderful vision. He had seen white soldiers 'falling like grasshoppers' into his camp while a voice said: 'I give you these because they have no ears.'

Victory was assured!

Custer also had visions – of his own glory. At the time of the Sioux sun dance, he was heading towards the Little Bighorn from Fort Abraham Lincoln, far to the east in North Dakota. Every night in camp, he would sit and write self-congratulatory dispatches to a New York newspaper. He also committed his 'private' thoughts to his diary – with, of course, a view to having them published later for posterity.

He wrote: 'In years long-numbered with the past, my every thought was ambitious. Not to be wealthy, not to be learned, but to be great. I desired to link my name with acts and men, and in such a manner as to be a mark of honour, not only to the present, but to future generations.'

This then was the man who arrived at the valley of the Little Bighorn, across the river from Sitting Bull's camp, on the night of June 24, 1876. Custer had with him just 611 men, 12 troops of the U.S. Cavalry – only a small part of the offensive force. But, in true Custer style, he had outstripped all other units and was far ahead of the field, ready for battle.

Straggling far to the south was General George Crook, leading 1,000 soldiers and 250 Sioux-hating Crows and Shoshonis from Fort Fetterman. They had been delayed – and all but defeated – in an ambush by Crazy Horse's Oglalas, who had made a daring sortie from their camp to halt the white men in the valley of the River Rosebud. In fact, under Crook's haphazard generalship, his force would have been obliterated but for the bravery of his Indian allies. As it was, his column was in disarray and had no chance of meeting up with the other forces descending on the Little Bighorn.

Custer knew none of this. He did know, however, that he was well ahead of the other two leaders who were also vying for the glory of wiping out the Indian 'hostiles'. They were Major-General John Gibbon, who had marched east from Fort Ellis, and General Alfred Terry, who had marched west from

Sitting Bull.

153

> Retired tailor Harold Senby had been wearing a hearing
> aid for 20 years but it never seemed to have done him much
> good. Harold, aged 74, discovered the reason why when he
> went to Leeds Hospital for a routine check-up . . . and was
> told that he had been wearing it in the wrong ear. Harold
> said: 'It appears there was a mix-up when it was first fitted.
> The aid was moulded to fit my left ear instead of my right
> one. I always thought it was pretty useless.'

Fort Abraham Lincoln to meet up with Gibbon on the Yellowstone River.
The two were now moving up the Little Bighorn with a combined force of
1,500 men.

Terry was Custer's superior, and the two generals should have been riding
together. But Terry, lacking experience in Indian fighting, had given in to
Custer's pleadings to be allowed to advance and reconnoitre the Sioux camp.
Fearful that anyone else might reach the camp before him, Custer turned
down Terry's offer of extra men and Gatling guns and raced ahead, boasting:
'I could whip all the Indians on the continent with the 7th Cavalry.'

Custer's confidence had never once deserted him. He had driven his 12
troops of men mercilessly – they had made 60 miles in just two days – and he
was unperturbed even when he discovered the true size of the force he was
seeking to take on in battle. The first clue to the strength of the Sioux came
when Custer's men encountered the tracks that the Indians had left when they
had moved their camp sites a few days earlier. The tracks, beaten up by the
hoofs of their ponies and the dragging of their tepee poles, were more than a
mile wide.

The second clue came from Custer's own Indian scouts. They begged their
leader to hold back for two days until Terry and Gibbon were due to arrive.
But Pahuska, the arrogant glory-seeker, could not wait – and his vanity was
his undoing.

Custer's plan was to split up his 12 troops into three battalions, which would
launch simultaneous attacks on the Indians' camp from different directions. So
at first light on June 25, he gave three troops to Captain Frederick Benteen and
three to Major Marcus Reno, took five himself, and left the remaining one
with the supply train.

Sitting Bull's scouts kept a careful watch on the slow progress of Custer and
his main force of 225 men, who were moving down the river valley but hidden
from the river itself by a long bluff. Custer was looking for a suitable crossing
place for a surprise attack on the village – but the Indians knew that he would
not find one.

At the other end of the camp, the Indians were less vigilant. While their attention was focused on the main cavalry force, Major Reno's modest battalion of 140 men crossed the river and attacked on schedule from the rear – taking the Indians largely by surprise. As he led his charge, Reno confidently expected Custer to be attacking the other side of the village at the same time. He had no way of knowing that Custer's battalion was still stumbling down the valley some four miles away.

Reno surprised the Oglalas, Hunkpapas and Blackfoot Sioux in their villages at the southern end of the great encampment. Women and children fled from their tepees under a hail of bullets. A young Hunkpapa named Gall, an orphan who had been adopted by Sitting Bull as his chief lieutenant, saw his wife and children cut down before he was able to rally his warriors for a counter-attack.

Gall led his men around Reno's flank and, when the cavalry momentarily faltered and failed to press their charge, he caught them from behind. Outflanked and outnumbered, Reno's soldiers, by now exhausted from their forced march, retreated to the comparative safety of nearby woodland to shelter until Custer's attack had drawn off the full fury of the Indians.

But Custer had still not attacked. Nor had the third column, under Captain Benteen, who was still some miles from his target. After only 30 minutes of battle, Major Reno's withdrawal was turned into a total rout. The Indians could now concentrate their full attention on the hated Pahuska. . . .

Sitting Bull stood in front of his tepee and directed the battle through a continuous stream of pony messengers. Gall, Crazy Horse and Cheyenne leader Two Moons galloped the three-mile length of the encampment, rallying the warriors to the battle about to commence.

Crazy Horse cried: 'Hoka-hey! It's a good day to fight. It's a good day to die. Strong hearts, brave hearts to the front . . . weak hearts and cowards to the rear.'

Custer's column was still hidden from Sitting Bull's camp by the hills. The general was advancing carefully but confidently, seeking the ideal break in the bluff through which to charge the Indian villages across the river. But unknown to him, the river had already been forded – by Gall's men. They swept through a ravine and hit the rear of the cavalry column. Custer was

---

When ad-men for Pepsi-Cola had their slogan 'Come alive with Pepsi' translated into Mandarin Chinese, the translation turned out to mean: 'Pepsi brings your ancestors back from the grave.'

taken completely by surprise. He ordered his men to race for a nearby hill and take up defensive positions. But when still only half way up the rise, the general saw a sight that must have made him realise for the first time that he was not invincible.

There, on the top of the rise that is now called Custer's Hill, appeared Crazy Horse – and 1,000 mounted warriors. For a moment, they peered down disdainfully at Custer and his straggling band of exhausted cavalry. Then, whooping and shouting and screaming, they charged down the hill.

The cavalry were surrounded within seconds. The soldiers dismounted and set about defending themselves on open ground with hardly a hint of cover. They fought bravely, trying to hold on to their horses. But as the shrieking Sioux closed in, the cavalry had to let their mounts go. There was now no hope of escape. The proud cavalrymen were reduced to a handful. On the edges of the battle, a few wounded soldiers held up their arms and asked to be taken prisoner. But there were no prisoners taken that day. The wounded were shot or hacked to death.

Custer was one of the last to die. As his ranks thinned and the Indians got nearer to him, they saw that Pahuska no longer had shoulder-length hair. He

had had it cut, which was why the attackers had failed to recognise him instantly.

The general stood at the centre of a pathetically small group of survivors. Sitting Bull said: 'Where the last stand was made, the Long-Haired One stood like a sheaf of corn with all the ears fallen around him.' Then Custer was covered by a wave of Indian warriors.

Many Indians claimed later to have been the one who had killed the hated Pahuska. It was a proud boast. In Washington, however, Custer's Last Stand was labelled a savage massacre. A stronger force was sent against the Indians, who quickly scattered.

Crazy Horse moved to a reservation and surrendered. But he was arrested and bayonetted to death while trying to escape from Fort Robinson in 1877. His last words were: 'Let me go, my friends. You have got me hurt enough.'

Sitting Bull fled with 3,000 warriors to Canada, the 'Land of the Great Godmother', Queen Victoria. He returned to the U.S. and surrendered in 1881. He spent two years in prison before being allowed to rejoin his tribe at Standing Rock reservation, North Dakota. He was the star of Buffalo Bill Cody's Wild West Show for a while but, after returning to his tribe once again, he was accused by the army of inciting unrest. When Indian police arrived to take him to jail on December 15, 1890, Sitting Bull resisted arrest and was shot in the back.

The vanquished Custer, on the other hand, received greater honours than the persecuted victors. His body was recovered and given a hero's burial at West Point. Even the lone survivor of the bloodbath - a cavalry horse ironically named Comanche - was honoured as the 7th Cavalry's mascot, always appearing on parades saddled but riderless.

Custer left for posterity a self-congratulatory book, *My Life On The Plains*, a phoney legend of heroism that it took a century to dispel. There is also devoted to his memory a small but thriving business at the Little Bighorn. It sells bottles of 'The Dust That Custer Bit'.

The Oxford University dons who turned up for a lecture by the eminent psychologist Dr. Emil Busch were puzzled but impressed. The man they had come to see after answering an advertisement in an Oxford newspaper had a flowing beard, a strong German accent and a strange way of haranguing his audience so that most of what he said was unintelligible. They learned later that 'Dr. Busch' was one of their undergraduates and that his entire speech had been gibberish.

Left. General Percival on his way to surrender Singapore to General Yamashita.

The fall of Singapore

How the Japanese took the 'Bastion of the British Empire' by bluff

Black rain fell on Singapore on Sunday, February 15, 1942. It fell through clouds of smoke billowing from the blazing oil storage tanks that the British had ordered to be burnt so that they would not fall into the hands of the invading Japanese. The British would not be needing the oil any more. They were surrendering.

The capitulation of the 'impregnable' natural fortress island of Singapore was the end of a long invasion road for the Japanese. But it was the end of an even longer road for the British. For when the Allied troops – outwitted, outfought and outmanoeuvred – handed over Singapore to the Japanese, they were also handing over imperial control in Asia. Above all, they were presaging the end of the British Empire – the destruction of the myth that Britain could protect her far-flung colonies from all comers.

And it need not have been so. When the Japanese invasion forces landed and began their long sweep down the Malay Peninsula, they were heavily outnumbered by the British, Australian and Indian forces who stood in their path. The Japanese, commanded by General Tomoyuki Yamashita, started out with no airfields, no naval cover and an inferior armoury. They made up for it with determination, imagination and brutality.

The Japanese overcame resistance by going around it. Whenever the Allies drew up new defence lines, the Japanese took to the sea in stolen boats and landed further down the coast. The Royal Navy was nowhere to be seen. The promised ships for the defence of Malaya and Singapore, Britain's primary naval base in the Far East, never arrived. Nor did the promised air reinforcements. There was nothing to stop the Japanese.

For most of their journey south towards Singapore, the enemy were able to pedal on bicycles along tracks through what was thought to be impenetrable jungle, guided by no more than school atlases. At the beginning of February 1942 they arrived, along with their captured planes, guns and trucks, at Johore, at the foot of the Malay Peninsula, and looked across the narrow Johore Strait at the stronghold they were determined to win – Singapore.

Singapore is an island about 20 miles long by 10 miles wide, joined to the mainland by a 1,100-yard causeway. To the south of the island, facing out to sea, is Singapore City, peopled by Malays and Chinese. To the north, facing the mainland, was what was then thought to be one of the most important military strongpoints in the world – the Royal Navy base.

For a century, Singapore had been the cornerstone of Britain's supremacy in the Far East. It was labelled the 'Gibraltar of the East' and the 'Bastion of the British Empire'. But it was neither of these. Because of the strange military blindness that seems to have afflicted so many of Britain's wartime leaders, Singapore was fortified against an attack from the sea but was wide open to a landing across the Johore Strait.

Singapore had slumbered for too long to be in any way prepared for the barbarous, murderous, raping, looting army that was about to overwhelm it. Not until two days before Christmas of 1941 did Lieutenant-General Percival, leader of the British Malaya Command, order a survey of the north coast of the island to plan defensive works. No action was taken on his order for two weeks.

Winston Churchill was not fully alerted to the risible state of Singapore's defences until January 16, when he received a telegram about them from General Wavell, who had recently been appointed Supreme Commander of the area. Churchill immediately sent a long and urgent directive to his chiefs of staff:

THE WORLD'S GREATEST MISTAKES

Fire-fighters labouring to quench the flames created by Japanese bombers.

'I must confess to being staggered by Wavell's telegram. . . . Merely to have seaward defences and no forts or fixed defences to protect the rear is not to be excused on any ground. I warn you this will be one of the greatest scandals that could possibly be exposed.

'Let a plan be made at once to do the best possible while the battle on Johore is going forward. This plan should comprise: an attempt to use the fortress guns on the northern front by firing reduced charges; mining and obstructing possible landing places; wiring and laying booby traps in mangrove swamps and other places; placing field batteries at each end of the Strait; forming the nuclei of three or four mobile counter-attack reserve columns upon which the troops, when driven out of Johore, can be based; and employing the entire male civilian population on constructing defence works, the most rigorous compulsion being used.

'Not only must the defence of Singapore Island be maintained by every means, but the whole island must be fought for until every single unit and every single strongpoint has been separately destroyed. Finally, the city of Singapore

VICTORS AND VANQUISHED

must be converted into a citadel and defended to the death. No surrender can be contemplated.'

His exhortations came too late for the defenders of Singapore. The defence works had not been put in hand soon enough. The civilian population was in such disorder that few construction projects could be started. The labourers had fled. Even some of the British and Australian troops had deserted and fled to other islands. There was also a strong fifth-column of Japanese businessmen in Singapore City. The scene was set for a military disaster.

Wavell believed that, even after the loss of Johore, Singapore could hold out for months. By then, American reinforcements, including aircraft carriers, would be in the area. Such a delay to the Japanese advance would allow time for a spring counter-offensive to be launched from the Dutch East Indies.

Yamashita had other ideas for his Japanese 25th Army. He wanted to sweep through the Indies and invade Australia. His key targets were Sydney and Brisbane, and he foresaw no major obstacles to their capture. But first: Singapore. And Yamashita knew that Singapore would have to be taken quickly, otherwise his long-stretched supply lines would be unable to sustain the offensive. His soldiers each had only 100 rounds of ammunition.

On January 31, the last British and Australian troops crossed the long causeway from Johore to the island. They were played across by the only two surviving pipers of the Argyll and Sutherland Highlanders; more than half of the pipers' regiment had been wiped out on the long retreat south.

After the last remnants of the fleeing forces had crossed, charges were set on a bridge section of the 70-foot wide causeway, carrying a road and railway. The causeway was breached. But when the Japanese examined it at low tide, they found that the sunken structure was only four feet underwater. If they wished, they could wade across.

Yamashita set up his forward command post in the tower of the palace of the Sultan of Johore. From there he watched the Japanese Air Force, outnumbering the Royal Air Force planes ten to one, pound the British and Australians, who were desperately trying to build their inadequate defences. Yamashita's tower was never shelled because it was considered too obvious a target for an enemy to occupy. While the Japanese general watched the action first-hand, Wavell

An undercover marshal seeking a witness to a crime in Dallas, Texas, sidled up to a girl standing provocatively in a darkened street and began sweet-talking her. The girl slapped a pair of handcuffs on him and marched him off to jail. She too was an undercover cop.

161

was far away in his Java headquarters, hampered by abysmal communications. The tactics for the defence of Singapore were left in the hands of General Arthur Edward Percival.

Percival decided to stretch his forces along the northern coastline to ward off the Japanese before they could land on the island. Churchill's idea for a strike force to repulse the enemy once they had landed was not thought by Percival to be the best policy. He knew that the morale of his troops was low and that the morale of the civilian population was lower. It did not help when soldiers saw the naval base installations that they had fought for so long to protect being blown up by their own side to prevent them from falling into the hands of the Japanese.

Percival had 85,000 men on Singapore, 15,000 of them non-combatants. They faced between 30,000 and 50,000 crack Japanese troops across the Strait. In terms of firepower, the two sides were well matched. But in all other respects the Japanese held the advantage. They ruled the skies. Their morale was higher: they were elated by victory, and they relished their glorious task

British soldiers taken prisoner by the Japanese.

of 'liberating' Singapore from white colonial domination. They would carry it out with fanatical zeal.

Wavell visited Singapore on January 20 to discuss defence plans with Percival. Wavell said he thought the enemy would land off the north-west of the island. Percival disagreed. He believed the attack would come from the north-east, and he decided to put his freshest troops there. The battered Australians would defend the north-west coastline. On February 8, after days of fierce air and artillery bombardment, Wavell was proved to have been right.

At 10.30 p.m. the Japanese landed in the north-west sector, held by the Australian Brigade. The coast at that point was covered by searchlights but the troops were told to keep them switched off, so as not to give away their positions, until an order to the contrary was issued. But the artillery barrage had cut all telephone lines, and so the order was never given. The invisible enemy came ashore and formed a strong beach-head. By 3 a.m. they were four miles inland. The Australians fell back to agreed lines, but in the darkness and the confusion, many went astray. A planned counter-attack had to be cancelled.

When the news was reported to Percival, he was visibly shaken. But there was worse to come. A further string of landings was reported. Because of lack of communications, units who feared they were in danger of being encircled pulled out of their strong positions without ever coming under attack. The whole front was falling apart. Finally, enemy tanks were sighted south of the causeway and on the main road to Singapore City.

The battle seemed to have been lost within a matter of hours. But the Japanese took time to build up their supplies from across the Strait. By the evening of February 9, about 25,000 men had crossed the Johore Strait in an armada of tiny boats, rafts and rubber dinghies. Many had swum across. It was a remarkable feat – no less remarkable than the disorganised state of the defending forces. The battle-weary Australians of the 22nd and neighbouring 27th Brigades fought hard, but they were badly organised. With them were the Japanese-hating Chinese civilian defence units, who refused to fall back even when the regular soldiers were ordered to do so.

Notorious gangster John Dillinger thought he had a sure-fire way of evading arrest. U.S. federal agents had a record of his finger-prints, so Dillinger decided to acquire new ones. He dipped all his fingers and thumbs in a saucer of acid and had to endure a period of agony before they healed again. After several weeks, Dillinger tested his new fingerprints – and found that they were exactly the same as the old ones.

THE WORLD'S GREATEST MISTAKES

At one stage of the battle, the Australians prevented further Japanese landings by draining oil storage tanks into the mangrove swamps – then setting fire to them. Many of the enemy were burned alive, and the invasion of the island was delayed. The Japanese took their revenge. They beheaded 200 wounded soldiers.

Then came two major errors which sealed the fate of Singapore. Just as the Japanese Imperial Guards Division was seeking permission to abandon its positions near the causeway because of intense opposition from a battalion of the Australian 27th, the Australians pulled back. The decision has never been explained. But it left a 4,000-yard gap through which the enemy poured unimpeded. At the same time, Percival drew up contingency plans which involved falling back to reserve lines around the perimeter of Singapore City. The intention was that the plans should be studied but not acted upon. But somewhere along the line the message got garbled – and the Australian 22nd Brigade, which was bearing the brunt of the attack, pulled back to the reserve lines. The 12th Indian Brigade, finding itself isolated, also pulled back to new positions.

On that day, too, the last RAF fighter flew out of Singapore. Had the RAF remained, it was said, it would have been obliterated as Japanese dive-bombers wrecked the airfields. Unhindered, the enemy aircraft turned their entire destructive power on Singapore City, with its population doubled by refugees to one million. The closely packed buildings were swept by fire, and the streets literally ran with blood. The water supply was almost entirely cut off by bomber attacks. Bodies lay in the gutters. An epidemic was now a certainty.

On February 10, Wavell flew in from Java for the last time and ordered an immediate counter-attack. Percival resisted the order. But on Wavell's insistence, the attack went ahead – and failed miserably. It had been launched too late.

Churchill cabled Wavell: 'I think you ought to realise the way we view the situation in Singapore. Percival is reported to have over 100,000 men, and it is doubtful whether the Japanese have as many in the whole Malay peninsula. In these circumstances, the defenders must greatly outnumber the Japanese forces and in a well-contested battle they should destroy them. There must at this stage be no thought of saving the troops. The honour of the British Empire and the British Army is at stake. The whole reputation of our country and our race is involved.'

Churchill's estimate of 100,000 British troops was an extreme exaggeration, but the war leader's anger got through. Percival told his officers: 'In some units, troops have not shown the fighting spirit expected of men of the British Empire. It will be a lasting disgrace if we are defeated by an army of clever gangsters, many times inferior in numbers to our own.'

Wavell also weighed in: 'It is certain that our troops on Singapore heavily outnumber Japanese troops who have crossed the Strait. We must destroy them. Our whole fighting reputation is at stake, and the honour of the British Empire. It will be disgraceful if we yield our boasted fortress of Singapore to inferior enemy forces.'

But the exhortations were in vain. Many of the soldiers, who through the length of the Malay Peninsula had fought so valiantly, had suddenly lost the will to fight. There were disgraceful scenes as armed deserters roamed the streets, looting stores. They even fought women for places on the last small boats leaving Singapore harbour.

The Governor of Singapore, Sir Shenton Thomas, ordered all liquor in the city to be destroyed so that victorious Japanese soldiers would not go on a drunken orgy of murder and rape. Percival ordered the Military Nursing Service to be evacuated by boat so that they would not suffer the usual sordid fate of white women prisoners of the Japanese. (When the Japanese did capture a hospital on the outskirts of Singapore City, they bayonetted patients and staff.)

On February 13, Percival called a meeting with Lieutenant-General Sir Lewis Heath, of the 3rd Indian Corps, and Major-General Gordon Bennett,

General Yamashita inspecting the devastation in Singapore.

Left General Yamashita.　　　　　*Right* Lt.-General Percival, aged 76.

of the 8th Australian Division. Both said that a counter-attack would certainly fail. Both advocated capitulation.

Percival held out, hoping for a miracle – that if the Japanese ran their supplies too low they might have to ease up the barrage that was crippling the city; and that this would allow time for reinforcements to arrive by sea. But on the afternoon of February 15, the Chinese New Year's Day, he gave up hope. A Japanese plane had dropped a package near his headquarters. It was tied with red and white ribbons which streamed out behind it as it fell to the ground. Inside was a message from Yamashita. It began: 'In a spirit of chivalry, we have the honour of advising you to surrender. . . .'

Percival knew that the city had only a week's food supplies left, and only a day's water. He knew that if the fighting continued, tens of thousands of the frightened civilians besieged there would soon be dead. And he took seriously a veiled threat in Yamashita's note: 'If you continue resistance, it will be difficult to bear with patience from a humanitarian point of view.'

Under a pall of black smoke and a downpour of blackened rain, Percival drove out of the city to meet his stony-faced Japanese counterpart across a table at the island's Ford car assembly plant. There, the tall 55-year-old British general unconditionally surrendered the 'Bastion of the British Empire'.

Yamashita bowed formally – and breathed a secret sigh of relief. He later wrote in his diary: 'My attack on Singapore was a bluff. I had 30,000 men and was outnumbered more than three to one. I knew that if I had been made to fight longer for Singapore I would have been beaten. That was why the surrender had to be immediate. I was extremely frightened that the British would discover our numerical weakness and lack of supplies and force me into disastrous street fighting. But they never did. My bluff worked.'

The hills of Hell

Eight months of killing ended with neither side the victor

Sir William Birdwood.

It was the most daring strategic plan of World War One: in one move, to break the terrible stalemate in the trenches of France by opening up a new front in the east. The plan was Winston Churchill's. The First Lord of the Admiralty, as he then was, believed that by attacking Germany's ally, Turkey, he could slit 'the soft underbelly' of the Kaiser's Europe. He would do it by smashing through the Dardanelles Strait, cutting off the Turks from the Germans and linking Britain with her ally, Russia, through the Black Sea.

167

THE WORLD'S GREATEST MISTAKES

It was a brilliant plan whose success relied on surprising the Turks on both land and sea. It required a strong naval force to sweep through the Dardanelles, plus an amphibious force to secure the heights on either side.

But for all the scheme's brilliant conception, the execution of it was a disaster. For the Turks were well warned of the British intentions.

On November 3, 1914, Royal Navy ships sailed up the Dardanelles Strait and launched a ten-minute bombardment on the Turkish forts. That ten minutes caused little damage but gave the game away entirely. The Turks, under German military guidance, began mining the Strait and reinforcing the defences along the difficult, mountainous country of the Gallipoli peninsula. They were able to do this at their leisure, because they were not bothered again by the Allies for a further three months.

On February 19, 1915, a much larger force of British and French ships began again bombarding the Turkish forts. The Turks immediately moved out of range of the naval guns, waited patiently for the bombardment to end, then returned to their positions. The attack availed the Allies little – and lost the British and French three battleships sunk by mines and three more disabled. The First Sea Lord, Admiral Fisher, reported: 'Things are going badly at the Dardanelles. We are held up for want of soldiers.'

Back in London, many of the War Cabinet wondered whether it was worth proceeding with the plan to take the Dardanelles. Not Churchill. He never wavered, and his enthusiasm for the project carried the majority of the war leaders with him.

So, in the early hours of April 25, 1915 – five months after the first warning shots were fired – the biggest amphibious force the world had known headed for the Gallipoli beaches.

There were 1,500 Australians and New Zealanders in the first assault. They were disgorged from three battleships into small boats, and at 4 a.m. they began rowing towards the black shore. In the early dawn light they approached the cove of Ari Burnu – but instead of seeing the wide, gently sloping beach they had been led to expect, all they saw were precipitous cliffs and barren hills. From the top of those hills a flare went up and suddenly a rain of bullets poured down on the little boats. The soldiers leaped into the sea and struggled ashore, weighed down by their packs. Many failed to make the beach, but those who did fixed their bayonets and stood waiting for the mass of Turks who were now running, slipping and tumbling down the hills in front of them. The battle had begun within yards of the water's edge of what was to be known for ever after as Anzac Cove.

The Australians and New Zealanders were all volunteer soldiers who had answered the call to defend the British Empire, of which they were the furthest-flung members. They were raw and not expected to put up a sustained

---

**Police opened the back of a refrigerated truck after
complaints that it was parked without lights in a London
street. Inside they found the nearly frozen driver, who had
locked himself in three hours earlier.**

---

fight. But their heroism, tenacity and sheer guts at Anzac Cove became a
legend. They pushed the Turks back off the shoreline and pursued them with
flashing bayonets up into the hills. The grand battle plan had broken down
into a series of bloody skirmishes. But by mid-morning the Anzac force had
advanced as far as a mile inland.

And that was when the bravery of the Anzacs was betrayed by the incompetence of their leaders. The Commander-in-Chief of the entire Gallipoli
expedition was General Sir Ian Hamilton, an ageing, ineffectual leader who
decided to run the operation from the comfort of the battleship *Queen Elizabeth*
three miles off-shore, completely out of touch with his two corps commanders
and the men on the beaches. Not that the corps commanders themselves were
on the beaches. They were ordered to command their operations from ships
standing off-shore, and, because communications quickly broke down, they
too had little idea of what was going on.

Commander of the Anzac corps was General Sir William Birdwood, able
and resourceful, but hampered by his unworkable orders. The other corps
commander was General Sir Hunter Weston, in charge of the 29th Division of
British and French troops, in whom Hamilton pinned his main hopes. Weston's
men were landed on five beaches on Cape Helles, at the tip of the Gallipoli
peninsula. They also carried out two decoy operations to divert Turkish troops
into other areas miles away from the main front.

At Cape Helles, the first force of 2,000 British soldiers approached the shore
inside an innocent-looking collier, the *River Clyde*, which was run aground on
Sedd-el-Bahr beach. The attack was launched more than an hour after the
Anzac landing. The British came ashore in broad daylight and ran into a hail
of bullets from the waiting, well-entrenched Turks. Hundreds of men were
shot dead as they crowded like sardines on the gangways that led ashore
from the collier. The few who got on to the beach were picked off one by one
as they scurried around seeking some shelter from the incessant enemy guns.

Four hours after the first landing, only about 200 Britons had scrambled
ashore and survived. The pilot of a spotter plane which flew over the beach
that morning described the sea as 'a horrible sight – absolutely red with blood'.
The battle of Sedd-el-Bahr was lost before it was begun.

THE WORLD'S GREATEST MISTAKES

Within a stretch of a few miles, four other assaults had been launched on Cape Helles, and these had more success. On three beaches, the British troops landed and met little resistance, so they captured the commanding hillsides and sat down waiting for further orders. They never came.

On the other beach, Y Beach, there was no resistance at all. Two thousand men landed, climbed the cliffs and wandered around the prickly scrub unhindered. They sat on the hilltops and listened to the sound of their comrades being annihilated just an hour's march away. The Y Beach troops outnumbered the entire Turkish force in Cape Helles. They could have encircled and overrun the enemy that very day. But when their officers asked for permission to advance, the plea was refused.

The 2,000 men who had landed on Y Beach sat and waited for further orders throughout the whole of that bloody day. Until, in the evening, Turkish reinforcements arrived on the scene – and attacked them. The Britons, who had expected at any moment to be given orders to march onward, had not bothered to dig themselves in against an attack. And when that attack came, half of the invaders began to file back to the water's edge, where they came under fire. Since there was no word from their senior officers, these troops now took to their boats and began to evacuate Y Beach.

Meanwhile, the other half of the Y Beach force had pushed further inland, where they fought throughout the night. At dawn the next day they found that they were alone and unsupported, but they fought so well that by midmorning the Turks had fled.

Yet the great chance of victory was gone. The Allies in Cape Helles had outnumbered the Turkish defenders six to one, yet because there was no senior officer who could order a combined attack, the Allies had failed to press home their advantage. The Turks withdrew, but so did the British. The result was stalemate.

The only part of the whole operation which could be classed as a success was the French diversion on the other side of the Dardanelles Strait, at Kum Kale. There, with a regiment of African colonial troops, the French, in hand-

> A tourist in Stockholm could not catch the restaurant waiter's eye, so he stepped outside, took all his clothes off and re-entered shouting: 'You Swedes only pay attention to nudes. Now will you serve me?' He was arrested for indecent behaviour.

to-hand fighting, had captured a major Turkish fort guarding the entrance to the Strait. The Turks had fled. But, in their moment of victory, the French had been ordered to withdraw and sail to Cape Helles. Kum Kale was, after all, just a diversion.

By midday on April 26, no fewer than 30,000 men had been landed on the Gallipoli peninsula . . . and none of them had been allowed by their leaders to achieve the victory that was in their grasp.

The original Anzacs had been reinforced by a further 15,000 men. But the enemy had not wasted their time either, and the main Turkish force was now concentrated on the hills around the Anzacs. By dusk of that day, the Anzac corps were all under siege on one tiny beach, without cover. At midnight Birdwood managed to get a message through to Hamilton's battleship asking for permission to evacuate his force.

He reported: 'My divisional generals and brigadiers have represented to me that they fear their men are thoroughly disorganised by shrapnel fire to which they have been subjected all day after exhausting and gallant work in the morning. Numbers have dribbled back from the firing line and cannot be collected in this difficult country. Even the New Zealand Brigade, which has only recently been engaged, lost heavily and is to some extent demoralised. If troops are subjected to shellfire again tomorrow there is likely to be a fiasco, as I have no fresh troops with which to replace those in the firing line. I know my representation is most serious but if we are to re-embark it must be at once.'

Thousands of lives could have been saved at that moment as Hamilton studied Birdwood's words aboard the battleship. But the tide of events turned on a second message that Hamilton received before he had made up his mind how to answer the first one.

This second report was from Lieutenant-Commander Huw Dacre Stoker, captain of the Australian submarine AE2. He had entered the Dardanelles Strait and, remaining on the surface to maintain his batteries, had passed into the Narrows under the guns of the Turkish forts. Shellfire made him submerge and he decided to pass beneath the Turks' floating minefield. He had to risk his submarine by surfacing twice in the middle of the minefield to check his position, and each time shells exploded around the craft. Finally Stoker came upon the main Turkish naval force sheltering behind the minefield, and he fired a torpedo at one of the cruisers, crash-diving just before the cruiser was able to ram him. But the torpedo hit home. Stoker kept the AE2 on the bottom for 16 hours, reading prayers to his men because it was a Sunday. Eventually, as the Turks gave up their hunt for the sub, he headed back down the Strait and radioed his success to the flagship *Queen Elizabeth*.

The vacillating Hamilton received the message and seized upon the only hopeful news of the day. He decided to send this reply to Birdwood's earlier

> The court was told that soon after the party came into
> Maloney's Bar, Milligan spat at O'Flaherty and called him
> 'a stinking Ulsterman'. O'Flaherty punched Milligan, and
> Rourke hit him with a bottle. Milligan kicked O'Flaherty in
> the groin and threw a pint of beer in Rourke's face.
> This led to ill-feeling, and they began to fight.
>   – County Louth (Eire) newspaper

appeal for an evacuation:

'Your news is indeed serious. But there is nothing for it but to dig yourselves right in and stick it out. It would take at least two days to re-embark you. Meanwhile, an Australian submarine has got up through the Narrows and has torpedoed a gunboat. Hunter Weston, despite his heavy losses, will be advancing tomorrow, which should divert pressure from you. Make a personal appeal to your men to make a supreme effort to hold their ground. You have got through the difficult business. Now you have only to dig, dig, dig until you are safe.'

And dig, dig, dig they did. With the 100-yard beach littered with 2,000 casualties and the hills above them covered with about as many Turks, the Anzac troops dug their burrows into the cliffsides, and the enemy did the same. The grand Gallipoli plan had, within hours of being launched, settled down into the same appalling system of trench warfare that was wasting millions of lives in the fields of France.

The men at Anzac Cove and Cape Helles were to stay in those trenches and dug-outs for eight more months, and the Allied casualties were to climb to a quarter of a million before the pride of their leaders was sufficiently deflated to allow them to admit defeat and pull out.

By April 29, news got back to London that the Gallipoli offensive was not proving as successful as had been hoped. The news did not come from Hamilton, who prevaricated as his assault became bogged down. The news of the impending disaster was relayed instead by the Royal Navy.

Reinforcements were urgently needed – and they were available. In Egypt, where the original force had been assembled, fresh troops idly stood by, waiting for the call to sail to Gallipoli. But Hamilton never called them – either because he did not know they were available to him, or because of his pride. No one knows. Eventually, the reinforcements did sail, under direct orders from London. But by then the Turks too had summoned their best regiments to the narrow front.

Two weeks after the landings, Weston had lost 6,500 men at Cape Helles and had achieved nothing. Men were dying from lack of medical care, and ammunition was perilously low. Bayonet attacks and small sallies across trenches, producing heavy casualties, were the order of the day.

The scene at Anzac Cove was, if anything, worse. Each man was rationed to two bullets a day unless under prolonged attack. Along the ragged front lines, the opposing trenches were in some places less than 30 feet apart. Men lived like rats in holes in the hills, while on the beaches the maimed died on their stretchers under the constant barrage of Turkish shells.

On May 18 there took place at Anzac Cove the bloodiest battle of the campaign. The Turks had brought in fresh forces and now outnumbered by three to one the remaining 12,000 Australians and New Zealanders still able to fight. At 5 p.m. the greatest artillery barrage the Anzacs had yet seen burst around them. It continued into the night as the beleaguered soldiers huddled in their burrows. At 3 a.m. Birdwood ordered all his men to stand by for an expected attack. No sooner had they taken up their positions than the firing ceased. The front lines fell silent. There was a single bugle call – and a solid mass of Turks left their trenches and descended on the Anzacs. Wave after wave of Turks entered no-man's-land and were mown down before they could cross the narrow gap. The few who did cross were bayonetted as they fell into the Anzac trenches. The charges continued throughout the night and right through until midday. Every time a wave of Turks fell before the concerted fire of the Allies, another wave rose from the parapets of their trenches and charged to their deaths.

When the Turkish commanders called off the attacks, 10,000 of their men had fallen, half of them only yards from the Anzac trenches.

In the hours and days that followed, as both sides retreated to their trenches, the lines again fell relatively quiet. But throughout the day and night came moans and screams from those who had fallen in no-man's-land. With so many bodies putrefying, the danger of disease increased daily, and the Anzacs pressed Hamilton to negotiate a ceasefire so that the dead could be buried. Hamilton

---

A glossy American cookbook contained a recipe for Silky Caramel Slices: put an unopened can of condensed milk in a pot and leave it on the stove for four hours. The publishers later recalled all the books at vast expense, when they realised they had just invented the first exploding pudding - they had forgotten to mention that the pot should first be filled with water.

refused, saying that the request must come from the Turks.

But on May 20 the volunteer soldiers from Down Under took matters into their own hands, and raised a Red Cross flag above the front line. It was immediately shot at by the Turks, and the flagstaff was shattered. Then the most extraordinary thing happened. . . .

It was certain death to raise your head above the trenches of the front lines. Yet a lone Turkish soldier leaped up and began running across no-man's-land towards the Australians. He stopped above their trench and, in stumbling French, apologised for the shooting. Then he ran back again. Minutes later, Red Crescent flags appeared above the enemy trenches. General Walker, Commander of the 1st Australian Division, stood up and began slowly walking towards the Turkish lines. Not a shot was fired. Five Turkish officers came forward to greet him and they all chatted in French, exchanging pleasantries and cigarettes. After about ten minutes they parted, agreeing to meet again that evening to discuss an amnesty.

On May 24 there was a 'suspension of arms' so that each side could bury its dead. The enemies stood shoulder to shoulder and dug mass graves, all under the direction of Australian officers. Author Compton Mackenzie, who was an officer on Hamilton's staff, came ashore for the day and described the scene. 'Everywhere Turks were digging and digging graves for their countrymen who had been putrefying in heaps in the warm May air. The impression that scene made on my mind has obliterated all the rest of the time at Anzac. I cannot recall a single incident on the way back down the valley. I know only that nothing could cleanse the smell of death from the nostrils for a fortnight afterwards. There was no herb so aromatic but it reeked of carrion.'*

The truce was to end at 4.30 p.m. on May 24, and about half an hour before the deadline Turkish and Allied troops exchanged cigarettes and fruit and small gifts. They shook hands, parted with wide grins and returned to their

* *Gallipoli Memories* by Compton Mackenzie (Cassell, London)

Mr. Michael Vanner, of Bexhill Road, St. Leonards, a defendant in a recent case at Hastings Magistrates' Court, wishes to state that Mr. Melvin Peck, whom he pleaded not guilty to assaulting, was not a passer-by, as stated, but a friend of his.

– Sussex newspaper

> **In the Nuts (unground) (other than ground nuts) Order, the expression nuts shall have reference to such nuts, other than ground nuts, as would but for this amending Order not qualify as nuts (unground) (other than ground nuts) by reason of their being nuts (unground).**
>
> – Amendment to British Parliamentary Act

own trenches. Shortly after 4.30, a Turkish sniper opened fire and the Anzacs blasted back. The war had begun again.

There was little respite for the next seven months. On August 6 Hamilton launched a fresh assault on Suvla Bay, north of the Anzac positions. The enemy was totally outflanked and fell back in disarray. By the end of the day, the Turks in the area were outnumbered 15 to one. But again the orders to push forward did not come. The Turks regrouped and sealed off the beach-head. It was the same old story: stalemate.

As 1915 dragged on, life became a living hell for the men on Cape Helles. Dysentery spread through the army, and 1,000 soldiers a week were shipped out suffering from it. Three-quarters of the Anzacs were seriously affected by it. More than half of them also suffered from skin sores through living in filthy trenches. The food was bad. And there was no fresh water in Anzac Cove – it had to be shipped from Egypt 750 miles away. Throughout the summer, there was a plague of flies over the camp, which helped spread disease. And finally the winter produced a new horror – frostbite for 15,000 soldiers.

In October the disastrous Hamilton was recalled and General Sir Charles Monro took over. He reported to the War Cabinet in London: 'The troops on the peninsula, with the exception of the Australian and New Zealand Corps, are not equal to a sustained effort owing to the inexperience of the officers, the want of training in the men and the depleted condition of many of the units. I am therefore of the opinion that another attempt to carry the Turkish lines would not offer any hope of success. On purely military grounds, I recommend the evacuation of the peninsula.'

The politicians argued the matter over until the middle of November before finally agreeing to give up the grand plan. Churchill resigned. He described Monro's part in the campaign thus: 'He came, he saw, he capitulated.'

Suvla Bay and Anzac Cove were evacuated in December 1915, and Cape Helles early the following month. One of the costliest blunders in history had come to an end. Half a million Allied troops had fought half a million Turks for eight months. And the result was 252,000 Allied casualties and 251,000 Turkish casualties. Even in death and injury there was stalemate.

U.S. *Arizona* after the Japanese attack.

Fiasco at Pearl Harbor

Warnings that were ignored could have prevented disaster

December 7, 1941, is a date that will for ever strike bitterness into the hearts of Americans. It was described by President Franklin D. Roosevelt as 'a date which will live in infamy' – the date on which Japanese aircraft swept out of the blue to bomb the pride of the American Pacific Fleet in Pearl Harbor.

The planes – almost 400 of them, launched from a vast carrier strike force – caused unimaginable damage, havoc and death on the wholly unprepared Hawaiian island of Oahu. But their coming had not been without warnings that, had they been heeded, would have at least halved the damage and the death toll that day.

The Japanese masterplan to cripple American opposition in the Pacific started being put into operation in mid-November of 1941. American agents in Japan reported that, one by one, major ships of the imperial navy had slipped out of their home ports and disappeared. The ships were assembling in Tankan Bay, along the string of islands that stretched into the icy waters of northern Japan.

From there, on November 26, sailed a vast force: six aircraft carriers, two battleships, three cruisers, nine destroyers, eight tankers and three submarines. An advance force of about 25 submarines, five of them carrying midget submarines, had gone ahead.

The main force had a journey ahead of it stretching halfway across the Pacific Ocean, and it was vital to the success of its mission that no one else should even know of its existence. To this end, radio silence was maintained, no garbage was dumped overboard, only low-smoke fuel was used, and there was a strict black-out. The cover-up was taken to such limits that ships remaining in Japanese home waters increased their own level of radio communications to a constant chatter in order to persuade U.S. eavesdroppers that the full fleet was still in the area.

On December 1, a mysterious message was broadcast from Tokyo. It was simply: 'Climb Mount Niitaka'. Only the commander of the strike fleet, Vice-Admiral Chuichi Nagumo, knew what it meant: the Imperial Council had decided on war, and the attack on Pearl Harbor was to proceed. Even so, the commander's instructions were that if the fleet were to be spotted on any day up to or including December 6, it should turn back, having lost the element of surprise. If it were sighted on December 7, the commander of the strike force would decide whether the attack should still go ahead – at 0800 hours, Sunday, December 7.

Apart from the strange disappearance from port of so many ships of the Japanese Navy, the first warning that could have helped the American authorities avert a major disaster at Pearl Harbor came on December 5. The local FBI branch in Hawaii tapped a phone call between Tokyo and a Japanese dentist living in Honolulu. The conversation ranged over the subjects of aircraft, defences and the number of ships in Pearl Harbor. But most of the time was spent talking about flowers. 'The hibiscus and poinsettia are now in bloom,' was how the conversation ended. The message was thought to be a code, but no great weight was attached to it. After all, a Japanese attack on Pearl Harbor was out of the question. Washington had warned that a declaration of war was expected from the Japanese, but an attack was believed to be coming in the Far East – probably in Borneo or the Philippines.

Washington had been well alerted to the possibility of war. The Americans had broken the secret code used in messages between Tokyo and the Japanese Embassy in Washington, and they had translated a long declaration that was evidently destined to be handed over by the Japanese envoys. The final part of the document, actually declaring war on the United States, would have completed the message that would plummet the Americans into World War Two. The curious Japanese sense of honour would have been satisfied if the declaration had been presented just before their strike force hit Hawaii. But it was not received from Tokyo in time.

So, on the morning of December 7, the Americans on the Hawaiian islands were not alerted to the fact that they could be a target for the Japanese. There had been mildly voiced fears of sabotage by the large Japanese civilian population of Hawaii if war were declared. But Pearl Harbor in the front line? Never!

Early in the morning of December 7 American military personnel went to bed after Honolulu's Saturday night parties and dances, while two dozen submarines of the Japanese advance force closed in around Pearl Harbor. Their job was to torpedo any ships that tried to escape the airborne attack that was to be launched. From five of the subs, two-man midget submarines, each bearing twin torpedoes, were to be launched against warships inside the harbour at the same time as the planes.

Then came another of the warnings that should have alerted the Americans. At 3.30 a.m. the minesweeper *Condor* sighted a submarine periscope heading towards the entrance to Pearl Harbor. The *Condor*, which was patrolling just outside the harbour, signalled the destroyer *Ward*, which was on duty nearby. Battle stations were called and held for an hour, but the submarine was not sighted again.

Shortly before 5 a.m., the *Condor* went off duty. The anti-submarine net across the harbour mouth was drawn open to allow the vessel back inside. The net was not closed again because other ships were expected to be moving in and out of the harbour over the next few hours. Pearl Harbor was wide open to the midget submarines which were even then moving towards the 96 warships lying snugly inside. The net was left open because neither the *Condor* nor the *Ward* reported to shore that a submarine was in the area.

At 6 a.m., in high seas 250 miles north of Oahu, six Japanese aircraft carriers turned their bows into the wind and a swarm of aircraft, laden with bombs and torpedoes, roared into the dawn sky to the cheers of the crews. The plan was to

---

Delays and confusion mean that solicitors either have to work for nothing or tell an inarticulate client that he must conduct his own ass.

– *Times*

Pearl Harbor at the height of the fire.

launch 350 planes in two waves, one at 6 a.m. and the other at 7 a.m. Another 80 planes were split between reconnaisance missions, defence of the fleet and reserves.

Most of Pearl Harbor still slumbered. But at 6.45 a.m. the first shot of the battle was fired. The destroyer *Ward*, still on patrol, spotted a midget submarine at the harbour entrance and opened fire on it. Then it ran at the sub as if to ram it, dropped a depth charge as it passed – and blew it up. A quarter of an hour later a second sub was sighted. More depth charges were dropped and this sub, too, was thought to have been destroyed. It was shortly after 7 a.m. that the second wave of Japanese planes took off from the carriers to the north. But in Pearl Harbor the only concern was that the early-morning 'exercises' taking place off-shore were not helping the hangovers suffered by the sleepy party-goers of the previous night.

The *Ward* radioed ashore to report the encounters with the submarines, in two messages, both in code. But it was at 7.15 a.m. that, because of delays in decoding, the first message reached the only man on duty at U.S. naval headquarters at Pearl Harbor. He was a veteran reservist, Lieutenant-Commander Harold Kaminsky, who spent the next 20 minutes raising some

Wanted: SINGLE MAN OR GIRL for STUD FARM. Girl must be 25 or over and experienced.

– *Belfast Newsletter*

of the navy top brass at their homes. But aboard the warships in Pearl Harbor, all anyone was concerned with was the hoisting of the morning colours.

Another wasted warning had come just before 7 a.m. Army radar stations on Oahu picked up the blips of two aircraft heading in from the north. They were probably Japanese reconnaissance aircraft flying ahead of the first wave of dive-bombers and torpedo planes. The reports went into the island's information centre for plotting. Unfortunately, at 7 a.m. everything stopped for breakfast, and this one-hour warning of impending disaster was also ignored.

At 7.05 a.m. Opana radar station on the northern tip of Oahu island picked up the first clear-cut sign that a major attack was about to take place. Dozens of aircraft showed up on the screen. The men at Opana were also supposed to have stood down at 7 a.m. but they stayed on duty to track the vast formation which was now only 100 miles away and closing fast. Bewildered, they put through reports to the information centre. But the centre had virtually closed down for breakfast, and the only two men on duty were the switchboard operator and one officer who was waiting to be relieved so that he too could get his coffee and a bite to eat. The men at Opana became fed up with passing through reports that were seemingly being ignored, so they also packed up and went off for breakfast.

The first wave of Japanese planes was now over the coast.

On the battleship *Nevada* lying in Pearl Harbor the ship's band began playing *The Star Spangled Banner* as part of the regular Sunday morning ceremony of hoisting the colours. Just then, a plane with a bright red circle on each wingtip swooped out of the sky, dropped a torpedo and skimmed over the *Nevada*'s decks. The plane's rear-gunner fired on the bandsmen but succeeded only in shredding the American flag to tatters. The band finished playing then fled for cover. The attack on Pearl Harbor had begun. It was 7.55 a.m.

At 8 a.m. a message was radioed to Washington, to the Atlantic and Pacific Fleets and all U.S. warships at sea: 'Air raid on Pearl Harbor – this is no drill.'

For the next two hours, wave upon wave of bombers, dive-bombers and torpedo aircraft pummelled Pearl Harbor and its surrounding air bases. Almost 200 American planes were destroyed, most of them on the ground. In the middle of the attack a flight of U.S. B-17 bombers arrived over Oahu

VICTORS AND VANQUISHED

on a routine mission. They found themselves in a maelstrom, were shot up, and crash-landed wherever they could.

The Japanese lost 30 aircraft, as well as all five of their midget submarines and one of the large subs. Fewer than 100 men in all. Their losses were so low because they had maintained the element of surprise. As for the Americans, having failed to read the warning signs, their losses were huge by contrast.

In Pearl Harbor itself, thick black smoke from a sea of burning oil obscured the carnage. Five torpedoes slammed into the battleship *Oklahoma*. It turned turtle. Its sister ship, the *Arizona*, exploded spectacularly from a direct bomb hit and sank, entombing 1,100 men. Three other battleships were seriously damaged but later salvaged. The *West Virginia* was hit by six torpedoes and sank. The *California* was hit by two torpedoes. The blazing *Nevada*, with a torpedo in its side and two bomb hits, made a dash for the harbour mouth but ran aground. The battleships *Tennessee*, *Pennsylvania* and *Maryland* were also damaged.

The target ship *Utah* was torpedoed and capsized. The cruiser *Helena* suffered the same fate. The minelayer *Oglala* was sunk by the same torpedo that holed the *Helena*. The destroyer *Shaw* exploded in dry dock. Its sister ships *Cassin* and *Downes* were totally destroyed in dry dock. The cruiser *Raleigh* was holed but remained afloat. The cruiser *Honolulu* was put out of action.

Eight miles away, the city that the *Honolulu* was named after suffered only mild damage. It was hit by one Japanese bomb – and about 40 U.S. Navy shells fired by ships in harbour at the attacking aircraft.

Sixty-eight civilians died that day and 2,335 American servicemen – almost half of them lost aboard the battleship *Arizona*.

Shortly after 3 p.m. on the afternoon of the attack, a cable from Washington was delivered to Lieutenant-General Walter C. Short, commander of the U.S. Army ground and air forces in Hawaii. Its message was that the Japanese were planning to present an official declaration at 7.30 Honolulu time that morning. It added: 'Just what significance the hour set may have we do not know – but be on the alert.' This warning would have been delivered to General Short earlier but it had been delayed because of the need to decode it, because of the air attack and because it was a Sunday. The cable had been received at 7.33 that morning.

Firemen paraded proudly for the opening of their showpiece headquarters at Barnsley, Yorkshire. Then factory inspectors moved in and ordered a vital addition to the building – a fire escape.

Massacre of the Light Brigade

The tragic charge into the Valley of Death by 'the noble six hundred'

C'est magnifique, mais ce n'est pas la guerre' ('It's magnificent, but it isn't war'). The remark was made by French General Bosquet as he watched the famous Light Brigade of the British Army charge to their destruction in the Crimea in 1854. And the comment has gone down in history as the truest verdict on a spectacular blunder that both shocked and inspired a nation.

The Charge of the Light Brigade resulted from the enmity, jealousy, suspicion and, above all, the conflicting pride of three men.

Lord Raglan, a soldier since the age of 15, was supreme commander. He was a popular leader and had served at Waterloo 39 years earlier, when he had watched with clenched teeth as a field surgeon amputated his right arm.

Under his command was Lord Lucan, who, as the young George Bingham, had bought himself the command of the 17th Lancers and had proved himself such a stickler for dress and discipline that his men were called Bingham's Dandies. He was tireless and brave but uninspiring, and he was hated by his officers for his pettiness and by his men for the floggings he was so keen to order.

No one hated Lucan more than his brother-in-law, Lord Cardigan, who commanded the 11th Hussars. They spoke hardly a word to each other. Cardigan had seen little war service, was also an enthusiast for floggings, and isolated himself from his officers by living aboard his private yacht off Balaclava. Yet he was a more flamboyant and colourful character than his brother-in-law and he inspired strong loyalty in the ranks.

The ill-fated Charge of the Light Brigade took place shortly after an earlier attack by the rival Heavy Brigade. The riders of the Heavy Brigade had routed an overwhelmingly superior force of Russian cavalry near Balaclava. The generals commanding the Light Brigade had watched the Heavy Brigade in action, but had been denied permission to join in and complete the rout. They felt cheated of a share in the glory.

After the Heavy Brigade's action, the Russian forces regrouped at the end of a long narrow valley which was bounded on two sides by hills, at the western end by the Chersonese Plateau and at the eastern end by the River Tchernaya. The Russian cavalry was drawn up at the eastern end of the valley, behind a solid line of cannons. Russian artillery flanked the valley in commanding positions on both sides -- on the Fedioukine Hills to the north and the Causeway Heights to the south.

The Russians had already been driven out of some of their previously held positions on the Causeway Heights, and the British infantry, along with their French allies, were preparing to evict them from the others. Raglan, whose headquarters were on the Chersonese Plateau, had a clear view down the length of the valley and could see clearly how the battle lines were shaping up.

Raglan decided that his infantry should winkle the enemy out of their emplacements on the hills while his cavalry should enter the valley to attack

---

The chairman reported that Bradford Council would not be able to repaint yellow No Parking lines in the village until the man who did the job had used up all the white paint in his bucket.

— Yorkshire newspaper

the retreating Russians as, one by one, the small pockets of resistance gave out. The plan was logical – the enemy gunners would be forced down from the hills on to the valley floor and the Light Brigade would pick them off with impunity.

But that was not how it happened.

On the southern side of the valley, the 1st Division of infantry advanced towards the Causeway Heights. On the other side, the 4th Division also advanced, but much more slowly. In the middle, the 600-strong Light Brigade, raring for action after jealously watching the success of the Heavy Brigade, moved forward too.

> *Half a league, half a league,*
> *Half a league onward,*
> *All in the valley of Death*
> *Rode the six hundred.*

So begins the famous poem by Alfred, Lord Tennyson, which describes the action and has immortalised the brave cavalrymen who took part in it.

The Light Brigade were far ahead of the infantry, and historians have argued that they should have been ordered to wait until the 1st and 4th Divisions caught up with them. But, due to a series of misunderstandings, they were launched on a spectacular but insane course of action.

The catalogue of chronic blunders began when Raglan, from his vantage point high on the Chersonese Plateau, saw that the Russians had already begun to pull out of some of their positions on the Causeway Heights and were hauling their cannon down the valley to the safety of their main force. There was no need for the British infantry to winkle them out – they were already sitting targets for the cavalry.

Raglan issued his first order to the Light Brigade: 'Advance and take advantage of any opportunity to recover the Heights. You will be supported by the infantry.'

Lucan received the order by messenger and thought it characteristically vague, which indeed it was. He interpreted it to mean that he was to wait for the infantry. So he moved the Light Brigade to the head of the valley, ordered a halt . . . and waited.

Raglan spluttered with rage and impatience when he saw the cavalry idling on the valley floor. He watched through his telescope as the Russians moved around without hindrance at the far end of the valley. Raglan called for his chief of staff, General Airey, and asked him to send off a further order to Lucan.

This order Airey took down on a flimsy scrap of paper as he stood before

THE WORLD'S GREATEST MISTAKES

the supreme commander. The order was: 'Advance rapidly to the front to prevent the enemy from carrying away their guns.' Airey gave the vital scrap of paper to his own aide de camp, Captain Nolan, and as Nolan wheeled his horse around to deliver the note personally to Lucan, Raglan shouted after him: 'Tell him to attack instantly.'

Nolan sent his horse slithering down the precipitous slopes to the valley below to pass the crucial message to Lucan, a leader whom he despised for his superior airs and inferior experience. Eventually, his horse bathed in sweat and dust, Nolan drew up alongside Lucan's horse and passed over the now-grimy slip of paper.

Lucan read the note nonchalantly and put it aside. He commented lightly that it seemed a foolhardy order, and he leaned back in his saddle to contemplate the situation as if he had all the time in the world.

This was too much for the fiery Nolan, an outspoken individualist but respected by his superiors as a battle-hardened officer.

'My Lord,' shouted Nolan, 'the orders are for the cavalry to attack instantly.'

Lucan was taken aback. He rounded angrily on his junior officer and remonstrated: 'Attack? Attack what? What guns?'

Nolan lost all patience. He pointed down the valley and shouted: 'There, my Lord, is your enemy. There are the guns.'

But Nolan was not pointing at the struggling Russians trying to pull their artillery out of their isolated positions on the Causeway Heights. He was pointing straight down the long valley to the massed Russian forces at the far end.

Dismissively, Lucan shrugged his shoulders and turned his horse away. He trotted over to his brother-in-law and ordered him to attack the Russian artillery immediately. Cardigan remonstrated with him, but the conversation was curt and unproductive.

'Allow me to point out, sir,' said Cardigan, 'that the enemy have a battery in the valley in our front and batteries and riflemen on both flanks.'

Lucan replied: 'I know it, but Raglan will have it. We must obey. Advance steadily.'

Lucan rode back to brigade headquarters. Cardigan rode off to rally his officers.

Cardigan drew up the Light Brigade at the head of the valley. On the right he placed the 13th Light Dragoons. On the left was Lucan's regiment, the 17th Lancers (in the temporary command of Captain Morris, while Lucan stood by with the Heavy Brigade). Cardigan's regiment, the 11th Hussars, formed a second line of cavalry. In the rear, the 8th Hussars and the 4th Light Dragoons formed up under Lord George Paget.

Up front, Cardigan ordered: 'Sound the advance', and a trumpeter sent the 607 horses first into a walk and then into a trot.

> *'Forward the Light Brigade!*
> *Charge for the guns!' he said:*
> *Into the valley of Death*
> *Rode the six hundred.*

Cardigan was out in front of the brigade on his chestnut charger. Nolan, the man who had passed on the fatal orders to Lucan, was nearby. He had asked to be allowed to ride with the 17th Lancers. When he realised the direction in which the brigade was heading, he left his place in the ranks and galloped forward to warn Cardigan of the error, but almost as soon as he reached the head of the mass of men and horses a Russian shell burst near him. Shrapnel hit Nolan in the chest and he and his horse collapsed in the dust.

The trumpeter, riding next to Cardigan, was ordered to sound the gallop. He had barely done so when he too was killed.

The Russian guns on the riders' flanks were now firing incessantly and the leading lancers were already falling like flies. But the target of the charge, the main body of the Russian force, was still more than a mile away. . . .

> *'Forward the Light Brigade!'*
> *Was there a man dismay'd?*
> *Not tho' the soldier knew*
> *Some one had blunder'd:*
> *Their's not to make reply,*
> *Their's not to reason why,*
> *Their's but to do and die:*
> *Into the valley of Death*
> *Rode the six hundred.*

There was now no trumpeter to sound the charge. But the eagerness of the men to pass through the rain of bullets and shells and reach the end of the valley as quickly as possible forced the pace. The charge began unordered.

'Steady the 17th Lancers,' called Cardigan as his men threatened to overtake their leader. Riders and horses fell one after another but the lines were immediately closed and the solid mass of men and chargers galloped up the dusty valley floor. Some horses, by now riderless, continued to charge until they too were hit.

> *Cannon to right of them,*
> *Cannon to left of them,*
> *Cannon in front of them*
> *Volley'd and thunder'd;*
> *Storm'd at with shot and shell,*
> *Boldly they rode and well,*
> *Into the jaws of Death,*
> *Into the mouth of Hell*
> *Rode the six hundred.*

The hail of shot and shell had become a murderous crossfire as the brigade was fired on from three sides. One man had his head cleanly severed but his torso continued in the saddle, his lance still pointing ahead to its target. Cannon fire began to knock out as many as four chargers at a time. One horse tore out its own entrails with its galloping hooves.

Suddenly the dust and smoke thickened and Cardigan, still at the head of his men, vanished into the midst of it. The Light Brigade were upon the Russian guns. Lances struck home, swords cut down the enemy gunners.

The brigade swept through the guns and into the thick of the waiting cavalry ranked behind them. The fighting was wholly disordered. Cardigan was involved in a hand-to-hand skirmish with a dozen Cossacks. But many of the British swept clean through the enemy cavalry and then had to fight every

inch of their way back again. Many were captured.

> *Flash'd all their sabres bare,*
> *Flash'd as they turn'd in air*
> *Sabring the gunners there,*
> *Charging an army, while*
> *All the world wonder'd:*
> *Plunged in the battery-smoke*
> *Right thro' the line they broke;*
> *Cossack and Russian*
> *Reel'd from the sabre-stroke*
> *Shatter'd and sunder'd.*
> *Then they rode back, but not,*
> *Not the six hundred.*

The dreadful hail of death from three sides had to be faced all over again as the tattered remnants of the Light Brigade rode back up the valley towards their own lines. But on the return journey there was an added hazard – they were pursued by Hussars and Cossacks.

> *Cannon to right of them,*
> *Cannon to left of them,*
> *Cannon behind them*
> *Volley'd and thunder'd;*
> *Storm'd at with shot and shell,*
> *While horse and hero fell,*
> *They that had fought so well*
> *Came thro' the jaws of Death,*
> *Back from the mouth of Hell,*
> *All that was left of them*
> *Left of six hundred.*

Private John Wightman, whose father had been Cardigan's riding master, was one of the survivors of the 17th Lancers. He left for the history books a graphic account of the futile battle.

On the charge down the valley Wightman had been shot through the right knee and shin but he refused to pull out and continued into the Russian lines, where a Cossack stuck a lance through his right thigh. Wightman killed the Cossack before he could do further damage. The private's horse was riddled with bullets but Wightman managed to coax it back through the enemy lines and 400 yards down the valley towards safety before it dropped dead.

As Wightman lay on the ground, a pursuing Cossack drove a lance at least eight times into his neck, back and through his right hand. But Wightman survived to spend the rest of the war as a prisoner.

Cardigan got back to his own lines and was cheered by his men. The main blame for the whole terrible episode was laid on his hated brother-in-law.

Lucan had begun to lead the Heavy Brigade down the valley in support of of the beleaguered Light Brigade but, seeing the futility of the effort, he drew his men up and retired, himself wounded in the leg.

Cardigan was proclaimed a hero. He said: 'It was a mad-brained trick but it was no fault of mine.'

A tubby Chicago garbage collector, Ruffs Jackson, was warned that he would be fired unless he slimmed. He dutifully crash-dieted and lost 200 pounds. But that was not all he lost. He fell ill, found that he could not lift the bins, was given the sack anyway, and his wife fell out of love with him.

It was Tennyson who was to leave the most enduring tribute to the Light Brigade.

> *When can their glory fade?*
> *O the wild charge they made!*
> *All the world wonder'd.*
> *Honour the charge they made!*
> *Honour the Light Brigade,*
> *Noble six hundred!*

But for most of the Light Brigade, that tribute was also an epitaph. Of the 'noble six hundred', only 329 returned that day from the Valley of Death.

The World's Greatest Blunders

Contents

Acknowledgements

The publishers would like to thank the following for their kind permission to reproduce the photographs in this book:

Gale Carlill 61

Popperfoto 12, 32, 109, 134, 140, 159/Reuter 128 top and bottom, 153/UPI 76, 144

Rex Features 23 top right, 85, 85 inset, 98

Syndication International 89

Topham Picture Library 23 top left and bottom, 49, 70, 117, 119, 124, 140 inset

Trivial Pursuit 83

Preface

We giggle at gaffes perpetrated by others in light relief that they are not our own. Who would want to be responsible for the hurricane howler of 1987, or to have dropped clangers on the air before an audience of millions? Who would want to be the historian who fell for the hoax Hitler diaries – fakes written on postwar paper – or the US president who told his bewildered Brazilian hosts how pleased he was to be visiting Bolivia – and have the bloomer broadcast world-wide?

When it comes to mistaken identity blunders have more serious, sometimes tragic, consequences and giggles turn to gasps. When heroic endeavour or human error become a matter of life and death we can only mourn the resulting disaster.

Chapter One

SHORTS

This cornucopia of quickfire cock-ups begins with some expensive advertising blunders and a handful of hair-raising motoring stories, in which the 'infernal machine' displays a mind of its own.

As always, the language barrier creates its own confusion and, as this chapter illustrates, certain words just don't mean the same thing in translation!

Bloomers in brief

A top store aimed a sales promotion at their account customers – which included Prince Charles. He received a missive addressed by computer to: Mr. HRH Prince, Charles Buckingham Palace, The Mall.

The letter from the impertinent machine began: 'Dear Mr Prince, what would your neighbours in the Mall think if you pulled up outside Charles Buckingham Palace in a brand new red Ford Fiesta, complete with sunroof and alloy wheels?'

Playing the milkman in a television advert nearly cost British comedian Benny Hill his life. His milk float was meant to disappear as if by magic when his back was turned and a crane was hired to whisk it out of sight.

But as Benny, chosen for the part because of his hit song *Ernie – the Fastest Milkman in the West*, feigned amazement and began to walk back to where the float had been standing, the crane's hook snapped and it crashed to the ground. A few seconds later and Benny would have been the Flattest Milkman in the West.

Worried by the growing number of vegetarians, the U.S. red meat industry fought back with an advertising campaign – but without much luck.

First they used American actress Cybill Shepherd . . . until she confessed she never ate the stuff.

Then they tried showing actor James Garner carving his way through roasts and grills . . . until the celebrity was suddenly rushed to hospital for heart surgery.

At this point, they gave up the idea of using a celebrity to beef up their product. Instead they produced a poster of an all-American boy holding the Stars and Stripes . . . until someone pointed out it was almost identical to an old Nazi recruiting poster.

An international airline advertised its 'rendezvous lounges' in Brazil and discovered, too late, 'rendezvous' is slang for sex in that country.

A baby-food company marketing its product in an African country labelled it with a picture of a cuddly infant.

The population took it literally and boycotted the stuff. They thought the jars contained minced babies!

A 30-second Schweppes advert starring William Franklyn and filmed off the southern coast of Spain turned out to be a costly commercial mistake.

The script called for a desert island but, unable to find one, the admen made their own by piling sandbags on to submerged rocks. They covered the bags with a yellow tarpaulin sprinkled with sand so that it looked like the real, tropical thing.

Rain and gales swept the sandbags out to sea and delayed filming, but finally the commercial was 'in the can'. It showed a marooned Franklyn tossing a tonic water bottle containing a message into the sea. But when it hit the screens, viewers complained it encouraged seashore litterbugs.

The advert had to be taken off after only two flightings.

A canal boat scene for an Andrex toilet tissue advert took almost a year to shoot because of the unpredictable British weather.

For the next commercial, which showed a family sitting on the lawn on a summer's day with the famous puppy romping around them, the ad agency decided to go to California to find the perfect sunny 'English' garden.

But it rained solidly and they had to plant 200 fake daffodils and use floodlights for sunshine.

One of the biggest commercial cockups of all time was the promotion for Strand cigarettes.

Using the slogan 'You're never alone with a Strand', the ads featured actor Trevor Brooke as a lone figure with just his cigarette for company. The public understood this to mean no one would want to know you if you smoked Strand cigarettes.

The haunting theme tune made the music charts and Brooke became a celebrity – but the cigarettes stayed on the shelves.

The brand was withdrawn in 1961, just 18 months after the costly campaign was launched.

Yorkshire viewers were in stitches the night the commercials' soundtracks got mixed up.

The words and pictures went like this:
Voice: 'Clean your teeth with this.'
Picture: A sausage.
Voice: 'Give this to your cat.'
Picture: A bottle of Babycham.

Voice: 'This will make your hair gleam.'
Picture: A tube of toothpaste.
Voice: 'Lubricate your car with this.'
Picture: A bottle of beer.
Voice: 'That's my husband.'
Picture: A contented cat.

In the early days of commercial television, many ads went out live, giving disaster plenty of scope to strike.

One commercial called for a close-up of a slice of Spam covered with mayonnaise. At the very instant the meaty morsel filled the nation's TV screens, a portly bluebottle landed on it, looking, after the admen's magnification, like some hideous monster from outer space.

Barclays Bank bosses blushed when they got their vicars in a twist in a £1,750,000 campaign aimed at newlyweds. The clergyman, shown marrying a young couple, was dressed for burying them, in a black funeral stole!

A clanger in a television commercial was spotted in time to save the Royal Family's blushes.

The ad, for Unipart car spares, was to have asked: 'Do you know how to fit a coil in a Princess?' It had nothing to do with the Royal birth rate. It was advertising a part for an Austin-Rover car.

The Princess in question.

12

A tea company landed in hot water with a competition designed to boost their teabag sales. It succeeded beyond their wildest dreams. Syndicates devised a way of winning £20 on every box of 160 bags and bought them by the lorryload. One 100-strong London group stood to collect £80,000 for an outlay of £8,600 on 4,000 boxes weighing eight tons.

Their leader explained: 'You had to scratch panels off cards to reveal six hidden teacups. We thought the cards must be quite expensive to print, so that there would be only a limited number of diagrams. We reckoned if we scraped off enough cards we would end up with a key to every diagram in circulation. After that, every card would be a winner. And that's how it worked out.'

There was just one snag. The tea company was prepared to pay out, but its insurers refused, on the grounds that the syndicate competitors had broken the rules by not using their 'skill and judgment'.

Some would argue they had displayed plenty of both.

The Parker pen company in America promised customers they could 'prevent embarrassment' by using a new leak-proof ink.

In Mexico 'embarrassment' was translated as *embarazar* which means 'getting pregnant'. Dealers were besieged by buyers hoping for a new birth control device.

The slogan 'Come Alive with Pepsi' was a huge success in America. But when the company plastered it on poster sites all over Germany the translation read: 'Come alive out of the grave with Pepsi.' Another version proclaimed: 'Pepsi brings your ancestors back from the dead.'

A Lincolnshire man who complained about drivers speeding near his home became the first victim of the radar trap police had set up to catch them.

Angela Harper believed her luck had run out when her van's fan belt snapped on the M6 motorway.

Thinking fast, she took off her tights and used one of the legs as a replacement. It tore as she drove into the next service area, where she bought an emergency belt. A few miles on, that snapped too, and so did the other leg of her tights.

Finally, she slipped off her knickers, and, using them as a frilly fan belt, coaxed her van into Penrith.

'I was beginning to think I'd run out of clothing,' Angela said.

Only then did the 29-year-old driver of Kendal, Cumbria, look in her toolkit . . . and find a spare fan belt.

13

Lincolnshire businessman Oscar Ejiamike's mistake was to mount a nocturnal expedition to poison moles who were digging up his lawn.

He decided to use the headlights of his XJ4.2 Jaguar to light the scene for his night assault. When the lights dimmed, he started the engine to charge the battery.

Without warning, the automatic car shot backwards and crashed through the wall of his house and into the sitting room, damaging the Jaguar's petrol tank and dislodging a wall-mounted electric heater.

Sparks from the heater ignited the leaking fuel and the car burst into flames. The room was wrecked, the Jaguar gutted, and Oscar's wife Lindy had to flee from the house in her nightclothes.

He spent the next day explaining his £6,000 mistake to the insurance company . . . while the moles carried on undisturbed.

Two Irish roadmen at Hatfield, near Doncaster, made the mistake of trying to save electricity while they had their lunch break.

They switched off the temporary traffic lights at their roadworks on a blind bend. Traffic jammed up for miles until the police arrived to sort out the mess. Said an officer: 'The men felt a bit sheepish when they realized their good deed had gone wrong.'

Drivers who filled up at an Irish filling station found their cars spluttering to a halt after a few yards.

The AA, RAC and police were called out to scores of breakdowns at Lurgan, County Armagh, and discovered the cars had been tanked up with water. The garage had just taken delivery of 'petrol' from a tanker which had been filled up with water to clean it.

No one had remembered to empty it and refill it with the right stuff.

An Exeter AA inspector, called to give a second-hand Mini the once-over, accidentally knocked the automatic gear shift into reverse, and the car went backwards into a brick wall. Then he put it into drive instead of neutral. It hurtled forward into a building. The inspector's call ended up with one written-off small car.

The Japanese Ambassador must have glowed with national pride as he headed for the Birmingham Motor Show to see his country's many exhibits.

But his £20,000 limousine, specially imported from Tokyo, broke down, and he had to wait at a motorway service station for a hired Ford Granada to take him the rest of the way.

14

Marine engine expert Peter Latham thought fixing his Mini's starting trouble would be child's play.

But three months later, Peter, of Dronfield, Derbyshire, was about to admit defeat. He had spent a fortune on new batteries, chargers, plugs and points. Then he discovered that instead of operating the choke, he had been pulling at the heater control.

An elderly woman was spotted in the loo of a West Country motorway service station trying to dry her hands on the machine next to the wash basin. But no matter how she pushed and pulled the knob, the contraption refused to blow out hot air. 'Thems aren't for drying hands,' she complained.

And she was right. 'Thems' were condom dispensers.

An expensive mechanical advertisement erected by the AA in the Cromwell Road in London showed a three-dimensional front of a car, complete with real steam belching from the grill and hazard lights flashing. A few hours after it was put up, it broke down.

A French doctor driving home to Paris from holiday heard an SOS on his car radio – and realized he had left his wife at a garage 200 miles back. He hadn't realized she had gone to the toilet when he stopped three hours earlier.

'I didn't miss her because we don't talk much while travelling,' he explained.

What's red and yellow, costs £50,000 and won't move?

Answer: A new Irish single-decker bus.

When the Irish State Transport Company took delivery of their new vehicle, the first of a fleet of 50, the transport minister himself took the wheel for a special ceremony.

But the bus wouldn't start. And a change of batteries didn't help to get the vehicle on the road.

And when the minister tried to launch it with Champagne, the bottle simply bounced off the bonnet. At his second attempt, he soaked the mayor of Limerick and injured him with flying glass.

Eventually engineers got the bus moving.

But it broke down a mile away.

American Frank Perkins decided, for reasons best known to himself, to set a new record for squatting at the top of a pole.

Frank, of Los Angeles, earmarked a flagpole in San Jose, California, for his record-beating venture. He was determined to perch there for 400 days.

But life on the ground changed quite a bit while Frank squatted on high. First, the firm sponsoring him went broke. Then his girlfriend went off with another man. When Frank finally made his descent, he found his phone and electricity had been cut off.

That wasn't all. He was still two days short of the world record.

On the day the new station of Sandwell and Dudley, near Birmingham, was opened, a top British Rail official turned up to wait with 30 early-morning passengers for the first train scheduled to stop there.

With a mighty roar, the historic 6.36 am whistled through the station at 70 miles an hour and disappeared into the distance.

No one had thought to tell the driver to stop.

The world of sound should have been music to Mervyn Stoneman's ears. Instead, the 51-year-old printer of Plymouth, Devon, wished he had never had the operation which successfully restored his hearing after a lifetime of silence.

Mervyn had had to wait 10 years for the implant of a special hearing aid, but he realized it was all a mistake when he had to lie awake night after night listening to his wife snoring.

'I often saw her puffing out of the side of her mouth when she was asleep, but I didn't realize she made such a racket,' he said.

Wife Wendy drove him into the spare bedroom with her nocturnal noises. 'He wakes up all the time,' she explained.

She lost out on Mervyn's newly restored hearing too – she could no longer swear at him and get away with it.

Things did not feel quite right when the 81-year-old driver pulled up outside his usual supermarket. The car park seemed to be bigger and emptier then he remembered, and a lot of people seemed to be getting into a flap. What was even more confusing was the sight of a huge aircraft hurtling towards him.

The pensioner had in fact mistaken the airport buildings at Palma, Majorca, for his local supermarket. He had innocently joined a convoy of official cars taking a Spanish government VIP to his plane, thinking it was the usual supermarket car park queue.

Air controllers were speedily alerted to the danger and were able to stop the holiday jet from landing while ground staff hastily redirected the startled shopper to a real supermarket.

When Clara Price was born prematurely, the doctor gave her only two days to live. The frail newborn went on to celebrate her 100th birthday in Newport, Gwent, in October 1988.

Vandals wrecked Northampton pensioner Bob Onn's car . . . while he was giving a talk at a residents' meeting on keeping bored teenagers out of mischief.

An over-enthusiastic police sergeant slapped a parking ticket on a bomber which overshot the runway at RAF Abingdon in Oxfordshire – and fetched up on the roadway.

Chief Superintendent Ken Diccox, head of the Newbury Division of Thames Valley Police, waived the customary £12 parking fine. The sergeant concerned was not named.

The new wine was ready, waiting for the verdict of connoisseur Guy Pelegrin. He climbed a ladder to peer into the vat, lost his balance and fell in. Monsieur Pelegrin, 44, died after being overcome by fumes during the testing of the new grand crû at his home, a castle near Bordeaux, France.

Helpful pensioner Thomas Basil lived to regret his good deed, when he took his wife shopping at the supermarket in Minneapolis, Kansas.

First, Thomas drove into the back of a stationary car, ramming it into the back of another. He immediately pulled over to apologize – and struck another vehicle. His wife, greatly distressed, leapt out of the car. She was run over by her husband.

The shopping trip ended with Mrs Basil in hospital and Thomas heading back home. On the way he drove into an office block.

The owner of a house in Memphis, Tennessee, was shocked when he came home and found the house had been burgled.

Among the debris discarded throughout the house he found his Polaroid camera, complete with a recent picture of a rather startled burglar. The thief had snatched the camera and accidentally taken his own picture, and had forgotten to take the evidence away with him.

The owner took the instant Identikit to the local police and the bungling burglar was arrested soon afterwards.

Newlyweds Sandy and David Ison knew getting married was the right thing for them.

Their honeymoon wasn't.

The brand new Porsche they'd given themselves as a wedding present broke down as they motored through France. It cost them £100 to get it fixed. When they awoke the next morning it had been stolen.

They believed love would conquer all and hired a car to travel further. The car developed gear trouble.

Poor Sandy didn't get to see much of Europe. She was allergic to her wedding ring, and suffered from travel sickness, food poisoning and sunstroke. Enough was enough, the couple decided. They headed for the safety of their home in Oxfordshire, but fate had not finished with them. At Dover, Sandy discovered her purse containing £100 had been stolen.

They eventually made it back to their house, to be woken in the early hours by police reporting that the pet shop they owned had been broken into. David staggered out of bed, went to the shop and discovered a chinchilla had got out of its cage and set off the burglar alarm.

Just as David made it back into bed, there was a real break-in.

The couple never even got to see their holiday photographs. The films went missing.

A British diplomat attending a luncheon party at the American Embassy became involved in an animated discussion with his host.

As he gesticulated to emphasize a point, his arm brushed the head of his hostess, knocking her wig across the room and showing all the world she was completely bald.

Sir Thomas Beecham felt satisfied but exhausted after conducting the Hallé Orchestra in a triumphant performance in Manchester in 1939. He was eager to get to bed after the concert but felt he should linger a little, for the sake of politeness, to greet a woman in the hotel foyer whose face seemed familiar, but whose name he could not for the life of him recall.

They exchanged a few pleasantries and Sir Thomas was about to continue on his way to his room, when something jogged his memory.

'And tell me, how is your dear brother?' Sir Thomas inquired hopefully.

'He is very well, thank you, Sir Thomas,' came the polite reply.

'And what is his business now?'

'Oh, he's still King, you know,' the woman said sweetly.

'A set of traffic lights has been stolen from a main road junction in Exeter. A police spokesman said: "Some thieves will stop at nothing."' – *Exeter Express & Echo*

'Deep freeze meat. Best Scotch meat from Wales.' – *Edinburgh Evening News*

'Why only twelve disciples? Go out and get thousands!' – American movie mogul Samuel Goldwyn

The goose-step, that cocky, strutting march associated with Prussian military precision, was not invented by the Germans. It was introduced by the British Army when a commanding officer created a step which would show him at once if any of his men were drunk.

'English shorthand typist. Efficien. Useless. Apply otherwise.' – Spanish newspaper advert

'To move the cabin, push button of wishing floor. If the cabin shud enter more persons, each one should press number of wishing floor. Driving is then going alphabetically by natural order. Button retaining pressed position shows received command for visiting station.' – Instructions in a Madrid lift

'Hand your baggage to us. We will send it in all directions.' – Advertisement in a Belgian forwarding office

> 'Erected to the memory of
> JOHN PHILIPS
> accidentally shot
> as a mark of affection
> by his brother'
> – *tombstone tribute*

Two bickering Frenchmen decided to settle their differences with a duel, but not in the accepted style of the 19th century. They chose to fight with blunderbusses from hot air balloons above the Tuileries gardens.
   Simultaneous shots brought down both balloons, killing both men outright.

You could say David Lloyd George was completely bananas. At the Peace Conference at Versailles in 1919, he came up with the idea that the Italian government should replace commercial losses suffered during the war by increasing banana output. It might have worked – if bananas grew in Italy.

'Raise your glasses and join me in a toast to Prince Charles and Lady Jane.' Businessman Peter Balfour dropped this clanger when he toasted the engagement of the royal couple, in the presence of the then Lady Diana.

19

It was only after the Duke of Monmouth was beheaded in 1685 for plotting to overthrow King James III that it was discovered an official portrait of the traitor had not been painted.

The powers that be decided to remedy this oversight and ordered the Duke's body to be exhumed. The head was reattached and the body dressed in the Duke's finery so that a formal portrait could be completed.

Gustav III of Sweden believed not only that coffee was bad for you, but that it was poisonous. The Swedish king was so sure of this that he ordered the drinking of coffee as a punishment for a convicted murderer. The killer drank, drank and drank. And lived.

It's not every day a forgetful passenger leaves a fortune in a taxi.

Kevin Butler was behind the wheel of his London mini-cab when he was hailed by Kizoto Idehem, a Nigerian businessman. He wanted to go to a bank to withdraw money and Butler waited patiently while he transacted his business. On his return, Idehem placed a bulging black bag containing £241,000 on the back seat of the taxi. Then the trusting tourist made a costly mistake; he asked Butler to hang on for a moment while he popped into a shop. Butler didn't.

Nothing is too much trouble for the attentive staff of New York's Waldorf Astoria hotel. And when the hotel detective saw a man trip and fall as he made his way downstairs one night, he was there in a flash to assist.

The man's suitcase burst open and out tumbled a load of beautiful jewels. The detective helpfully scooped them all up and discreetly hailed a cab for the wealthy guest. Back at his post the receptionist called to report the theft of more than half a million dollars' worth of gems from one of the rooms.

For a brew that was meant to be mild, it had explosive results. The drink was called Smiles and it certainly put a contented grin on the faces of regulars at a pub in Congresbury, near Bristol. So John Parsons, the landlord of the Old Inn, had a glass himself. It went straight to his head.

Workers at Bristol's Smiles Brewery had accidentally put a 'mild' label on a barrel of their extra strong exhibition ale, 8p more expensive per pint than the mild. Said John, 'By the time we realized the error it was too late. Everyone was either wobbling around with broad grins or snoring in front of the fire. I had to order a fleet of taxis to get them home. Most of the tipplers had pretty thick heads the next morning and one chap couldn't manage to go to work.' But at least the misguided drinkers had value for their money.

Chapter Two

MISTAKEN IDENTITY

The often-tragic results of mistaken identity are explored in this chapter. An innocent man is shot through being in the wrong place and the wrong time, newborn baby girls are muddled up in a Nottingham nursing home and given to the wrong mothers, others are accused of crimes they did not commit, publicly honoured in someone else's place or erroneously reported dead.

MISTAKEN IDENTITY

Stephen Waldorf

It was 14 January, 1983, the kind of typical winter's evening in London when you have your car heater turned on full. The commuter traffic crawled its way through the city. It was 6 pm, a Friday, and everyone's aim was to get home and put the week's work behind them.

Freelance film editor Stephen Waldorf was sitting in the passenger seat of a bright yellow Mini, stuck in a traffic jam. He chatted amiably with his companions, Sue Stephens and Lester Purdy, who was driving. They idly gazed out of the car window and at the traffic beside them, exchanging indifferent glances with other drivers.

They never realized, for one moment, that they were being stalked, nor that they were the target of an undercover police hunt for a dangerous gunman. They had no idea that their yellow car, inching its way in the heavy traffic, had gunmen's eyes trained on it all the way. Nor could they have known that a desperate alert had been sounded calling crack-shot police officers to spring into action.

The yellow Mini stopped near the junction of Pembroke Road and Earls Court Road, Kensington. Its occupants patiently waited for the traffic to clear. It was then that the shots rang out, like a scene from a TV film drama. A few moments after 6 pm, Stephen Waldorf lay in the seat of the yellow Mini, close to death. It was only after the bloody ambush was over and the streets were cleared of confusion that the crack CID team realized they had made a terrible mistake: they had shot the *wrong man*.

'It was all over in seconds,' said witness Malcolm Hill, who had heard the shots from his home in Pembroke Road. To Hill, it had sounded as if someone was trying to break down his own front door. What he saw, when he cautiously looked out into the street, seemed too incredible to be true. There were two men crouched beside a Mini, one at the front near-side of the car, the other at the back. They both held guns, gripped military-style with both hands and at arm's length. They were motionless, not making a sound. Hill stared in disbelief as several other men ran from behind the car and crouched down in the same position. As onlookers began to approach, a man called out, 'Get away, we're the police.' It was only then that Mr Hill and the other horrified passers-by realized who the 'hit men' really were. Wearing blue sleeveless flak-jackets, not easily noticed in the dark, the police team looked like gunmen who had found their prey.

David Martin and lookalike Stephen Waldorf; the shot-out mini.

By this time, both doors of the Mini were wide open; the passenger seat was empty. 'At first, I didn't realize there was a girl in the back,' continued Hill. 'There was no sound coming from the car and I think she must have crouched down.'

The policeman at the front of the car knocked out the window of the passenger door using the butt of his gun, as if to get a better view. He then immediately reverted to his original stance, with the gun held in both hands and out in front of him, while, 'very slowly and deliberately', more policemen approached the car. Little did they know that neither the driver, Lester Purdy, nor the man they had shot, Stephen Waldorf, was the killer they were after.

For the top officers who were hunting hardened criminal David Martin, it was all a tragic fiasco. Martin, aged thirty-five, had escaped from a cell at Marlborough Street Magistrates Court on Christmas Eve 1982, where he was awaiting trial on charges of attempted murder of a police officer, possession of a firearm and other charges, including one concerning a £25,000 bank robbery. Martin was a police-hating gunman, who would shoot if approached. He had to be caught.

That night, CID officers had been convinced they had spotted Martin in the yellow Mini. When the Mini stopped, they had decided to make their move, fearing their target might soon be swallowed up in the rush-hour flow of traffic. They knew they could not afford to take any chances; they had to get their man. But they made a near-fatal error, and when the shooting had died down, it was Stephen Waldorf – not David Martin – who slumped out of the car door.

Amazingly, Stephen's fellow passengers, Sue Stephens and Lester Purdy, escaped serious injury. Purdy ran 'petrified' into the night, through a hail of police bullets. But the real miracle was that Stephen Waldorf escaped death. His body was riddled with bullets. One had entered him just above the right hip, narrowly missing his spine and nerve cord, on one side, and the aorta (the main body artery) on the other. Had the bullet hit the spine, Stephen would probably have been paralysed for the rest of his life; had it hit the aorta, it would almost certainly have killed him. There were also bullet wounds in Stephen's shoulder and thigh, and there were cracks in his skull. Stephen was lucky not to have suffered brain damage.

The speed and expertise of surgeons and nursing staff at London's St Stephen's Hospital saved Stephen's life, but it was a twenty-five-year-old off-duty nurse, Jane Lamprill, to whom much of the credit was due. Jane had heard the commotion from her house just 20 feet away from where the shoot-out occurred. It was she who bandaged his arm and held a dressing to his chest until he arrived at the hospital. Doctors said later her actions had been vital in saving the young man's life.

While Stephen lay in agony in Pembroke Road, questions were already being asked: Why had an innocent motorist been gunned down? Scotland Yard began to give its side of the story. According to the police, one of their team had shot the left-hand rear tyre of the Mini to stop it from moving off. This single shot was followed by a barrage of perhaps 13 others, which shattered the windows of the car and severely wounded Stephen. Perhaps, they said, the very first shot had been mistaken by their team as having come from somebody inside the Mini.

The Yard wanted to emphasize that a police team on an operation as dangerous as the hunt for David Martin would consist of highly trained men who were primed to react instantly. Perhaps it was because of this that the gunmen acted without restraint.

The police had a detailed description of the man they were looking for. Martin, a known bisexual, had blond hair and a distinctive hooked nose. It was also known he sometimes disguised himself as a woman, complete with stockings, and that he got some kind of kick from tucking a gun into his suspenders.

Stephen Waldorf bore only a slight facial similarity to Martin, but there the physical similarities ended.

There was, however, one link. Sue Stephens, his fellow passenger that night, was David Martin's former girlfriend. Police had already staked out the flat in Hampstead which she shared with a girl friend. They had kept watch over Christmas, hoping Martin, on the run and with few friends, would try to make contact with her.

After the shooting, Sue Stephens, falsely claiming she, too, had been hit by a bullet, was handcuffed and taken away by police and interviewed at Kensington police station, only a hundred yards away from the ambush.

Her flatmate was also brought in for questioning. Later, both Sue Stephens and Lester Purdy were charged and jailed for handling stolen goods for Martin. At the trial it was stated that some of the stolen items had been found in a flat once occupied by Stephen Waldorf. Stephen, however, denied that he had ever met Martin.

In October 1983, two of the detectives involved in the ambush, Constables John Jardine and Peter Finch, were acquitted at the Old Bailey of attempting to murder Stephen Waldorf and of wounding him. Although disciplinary charges were brought, Mr Jardine was quietly posted to the Yard's Criminal Intelligence branch and Mr Finch returned to uniformed duty.

The one acknowledgment that something had gone drastically wrong that January night, was that neither of the two constables was permitted to carry guns again.

25

Stephen, who had been struck by five bullets and suffered head injuries, made a miraculous recovery. He fought back from the brink of death and was in hospital for six weeks. It was an extraordinary recovery, said Mr Hoile, the surgeon leading the team at St Stephen's. Emergency treatment had included calling in doctors from another hospital, the Brompton Chest Hospital, to drain one of Stephen's blood-filled lungs. His life had hung by a thread for four days and nights. Then he was able to breathe without a ventilator.

Five days after the shooting he was eating solid food. One week later he could actually get out of bed and sit in a chair. And even talk.

In February 1984, Stephen was awarded nearly £150,000 compensation by Scotland Yard. It was, they admitted, a disastrous blunder on that bitter January night. But they also argued that Stephen may have placed himself in jeopardy by associating with friends of David Martin. Said Stephen as he picked up the cheque: 'I suppose it is a fair sum. But nothing could really compensate for the horrors I went through. I thought I was going to die.'

Months after the shooting he admitted he still suffered horrific nightmares. In them he saw guns pointed at him and flashes.

'Sometimes I wake up in a cold sweat shouting "No, No don't shoot." I believe I am back in that car with the police firing at me.' He also said he bore no grudge against the police who shot him. 'I hold no bitterness against them as individuals.'

It was the system, he said, that was to blame.

And he had no harsh feelings about Constables Jardine and Finch not being jailed. 'Like me they will have to live through that nightmare. I will never forget what happened but nor will the gun cops.'

WHAT JUSTICE FOR THE HUNTED MAN?

David Martin was jailed in October 1983. He was found guilty of shooting at a policeman and of firearms offences. The sentence was 25 years in prison.

Martin had been caught 35 days after he escaped police custody. His former girlfriend Sue Stephens had tipped off Scotland Yard. Martin went on a hunger strike and took an overdose in an attempt to get his ex-lover to see him in jail. She refused.

On Tuesday, 14 March, 1984, David Martin hung himself in his cell at Parkhurst Prison on the Isle of Wight. A prison officer had looked in on him just moments before.

The yellow Mini, a colourful but macabre exhibit, kept in police custody in case it was required during the court hearing, was put up for sale. But only when its bodywork was repaired of bullet holes.

The case of the nursery mix-up

From the moment a baby draws its first breath, any mother can tell her newborn's cry from a roomful of other fractious infants, and any mother knows at once that the tiny bundle in her arms could belong to no one else. This makes the tale of the mixed-up babies one of the most heart-rending cases of mistaken identity.

The story of the tragic tots goes back to a crisp autumn night in Nottingham in the 1930s. No one believed Margaret Wheeler when she told them the newborn baby they had given her to hold was not hers. Margaret's own baby daughter, delivered at term on November 18, 1936, was longer, thinner – and redder.

The newborn baby Margaret was handed by a nurse soon after she had given birth was quite different. It was a girl, but there the similarity ended. This baby was obviously premature; Margaret noticed the little nails were not fully developed.

In distress, she summoned another nurse and other medical staff, but they scoffed at her claim. No hospital in the world would make a mistake like that.

'But I'd seen my own baby in the delivery room,' Margaret recalled years later. 'The baby they gave me when I got back to the ward had clearly been born early.'

She was right. The infant had been born six weeks prematurely to Margaret's ward neighbour, Blanche Rylatt. The two women had given birth at almost the same time.

Margaret, having failed to convince the hospital that she had been given the wrong baby, approached Blanche in anguish. But Blanche refused to consider the possibility that a hospital could be so seriously at fault and Margaret had to watch distraught as another woman cuddled and nursed a baby girl that she herself had borne.

It was in great distress that Margaret left the Nottingham nursing home with a child she firmly believed belonged to another woman. She tried gallantly to wipe her doubts from her mind and for seven years gave the little girl all the love a mother could bestow on her offspring. But the

27

terrible conviction that the little girl she was nurturing was not hers continued to fester.

Eventually Margaret mustered all her courage and went to see Blanche again. She suggested that they should go back to the hospital to look at the birth records so that they could be sure, once and for all, that nothing had gone wrong.

By this time, the women shared a close, if somewhat strained friendship. Each little girl called her mother's friend 'aunt' – and it was uncanny how much they resembled their aunties.

Blanche agreed to what she considered a rather unnecessary check, but she was shocked when she and Margaret returned to the Nottingham nursing home they had left seven years before with their babies. They were allowed to examine records. No one could argue with what had been written in black and white. It was clear the babies had been swapped.

The wrong doctors' names were on the forms; notes of the labour, medication given, and the time of birth of each baby related to the wrong mother! Blood and saliva tests proved conclusively what Margaret had tried to tell medical staff all those years before.

The baby blunder was bad enough, but the decision Margaret and Blanche made afterwards was even more dramatic. They agreed they would carry on bringing up each other's daughters. Little Peggy, Margaret's daughter, was to be raised by Blanche and her husband Fred, while Valerie, Blanche's daughter, would continue to be cared for by Margaret and her husband Charles.

The mothers decided not to tell Peggy and Valerie the truth, but agreed to keep in touch. That meant each mother could lovingly monitor her own daughter's growing-up, even though she had no part in it.

It was a touching pact, made because both women thought it would be too disruptive for the children to be taken from the homes they considered theirs.

'We agreed, on counsel's advice, that the children should stay as they were,' said Margaret.

For a while, Margaret was deeply upset by the heart-rending decision she had made. She admitted there was a time when she wanted both children – a desire also experienced by Blanche.

It was only a matter of time before the little girls would grow into intelligent young women, and eye their mothers and 'aunts' suspiciously.

Peggy is now 51, but she still remembers the first moment she started wondering about her parents. She was about 10 and stared longingly at her 'father's' hands, wondering why she hadn't inherited his slender fingers. She couldn't help noticing that Blanche and Fred were both slim, fair-haired

28

and blue-eyed, while Peggy was a brunette, brown-eyed, and, in her own words, 'large and gawky'.

'I was always puzzled by how different I was from my parents,' she said.

Eight years later she found the courage to express her doubts. She was now a junior civil servant. Her 'Aunt Margaret' and 'Uncle Charles' had popped in to see her as she sat munching her sandwiches on Nottingham Castle green one lunch hour. The couple paid regular visits from their home in Cumbria.

'Aunty Margaret showed me a photograph of her other daughter, Denise, born three years after me. I looked at it and then at her.

'I simply said, "You're my mother aren't you?"'

The truth was finally out. Both Margaret and Blanche were relieved, because it had been inevitable and because it had come from one of the girls themselves.

For Peggy, many mysteries were solved that day. 'The likeness of that photograph was incredible. I just knew Denise was my sister. It cleared up all the things I had been puzzling over for years.'

Valerie was told the truth while on a course at a teacher training college. When she qualified she had to say a painful 'goodbye' to Margaret and Charles and begin to pick up the pieces of a new life with her real parents, Blanche and Fred.

'I'll never forget the moment when I opened the little gate that led to the path to the front door or the feeling of waiting for that door to open,' she recalls.

For Margaret and Blanche, all those years of living a lie were over. But they still feel, as only mothers can, that what they did was the right thing for their children. Peggy and Valerie are both married and each has two children of her own, which has made it easier for them to understand that tragic decision. Valerie lives in Andorra with her two youngsters. Peggy lives in Nottingham, with her family. The two women consider themselves sisters, and are as close as real sisters could be. The muddled-up babies harbour no resentment for their 'lost' teenage years.

For Margaret, now 79, and Blanche, now 74, mother love finally won through. Blanche often thinks back to that moment in a Nottingham nursing home, when she was asked by a nurse, holding Valerie: 'Is this baby yours?'

Catching up with the Joneses

Having the same surname as thousands of others can bring problems enough. But one luckless woman, Susan Jones, also shared her christian name, date of birth and home town with someone else – and ended up in court as a result.

Susan Jones's troubles began when she returned to her home in Barnsley and found a police squad car waiting for her.

An officer handed her a summons to Bristol magistrates' court to face a charge of owning a dangerous dog, which had viciously bitten a woman. There was another charge of keeping two dogs without a licence. The charges related to offences allegedly committed in Bristol 18 months previously. Susan Jones knew it couldn't possibly have anything to do with her. She'd lived in Barnsley for six years, had never been to Bristol in her life and the only dog she'd ever owned was a little Jack Russell that had died the year before.

But Susan Jones had not reckoned with the determination of the boys in blue. To them it was a fair cop. The more she protested her innocence, the more the police insisted she was the person they were after. They suggested she wrote to the court. Susan did as they suggested but received no reply. She telephoned – and was told to put her complaint in writing!

The only response was a letter saying the date of her hearing had been changed, and warning that the case would go on if she didn't turn up.

By this time, pregnant Susan was in great distress. 'That was when I broke down and cried,' she said.

Two months after her ordeal began, she was found 'innocent'. The prosecution explained that police had answered a complaint from a woman who had been badly bitten by a dog, and found its owner, another Mrs Susan Jones, had moved to Barnsley.

Susan eventually received an apology from the chief superintendent of Avon and Somerset Constabulary, admitting their 'regrettable error'. What cleared Susan's name in the end? She was working in a shirt factory in her home town on the day she was supposed to have been in Bristol. Her employers confirmed it. And the police went on the Jones hunt again.

Tragic coincidence

By tragic coincidence, the two girls who were injured in a bad car crash near Seville in Spain looked remarkably similar. One girl later died. The other, terribly scarred and with facial injuries which made her virtually unrecognizable, lived, but suffered from loss of memory as a result of the accident.

The parents of the one girl were grief-stricken and went into deep mourning, while the other couple prepared themselves for the long fight to help their daughter to get back to normal. As she recovered, the sickening truth dawned on them – she was not their daughter. In the confusion of the accident, the hospital had mixed up the girls' handbags, and, as a result, their identification.

Two months after the crash in 1978, the grieving family were re-united with the daughter they thought they had lost. The patience and love of the other family turned to despair when they learnt they had been nursing someone else's daughter – and it was theirs who had been buried.

Heinous errors

There were celebrations all round when, in 1976, Young Liberals' president Peter Hain was acquitted of a robbery. The case was widely publicized because it hinged on a question of identity.

Peter Hain, charged with stealing £490 from Barclays Bank in Putney, West London, was picked out in an identity parade. Hain strenuously denied the charge, but three of four schoolboys who saw the chase after the robbery were convinced they had seen him, and at a police identity parade four days after the incident on 24 October, 1975, cashier Lucy Haines pointed him out.

An unjustly charged Peter Hain.

It took an Old Bailey jury four hours and 55 minutes to bring in a verdict of 'not guilty' on 9 April, 1976. Hain's wife Pat and his family were naturally overjoyed at the acquittal which ended months of speculation and suffering.

'I feel absolutely insulted and degraded that even one person could think I might have been a thief,' Hain said after his acquittal. But he was one of the luckier ones.

He escaped being jailed for a crime he did not commit.

In December 1974, an innocent man was offered £17,500 compensation after spending five years in prison. It was the largest pay out ever for someone jailed in error.

The victim, Laszlo Virag of Windsor, Berkshire, had been wrongly accused of stealing parking meter coin boxes in Bristol and Liverpool, shooting and wounding a police officer and resisting arrest. He was convicted by a jury at Gloucester Assizes and sentenced to ten years at Parkhurst prison.

Virag, a 35-year-old Hungarian, was identified by several policemen and other witnesses, but he maintained he was in London, 130 miles from Bristol, at the time of the alleged offences.

Nine witnesses had testified to this at his trial.

Later, another man was found to have used the gun involved in the case.

32

Electrician Alphonso Eric Douglas, 30, spent 36 days in custody in 1977 for a crime he did not commit. He was also pointed out at an identity parade. Douglas was accused of an £8,750 armed robbery.

Said Douglas: 'I don't think it is right that a person should be charged on just identification evidence alone. I think there should be other evidence. The past six months have been a nightmare for me and my family with these terrible charges hanging over my head.'

In March 1968, lorry driver Albert Chapman was released after 17 days behind bars at Leeds prison. Chapman, 33, won freedom for a crime he didn't commit, after a confession from the real villain, Roy Roberts, 25. The two men were similar in appearance.

Chapman was jailed for nine months at Bradford Quarter Sessions after being wrongfully convicted of driving a van while knowing it to be stolen and for assaulting a police officer. His conviction rested on his identification by Bradford PC David Hemsley. Roy Roberts was in prison for other offences when he heard of the mistake, and confessed.

The lorry driver later went to see Roberts' wife, Maureen, so that she could pass on his thanks. 'If he hadn't owned up, I'd still be in jail,' he told Maureen.

Yet another case of criminal mistaken identity involved 41-year-old Leonard Everington, a labourer of Ipswich, Suffolk. He spent four weeks in prison awaiting trial on three theft charges.

He was discharged at Ipswich Quarter Sessions when Mr William Howard QC said: 'This case illustrates the dangers of identification through photographs alone.'

Everington, charged with stealing from Ipswich churches, had in fact confessed to the crimes. He had done so, he said, 'under pressure'.

Two men who did not confess after being wrongly identified still had their freedom taken away from them. Both cases occurred in 1968.

Harry Wimpress, 60, a night watchman, was alleged to have attacked a nurse and stolen her handbag. He was picked out at an identity parade by another nurse, but a stranger, Francis Holden, 20, owned up after Wimpress had spent 21 hours in a cell.

Patrick Crundal, 20, a shop assistant, was alleged to have stolen bank notes from women in Bradford. Six women identified him in court as the one who had nicked their money.

This time, 17-year-old Jeremiah Delaney owned up, but only after Patrick had spent four weeks in custody. They were said to look alike.

33

The strangest case of mistaken identity must be that of a man accused of a street robbery which took place while he was in a police station to report that he had been assaulted!

William McRoberts, 37, spent seven weeks in jail because of an amazing mix-up. It happened like this. A Mr Kenneth Jennings was attacked by four men and robbed of £10 at Victoria Station in London.

At that moment, McRoberts was at his local police station in Sutton, Surrey, telling police how *he* had just been assaulted.

A few nights later, McRoberts was at Victoria Station, when Jennings saw him and mistook him for one of his previous assailants. He called the police and McRoberts was arrested.

Unfortunately, he couldn't at first remember exactly where he had been at the time of the four-man attack. Eventually, and luckily for him, he did. From behind bars he sent a message to his solicitor. A police sergeant from Sutton went to Brixton Prison and confirmed McRoberts' alibi.

The one-minute beauty

It was the moment every beauty queen dreams of, when her name is announced as the glamorous golden girl – the winner.

Beautiful blonde Sharron Gardiner of Cardiff was overjoyed to be acclaimed as Miss Wales in the Miss World heat in 1987.

Her glory lasted just one minute. Sharron, 23, was walking up to be crowned, applause ringing in her ears after being told she had won the contest at Pontypridd Municipal Hall in Mid Glamorgan, when the bad news was broken by Miss World chairman Eric Morley. He hastily explained that there had been a mix-up in the scrutineer's count. The real winner was 18-year-old Nicola Davies from Merthyr Tydfil who won £2,000 and a holiday in Greece. She would also go on to represent Wales in that year's Miss Universe contest in Singapore.

Said Sharron's father: 'It was a terrible blow. She has been taking part in beauty contests since she was 15. Representing Wales in the Miss Universe contest was to be the pinnacle of her career. She put everything into preparing for it.'

Eric Morley did give Sharron £1,000 compensation for her disappointment. 'I was handed a piece of paper. When I announced the result the scrutineer suddenly realized he had made a mistake, ran across and gave me the right result,' he said.

Sharron accepted her consolation prize philosophically.

'At least I can say I was Miss Wales, if only for a minute. I felt so humiliated. I don't think I'll ever enter a competition again,' she commented sadly.

The spy who stayed out in the cold

The spy who fooled the world made history and hit the headlines as a hero before his cover was finally blown – by his own brother.

Everyone knew of Charles Henry Evans, Britain's wartime master spy who had infiltrated the Nazi hierarchy. He even had the temerity to write to intelligence expert and author Nigel West to correct his references to MI6 in a book, and he brazenly took part in a BBC-TV news interview, his face half-hidden behind a venetian blind to protect his identity.

The world heard how Evans had been recruited into MI6 while still at Marlborough public school, had studied medicine at Heidelberg University and had later adopted a German identity. He described how he became a colonel in German Military Intelligence and went on to win an Iron Cross, all the while busily feeding Nazi secrets to Britain.

It was all too much for his brother Gerald, who decided to speak up in 1985 after a blaze of publicity.

Charles did not go to Marlborough, but to Kilburn Lane High School in North London, he declared. He was never involved with MI6, nor was he a doctor. He had been a ship's trainee purser, an office clerk and a pub barman.

Gerald conceded that Charles had seen service – as a dispatch rider in the British Army. And his contact with the enemy took place when, as a humble private, he was captured in France and spent five years as a prisoner of war in camps in Poland.

'The only gong he got was his service medal from the British Army,' Gerald said. 'And he must have been exhausted coming home to Paddington every night when he was supposedly studying medicine in Germany.'

Charles needed medical help, Gerald stated.

But one fact of the bogus spy's amazing life story was true, or nearly true. It appeared he had been to Marlborough – to buy an old school tie for a friend.

After these family revelations, Charles Henry Evans did not dare to come in from the cold.

Grave error

A graveside funeral service was held up for half an hour when the vicar realized he was burying the wrong body. He noticed, as wreaths were removed from the coffin top, that it bore a man's name – and not that of great-grandmother Nora Boote.

Relatives waited in the church while embarrassed funeral directors rushed off to collect Mrs Boote's body and coffin so that the service at St Michael's Church in Bishops Hitchington, Warwickshire, could continue.

Dead or alive?

Ethel Clunas faced a heart-breaking task. She had been called by the police to identify her son, killed in a climbing accident in Scotland. She had been shocked to read about the fatal accident in the newspapers. Police could put no name to the body two other climbers had found in the Cairngorm foothills in Scotland. Ethel noted the age of the unidentified victim, about 25, his description, and the fact he was wearing a gold Timex watch with a brown leather strap.

Her heart sank. It had to be her son Stephen.

She travelled from her home in Inverness to make the formal identification. Yes, she confessed in tears, it was Stephen. The grief-stricken family went through the harrowing ordeal of registering the death and making funeral arrangements. Then Stephen rang to say hello.

Ethel had identified a complete stranger as her son.

The sad tale turned to overwhelming relief because a family friend had read about Stephen's 'death'. Pat Harvey thought it strange that Stephen's body could have been found on a Saturday, when she had chatted to him in Aviemore the day after. Pat, who used to work with Stephen in the laundry department of a local hospital, knew for certain she couldn't be mistaken. 'I told the police that if Stephen was dead I must have just had tea with a ghost,' she said.

Police paid the Clunas family another visit, then Stephen's brother-in-law Fraser Ross and his father Angus went to the mortuary to see for themselves. This did not help to clear up the confusion for the now distraught family.

Said Ross: 'I thought it was Stephen although I was not sure because people change after they die. But his father thought so too.'

Police at Inverness had to step in. They took fingerprints from Stephen's home and matched them with the corpse's. They were not the same. They scoured hotels around Aviemore after hearing Stephen had been staying there and finally found him – alive and well.

Said Stephen: 'I am glad to be back home but I did not know anything was wrong until the police contacted me. I tried to phone home but couldn't get through.'

'It has been an awful shock,' Angus Clunes said. 'One day our boy was dead, the next he was alive. It was like having him brought back from the dead.'

It had all been an amazing but tragic coincidence. The clothing on the body made Ethel Clunas sure it was her son. The face was remarkably similar and so was the hairstyle. Later, happily reunited with her son, she said: 'This has been a terrible mix-up. You would have to have gone through what I have to know how I feel.'

Identical twins

Identical twins Simon and Peter Eubanks had Sussex police seeing double. Simon, 26, a professional boxer, was charged with theft from a Brighton store. But the case was withdrawn when no one could be sure which brother had actually turned up in court.

Simon had denied the charge and prosecutor Trevor Small thought it unwise to proceed. Peter Eubanks was also a professional boxer.

Crash victim

The life support system for teenage car crash victim Kristine Bailer was turned off – on the orders of another girl's parents.

The couple's own daughter, Wendy Liby, was killed outright in the same accident in Fort Wayne, Indiana. Kristine was critically injured.

Officials confused the names of the two victims and mistakenly called Kristine's friend's parents to ask for permission to switch off the life support system. They gave it.

Spitting image

Wherever he went, the little boy was treated like Royalty. Children would beg their parents to be allowed to say 'hello'. Grown-ups stood aside, looking on in awe. It was not everyday, they all thought, you clapped eyes on the future King of England. Only it was not the eight-year-old Prince Charles.

Way back in 1957, the right royal recognition caused a big problem for proud mum Mrs Betty Shepherd. Her son Martyn was the spitting image of the little prince. They were the same age, had the same shy smile and wore their hair parted in the same way. Naturally, the similarities caused confusion.

When Mrs Shepherd and her husband took Martyn to a hotel in Sussex the hotel owner promptly called the local police to report his fears that Prince Charles had been kidnapped.

The constable who turned up took a lot of persuading that Martyn Shepherd was not a Royal kidnap victim.

'Since he was six months old people said how closely he resembled the Prince,' said Mrs Shepherd. 'Children in parks ask their parents if they can speak to the Prince.'

The similarity for the Shepherds, who lived in Morden, Surrey, did not end there. When Charles got flu, Martyn had a temperature too. Mrs Shepherd had a curious theory about her son. She believed that her great interest in the Royals, especially the Queen, could have influenced Martyn's looks. 'I read everything I can about the Royal Family. If Martyn misbehaves, I tell him Prince Charles wouldn't do that.' Martyn would sometimes reply: 'I bet he would!'

Said Mrs Shepherd: 'He's proud of being like the Prince and although he's so young he seems to have the feeling that he has something to live up to. I want him to show the same fine, sturdy qualities that we see in Charles,' she went on. 'But if he got conceited we'd stop it very quickly.'

Boeing horror

In a tragic air crash, a Boeing 727 struck a mountain in northern Cyprus, killing 15 people – and causing unnecessarily prolonged anguish to the families of the three air hostesses who perished.

British crew Andrea Pegg, 23, of Bournemouth, and Sharon Simcock, 29, of Blackpool, worked for the Turkish airline Talya whose flight was on its way to Nicosia when the plane crashed. Sharon's body was not returned to Britain, because it was mistaken for that of a Turkish air hostess and buried in a communal grave in Istanbul. Andrea's corpse was sent in error to a Blackpool mortuary, where Sharon's body should have been sent. And the horrifying mix-up was complicated further when the body of Turkish air hostess Mensah Banu was thought to be that of Andrea and was sent to the British girl's home town of Bournemouth.

The mistake came to light only when RAF pathologist Wing Commander Ian Hill noticed the dental records of Miss Banu did not match those of Miss Pegg. He travelled to Blackpool to make the correct identification while officials in Istanbul faced the terrible task of exhuming Andrea's body.

'The only forms of identification on the crash victims were plastic adhesive labels,' the pathologist reported. 'The whole business should have been carried out by people who knew what they were doing.'

Chapter Three

AGAINST ALL ODDS

This chapter contains some of the most embarrassing moments in history. Burglars who do nothing but bungle, intimate amorous adventures that suddenly become public performances and experts who seem to attract disaster create the kind of unbelievable situations recounted in these pages, which seem to occur against all odds.

Don't count on it

Derek Howell paid £85,000 for a newsagent's shop in Hastings, Sussex, just to have access to the parking space for his Rolls-Royce. Then he discovered his £40,000 pride and joy was too wide to fit it.

Customers were delighted with the bonus they received from a cash dispenser at a New York bank. A cashier had put 20 dollar bills in the five dollar slot and card holders got four times what they asked for. No one got away with it though. Their names had all been recorded with their transactions.

Father of two Matt Casey hit the roof when he received his building society statement, claiming he owed nearly £1 million on his three-bedroom semi in Washington, Tyne and Wear. A computer hiccup had sent similar letters to more than 200 customers of the Northern Rock Building Society.

Two guard dogs worth £350 were stolen from the house they were supposed to be protecting in Whaplode Drove, Lincolnshire. Their owner, Rosemary Cormack, said: 'We hoped the dogs would scare people off.'

A Swiss bank desperately offered a £2,000 reward to trace a lucky customer who had been paid out £46,000 by mistake. A girl cashier had confused Austrian schillings with German marks which are worth twice as much. She rushed after the customer but he vanished in the crowds.

The bungling bandit was as blind as a bat without his glasses, and that was how he came to make a spectacle of himself. He decided a disguise was called for when he went to rob a jeweller's shop and put on a new suit and a false beard for the occasion, but left off his specs. The myopic marauder burst into the shop, snatched a tray of rings and ran off – smack into a parked car just outside. Staff at the shop in Brighton, Sussex, soon overpowered the confused thief.

A Durham museum hurriedly removed a Roman coin from display when a little boy spotted it was a free plastic token from a soft-drink company.

A mugger thought he was on to a winner when he tackled a betting shop worker carrying two plastic bags. He was able to snatch only one, and made off down the road with his takings. When he felt safe, he took a look at his haul and found he had stolen a bag of dirty washing. The day's takings from the shop were in the other bag.

Inventor Lieutenant Ivan Saevas was awarded 40,000 dollars for designing a training device that saved the Swedish Air Force nearly eight million dollars. First the tax authorities took 30,000 dollars off Saevas then they decided he was now in a higher tax bracket so deducted another seven thousand dollars.

Finally they said he was liable to social security and other taxes so demanded 16,000 dollars more. Saevas was left 13,000 dollars worse off after inventing the money-saving device. The tax people said they would investigate his case.

The parents of Anton Grellier were sorry they ever called him stupid. When he grew up and became a wealthy Belgian businessman, Grellier sent them generous cheques – incorrectly made out so they couldn't be cashed.

Once bitten . . .

W hen farmer Lawrence Littley went muckspreading, he was a little too generous and caused quite a stink.

Littley forgot to turn off his sprayer as he towed it home behind his tractor – and coated the picture-postcard village of Musbury, Devon, with a layer of evil-smelling sludge. In his sound-proofed cab, the farmer was unaware of the chaos he left in his wake as he showered fertilizer on eight cars, seven houses, several angry locals and the post office.

The blunder would have been embarrassing for anyone, but especially so for Littley, who was chairman of the local parish council. That night the red-faced farmer went back to the village to clean it up.

43

Escapologist Eric Ward finally had to admit defeat – in a British Rail toilet. One of Eric's tricks was to be chained in a straight-jacket, then hauled 100 feet up on a rope by a crane. The rope would be set alight and Eric would be out of the jacket and on to the crane in seconds.

Another feat consisted of his being tied to the frame of an advancing circular saw and freeing himself before he could be sliced up.

But he was helpless when the lavatory lock jammed on an inter-city express taking him from London to Stoke-on-Trent.

Said Eric, 39, of Woking, Surrey: 'It was the most embarrassing moment of my life and I was hoping to keep it quiet. I tried every trick I knew but the lock wouldn't budge.'

The escapologist was still trapped when the train left Stoke. His ordeal lasted an hour before his knocking and cries for help were heard.

A director filming a river scene for a television commercial wanted to include a group of ducks, but they kept swimming out of the picture – until someone had the bright idea of anchoring them with bricks and lengths of string tied to their legs. The admen decided to move upstream to a better location, taking the co-operative ducks with them, but the new stretch of water was deeper and the string too short.

Weighted down by their bricks, the poor ducks sank. As one adman, the entire crew dived in and rescued them.

When Joseph Begley of Evesham, Worcestershire, sent off 2,000 cigarette coupons for a watch, nothing happened. He wrote to complain, and within three days, 10 parcels had arrived from the cigarette company. The next day there were 18. The next day, 10 more. By this time, Begley had received three tape recorders, a golf bag, a pressure cooker, two electric blankets, a baby's cot, a doll and many other things he didn't really want. Running out of space, he asked the company to stop sending him gifts. They replied – with a letter of apology and 10,000 coupons to make up for his inconvenience.

He sent them off, ordering tools and a bedspread. By return came two ladders and a plant stand.

Mr Begley swapped his brand of cigarettes.

The picture decorating the lids of tins of biscuits for the Christmas market showed a colourful scene of an old-fashioned tea party in an English country garden – just the thing to give to granny with a bottle of sherry. But if granny had good eyesight, she would have choked on her sherry and custard cream. Just a step away from the elegant ladies pictured sipping their tea, two terrier dogs were busy engaging in something very rude and across the lawn could be seen the naked limbs of a couple seeking more excitement than tea and biscuits.

Thousands of the tins had gone out to the shops before a Middlesex grocer spotted the saucy scenes. Huntley and Palmers, who made the biscuits, said it must have been an agency artist's idea of a joke and scrapped the remaining stock at a great loss.

Every newspaper takes pains to prevent it, but sometimes the same item is published twice. *The Scotsman* seems to have gone one better. An Edinburgh reader wrote this letter to the editor. 'Sir, I note with interest that you have published my letter of 13 June three times (so far) this week. I'm pleased that you like it so much but if the letter is to become a regular feature in *The Scotsman* I'd appreciate a small fee by way of acknowledgement. May I add that I approve of your use of different headings each time the letter is published. This stops it becoming too stale or repetitive. Let me know if your readers grow tired of the letter and I'll send you a fresh one.'

Reluctant soldier Peter Lenz of Nuremberg, West Germany, thought he had the perfect ruse for dodging call-up. He went for his medical with a urine sample from his girlfriend, a diabetic. But a few days later, Peter received orders to report for duty. A covering letter said: 'We would have believed you were a diabetic – but not that you are pregnant.'

Would-be worshippers dialling London's Westminster Abbey for times of services were taken aback by an angry female voice saying: 'It hasn't come out yet. Sod it.' Hundreds of callers heard the unholy slip, made by the receptionist who recorded the tapes for the answering machine, but no one at the Abbey noticed for two days.

An Abbey spokesman said: 'She was trying to record a message when several people were demanding attention at the reception desk and phone calls were flooding in. She suffered acute embarrassment afterwards and was in a state of near collapse. But the clergy have heard much worse language. They took a light-hearted view of it.' Showing true Christian tolerance, they forgave the red-faced receptionist.

Shipbuilders scratched their heads when they surveyed their latest bit of work on a nuclear submarine. Something didn't look quite right. Then the awful truth dawned. They had welded a large section upside down! A senior union member of Vickers in Barrow, Cumbria, described the mis-match as a 'monumental cock-up'. The mistake is thought to have happened when a section of the vessel arrived without proper identification. Workers had to re-weld the part. Ironically, the submarine was named *Triumph*. 'It was very embarrassing,' said a Vickers spokesman, and declined to say what the mistake cost the taxpayer.

Jumble sale organizer Judith Fraser-Smith was floored when she realized she'd sold off the local town hall carpet by mistake. The carpet was kept in Bakewell Town Hall, Derbyshire, and unrolled only to deaden the sound of footsteps when the magistrates' court was sitting. Members of St Giles's Church in the Peak District village of Great Longstone had taken it thinking it was jumble. Judith contacted her helpers but no one knew the young couple who'd made the £1 bargain buy. A notice was pinned outside the church hall and an advert placed in the local newspaper. A week later the couple rang to say it was they who had the town hall carpet, and they'd cut it up to fit their staircase.

The man from the ministry was just explaining why he didn't consider a notorious blackspot dangerous. But his firm words: 'I will not accept that this is a highly dangerous road' were interrupted by three cars piling up behind him. Jim Davidson from the Ministry of Transport carried on talking as first a blue estate car in the background ran off the road and up a steep grassy slope, followed by a screech of brakes as the second car, swerving to avoid the estate, smashed into the back of another vehicle. The whole scene was captured on TV and broadcast to millions of ITN early evening news viewers. Mr Davidson's crash course took place when he visited the A19 near Peterlee, Durham.

Nadine Williams of 13 Newall Crescent, Fitzwilliam, West Yorkshire, was delighted with her new bathroom. She thought it was a birthday surprise from her husband. But he knew nothing about it. Plumbers should have called at Number 30 Newall Crescent. By the time they realized their mistake they had ripped out the Williams's old bath, wrenched off the wall tiles and completed the £450 renovations.

Passengers on a Britannia Airways flight from Zurich to Gatwick listened in horror as a stewardess announced the plane was about to ditch in the sea. She explained the emergency procedure, as white-faced passengers listened in terrified silence for two minutes.

Then the voice of the captain came over the intercom. 'It was a mistake. We were meant to tell you we were about to serve the duty frees.' The wrong pre-recorded tape had been played.

46

The binmen's blood ran cold when they heard a baby crying inside their dustcart. Driver Stan Anderson, horrified that someone could dump an infant, immediately called his council depot boss Alex Patterson who said: 'Search the lot.' The refuse team at Luton, Bedfordshire, tipped five tons of rubbish out into the street and frantically began their mercy hunt.

After clawing through mountains of garbage, they found the crying child – it was a talking doll. The toy's battery had somehow been switched on when it landed in the back of the cart. Said Mr Patterson: 'The cries were incredibly life-like and it gave the men a real scare.'

Irishman Brendan Murphy, 25, was caught on the hop when he raided a shoe shop in Bedford. He swopped his worn-out training shoes for a classy £29 pair of cowboy boots. But staff had no trouble spotting him when he tried to make a getaway, wearing two right boots, one a size nine, and the other a size 11. Murphy was put on probation by the town's magistrates.

Love on the rocks

B ritain's oldest married couple in 1988, Ted and Florrie Bradley, postponed their 100th birthday parties when they discovered they were both only 96.

For Karen Bowen, it seemed a naughty but nice way to end a fun evening out at a nightclub in Windsor, Berkshire. The tall, dark, handsome and obviously wealthy stranger invited her back to his luxurious home, to romp in a whirlpool bath and on a king-sized bed. When Karen woke the next morning her Romeo had gone. The three people staring at her were the estate agent and two prospective buyers of the show house.

Newlyweds Kenneth and Donna Kiehn posed for just one more picture at their wedding reception – and fell off the balcony to crash down 30 feet into an indoor fountain. 'They were still holding hands when we pulled them out,' said a friend.

A Californian couple decided to spice up their sex life. They checked into a Santa Barbara hotel for seven days of fun and frolics – which they videoed and replayed endlessly. They couldn't understand why the staff gave them flowers and champagne and the manager halved their bill when they checked out. Then they learnt their home movies had accidentally been transmitted all over the hotel, entertaining staff and guests.

Engineers were baffled by a real-life Agatha Christie mystery on the Orient Express. They were called in because the train refused to budge when the stationmaster waved it off at Innsbruck station in Austria on its Paris-Venice run. They began working through the train . . . and found the cause of the trouble in the very last compartment. A young couple making love were blissfully unaware that the girl's foot had become entangled in the communication cord, automatically jamming on the brakes.

A London publisher took his mistress to Normandy, leaving his wife under the impression that he had been called away to Brussels on business. The sneaky pair spent a blissful week together in an olde-world hotel, soaked up the sun and wined, dined and loved in fine style. They returned home, convinced that their sexy secret would never come to light.

A year later the publisher, perhaps with a pang of conscience, took his wife to a travel agent to arrange a holiday for just the two of them. Browsing through the brochures, she came upon one extolling Normandy as the place to unwind. The cover showed a happy, laughing couple leaning against a harbour wall with their arms around each other, unaware that they were being photographed by the French Tourist Board. It was the erring husband and his girlfriend.

A police hunt for an IRA bomb suspect netted a cheating husband. He had told his wife he was going fishing but went away with a girlfriend instead. He sparked off a security alert while tucked up with his lady love, for he had left his car parked outside the Grand Hotel in Brighton, the target of IRA bombing in 1984.

Police became suspicious, found the car owner's name and address in Wiltshire and rang his wife. She said he couldn't possibly be in Brighton, but in Dorset fishing with friends.

This alarmed the police even more. They sealed off the hotel, a helicopter hovered and sniffer dogs were sent in. The two-timing husband and his lady arrived in the middle of it all. They were taken away and questioned but later released. 'He'll be entering another sensitive area when he gets home,' a policeman remarked wryly.

The sensitive zone that exposed a two–timing husband.

Suah Shaheen was looking forward to her wedding night with new husband Mohamed Saleh. Not until it was too late did she find out he was really a 'she', married to a man, and with two children of her own. Police were called and had to break the news that Saleh, 29, liked to wear men's clothes. The registrar who had conducted the marriage ceremony was arrested. Police said he should have noticed!

The woman boss of a West German building firm refused to pay a £130 fine for speeding in her BMW, insisting it was a company car and anyone of 16 staff could have been driving it. Miffed at having their word doubted, the police sent photographs taken by their radar equipment to her home. The snaps showed her doing 86 miles an hour, with a young man nuzzling up close to her as she sped along. Her husband declared that he was to divorce her and would use the snaps as evidence. The attentive boyfriend faced a charge of endangering road safety.

When Zaza Kimmont returned to her New York home after a holiday she found a strange toothbrush next to her husband's in the bathroom. There were traces of lipstick on the bristles. Zaza was furious. Convinced there was another woman, she angrily smashed up the home, shattering lamps, china, vases and ornaments, gouging furniture and slashing paintings. She stormed back home to mother . . . where she learned the truth. Her husband had invited his mother to stay while she was away, and the toothbrush belonged to her. The insurance company refused to pay out for the thousands of dollars' deliberate damage to the apartment.

A seven-year-old boy living on a top-security base near Ipswich, Suffolk, dialled 999 and said his parents were having a terrible fight in the next room. Military police stormed in and found a red-faced mum and dad making love not war.

The earth moved for a courting couple parked on the beach at Weston-super-Mare, Avon, when their car began sinking in the sand. A garage recovery vehicle sent to pull them out also got stuck. Then a second rescue truck got bogged down. All three were hauled out the following day by four vehicles linked together.

A pair who got overheated in the snow started a full-scale emergency alert when an old lady saw a pair of legs sticking out of a snowdrift under a hedge. She ran to the nearby post office and said she had found a body. A 999 call went out and police and ambulancemen raced to the field at

Nuneaton, Warwickshire – and flushed out a young couple who leapt up and ran off naked, clutching their clothes. Police described the lovers as 'cool customers'.

Two teenagers kissing in a car at traffic lights in Rio de Janeiro held up traffic for two and a half hours when their dental braces became entangled.

In Sicily, 64-year-old Duke Giuseppe Avarna made sure everyone knew when he was making love to his beautiful 29-year-old girlfriend . . . by having the village church bells rung. But sleepy locals did not appreciate the nightly ding-dongs. The Duke was fined £15 for disturbing the peace and £70 for 'insulting' his estranged wife. His lawyers said: 'He is crazy about his girl and wants the entire dukedom to share his happiness.'

A sexy secretary's search for Mr Nice Guy attracted far more male attention than she had expected, when a letter she had written to a friend found its way to government and newspaper offices throughout Canada.

The love-lorn secretary had dictated her desires into a computerized office printer at the state government offices in Quebec, and the machine, which could not tell the difference between official and private correspondence, immediately sent copies to every member of the government, the press, and all the other secretaries.

They were bemused to read the memo which said: 'My love life is a bit dull. I haven't seen him for two weeks. Men, they're not easy to understand. Tell me if you meet a nice, good-looking guy. I'd be happy to meet him. Solitude is a heavy burden.'

'It was a technical error,' said Jacques St Onge, the woman's departmental head.

It's criminal

A man handed a bank cashier in Del Ray Beach, Florida a badly spelt note reading: 'I got a bum. I can blow you sky height.' The cashier showed it to his colleagues and they all fell about laughing. The would-be raider was so embarrassed he ran away.

After robbing a garage in Reno, Nevada, a gunman allowed the owner to make just one phone call. He did – to the police.

Robbers used too much explosive on a bank safe in Munkebo, Denmark, and demolished the building. When they finally managed to crawl out they found the safe, still intact.

A burglar unwittingly became an advertisement for a security equipment firm he raided in South London. An infra-red device detected his body heat and set alarm bells ringing. Police arrested him within two minutes.

Finding his victim had no cash, an Essex mugger forced him to write a cheque. 'My name is Andrew Cross. Make it out to me,' he ordered. His victim promptly went to the police, armed with the name of his assailant.

A policeman was amazed when a thief waved at him from the Bristol shop he was burgling. The crook had mistaken the policeman for his accomplice.

A burglar broke into what he thought was a block of flats and found himself in the lap of the law, in Knightsbridge Magistrates' Court, London.

Hoping to cut his electricity bills, a County Tyrone man tampered with his meter. But he fiddled it in the electricity board's favour, and clocked up thousands of extra units and a £600 bill.

A burglar planning to raid an off-licence broke into the wrong shop, took nothing, was arrested within minutes and suffered the indignity of a judge telling him: 'Give up crime, you're no good at it.'

Two raiders out to rob a Buckinghamshire post office tricked the postmistress into opening the security window by asking her to change two £50 notes. She snatched their money and slammed the window shut and they fled empty-handed – and £100 worse off.

Police soon caught up with a thieving motorist who drove off from a Midlands petrol station without paying – and spluttered to a halt less than a mile up the road. He phoned the AA who diagnosed the problem. He had filled up with diesel fuel instead of petrol.

Two handcuffed prisoners leapt from a prison van in Luton, Bedfordshire, and made a dash for freedom. But the shackled pair were stopped short when they ran past a lamp-post, one on either side of it. They were yanked off their feet, collided in mid-air and crashed to the ground in agony. They were rushed to hospital with dislocated arms and crushed ribs.

Two lovers running drugs for a gang discussed their mission as they cuddled in a Worcestershire hotel room – not realizing the baby alarm was on and everything they said was being broadcast to the reception desk. The desk receptionist promptly called the police.

Three prisoners from Lincoln were hitching a lift when a bus stopped for them – and out jumped seven warders from their jail who recaptured them. The warders were escorting a group of prisoners to court.

The 75 convicts who tunnelled out of jail at Saltillo in northern Mexico slipped up on the planning. After six months of hard digging for freedom, they emerged in the nearby courtroom where most of them had been sentenced.

Forgers are often caught by their printing mistakes. But a Kenyan crook who produced near-perfect banknotes was easily identified, thanks to his vanity. Instead of a portrait of the president, he used a picture of himself.

When a would-be robber pushed a note demanding cash across the counter of a wine shop in Yorkshire, shopkeeper John Patterson had to laugh. Neatly printed at the top was the man's name, address and postcode. When the thief produced what appeared to be a gun in a handkerchief, Patterson pelted him with sweets from a jar, then chased him out of the shop armed with a bottle of Coke. Detectives caught up with the hapless thief less than an hour later.

An Irish thief broke into a London electrical shop to steal television sets, but drove off with three microwave ovens by mistake. In court, the judge suspended the man's 18-month jail sentence because of his 'crass stupidity'.

Richard Richardson barged to the front of the queue in a Texas bank and shouted: 'This is a stick-up. Give me the money!' The 20-year-old cashier retorted firmly: 'You're in the wrong line. Wait over there.' Richardson meekly waited – until the police turned up.

An Oregon bank robber pushed a note to the cashier reading: 'This is a hold-up and I've got a gun. Put all the money in a paper bag.' After reading the note, the cashier wrote on it: 'I don't have a paper bag.' The thwarted thief walked out shaking his head.

Nothing went right when an Italian decided to rob a bank in Milan. He tripped on a door mat as he burst in and fell. His mask dropped and his revolver went off. He got up, ran towards a cashier, slipped and grabbed the counter for support, dropping his gun. With staff and customers laughing, he rushed out humiliated – straight into the arms of a policeman who was writing him a parking ticket.

A cool Southampton crook strolled into a city supermarket and filled a basket with goods. He went to the checkout and gave the cashier a £10 note, intending to snatch the contents of the till when she opened it. But the till contained only £4.37, which he took, losing £5.63 on his robbery.

Tourist traps

A pretty girl on holiday from London was admiring the grand pre-Revolution buildings of Red Square in Moscow when a fur-hatted comrade sidled up to her. Furtively he pressed a note scribbled in Russian into her hand. It was, she was sure, a top-secret message for British Intelligence that she had to guard with her life. Her heart pounded as she passed through security checks at Moscow airport, but her secret remained undiscovered and, back home, she took it straight away to London University to be translated. The note read: 'You ugly English cows are all the same.'

A woman asked for a refund on her new passport at Reigate, Surrey. She was unhappy, she told post office staff, because she'd discovered the Lake District was not in Holland.

It's easy to forget something when you're packing for a holiday. And housewife Susan Grove of Cheshire forgot her birth control pills. She remembered as she and her husband, with their baby daughter, were heading for Dover to catch the cross-Channel ferry, and they pulled off the motorway to visit a chemist's. While they were away from their car, it was stolen, complete with their luggage and £800 spending money. They spent the next fortnight at home – gardening.

A German couple sunbathing nude on a beach at Tropea, Italy, were arrested under a bylaw which allows bare bottoms only if they meet 'the highest standards of classical beauty'.

A British Rail guide to scenic railways in Devon had cover pictures of Selworthy village, which is in Somerset, and cannot be reached by train.

Publican John Weller snapped away enthusiastically on his holiday in Yugoslavia. But back home in Long Whatton, Nottinghamshire, he was shattered when his prints arrived. He had 24 perfect shots of his left ear. 'I must have held the camera the wrong way round,' he said sheepishly.

It was the height of embarrassment for British Airways when they flew their beauty queen Kim Turner to Cyprus to promote their image. As Kim, 23, landed safely at Nicosia, her luggage was being expertly unloaded at Zurich. Her suitcases, containing her uniform and cocktail dresses vital for her six-day tour, reached her a day later.

Expertease

B uilder Stan Gordon spent a day bricking up a doorway, stood back to admire a job well done – and still didn't spot his mistake. He had walled himself in. Red-faced Stan of Daventry, Northants, discovered the blunder when he tried to leave. There was another door, but it was locked. He finally escaped after shouting for help to a shop assistant across the road.

Workmen were called in to improve security at a Birmingham block of flats for the elderly. They were told to fit entryphones so that callers could identify themselves. But the workmen installed them on the inside of the doors and no one could get in.

A builder's blunder at a new jail on the Spanish island of Ibiza made it easy for prisoners to escape. He put in cell door locks which could only be opened from the inside. The prisoners had to promise on their honour not to escape.

Builders of a new primary school at Taunton, Somerset, made a glaring error when they put clear glass in the lavatory doors. Parents helped replace the glass so that the school could open as scheduled in September 1984.

There was a bigger problem with the loos at Northamptonshire County Council's new nuclear fall-out shelter. It didn't have any. Officials controlling emergency services would have to risk radiation by nipping outside to spend a penny.

A house taken over by Channel 4 for a do-it-yourself series was left in an unlettable condition by the television experts who renovated it. Inspectors from Milton Keynes Development Corporation gave the semi the thumbs down after the series *Anything We Can Do* ended. A spokesman said: 'It looked great on television, but not if you had to live in it.'

Firemen at Barnsley, Yorkshire, had faces as red as their engines when magistrates refused to issue a 10-year registration certificate for their new social club. It had no fire escape.

Equally embarrassed was the senior London Transport engineer who took the first £50,000 bus of a new fleet on a test run . . . and tried to drive the 20 foot double-decker under a 13 foot bridge, slicing the entire top off the vehicle. The only injury was to the driver's pride.

Demolition experts sometimes blow it too. Like the Irishman and his pals who were demolishing a pier at Greenock, Strathclyde. They had to be rescued by an RAF helicopter because they had started work from the wrong end.

A team at Reutte, Austria, blew up the wrong railway bridge – the new £1 million structure that had been opened only three days before.

A demolition team turned up at the home of Barbara Worthington in Cheshire. She arrived back from shopping to see them tearing her place down. They had come to the right street – and the right number. It was the town they got wrong. The workmen should have been knocking down 54 Brookside Avenue, Poynton, but instead, they set to work smashing up the same address at nearby Offerton.

When a Swiss hotel chef lost a finger in a meat-cutting machine, he submitted an insurance claim. The company, suspecting negligence, sent an expert to see for himself. He tried the machine out to prove it was safe – and lost a finger too. The chef's claim was approved.

To check whether curtains in a hotel ballroom were flame resistant, a Vienna fire prevention officer held a lighter to them. He thought he had safely extinguished the fire that resulted, but minutes after he had left, the room was ablaze, ruining the stage, valuable paintings and part of the roof – and no doubt the fire officer's reputation.

The head of the Royal National Lifeboat Institute museum at Bristol capsized while out sailing. A lifeboat was sent to rescue him.

A man in Rochester, New York, cancelled all engagements while his three-day bout of hiccups lasted. 'They're kinda embarrassing in my line of business,' he said. He was area director of the National Council on Alcoholism.

An Irish contact lens manufacturer was awarded £45,000 damages when he walked through the glass door of a golf club, injuring himself badly.

57

Soon after qualifying as Britain's first woman train driver, Anne Winter had her first crash . . . when the miniature steam engine she was driving at an Oxfordshire school fete came off the rails at three miles an hour. Organizers discovered it was caused by children leaning out and a blushing Anne said: 'Thank heavens it wasn't my fault.'

Electrical expert Phil Sunderland was covered in confusion after getting his wires crossed on BBC breakfast television. Viewers jammed the switchboard when he connected the live wire to the earth pin while demonstrating his firm's new plug.

Within minutes, presenter Selina Scott warned viewers not to make the same dangerous mistake but to leave it to the experts.

A group of Harwich lifeboat men who hired a boat to go on a river trip with their families ran aground on mud flats. They had to be rescued by their own lifeboat manned by a reserve crew.

Dr Yvonne Hodges was delighted to find she was unexpectedly expecting a baby . . . and embarrassed too. She ran a family planning clinic near her home in Axminster, Devon. Yvonne and her husband – also a doctor – declined to confess which birth control method had failed them.

A policeman's lot

Policeman Jimmy Landels will never forget the first time he locked someone in his shiny new handcuffs. It was his grandmother, and he had to send for the police to free her.

Jimmy, 19, was on holiday at home in Brora, Sutherland, after graduating from police college. His 77-year-old grandmother asked him how the handcuffs worked and he proudly demonstrated – on her. Then he realized he had left the key at Inverness, 75 miles away.

He said: 'I had to phone the local police for help, but granny saw the funny side and sat there laughing until tears came to her eyes.'

58

There were red faces all round when Warwickshire policeman Eric Clegg, on holiday with his wife in Sorrento, Italy, had a visit from the local police. They accused him of spending forged currency.

The fake cash had been handed to him in error by his bank back home, who swiftly wired out new funds.

WPC Fenella Whitehouse made an arresting sight as she ran naked from her house to chase a suspect. Fenella, 20, likes to sleep in the nude and when she heard someone trying to break in, she jumped out of bed and chased the intruder.

'It was only when I started running through the garden that it dawned on me I was starkers,' she said later.

Fenella failed to get her man, but male colleagues from her Bristol police station caught up with him later.

It was an embarrassed pair of bobbies who took their brand new Panda car back to the station at Slough, Berkshire, with £200 worth of damage.

They had been ordered to catch up with three men driving a stolen dumper truck, and they soon spotted it chugging along at 10 mph. Just like the telly cops, they roared past and blocked the road. The villains jumped off and ran, with the two constables in hot pursuit. Meanwhile the dumper truck continued on its slow but steady course – slap into the back of the police car.

Nottingham detectives who had handcuffed a youth to the wheel of their car while they chased his friends returned to find their captive – and the car – gone. It was later found abandoned, with the handcuffs still attached to the wheel.

Then there was the blushing bobby who got lost on his own beat. Teasing colleagues nicknamed him The Mole because he was unable to find his way out of a network of subways in Birmingham. He was too embarrassed to radio for help or ask passersby for directions, and was eventually rescued by a search party.

Puffing runners in a half-marathon near Kirkcudbright wished they'd never seen the motor-cycle cop who escorted them. He took a wrong turning and the 10 leading runners behind him lost their chances of winning. They ran 19 miles instead of 13.

Another 60 behind them in the race clocked up an extra two miles before realizing they were on the wrong road.

59

Sometimes, police blunders call for real teamwork. Crack cops swung into action when a passerby spotted a safe dumped by the road. One man stood guard, detectives took fingerprints, and a Land-Rover arrived to carry it back to the station at Halesowen, West Midlands.

But try as they might, the burly bobbies just couldn't shift the thing. That was when they realized it was a junction box – firmly cemented to the ground.

Two policewomen in South Yorkshire are still trying to live down the day they took two prisoners by mistake – on a goodwill visit to a school. Julie Marshall and Jackie Lawrence let two youngsters handcuff themselves together, and found they didn't have a key to release the boys. They had to take the 12 year olds back to the station to be freed.

A traffic experiment for police in Bristol had embarrassing results too. Rush-hour traffic was found to flow more smoothly after police point-duty had ended.

When a sharp-eyed officer spotted a valuable stolen car in a South London side street, it was taken to the police station. But when fingerprint experts went to examine the £18,000, 150 mph Cosworth Sierra, it had been nicked again – from the garage behind the station.

The light-fingered talents of an arrested burglar got one cop out of trouble. When a PC drove up with the criminal, the duty sergeant at Preston police station went outside to open up the garage for him – and the station's door slammed shut behind him. With no key and no idea how to beat the sophisticated electronic security system, the two cops had to ask the burglar to open the door. He did so in just a few seconds.

An officer alone in the police station at Tuffley, Gloucestershire, locked himself in the loo, and had to radio for help on his walkie-talkie.

But policemen have their human side, as this tale shows. A lady driver pulled up at traffic lights in Hampstead, London, followed by a male driver and, behind him, a police car. As the lights changed, the lady moved away and then stalled.

The man behind her braked sharply and gave an angry blast on his horn. Whereupon the policeman behind him switched on his loudhailer and said: 'Come along sir, give the lady a chance.' By now very flustered, the woman driver started off again – and stalled once more.

60

Cops came unstuck trying to take a junction box into safe-keeping.

Back in the police car, someone had forgotten to switch off the loudhailer. An amplified groan was heard booming through the street: 'Silly cow's done it again!'

Security-conscious police towed away cars parked near a Glasgow hospital during a visit by Princess Margaret and left them in side streets. When the owners finally managed to track their vehicles down they found 'helpful' notes on the windscreens from a Sergeant Collins telling them where to find their cars.

And when prisoners escaped by helicopter from Gartree jail, police set up road blocks to catch them.

In a police campaign against car tax dodgers in Barnsley, Yorkshire, most of their own patrol cars were nicked for having out-of-date licences.

PC Graham Markwick lectured schoolchildren at Deal, Kent, on how to foil bike thieves and advised them to get their bicycles stamped with their postcode . . . then found his own had been stolen. It wasn't stamped.

In Salford, Manchester, 70 officers made a dawn swoop on a 13th-floor flat, rifles at the ready. But it was the wrong address. The two escaped convicts they were seeking got clean away from a neighbouring tower block.

It's not just British policemen who sometimes end up with red faces. Two New York officers who stepped out of their squad car to investigate suspicious loiterers on a river pier heard the crunch of wheels on gravel as the group fled.
    They turned round just in time to see their car rolling forward and plunging into the water. They had to catch a bus back to their station.

Two women agents from FBI headquarters in New York were sitting in Central Park when they were set upon by muggers who took their jewellery, cash and guns before leaving them handcuffed to each other with their own handcuffs.

Star-spangled clangers

Jackie Onassis became the golden girl of the literary world when she persuaded millionaire popstar Michael Jackson to write his autobiography for her employers, Doubleday publishers.

It was a publishing coup, because 'Wacko Jacko' rarely gives interviews at all, let alone baring his soul for a book. Surprisingly, the whole deal went off without a hitch.

Alas, poor Jackie was not so successful with other sign-ups. Having failed to persuade the elusive Hollywood legend Greta Garbo to write her memoirs, she turned her attention to another big name – sultry Italian star Sophia Loren.

Jackie sent an assistant to the home of the sex goddess in Lucerne, Switzerland. Would La Loren, the aide asked, write her autobiography – including her 'extraordinary love affairs and marriages'.

Sophia was not interested – but came up with a suggestion of her own. 'Tell Mrs Onassis to write a book about *her* extraordinary love affairs and marriages,' she retorted.

British television presenter Selina Scott will never forget the night she dropped one clanger after another in the presence of hundreds of VIPs.

By the time she'd finished presenting the Salute to the Falklands Task Force concert, she was wishing the ground would swallow her up. She had announced actor Denholm Elliot as Donald Sinden, another distinguished thespian; actor Richard Todd became Sir John Mills; and English rose Virginia McKenna was confused with Dame Anna Neagle.

Blonde TV action girl Anneka Rice hit the wrong note when she interviewed guest trumpeter Herb Miller on ITV's TV-am programme.

'Between your legs you have something to show us,' she said cheekily. Herb, brother of famous Glenn, burst out laughing at the saucy gaffe.

Sports presenter Jimmy Hill was worried about pronouncing the tongue-twisting name of a rugby player, Nigel Starmer-Smith. Before he went on air, he repeated the name over and over again to get it right.

On air Jimmy pronounced the player's name perfectly, and overcome with relief continued: 'He had seven craps as scum-half for England.'

63

Important officials waited in vain for Mastermind general knowledge quiz host Magnus Magnusson to turn up to open a restored windmill. The man with all the questions came up with the answer – he had completely forgotten about it.

Magnusson, who had been invited in his capacity as chairman of the Ancient Monuments Board, and had even plugged the event, at Nithsdale, Dumfriesshire, on radio, confessed afterwards: 'I just forgot.'

Sometimes a star learns the hard way that if you say the wrong thing it's best to move on to another subject. British comedian Michael Bentine was watching an audition for a stage show. After listening to the woman singer on stage, he turned to the man next to him and said: 'Isn't that awful?'

'That's my wife,' his neighbour replied.

Trying to salvage the embarrassing blunder, Bentine pressed on: 'I didn't mean the singer. I meant the song.'

'I wrote it,' came the reply.

Former motor-racing champion James Hunt was delighted to be invited to the launch of a new Mercedes model. The ace took it on a 100 miles an hour demonstration lap before an audience of motoring journalists, experts and Mercedes executives at Donington Park.

He handled the speedy vehicle with all the skill you would expect from an ace driver. Well, nearly all. Unfortunately he had forgotten to take the handbrake off and brought the gleaming £20,000 machine back to the pits with smoke pouring from the wheels.

The public likes to see the famous falter – and they got value for money from American TV announcer Ben Graver.

After an orchestral concert, he told millions of viewers: 'You have been listening to the New York Symphony Orchestra under the baton of Atosco Touranini . . . I beg your pardon, Otosco Tiscani . . . I mean Artuto Toscanni.'

Eventually he gave up and started again: 'Your announcer has been Ben Graver, ladies and gentlemen. Remember the name. You may never hear it again.'

But delighted viewers phoned in their hundreds, demanding that he should not be fired. He wasn't.

On the cards

Fate really put the boot in for the Wellington family. They won £100,000 in a football draw – but lost the prizewinning tickets.

John, Sally, and their son Mark, 19, could have kicked themselves when they realized they had misunderstood the rules. Mark had been given a ticket showing a picture of Liverpool star Ian Rush when he filled up with petrol at a garage taking part in the football game. To stand a chance of winning a fortune, Mark had to match his card up with another showing Liverpool's club motif, and they actually had the matching card in their home in Parragate, Cinderford, Gloucestershire. But the Wellingtons all thought they had to have two pictures on one card to win. So they chucked both cards out.

Three days' search of their local rubbish tip – with special permission from the council – failed to produce the cards and cost them the chance of scoring £100,000. The Wellingtons could only stare bleakly as all the rubbish was finally bulldozed into the ground.

'It was heartbreaking,' said Mrs Wellington. 'I tremble when I think how I put those cards into a rubbish bag.'

Matters were even worse for her husband John. His colleagues at work couldn't understand how a financial manager could have thrown away the chance of making a fortune.

Long-distance loving

Terry Jasper was pleased that his shy son had finally found the right girl. He thought it a little odd, however, that Damon, 19, never brought the girl home, although they chatted happily on the 'phone.

Girlfriend Donna had a very good reason for not popping round to the Jasper family home – she lived in Hong Kong. And the distance seemed even greater when Terry got the 'phone bill. Naturally, in view of the big part played by the telephone in Damon's romance, the lad's main wish was to get 'engaged'.

'When Donna's dad took her to Hong Kong that was bad enough but now my love life has turned into a terrible nightmare,' Damon complained. His father had ordered him to use the money he was saving for their wedding to pay for the 'phone calls.

Chapter Four

A FOOL AND HIS MONEY

Tales of some of the wealthiest people in the world being parted from their money – or at least some of it – make interesting reading. Are the rich really so gullible, or does greed make them temporarily blind?

Confidence tricks, frauds and hair-brained schemes to make money abound in these pages, along with one scheme that sounded daft but actually succeeded for the Canadian inventors of the hugely popular board game, Trivial Pursuit.

Oil's well that ends well . . .?

Count Alain de Villegas certainly impressed the directors of Elf, the French national oil company. This bizarre, but obviously brilliant Belgian seemed the answer to all France's problems. He had, he said, a remarkable solution to the country's oil shortage. With his colleague, an Italian scientist called Bonassoli, he had invented a machine so technically sophisticated that it could literally sniff out oil!

Because the Count had been introduced to them by Antoine Pinay, their country's former Prime Minister, the Elf executives had no reason to doubt his word. They conferred at a hush-hush meeting and decided that no less a person than President Giscard d'Estaing should be told of the discovery. The President, in turn, agreed that the project was so crucial to France's future that any money paid for the invention should come from special government funds.

The Count was duly handed a staggering 30 million pounds' worth of government money and set about building his magical black box. But the black box was such a sensitive secret, no one but he or Bonassoli were to be allowed to open it.

It was indeed an amazing piece of equipment. As reconnaissance planes flew over France's potential oil sites, the black box spewed out sharply defined maps showing where hidden oil deposits could be found.

The directors of Elf were ecstatic, and oil workers immediately began drilling umpteen bore-holes, expecting oil to gush forth at any moment.

But it was nothing like the 'digging for victory' they had anticipated. All the holes were bone dry. Not a single drop of oil was to be found.

Suspicions were aroused and, finally, the magic black box was forced open. Inside, all that was found was a set of maps . . . and a photocopier!

The French police immediately left for Belgium to apprehend the slippery con-man. But he proved as elusive as the supposed oil deposits – and was never seen again.

The gullible rich and towering deceits

It was back in the 1920s that the notorious 'Count' Victor Lustig and Daniel Collins 'sold' the Eiffel Tower. In fact, they had actually 'sold' it *twice* – to two separate scrap merchants. You would think no one would make the same mistake again; yet there was at least one man – a wealthy Texan – who had never heard the story.

Just after the Second World War, a con-man named Stanley Lowe offered the Eiffel Tower as scrap to the unsuspecting Texan. The Texan was on a visit to Paris when Lowe managed to convince him that the tower – one of the most famous monuments in the world – had been so badly damaged during the war that the city's officials had decided to sell it off as scrap. According to Lowe, the historic monument was up for sale at its scrap value – 25,000 dollars. The Texan bought the story lock, stock and barrel.

Luckily for the Texan – and for Paris – Lowe's con was discovered and he was sentenced to nine months in jail – an experience not entirely unknown to him. In fact, until his 'retirement', at the age of 50, he spent more than 16 years in prison for a variety of audacious frauds and cons. One was a spending spree in America, where he spent no less than 3,000 dollars of phony currency, crafted by a London counterfeiter named 'Johnny the Mask'. For that little jaunt, Lowe was deported.

Then there was the time he persuaded a Japanese tourist to part with 10,000 dollars to help restore London's St Paul's Cathedral. He had donned one of his large collection of clerical gowns for the occasion, just to add a bit of authenticity to the appeal.

Lowe fancied himself as a bit of a Robin Hood. 'I wanted to rob the rich,' he said. He claimed he simply couldn't help himself; people everywhere, it seemed, wanted to give him their money. And it could be so much fun, too. One day he would be Oscar-winning Hollywood producer Mark Sheridan, seeking investors for a new, guaranteed box-office smash; another day, he would become Group Captain Rivers Bogle-Bland and, despite the rather dubious double-barrelled tag, managed to convince people he was a war-time flying hero currently working undercover for the government on a secret mission.

69

The Eiffel Tower, sold to the man in the big hat at a knock-down price.

Lowe did not just extort from ordinary people; he would sometimes set his sights far higher – even as high as the Royal Family. Once, he smooth-talked his way into a job as a footman at Marlborough House, home of the late Queen Mary. Here, his plan was to steal as much as he could lay his hands on. But his taste for high living eventually betrayed him, when he arrived for work one day wearing a designer suit and driving a brand new Jaguar (which he had stolen) – a bit suspicious for a footman on £6 a week. When he was questioned by police, he explained, 'She (Queen Mary) is surrounded by priceless possessions, and I had nothing . . . It's not that I'm disloyal to our beloved Royal Family. I just decided she should be punished for her greed.'

Lowe, who had begun his life in an orphanage in north London and had developed into a small-time criminal, had the gift of the gab and was used to coping with tricky situations. Once, the owner of a Mayfair apartment caught him stealing. Cool, calm and collected, the con-man explained: 'Madam, this is an emergency. I was just passing when I saw a man attempting to hurl himself from the window.' Then, with his pockets full of jewellery, he swept past the astonished woman and was gone.

Stanley Lowe eventually ended his life living in a bed-sit. Gone were the days of hand-made shirts and shoes, the times when life revolved around magnums of champagne, weekends at the ritzy George V Hotel in Paris and luxury holidays in Bermuda – all paid for by clever cons involving the rich and gullible.

Under the hammer

Butcher Arthur Dawson thought he'd got a good price for the rusty old banger which had stood in his garage in Walsall for 30 years. He had sold it for £150,000 to a kindly car dealer – who didn't seem to mind about the bodywork falling apart and mice attacking the leather upholstery.

In fact, the 'rusty old banger' turned out to be a 1936 Mercedes-Benz tourer – a classic model of which just ten were made and only four still exist. And the 'kindly car dealer' had been John Price, who put his new purchase up for auction -- where it went for £1½ million.

The new, proud owner, millionaire Swedish property developer Hans Thulin, had spent the last 10 years scouring the world for the 500k Mercedes-Benz Special Roadster. 'I'll restore it and very soon it will be worth £5 million,' he said. 'But I'll never, ever sell it.'

All Mr Dawson could say was: 'I didn't do a very good deal, did I?'

Laughing all the way to the bank?

Chris Sandland, company secretary of Young's Brewery in Wandsworth, London, couldn't believe his eyes when he saw the latest bank statement showing that his company was £5 million in the black. 'We normally run with an overdraft of £2 million by the end of the year, so when the cashier mentioned the figure we didn't take too much notice – until we realized we were in credit.'

But Sandland's joy did not last for long. Five days later, he received a letter from a rather embarrassed customer services manager, Chris Green of the National Westminster Bank . . . asking for it all back! 'I was concerned,' Green had written, 'to learn that we have credited your account with the sum of 'five million pounds and no pence' in error. I can confirm that the necessary adjustment has been made to take the money back again.'

The bank had every reason to be embarrassed. Had they not picked up the error, in just those five days they stood to lose over £7,000 in interest payments!

Never trust a weatherman

Nearly two billion pounds was wiped off share values in February 1988, when reports of another Chernobyl nuclear disaster were flashed around the world.

The London stockmarket plunged, as dealers went wild at the news of a damaged Russian atomic plant spewing radioactive fallout all over Europe; America's White House was bombarded with frantic calls; the Swedes launched a fall-out alert along their border with Russia; while the Kremlin added to the chaos by refusing to deny or confirm the report.

Then red-faced weathermen in Britain had to admit it was all a false alarm. Staff at the Meteorological Centre in Bracknell, Berkshire, had dreamed up a bogus message to test the hotline to the International Atomic Energy Agency in Vienna. Somehow the message had appeared on a Telex machine and, suddenly, all hell had broken loose.

Said a Met Office spokesman: 'We can't figure out why the Telex message should suddenly appear and give people the fright of their lives.'

The big winner was the American dollar – it soared in two hours of frenzied trading.

Engineer turns property tycoon

Blundering engineer Bill Savin had gone along to a property auction in Bristol purely out of interest. He had just sold his own house and was curious to know what his money would buy. He came away the reluctant owner of a row of ten Regency houses worth £1.8 million!

Blundering Bill had raised his hand to scratch his nose, and before he had time to realize what had happened, his 'bid' had been accepted.

Bill was too embarrassed to tell the packed auction hall that he didn't want the prestige properties, or that he had nowhere near the money to pay for them. His confession came later, as the vendor's solicitors awaited their cheque for £1,800,000.

Bill finally got his own solicitor, Richard Castle, to get him out of the mess. Said Castle: 'Mr Savin is just an ordinary chap who does not have the money for such a property deal. It was just a terrible error. The vendor's solicitors seem to understand it was just a ghastly mistake.' Later, another auction was called to sell the houses, this time to a *bona fide* developer.

I am a camera – fly me!

It seemed like a great idea at the time – you bought a camera and got a cut-price flight. The promotional scheme, hatched by TWA and Polaroid in the United States, would sell cameras *and* fill airline seats. The customers would be getting a bargain, too. Yet the scheme went down as one of the biggest boobs in the history of sales stunts.

What the high-flying executives at TWA and Polaroid forgot to do was to add to the small print: 'Only one camera per person.' The result was that, for the price of a 20-dollar camera, snap-happy Americans could buy a cut-price airline ticket to anywhere they fancied. The more cameras they bought, the more tickets they could buy and the more money they saved.

Soon, travel agents were buying cameras by the thousand, giving customers huge discounts over and over again. Shrewd businessmen made fortunes by scooping up caseloads of cameras and selling the discount vouchers to companies with large travel bills: the McDonnell–Douglas Corporation bought 1000 coupons at 10 dollars each, and saved 200,000 dollars on their executives' travel expenses.

While Polaroid chiefs celebrated their massive boom in camera sales, TWA executives admitted ruefully: 'We left some big loopholes.'

Der Führer's secret life

Any newspaper in the world would have been happy to pay a fortune for the ultimate scoop: the private, unpublished diaries of Adolf Hitler, spanning a watershed in world history, from 1932 to 1945.

The German news magazine *Stern* could not afford to miss the chance of boosting its circulation sky-high – for an outlay of £2.5 million. This was the sum paid for exclusive world rights to the Nazi leader's intimate, day to day revelations. And for becoming the victim of what has been called the literary hoax of the century.

The 'Hitler Diaries', touted to the world as the scoop of all time, were all fake, the work of a con-man who became obsessed with his forgery and fooled hardbitten newspaper executives and historical experts.

It was in 1983 that *Stern*, and that most reputable British newspaper, *The Sunday Times*, announced the existence of volumes of Der Führer's wartime jottings. No one had any reason to suspect that their publication was the

75

Heidemann shows the books *Stern* claims are Adolf Hitler's diaries.

result of collaboration and collusion between two men, one of whom was a 53-year-old award winning journalist, Gerd Heidemann, who worked for *Stern*, the magazine he was to defraud.

The other was a small time forger, Konrad Kujau, 46, who had been running a profitable sideline in counterfeit luncheon vouchers. He was, in fact, a talented artist with a fertile imagination and a feeling for fantasy.

Kujau supplemented his living by selling antiques, especially war memorabilia. He never missed a chance to pull a fast one on eager collectors, cashing in on their cravings for material, and was not above manufacturing his own certificates of authenticity. He 'aged' the documents by soaking them in tea – a technique that was to earn him a fortune from news-hungry editors throughout the world.

Then he moved on to paintings, supposedly done by Hitler. This line was to lead to his relationship with another keen collector of Nazi memorabilia, Fritz Stiefel, which sparked off the Hitler diary hoax.

Stiefel often bought items for his collection from Kujau, who decided, in return for his faithful custom, to treat him to a real gem, a diary written in the Führer's own fair hand.

News of the startling find soon reached the ears of *Stern* journalist Gerd Heidemann, who was also obsessed with the Third Reich.

Heidemann never doubted the authenticity of the new discovery. As any experienced reporter would do, he embarked on background research and learnt, to his great excitement, that a courier aircraft had crashed near the Czechoslovakian border towards the end of the Second World War. The plane, flying from Berlin, had carried secret papers belonging to Hitler. There was every reason to suppose that the diaries had been among them.

Stern, when it published the astonishing diaries scoop, added that Heidemann had managed to obtain the historic material from 'East German contacts'. The papers had been discovered in a hay loft where they had supposedly been hidden after the plane crash.

Heidemann could scarcely wait to tell his superiors about his find, but senior editors Peter Koch and Felix Schmidt dismissed his scoop as yet another piece of obsessive fabrication.

It was Thomas Walde, a senior *Stern* journalist, who unwittingly became part of the hoax. He and Heidemann together succeeded in convincing *Stern*'s top management that they should offer Kujau two million German marks for the priceless diaries. Walde and Heidemann were assigned to follow up the story.

Kujau was beside himself with joy. He couldn't believe his luck, and set about his work with relish. If *Stern* wanted Hitler's war diaries, they would have them – as many as they wished. Such was Kujau's enthusiasm for the project that he compiled a prodigious output of 62 faked volumes.

It seems incredible now that *Stern* and a host of eminent academics could have been taken in by some of the entries.

'Friday, 13th: Ten thousand communists meet in Berlin Sports Palace, pledge will fight fascism to last breath. Demonstration, many arrests. By Jove, we must stamp out the Reds.

Saturday, 14th: Meet all the leaders of the storm troopers in Bavaria, give them medals. They pledge lifelong loyalty to the Führer, with tears in their eyes. What a splendid body of men!'

Kujau claimed smugly that 'Hitler's life' had taken him no time at all to record. As the money kept on coming, he had simply kept on writing, and with each fake entry his confidence grew.

Of the famous bomb plot against Hitler by the German Generals, Kujau recorded gleefully: 'Ha! Ha! Isn't it laughable? These people were bunglers. This scum, these loafers and good-for-nothings!'

The Sunday Times had in all good faith bought the rights and had started to publish extracts when the scandal broke. A correspondent, Frank Johnson, wrote in *The Times* in March 1985: 'At least when *The Sunday Times* published its first extract, your present correspondent, a lifelong amateur student of mid-20th-century European politics, had no doubt that the diaries were genuine; they were so boring.

Hitler exerts his fascination with his deeds rather than his prose. On that Sunday, those of us familiar with *Mein Kampf, The Collected Speeches* and *Table Talk* knew that this was the authentic voice.'

Kujau and Heidemann were arrested in May 1983 for faking up the world scoop. Heidemann, his record as a star writer ruined for ever, was charged with defrauding the magazine of £2.5 million, paid in instalments between January 1981 and April 1983. He maintained throughout the 11-month trial in Hamburg that he had believed the diaries to be genuine.

Kujau was charged with forgery which had earned him £415,000. He admitted guilt. Indeed, he basked in the attention he attracted during the court proceedings.

The prosecution's case against the forgers filled 4,000 pages and involved 62 witnesses and eight experts. Eminent historian Lord Dacre of Glanton, who had at first declared the diaries to be genuine, had the courage to admit his mistake. He attended a conference called by *Stern* in Hamburg in April 1983, where he expressed his doubts about the value of the scoop and he tried to warn *The Sunday Times* about the risks.

As the trial dragged on, fascinating evidence was heard, producing copy as riveting to readers as the fake scoop.

A Professor Eberhard Jaeckel had published some of Kujau's 'war documents' before the big scandal broke. Experts had seen through them straight away.

A *Sunday Times* reporter, Gita Sereny, had been dispatched to Germany after a tip-off about the diaries, but she had not been allowed to visit Jaeckel because of the extra cost it would have involved.

Stern executives had given a page of the 'diaries' to experts to study, without explaining why. The experts they had engaged did not know what they were looking for and passed the copies as authentic.

The ink and tea-soaked paper used for the diaries had not been tested until it was too late.

Kujau said he at first intended to write only three diaries in return for a uniform worn by Hermann Göring and which Heidemann had shown him.

'I had to have it,' he told the court. He had forged one Hitler diary in 1978 because it annoyed him that the Führer had apparently left no records of his life. Kujau said he was sure Heidemann had tumbled his trickery after he wrote the word 'helmet' in Hitler's script on a piece of paper which the reporter saw.

To prove the *Stern* reporter's obsession with Hitler, German police raided his home. They took photographs of objects which had once adorned Hitler's desk, including a swastika on a red background which Heidemann said was Hitler's 'martyr's flag'. Heidemann also had in his bizarre collection a pair of underpants that had once belonged to Idi Amin.

Heidemann told the court that Kujau had also offered him an unpublished volume of Hitler's autobiography *Mein Kampf*. 'When I heard the diaries were fakes, I wondered whether to shoot myself then or later,' Heidemann said.

Kujau claimed Heidemann had first told him he wanted the diaries so that they could be sent to Martin Bormann, Hitler's former deputy in South America. 'Heidemann said the diaries would help to rehabilitate Bormann but I began to doubt the story. Then in January 1982, Heidemann told me Bormann was seriously ill and I should hurry my work.'

Heidemann and Kujau's con was rumbled when experts at the Federal Archives in Koblenz were finally allowed to examine some of the writings. They declared them 'primitive fakes' on postwar paper.

Kujau had apparently outsmarted himself. Although he'd checked facts and dates about Hitler before creating the diaries, he did not realize, when he bought the Gothic letters in Hong Kong to stick on the diary covers, that he had mixed up the letters A and F. The imitation metal initials 'FH' instead of 'AH' adorned the volumes.

The court couldn't help but snigger when it heard that Kujau had once provided the obsessed Heidemann with fake ashes of Hitler, supplied by a friend who worked in a crematorium.

Heidemann and Kujau were both found guilty on 8 July, 1985. Heidemann was jailed for four years and eight months and Kujau for four years and six months.

Kujau's girlfriend, Edith Lieblang, had also been involved. She was accused of spending part of the ill-gotten gains and was given an eight-month suspended sentence. No one found out where all the money went.

Poor Thomas Walde was grilled in court for his gullibility.

The whole world knew the Hitler diaries were a fake.

Heidemann's friends said he had been used as a scapegoat by *Stern*, whose weekly circulation dropped by 100,000 when the deception was announced.

The Sunday Times had already agreed to pay £250,000 for the extracts. Too late, Lord Dacre realized his first assessment was wrong. In *The Times* of May 19, 1983, he admitted making 'a grave error' and claimed he had been misled by *Stern*.

Stern editors Peter Koch and Felix Schmidt were fired even though they had been kept in the dark about the diary dealings.

Gerd Schulte-Hillen, managing director of *Stern* owners Grüner and Jahr, had inherited the diaries from his predecessor Henri Nannen but had backed Heidemann, refusing to believe that he was involved in a major fraud. He was allowed to stay on at *Stern*.

Frank Giles, editor of *The Sunday Times*, retired to become 'editor emeritus'. In *Selling Hitler, the Story of the Hitler Diaries*, author Richard Harris tells how Rupert Murdoch, owner of *The Sunday Times*, justified Giles's new title. 'It's Latin. The 'e' means you're out and 'meritus' means you deserve it.'

Continues Harris: 'Murdoch, who ordered *The Sunday Times* to continue printing even when he had been told that Lord Dacre was sounding the alarm, commented: 'After all, we're in the entertainment business.'

All that glitters

To the aristocrats assembled in a Munich hotel, it seemed the golden opportunity they had been waiting for – a conspiracy of silence which was sure to make their fortune. All eyes were upon the stranger who had invited them to witness his amazing demonstration that night.

Hans Unruh spoke intently: 'I must ask you to treat what I am about to tell you with the strictest confidence. This is not a secret to be shared, but one we must keep strictly to ourselves. It is very important. And it could be dangerous.'

He picked up a salt cellar and brandished it before his captivated audience. He explained that the cellar contained a rare and very precious commodity. Gold.

Some guests sniggered, others sat in silent disbelief. But they all listened as Unruh continued.

He was a scientist, he went on. And he had discovered how gold was made. It came from the depths of the earth where it was created by a chemical action on ordinary salt. If some method could be discovered of reproducing this chemical change artificially, unlimited quantities of gold could be manufactured from the world's salt supplies.

He showed his enthralled audience a simple piece of apparatus – a green lampshade. Research had proved that if you treated salt with a special form of light it would turn into pure gold, he told them.

Unruh knew the good and wealthy people he was addressing would need proof of this miracle. He took hold of the salt cellar and gently tapped some of the salt on to a steel plate. Then he took the lamp and held it in such a way that the shade completely covered the dish.

He switched the lamp on and waited a few moments. When he finally removed the shade, the onlookers were speechless. There on the plate, where grains of salt had lain, bright flecks of gold dust were glittering. To emphasize the value of the little pile, Unruh scooped it up and tipped it into a small bag.

By now, disbelief had turned into avid interest. Unruh had his guests under his spell. This was the moment to explain that he was a struggling scientist and that his discovery had to be exploited to the full. Money would be needed to provide equipment for the large-scale manufacture of gold. 'You are wealthy, of proven integrity and have a great sense of responsibility. You have all been specially selected for this opportunity,' Unruh told his guests. 'I wish you to all become shareholders in my enterprise. Perhaps you would like to go away and think it over.'

Already, guests were inquiring how much the shares would cost. Little did they know it was Unruh, and not his gullible guests, who had struck gold. He made £3,500 from the evening's show, thanks to a simple trick which had completely fooled the sons and daughters of Germany's finest families. The 'gold dust' had been concealed in the green lampshade, and when Unruh tapped it, it showered down, covering the salt. Closer inspection would have given him away, because brass, with the light shining on it, looks just like gold.

81

Too trivial for words

Ray Loud and Steve Birch had to laugh when two quirky Canadians with whom they had been drinking sangria on holiday in Spain in 1974 tried to involve them in a hare-brained scheme to make an easy fortune.

The enterprising Canadians, Chris Haney and Scott Abbott, had invented a board game they were convinced was going to make them rich, and they wanted Ray and Steve to help them by writing down a lot of daft questions while the dice were thrown.

'We were playing this silly game on the back of a table mat at a barbecue in Spain,' Ray recalled. 'It was good fun but nothing more – or so we thought. We just burst out laughing when Chris and Scott asked us to be the writers of the British version of their game. We didn't want to be caught up in a crazy scheme.'

They might have changed their minds if they had known that they had just turned down a chance to share in the success of the world's biggest board game blockbuster of all time – Trivial Pursuit.

Less than ten years after its creation, the game was being played in four million British homes and in 50 million homes throughout the world. Trivial Pursuit earned Scott, Chris, and his brother John Haney £25 million and established a cult following from Hollywood to the White House. There was a 10-day Trivial Pursuit cruise on *QE2*; 78 editions went on sale in 17 different languages; and addicts in 31 countries, including Iceland and Japan, couldn't stop playing it. At the height of Trivial Pursuit mania, four students in Doncaster, Yorkshire, claimed an entry in *The Guinness Book of Records* for playing non-stop for five days.

The success story began when Scott and Chris sat idly over their beers one day, marvelling at the amount of money Scrabble must have made for its creators. Within 45 minutes they had come up with the basis for their own money-spinner.

'We wanted the game to be a kind of party in a box, with lots of fun for all ages and types, and we figured if we creased up laughing, others would too,' Chris said. 'To test our game, we dragged people off the street, gave them a glass of wine, and bombarded them with silly questions.'

The game ended happily for its clever creators, who were able to live in luxury, thanks to their bright idea.

The Trivial Pursuit that brought tremendous rewards.

Ray Loud and Steve Birch did not miss out after all. They were given a second opportunity to cash in, two years after the first approach. This time they jumped at the chance to write the questions for the British version, and went on to reap the rewards.

Goose down

This was one goose which would never lay a golden egg, not even for its creator, the fabulously wealthy Howard Hughes. To the billionaire, ploughing £18 million into a giant wooden flying boat, the *Spruce Goose*, seemed a good idea at the time. The eight-engined seaplane, commissioned in 1942 and designed to hold 700 troops, wasn't finished until the end of the war.

Hughes hit the heights at the controls of the *Spruce Goose* on 2 November 1947, in a maiden – the one-and-only – flight, which lasted for just one minute, over the waters of Long Beach Harbor. The *Spruce Goose* reached a height of 70 feet, then took a dive, never to see the light of day again.

It remained in a hangar in California gathering dust for 33 years. In 1980, four years after the death of the rich recluse, the city of Long Beach wanted the machine taken out of the hangar, so that the hangar could be used as an oil terminal.

The *Spruce Goose* was dismantled in such a way that nine museums throughout America could each have a part of the aircraft to display. 'The decision to do this was an emotional one for all of us involved,' said Fred Lewis, a spokesman for the Summa Corporation of America.

The goose that took a dive and its creator, Howard Hughes.

Prince – or pauper

The film star always had her eyes open for a man – preferably famous or rich – who would woo her. And she thought her ship had come in when a young man sought out her company during a holiday in Monte Carlo. For she'd heard him being paged – the call went out for Prince Urbano of Barberini. The two engaged in conversation and for several days the film star and the Prince were inseparable.

A yet deeper impression was made when he dropped the names of the local royal family into conversation.

Trying to do the right thing, the film star picked up the bills on a trip to Paris. She did not want to be seen as a gold digger. And they went Dutch when dining at exclusive restaurants. Only later did she discover the teenage Romeo was just an ordinary lad who'd always wanted to meet her.

Chapter
Five

CATASTROPHES

The 1980s will be remembered as a decade with more than its share of tragedy. Who can forget the horror of the Zeebrugge disaster, in which 193 people perished as the Townsend Thoresen ferry capsized, the American Independence Day error which cost nearly 300 innocent people on board an Iranian passenger plane their lives, or the death of teacher Christa McAuliffe and her six fellow astronauts in the ill-fated Challenger?

These quite recent happenings and the stories of catastrophes from earlier days lament the fate of the innocent victims of aggression and human error.

Zeebrugge

The trip to the Continent had been a fun day, the ferry passengers agreed. Now they were safely on board for the return crossing to Dover, with time to relax on board as the late winter's evening closed in.

Some of the 436 passengers stood on deck to watch the quay at the Belgian port of Zeebrugge receding as they sailed home; others gathered at the bar. Children scampered about, over-tired and excited, while their parents put their feet up in the lounges or prepared to enjoy a cup of tea in the restaurant of the 7,951 ton Townsend Thoresen ferry, *Herald of Free Enterprise*.

The ferry's 60 crew members made preparations to sail and to do brisk business in the bars and the duty free shop. David Lewry, the ship's captain, had made the trip many times before, and just after 6 pm his vessel was under way, with its passengers, 36 lorries and 84 cars all secure.

Moments later, the happy holiday ship turned into an icy tomb for hundreds of innocent men, women and children as the ferry capsized and the dark North Sea flooded in.

Many died instantly in the first minutes of horror. Screaming passengers were sucked out of smashed windows, others were crushed as furniture and fittings caved in, vehicles were hurled over the capsized ferry and people fought for their lives in a nightmare of rising sea water.

That night, 6 March, 1987, 193 people perished in what a survivor described as a scene from hell.

One passenger told his own story of the tragedy. He had been sitting in the top bar with a friend when they felt the boat keel over without warning. They sat for a moment, stunned. 'As she went, one of the windows nearest the waterline broke and people were pulled out of the window. We grabbed hold of the seats nearest to us and just held on to them.

'The ferry turned right over on her side and my friend and I were thrown into the water. He managed to get back and we scrambled on to the seats, just moving up with the water level until it seemed to have stopped rising.

'I got hold of one child who was passed to us to keep it above water level. Those who were able to do so climbed the tables and chairs to get out of the broken window and some were pulled up with ropes, hosepipes, anything they could get hold of.

The capsized *Herald of Free Enterprise* outside Zeebrugge.

'Finally, the rescue boats and helicopters arrived. The rescuers broke the windows. It seemed like an eternity but it was probably only 10 to 15 minutes before they came on the scene.'

Many of the passengers were taken to hospital at nearby Knokke. The ship's cook, Paul White, was one of them.

'I've been on that run for 14 years,' he said, 'but I can't understand what happened. It just went over. People started to scream. Some had put on life jackets in the darkness. It was the only thing they could see because of the fluorescent strips.'

Many passengers tumbled straight into the icy sea, 30 feet deep at that point. The ferry had only just passed out of the harbour entrance when disaster struck.

A 16-minute replay evokes the tragedy.

6.10 pm: Everyone aboard. The ship, which can accommodate 1,000 passengers, is less than half full.

6.11 pm: The *Herald of Free Enterprise* heads for home.

6.15 pm: Some lorry drivers and motorists make a last check to see if their vehicles are secure on the roll on-roll off vessel.

6.22 pm: The crew hear a strange coded message from the captain. The passengers are unaware of the emergency call.

6.25 pm: The ferry starts to list, and with a violent lurch is thrust on its side.

6.26 pm: Terror reigns as the North Sea grips the sinking ship.

A massive rescue operation was launched within minutes. Even though the *Herald* had only left the harbour, it was to take many exhausting, heroic hours before rescue operations were completed. Helpers were still racing against a rising morning tide the next day to find those still missing and to lift off the dead.

The floodlit scene after the disaster was sinister as the tug *Fighter* from Antwerp and its two sister vessels, working in adverse conditions, moved in to help. Helicopter searchlights cast an eerie, blitz-like glow over the scene of death.

Belgian and Dutch authorities had acted swiftly. Navy helicopters rushed to the scene. Experts from a Dutch salvage firm sent vessels and divers to Zeebrugge. Britain joined in the rescue effort as soon as it heard of the tragic plight of its people. Two RAF Sea King helicopters with divers were sent from the Culdrose Royal Navy base in Cornwall. The destroyer HMS *Glasgow* and frigate HMS *Diomede* joined the rescue teams. An RAF Nimrod aircraft with life saving equipment was on emergency stand-by.

While some of the ferry's passengers still fought for their lives, others were taken to hospital. Bodies, too many to count in the dark chaos, lay battered in the watery grave.

A hasty message, chalked up at Townsend Thoresen's embarkation point in the Zeebrugge terminal, stated bleakly: 'Due to an incident in the port, all sailings are temporarily suspended. You will be notified as soon as sailings are resumed.'

Many passengers waiting for the next ferry to Dover that night remained standing on the dockside, unsure why they were not allowed to embark. Their children tugged at their sleeves, too young to understand that a terrible tragedy was happening at sea.

Four men, including Captain David Lewry, were singled out for making the fatal mistakes that turned the 132-metre ferry into a watery tomb.

Mr Justice Sheen, chairman of the Zeebrugge inquiry in July 1987, stated the cause of the disaster clearly: 'The *Herald* sank because she went to sea with her inner and outer bow doors open.'

The assistant bosun, Marc Stanley, who was responsible for closing the bow doors before the ship sailed, had been fast asleep at the time. He awoke when he was thrown from his bunk as the crippled ferry turned on her side. Chief Officer Leslie Sabel was accused of being 'seriously negligent' for not checking that the doors were closed before sailing. The *Herald*'s senior master, Captain John Kirby, was told he must 'bear the responsibility for the disaster' for not issuing clear orders about closing the doors. And the inquiry found that Captain Lewry had also been seriously negligent in taking his ship to sea in an 'unsafe condition'.

Mr Justice Sheen, who had sat with four assessors for 29 days, ordered the immediate suspension of Captain Lewry's master's certificate for a year and Chief Officer Leslie Sabel's certificate for two years.

It had seemed at first, said the judge, that responsibility rested with the *Herald*'s captain and crew. But on reflection, blame lay higher up in Townsend Thoresen's management where 'cardinal faults' came to light. Mr Justice Sheen said the board of directors had not appreciated their responsibility for safety on their ships and that the directors lacked a proper understanding of their duties.

'From top to bottom, the body was infected by the disease of sloppiness,' was his indictment.

He criticized standing orders issued to the *Herald* by management for not including express instructions to close the bow and storm doors. This had led the captain to believe erroneously that the ship was ready to sail.

The inquiry noted that the ship's masters had in the past, in internal memos, expressed concern to management about safety. This had fallen on deaf ears ashore. The *Herald* was not the first of the company's ferries to sail with its cargo door open. This had happened on several other occasions, and these incidents had led one of the masters, two years previously, to suggest that indicator lights were needed on the bridge to show whether or not the doors had been shut.

The inquiry considered that if this had received 'the serious consideration it deserved', it was at least possible that the lights would have been fitted in the early months of 1986 and disaster prevented.

After a month-long inquest, it took a jury in Dover nine hours to reach verdicts of unlawful killing of the 192 victims who died that cold, bitter night. Another passenger had died some time later in hospital, bringing the death toll to 193.

The British Government called for changes at the International Maritime Organisation (IMO) to ensure that members' ships would have door indicator lights, TV monitoring of the vehicle deck and back-up emergency lighting. Following the inquest verdict, Britain's Department of Public Prosecutions prepared charges against Townsend Thoresen, to make sure a similar British sea catastrophe would not occur.

91

The heroes

Queen Elizabeth honoured 27 heroes of the Zeebrugge tragedy with personal thanks and medals for their bravery. They included Lieutenant Guido Couwenbergh of the Belgian Navy, a brave frogman who had singlehandedly saved the lives of 40 drowning people.

He was the first person to plunge into the icy sea and make his way to the sinking ferry's main café area where most of the victims were trapped. He received the Queen's Gallantry Medal.

At the Buckingham Palace ceremony he said: 'I thank God I managed to save so many but I can never forget the poor people who drifted away from me into the darkness to die.'

Andrew Parker, a Londoner, received the George Medal, Britain's second highest peacetime bravery award. He had helped save more than 120 fellow passengers by allowing them to use him as a human ladder to climb to safety.

The Queen honoured Belgian civilian diver Piet Lagast for saving the life of 15-year-old Nicola Simpson from Welwyn Garden City, Hertfordshire. Lagast received the Queen's Gallantry Medal after the monarch heard how he had rescued Nicola and eight others trapped behind a glass screen by shattering it with his diver's knife and cutting his hand to the bone in the process.

Nicola had suffered a heart attack as her body temperature dropped 25 degrees below normal. She became known as the 'Ice Maiden' after surviving four hours in the freezing waters. She was in fact certified dead on arrival at a Belgian hospital and declared clinically dead several times after her ordeal, but made an amazing recovery, only to learn that her mother had died in the tragedy.

The leader of the 40-strong Belgian Navy diving team, Lieutenant-Commander Alfons Daems, was also honoured for rescue work. 'There can be no joy here after being involved in such a major tragedy,' was his poignant response.

The hapless

The 42 crew members who survived were still suffering serious mental anguish a year later. Only two returned to sea, trying to forget their 38 dead colleagues.

The surviving crew underwent intense counselling to encourage them to talk about the horror of hearing their trapped friends screaming pitifully for help. Marriages foundered as men underwent personality changes in the aftermath of the sinking.

Children, especially, found it hard to forget what they had suffered. One little boy had recurrent dreams that his world had turned upside down and people were flying into the air.

One ferry hero, Londoner Colin Baines, was jailed for two and a half years after turning to drug dealing in the wake of the Zeebrugge tragedy. He had lost his brother-in-law and niece and was injured trying to save passengers from the stricken vessel. He had needed psychiatric help after the horror.

Baines was arrested after trying to sell £34,000 worth of cannabis, found in a bag belonging to his brother-in-law.

The horror

The Zeebrugge horror was re-enacted 18 months later when British and French rescue services created a similar tragedy to test contingency plans in the event of another shipping disaster.

The dark night was relived again at a memorial service 12 months after the ferry went down. Wreaths of flowers were lovingly tossed on to the waters off the Belgian coast by the grieving.

One touching card attached to a tribute read: 'Daddy – miss you.'

Those who could not bear to return to the scene that reminded them of lost loved ones attended a service at St Mary's Church, Dover, where a stained-glass window in memory of the dead was unveiled. Nearly 2,000 seamen marched in silence through Dover to the church.

The *Herald*'s captain continued to be haunted by the tragedy. 'I have been over it again and again so many times,' Captain Lewry recalled bitterly.

'I blacked out when it was happening but most of it stays with me. I wished I was dead. Sometimes I still do.'

His ship, the *Herald of Free Enterprise*, died a shameful death. A year after the disaster, the rusting vessel, renamed *Flushing Range*, was towed to rest in a Taiwanese breakers' yard.

All's unfair in love and war

The bitter fight between Iran and Iraq was at first called 'the whirlwind war' but after eight years the fighting was still fierce.

The battle that became the Gulf War started in 1980 when the Iraqi army sent its tanks across the international frontier from Basra into Iran. Iraqi soldiers believed they would be singing victoriously a few weeks later.

When they captured the bridge across the Karun River and that moment of glory ended in their blood-spattered bodies piling up in the dusty streets, the scene was set for a long-played-out conflict.

Vessels from Britain and America were called in to act as peace-keepers. Ironically, the mission earned Captain Will C. Rogers a tragic place in the history of the conflict. From his American warship, USS *Vincennes*, he gave an order to fire. Moments later, 290 innocent men, women and children were dead – in error. It was not an enemy fighter plane Captain Rogers's warship had blasted from the sky, but an Iranian jetliner on a scheduled domestic flight.

The tragedy happened on 4 July – Independence Day, traditionally a festive occasion for Americans. In 1988, it became a day of international outrage against their country.

The American cruiser detected Flight 655 to Dubai shortly after it took off from Bandar Abbas at 10.45 am. Captain Rogers and his US Navy crew had cause to feel threatened at the time. Earlier that morning a helicopter from the *Vincennes* had been fired on by Iranian fast attack craft.

A warning shot in the hostile atmosphere of the Gulf was not an unusual event, but tension was running particularly high that day. Western diplomats expected the Iranians to strike a blow against the Americans to coincide with the 4 July festivities, in order to focus public attention on their cause.

Captain Rogers was sure the attack on the *Vincennes* helicopter would lead to something more serious, and ordered his warship to retaliate, crippling two of the Iranian aircraft.

Five minutes after the Iranians' attack, the ill-fated A300 Airbus was picked up by the radar system on the *Vincennes*. It was later claimed that attempts were made to contact the Airbus on both military and civilian radio frequencies. The transponder on the Airbus should have identified the aircraft to the *Vincennes*. It was stated that at least six warnings were sent from the American warship, but no response, either friendly or hostile, came back.

Captain Rogers believed a US Navy ship was under threat by an F-14 fighter. At 10.51 am, the silent aircraft was declared the enemy. Three minutes later two standard ER2 missiles were fired at the target, destroying it at a range of six miles.

The 290 civilians who perished included 57 children aged between two and 12 years and nine babies. Passengers included not only Iranian but Indian, Pakistani, Italian, Afghan and Yugoslav nationals.

The Pentagon frantically issued statements to ward off international hostility. Officials said it had not been clear whether the plane was operating as a normal civilian airliner at the time of the shooting. The aircraft was flying well below commercial airspace and was broadcasting on a military frequency. It was descending upon the *Vincennes* when it was fired at, they claimed. Instead of climbing to the normal scheduled altitude above 20,000 feet it had levelled off at a dangerously low 9,000 feet.

The US Government was determined to portray the incident as a legitimate act of self defence 'when hostile intent was manifested', but some naval experts voiced their doubts. How could the highly sophisticated radar system on the *Vincennes* have failed to differentiate between friend and foe?

A less sophisticated source, the *ABC World Airways Guide*, widely used by travel agents, would have told those on board the *Vincennes* that the aircraft they were tracking had left within three minutes of the scheduled departure time of the fated Flight 655 to Dubai.

A former British anti-air-warfare officer later stated that any British warships in the Gulf would have records of civilian traffic patterns which would have been fed into a 'battle computer'.

A former US Navy officer said Iranian civilian aircraft had been challenged many times, but always gave the friendly response. No satisfactory explanation could be found for the fact that the Airbus was five miles outside the civilian air lane between Bandar Abbas and its destination of Dubai, or why the pilot allegedly ignored warnings.

It was suggested the Airbus might have been leading an Iranian fighter in its radar 'shadow' for an attack on the *Vincennes*.

Iran stated it would 'exploit to the utmost American barbarism as the innocent victim of the unprovoked massacre', but refrained from immediate retaliation.

No one will ever know the full story behind the Independence Day tragedy of 1988.

All hopes of piecing together those last few, fatal minutes must have sunk with the Airbus's flight recorder. Its recovery was never announced.

On 11 July, President Reagan announced America would offer compensation to the families of all 290 passengers. On 20 July, the Pentagon admitted errors were made by Captain Rogers and the crew of the *Vincennes*, but claimed the mistakes were not due to negligence. Defence Secretary Frank Carlucci said Captain Rogers had acted 'prudently on the basis of information available to him.'

No disciplinary action was taken against the warship's captain or any member of the crew.

Admiral William Crowe, chairman of the Joint Chiefs of Staff, said individual mistakes were not 'crucial' in the decision to attack the Iranian passenger plane.

'There was no culpable conduct displayed on board the *Vincennes*. This regrettable accident was a by-product of the Iran-Iraq war.'

But a senior Pentagon naval officer made his feelings clear. 'To hell with the Navy taking all the responsibility. Blame the politicians. They send us out there and tell us we can take anything in the sky which threatens us and then start raising questions when something goes wrong.'

Captain Rogers had made a poignant statement before sailing for the Middle East on the peace-keeping mission. 'If we are attacked or face hostile intent we will defend ourselves, but we are certainly not out there to create hostility.'

The 44-year-old Captain shouldered the deaths of nearly 300 innocent people on his own. 'I and I alone am responsible,' he said. 'This is a burden I will carry for the rest of my life.'

The *Vincennes* was relieved of duty in the Gulf later that year during a ceasefire between Iraq and Iran. American officials said the 96,000 ton warship was officially detached from the navy's Middle East joint task force. Shortly after the ceasefire was announced, machine guns opened fire on a Norwegian tanker in the Gulf . . . and the war continued, and with unjust, irrational actions.

Teaching from the sky

igh school teacher Christa McAuliffe could not contain her
exuberance at the thought of the big step she was about to take
for womankind. The 37-year-old mother of two had been
picked from among 11,000 eager American applicants to make
the epic space journey on board the US shuttle Challenger.

Dawn broke bitterly cold in Florida on 28 January, 1986, the day of the launch. Christa had kissed and hugged her children Scott, 9, and Caroline, 6, goodbye the night before. They were still sleeping but would soon, with their father Steve, and family and friends, witness at first hand the historic launch at Cape Canaveral. The McAuliffe children were the envy of all small girls and boys who have ever dreamt about becoming one of the elite band of American astronauts. The whole world was waiting with baited breath to see live televised broadcasts of Challenger blasting off into the blue.

Christa had enjoyed an early supper with her lawyer husband the night before and had kissed him goodbye at the crew quarters. It was not the happy occasion she would have wanted. With her six fellow astronauts Christa had had to accept with great disappointment the news that the launch had been postponed for 24 hours because of technical problems.

They had set off brightly past all the waiting newsmen who were waving and smiling. Then they all had to return to crew quarters to kick their heels as the freezing weather delayed the launch. The mission had already been postponed three times before.

Christa killed time by calling the teacher who was replacing her. She joked about how funny it was they were all due to be launched in a billion-dollar shuttle, and no one could find a tool box for last minute repairs.

Meanwhile, the temperature continued to plummet to sub-freezing. Arctic winds were blowing at the shuttle's proposed launch time of 9.38 am.

The launch-pad team grew increasingly worried about the ice forming around the shuttle. The temperature had dropped to 24° Fahrenheit, the wind chill to 10 below zero. The ground crew had kept the water running to prevent the pipes that fed the fire-extinguishing system from freezing.

Christa woke at 6.20 am on the day of the launch. She showered, pulled on her blue jeans and sneakers and joined the rest of the crew for a light

The Challenger lift-off.

breakfast. The cooks had prepared a special surprise for them – a white-frosted cake decorated with the Challenger's emblem and all their names. Christa's was there, together with shuttle pilot Michael Smith, Commander Francis Scobbe, Ronald McNair, Ellison Onizuka, Gregory Jarvis and female astronaut Judy Resnick.

At 7.20 am they received their final orders and a weather briefing. None knew just how bitterly cold it was . . . or how great a threat the freezing weather posed to their safety. A few moments later Commander Scobbe led the crew down the ramp past the roped-off throng of photographers. Christa's excitement mounted once more. This time they were off! Even the icicles, several feet long, hanging from the launch tower gave her no cause for concern. She was confident that nothing would go wrong and she laughed when someone in the crowd handed her a bright red apple, as red as her own cheeks in the freezing air. 'Save it for me and I'll eat it when I get back,' she shouted.

By this time Christa's husband and children, her sister, Betsy Corrigan, and her parents Grace and Ed Corrigan, were standing in a prime vantage area, waiting for the countdown and holding hands in their excitement.

They knew astronaut Judy Resnick would be the second woman in space, but their Christa was to be the first teacher in space.

The world was watching too and millions saw the expression on those faces, now shining with pride, later change to grief and horror, at what they saw. Betsy Corrigan screamed in despair and Steve hustled the children away in stunned silence after Christa and the rest of the Challenger crew were blown from the sky before their very eyes – turning the historic moment into tragedy.

The billion-dollar shuttle exploded at 1,977 miles an hour with the force of a small nuclear weapon one minute and 12 seconds after launch, shattering the lives of the crew and their close ones and destroying America's entire space programme in one almighty blast.

Christa and her space friends died in an explosion of 526,000 gallons of liquid hydrogen and liquid oxygen as the 90-ton shuttle shattered into thousands of pieces. At first the world was told they had all died instantly, but months later the full horror emerged. NASA's cameras and the American television networks recorded the disaster in terrifying detail.

Long after the original fireball that marked the explosion, a red-orange and white inferno that stunned spectators, came the smoking trails of debris etched across the clear wintry sky. So much debris was falling down that it was unsafe to send out search parties for nearly an hour. Frogmen later scoured the waters off the Florida coast, looking for bodies. They had been instructed to recover even the smallest fragments of what had once been

Challenger. Anything which could give a clue to the disaster would be needed.

Witnesses spoke of a tongue of flame near the base of the port booster rocket as the shuttle was throttling up to full engine power. Then a larger flame was seen near the base of the external fuel tank. Then came the explosion. There were contingency plans for rapid evacuation while the shuttle was still tethered to its launch tower – but it emerged that no one had prepared an escape route to be used once Challenger was airborne.

Until the explosion, routine dialogue was recorded between Challenger and Mission Control.

Mission Control commentator: '10-9-8-7-6, we have main engine start, 4-3-2-1 and lift-off. Lift-off of the 25th space shuttle mission. And it has cleared the tower.'

Pilot Mike Smith: 'Roll programme.'

Mission Control: 'Roger, roll, Challenger.'

Mission Control commentator: 'Roll programme confirmed. Challenger now heading down range. The engines are throttling down now at 94 per cent. Normal throttle for most of the flight is 104 per cent. We'll throttle down to 65 per cent shortly. Engines at 65 per cent. Three engines running normally. Three good fuel cells. Three good auxiliary power units. Velocity 22,057 feet per second, altitude 4.3 nautical miles, downrange distance three nautical miles. Engines throttling up, three engines now 104 per cent.'

Mission Control: 'Challenger, go at throttle up.'

Pilot: 'Roger, go at throttle up.'

Mission Control commentator: 'We're at a minute 15 seconds, velocity 2,900 feet per second, altitude nine nautical miles, range distance seven nautical miles.'

After an unexplained silence, the next words heard were from the NASA commentator: 'Vehicle has exploded . . . we are awaiting word from any recovery forces downrange.'

Months of inquiry followed. Former Secretary of State William Rogers chaired a presidential panel while NASA and the manufacturers of the shuttle booster, Morton Thiokol Inc, launched internal investigations.

Experts looked at the obvious possibilities of technical failure. A much earlier fear resurfaced, that the combination of the extreme weather and the shuttle's structure could have proved fatal. What sealed the fate of the Challenger and its seven crew on that bright January morning were vital rocket seals, never before put to the test in harsh, bitterly cold conditions.

The question of the rocket seals had been discussed the day before Challenger's fatal mission. Lawrence W. Wear, solid rocket motor project office manager at the Marshall Space Flight Centre in Huntsville, was in Florida for lunch. He called Boyd C. Brinton, manager of Morton Thiokol's project office in Huntsville who in turn called the Thiokol Wasatch Plant in Utah. There, the supervisor of rocket motor cases, Arnold R. Thompson, consulted with Robert Ebeling, the manager in charge of the solid rocket's motor ignition system and final assembly.

Ebeling sat down with Roger Boisjoly, of Thiokol's rocket-seal task force, and other engineers. They discussed how the shuttle would stand up to extreme weather no one had anticipated. The scientists wondered if previous incidents of booster-seal erosion had been directly linked to temperature. During a flight in October 1985, when the ambient temperature was 75°F, soot had been blown by a seal, which indicated a potentially dangerous situation. The same thing had happened again in January 1985, when launch temperature was 51°F. Roger Boisjoly argued there had been more visible damage to seals on the flight in colder weather. Thiokol engineers had calculated that the temperature of the internal rocket joints on that January mission was 53°F and that NASA could not afford to launch another shuttle in such cold weather, advice that was ultimately ignored.

At the time Challenger approached its final, fatal countdown the outside temperature was 36°F. Later, investigators discovered the temperature of the failed booster joint, chilled throughout the freezing night, was about 28°F at launch time.

According to Thiokol, the solid rockets had been tested and qualified for flight when the fuel temperature was between 40° and 90°F, but no separate guidelines had been established for more sensitive joints.

Roger Boisjoly had his own opinion. Cold weather made the seals, known as 'O-rings', less pliable. He was to say later that trying to secure a joint with a stiff O-ring was like 'trying to shove a brick into a crack versus a sponge.'

In Florida on the day before the mission, Allan J. McDonald, director of Thiokol's solid rocket motor project, was at the home of Carver Kennedy, vice-president of space operations at Cape Canaveral. Ebeling called McDonald there. He said his engineers were worried about the rocket seals and needed guidance. They wanted a further postponement of the shuttle launch, at least until late in the afternoon. NASA was not convinced. They wanted more people involved in the ultimate decision, and they were concerned about the mounting number of delays.

'They wanted scientific reasons for holding up the launch,' said Jack Kapp, a section supervisor of Thiokol. 'We had all made up our minds we should not fire.'

101

NASA was carrying out its own hasty research. Wilbur Riehl, chief of Marshall's non-metallic materials division, had been sent to look for data relating to O-ring performance in cold weather, but without much luck.

His colleague Robert Schwinghamer, director of the materials and processes laboratory, wanted tests done on the spot but Riehl didn't see how anything efficient and reliable could be done so quickly. 'We hadn't done any tests at low temperatures – or I'm pretty sure we hadn't,' Riehl said later. After searching, they came across reports indicating the rings were likely to be twice as stiff at 17°F as at room temperature – information that seemed to establish that weather was an important factor in rocket-seal performance.

'Should the outside temperature be lower than 20°F, we could be very uncomfortable,' Riehl pointed out. He said he had tried to alert Marshall's executives but the space centre chiefs were absorbed by a three-way telephone conference with other executives involved in the Challenger design and launch and didn't look at the newly discovered data.

At Cape Canaveral, Marshall booster manager Larry Mulloy stated that nothing in the data satisfied him there should be a launch delay. He was reported to have said: 'My God. When do you want me to launch – next April?'

George Hardy, science and engineering deputy at Marshall, said he was appalled at the idea of no lift-off. Later, he explained he was more concerned with Thiokol's presentation.

The Rogers Commission investigating the disaster concluded a seam in the booster rocket had failed but suggested strongly that there had been human error as well. Despite technical error which seemed to have haunted the rocket seal design for ten years, the commission reported, Thiokol engineers still had only a shaky understanding of how the crucial rocket booster joint performed, and of vital issues relating to launch temperature.

'Warnings were sounded and dismissed in these anxious pre-launch hours and the momentum preceding lift-off overpowered engineering concerns,' the commission found. 'Lacking hard evidence that a disaster was in the making, designers had to rely on their 'gut' feeling – not enough reason, in NASA officials' minds, to ground the flight. Management-level personnel, confronted with what they considered ambiguous data, opted not to rattle the chair of command. As a result, top NASA executives say they were unaware that the shuttle was flying against the advice of some of the very engineers whose careers had been dedicated to assuring its success.'

In harsh, practical terms, what had happened was that a seal on Challenger's solid rocket booster failed. Flames burst through a joint and then hit the ship's external fuel tank.

No technical jargon could bring comfort to Christa McAuliffe's family. Their sorrow turned to anger when evidence emerged that Challenger was doomed as a result of human error and not a technological fault.

Worse was to come. Everyone had believed that Christa and her fellow astronauts had died instantly at the time of the explosion. But weeks after the tragedy, Challenger's cabin and what was left of the crew was raised from the Atlantic ocean bed. This produced conclusive evidence that they had all survived at least several seconds after the explosion, and possibly until they struck the ocean surface.

William Shannon, former US Ambassador to Ireland, accused NASA of a cover-up. Why did it take them five weeks to find the sunken crew cabin? And five more weeks to bring it up from a depth of only 80 feet of water?

'The truth is the astronauts were alive and conscious for several minutes after the disaster occurred. They were probably making gigantic efforts to bring their craft under control. If the craft had been equipped, as it should have been, with ejector seats and parachutes, they could have saved themselves. There is a good chance they died only when their craft hit the water at 140 miles an hour and broke up because of the impact. They died because of NASA's false economies and incompetence,' stormed Shannon.

The Rogers Commission concluded the shuttle tragedy was due to mismanagement of the space agency. Challenger exploded because NASA executives ignored months of warnings about design and allowed the spacecraft to lift off in weather so cold it caused the O-rings between segments of its booster to fail.

The final technicalities no longer mattered to the 32,000 grieving residents of Christa's home town of Concord, New Hampshire. She was buried in the Catholic section of the town's public cemetery on 1 May, 1986 – exactly a year after the determined and adventurous school teacher of Concord High had declared: 'My philosophy is to get the most out of life as possible,' the statement that had won her NASA's teacher-in-space contest.

Her husband and children tried to carry on with their lives. Christa's mother came to live with them to help with the running of the household. A few weeks later, Steve flew to Louisville with the children to accept the Friend of Education Award, the National Education Association's highest honour – on Christa's behalf. He told 7,500 people at the convention: 'Christa was the most selfless person I have ever met. If you sit on the sideline, reflect on Christa as a hero, or as a glorious representative or a canonized saint, rather than putting your energies into accomplishing for her what she wanted to do, then I think her efforts will have been in vain.'

Then he flew back home with his children. He uttered no words of comfort for those responsible for the death of a much-loved wife and mother.

103

But the tragedy finally prompted aeronautical engineers to re-examine previous concepts. They modified the faulty joints and installed a heating system to protect them against extreme cold.

NASA developed a special escape system for its astronauts, who would henceforth have the final responsibility for allowing the launch to go ahead.

The improvements in design and human input were justified when the shuttle Discovery was launched on 29 September, 1988, while the world watched their TV screens, first in fearful anticipation, and then with sighs of relief as the graceful spacecraft soared up safely.

Flight KAL 007

The passengers aboard flight KAL 007 from New York to Seoul in Korea welcomed the chance to stretch their legs when the aircraft made its refuelling stop at Anchorage, Alaska.

The 246 passengers were mainly Korean, Taiwanese and Japanese, but included Americans, Canadians and Britons. With the crew of 23 on the long-haul flight to Korea, the Boeing 747 was carrying a total of 269 people.

It was 2.31 am American time at Anchorage, the busiest time of the airport's long night. The weather was dry that early morning of 1 September, 1983. There was a smell of autumn in the air.

The crew who left the Korean Air Lines flight at Anchorage to be replaced by three fresh flight deck personnel and 20 cabin staff were the lucky ones. It was the last day alive for all who took off on the last leg of the flight to Korea.

During that flight Captain Chun Byong-In allowed his craft to drift into Russian air space, even though his route was carefully mapped out. It was a specially sensitive flight, scraping the eastern border, and the off-course error proved fatal. The jet was blasted from the sky, mistaken by Soviet defence forces for an enemy aircraft. Flight KAL 007, with all its innocent people on board, became yet another casualty of war during peacetime, a political pawn whose fate caused anguished outrage throughout the world.

Captain Chun could not have been unaware of the danger of allowing his plane to deviate from the allotted flight path. He had a Russian-issued map clearly printed with the warning that the USSR reserved the right to shoot any aircraft that strayed too close to its military base on Sakhalin Island.

Every airline knew the Russians meant business. In 1978, another Korean Air Lines flight had violated Russian air space. The Boeing 707 was shot at, two passengers were killed and 13 injured. The plane was forced to make an emergency landing.

On the flight in 1983, neither passengers nor crew had any reason to fear that their eight-hour trip would provoke Russian retaliation. Captain Chun could not have failed to study his map and charts, but despite the warnings, he headed towards Sakhalin Island, a Russian military area.

The flight deck's inertial navigation system (INS) should have guided the 747 safely to its destination. An advanced computer programme pinpoints an aircraft's position accurately, and it was vital on flight KAL 007. But like all computer programmes, it relies on initial human input. If it had been incorrectly programmed after refuelling at Anchorage, it would have given a false reading. The INS has programmed 'way points', compulsory reporting points along the route. A minute before arriving at each way point, an amber alert warns the pilot he should get ready to report to ground to confirm his position. Two minutes later, the light goes off, to show the way point has been passed, and the pilot informs ground control of the time and position and estimated flight time to the next point.

The first major way point on the Boeing's route was a radio beacon at the hamlet of Bethel, 345 nautical miles away on the inlet of the Kuskowin River on the west Alaskan coast. As the plane made its way past this point, the captain reported normally. There was no hint of what was to come, yet the 747 was already 12 miles north of Bethel, and way off route. And as far as the captain and crew were concerned, the INS, linked to the automatic pilot which steers an aircraft on its proper course, was working perfectly.

But KAL 007 was by then heading dangerously towards Romeo 20, an air route which runs close to the Soviet Union's sensitive area of the Kamchatka Peninsula and Sakhalin Island. The area is under constant military radar surveillance by the Russians.

In the 747's cockpit, the INS appeared to guide the aircraft accurately towards its next way point, an imaginary aeronautical position called Nabie. By now the Korean plane was 40 miles north of its proper course. The aircraft continued to make reports at each way point, but unbeknown to its crew, the INS could not have been coupled to the autopilot. The early error would never have happened if it had been.

Passing another way point, the imaginary position of Neeva, the 747 had

105

strayed 150 miles off course. The Korean Air Lines craft was now flying unannounced in an area supervised by Soviet civil controllers.

Ironically, the presence of another craft, a US Air Force RC-135, detected by radar, did not give the Russians cause for concern. It was not uncommon for such craft to patrol the area, sometimes as frequently as 20 days each month. What disturbed the silent Soviet watchers was the Boeing 747 flying 75 miles behind the American military aircraft. It was much too close to the Kamchatka Peninsula with its missile testing sites, and to the port of Petropavlovsk, a nuclear submarine base.

The Russians alerted six MiG-23 fighters which took off in hot pursuit of the unsuspecting 747. Somehow the pursuers missed their target. The Korean aircraft moved out of the Russians' air space for a while and the MiGs had to return to their stations. But instead of entering Japanese air space, the 747, now 185 miles off course, headed towards the south coast of Sakhalin.

This time the Russians were determined not to let their prey escape. They did not know whether the intruder was another US RC-135 or a Boeing converted into a fighter plane, or a civilian plane deliberately flying off course on a spying mission. Soviet fighters were again alerted to block its escape route.

The Japanese and American intelligence officers, aware of the Russians' monitoring system, assumed the Soviets were indulging in an air defence exercise.

Fighters from Sakhalin Island were also alerted. The Russians had just 10 minutes before the 747 would cross their air space and be lost to them.

Three fighters were involved in the mission. It was a pilot with the call sign 805 who announced to his control: 'I see it.'

Despite his identification call, the 747 did not respond, possibly because Russian systems are incompatible with those of other airlines. KAL 007 flew on, totally unaware that it was being lined up for attack. The pilot was still making normal procedural contact, now with Tokyo, for permission to climb to a higher flight level.

Fighter pilot 805 radioed: 'I am closing in on target.'

KAL 007 was now 365 miles off course.

As it received Tokyo's clearance to climb, fighter pilot 805 fired 120 rounds in four bursts, as a warning to the unresponsive and ignorant intruder. Even then, it seemed, no one aboard the Korean Air Lines jet realized what was happening. The Russian fighter fired his missiles. Seconds later, the plane with its 269 innocent people on board broke up, spiralling into the sea just outside Soviet waters. There were no survivors.

'The target is destroyed,' fighter pilot 805 reported to control.

The world was stunned.

The Soviet Union's act was denounced, and retaliation was demanded. The Canadians immediately stopped Aeroflot's flights into their country. Other nations followed suit. President Ronald Reagan closed Aeroflot's offices in New York and Washington. A worldwide 60-day ban was ordered on all flights to Russia.

At first the Russians refused to admit their error, but later they issued a statement admitting that the 747 had been attacked because it was believed to be a spy plane. The plane, they said, had not responded to a call for identification, after it had been tracked on radar for several hours.

At the time no one knew the Russians were planning to test a highly secret weapon on the night KAL wandered off course and were specially sensitive about intruders.

The reason why the Korean Air Lines jet made its fatal detour can only be speculated upon. It could have been straightforward INS failure. Failure of all three INS systems on board seems unlikely. Captain Chun may have switched off his INS control and forgotten to link it in again. No one will ever know. The cockpit recorder and flight data recorder boxes were never recovered.

One positive result of the tragedy was the improved communications between military and civil air controllers at Anchorage, Khabarovsk and Tokyo. But the plans to prevent innocent deaths in future brought little comfort to relatives and friends of those who perished. They could only grieve for victims of aggression in peacetime.

Great Scott

For God's sake look after our people.' Those were the final, compassionate words written by one of Britain's most courageous explorers, Captain Robert Falcon Scott, on 29 March, 1912. With frostbite gnawing at his very bones, Scott lay dying in the bitter waste of the Antarctic. His tragic but heroic death ended a historic expedition. The world has forgiven him his error of judgment, but it has not forgotten his bravery.

Scott and his pioneering team of Dr Wilson, Captain Oates, Petty-Officer Edgar Evans and Lieutenant Bowers reached their goal, the South Pole, only to discover that a Norwegian team led by Roald Amundsen had already reached it. Amundsen hoisted the Norwegian flag and left two letters in a small tent. One was addressed to Scott, asking him to forward the other to Norwegian King Haakon, should his countrymen fail to return.

Yet the glory could have been Scott's, and Britain's. He could have got to the South Pole first and returned safely with his team to a hero's welcome. But it wasn't to be. Scott had made a fatal mistake during his preparations for his epic voyage to the South Pole. He decided to use ponies as his main form of haulage instead of dogs, which many thought were far more experienced, hardy and suitable. A small dog team went along only as back-up. This decision led to tragic consequences for Scott and his men.

Scott had upheld the family tradition by entering the forces. This pleased his father John Edward, whose ill health had prevented him from doing so. Instead he worked in a family brewery in Plymouth, taking a back seat while his brothers served their country. One was a naval surgeon, the other three were officers in the Indian Army.

Robert Falcon Scott was born near Devonport on 6 June, 1868. A governess taught him at home until he was eight, when he was sent to a day school. Later he went to Stubbington House, Fareham, Hampshire, before finally being entered as a naval cadet on the *Britannia*. He was just 13.

He joined the crew of the *Boadicea* as a midshipman, served two years there and then a short term on the *Monarch*. Afterwards he joined the *Rover*, one of the ships of the training squadron under Commodore Sir Albert Hastings Markham, the Arctic explorer, cousin of Sir Clements Markham, geographer and historian who, as president of the Geographical Society, was later to instigate the *Discovery* expedition.

Captain Scott before the start of the last expedition in 1911.

The young cadet could never have suspected that when Sir Clements came to the squadron as the guest of the Commodore he was already looking for a likely leader for the expedition to the Antarctic. But some time later, Sir Clements recorded one of their meetings. In his book, *The Lands of Silence*, he wrote: 'I had selected the fittest commander in my own mind in 1887. On the 5th, Scott dined with us. He was then 18 years of age and I was much struck by his intelligence, information and the charm of his manner. My experience taught me that it would be years before an expedition would be ready and I believed that Scott was the man destined to command it.'

Towards the end of 1888, Scott was transferred to the *Amphion*, then at Esquimalt in British Columbia. On the journey there he clearly displayed his leadership skills.

Because of bad snow on the railways he had to take a tramp steamer which was going to Alaska from San Francisco. The ship, packed with too many passengers, hit a mighty gale. Panic and chaos ensued, and women and children were lying prostrate with seasickness on the floor of the small saloon. Scott, a young sub-lieutenant aged just 20, took control. He organized the men – mainly rough Californian miners – into watches to wash, dress, feed and nurse the sick women and children. The men turned into a fairly disciplined crew, obeying his every order. Scott had shown flair at a very tender age for dealing with people and difficult situations.

He returned from Esquimalt a full lieutenant in 1891 and was posted to the *Vernon*, the naval torpedo school at Portsmouth, to specialize in torpedo practice, and finally to the *Majestic*, flagship of the Channel Fleet.

It was in June 1899, while on a shore leave in London, that he again encountered Sir Clements Markham. It was indeed a meeting of fate, recalled by Scott: 'Chancing one day to walk down Buckingham Palace Road, I espied Sir Clements Markham on the opposite pavement, and naturally crossed and as naturally turned and accompanied him to his house.

'That afternoon I learned for the first time that there was such a thing as a prospective Antarctic expedition; two days later I wrote to apply to command it.'

A year later his appointment as prospective leader of the expedition was announced. In June 1900 he was promoted to the rank of commander.

A sum of £92,000 was raised and the *Discovery* was built.

Scott was released from routine naval duties to superintend preparations for the expedition. It was thanks to his insistence, backed by the recommendation of high naval officers, that the ship's company, with the exception of the scientific personnel, was almost entirely recruited from the Royal Navy.

In the summer of 1901 *Discovery* set forth. The expedition surveyed South Victoria land, the interior of the Antarctic continent, rounded the Ross Sea and investigated the nature of the ice barrier. She returned in September 1904 after three years and three months.

Scott's reception was overwhelming. He was promoted to captain from the day of his return and was invited to Balmoral where he gave a lecture in the presence of the king, prime minister and other distinguished guests.

Foreign countries and their geographical societies awarded him their medals and decorations. *The Times* of September 1904 wrote of his work: 'It has been one of the most successful that ever ventured into the polar regions, north or south. True to the spirit of his instructions, he has done what he set out to do and even more. He has added definitely to the map a long and continuous stretch of the coast of the supposed Antarctic continent. His sledge expeditions, south and west and east, have given a part at least of the history of this land of desolation . . . Moreover, probably on no previous expedition has there been such unbroken harmony among its members.'

Scott's return on the *Discovery* that day heralded the beginning of the real expedition – when man would have to conquer the unknown, the vastness and harshness of the South Pole.

Scott was given nine months' leave to allow him time to record his first exploratory expedition. He had already written and sent home from New Zealand his report to the Admiralty.

His book, *The Voyage of the Discovery*, was finished in August 1905. Shortly before it was published Scott was appointed to a staff post as Assistant Director of Naval Intelligence at the Admiralty. Then came command of *Victorious* and *Albemarle* – and romance for Captain Scott.

After leaving the *Albemarle* in 1907, Scott returned to London. There he met a sculptress, Kathleen Bruce, daughter of Canon Lloyd Bruce of York. Their love blossomed and endured when he was posted to the battleship *Essex* in January 1908 and five months later to the *Bulwark*. In September that year, Kathleen and Robert married. He rejoined his ship after a short honeymoon at Etretat.

His comrades believed Scottie, as they called him, would now become a settled husband, abandoning all thoughts of a long, hazardous trip to the South Pole.

They were wrong. Plans were already being made for a new expedition. The British government and those of Australia, New Zealand and South Africa gave grants, but, inexplicably, the expedition was not an official one.

On the day Kathleen gave birth to a little boy, Scott was already working out his Antarctic goals. They were twofold: to undergo further exploration

111

of the Ross Sea area and to reach the South Pole. He assembled the strongest scientific team ever recruited for polar work. Dr E. A. Wilson, who had been on the *Discovery*, was zoologist, artist and chief of staff. Dr G. C. Simpson, director of the British Meteorological Office, was meteorologist. There were biologists, geologists, a physician and a parasitologist.

On 1 June, 1910, the *Terra Nova* left the Thames under the command of Lieutenant Evans. Scott went on to the Cape of Good Hope in a mail boat. The expedition left Cape Town under Scott on 2 September for Australia and reached Melbourne on 12 October. Here Scott received a cable from the Norwegian Amundsen informing him that he, too, was about to make the attempt to reach the South Pole. Scott's heart sank. Did he have a premonition of the disaster that awaited him in the frozen wastelands?

The *Terra Nova* sailed for the ice from Dunedin in New Zealand on Tuesday, 28 November, 1910. His wife stayed on board until the ship was past the Heads, when a tug took her ashore. Kathleen and Robert held each other close upon parting. It was their last embrace.

Scott's intention was to find a landing place at Cape Crozier on Ross Island, but the heavy swell prevented this and he sought another landing place at Hut Point. It was here that his ill-chosen animal haulage team was landed.

Scott had decided not to take a full team of dogs, but had preferred to take Manchurian ponies specially bought in Siberia for the expedition.

He had insisted the ponies had to be white because he believed them to be more hardy than brown ponies. This delighted the dealers. The asking price for these rare beasts was sky-high.

Why Scott was adamant about using ponies remains a mystery. Earlier trips across the Antarctic ice had shown how vulnerable they were. But Scott would not be swayed. His obstinacy was to prove a fatal error.

By 12 January, 1911, everything needed for the expedition had been unloaded from the *Terra Nova*. Captain Oates had charge of the ponies. All stores for the Pole were first collected at a base named Safety Camp. Scott himself oversaw every detail and prepared to lay depots for his journey.

The *Terra Nova* left New Zealand before the beginning of the long Antarctic night, but not before Scott learnt that Amundsen's party was at the Bay of Whales, 60 miles nearer the Pole than he was.

The groups laid up for the winter between April and September – a long, frustrating night-time – and a start was made on 1 November, 1911.

The journey was in three stages – to the snow plain of the Ice Barrier, then to the Glacier and finally to the bleak, barren summit plateau of dry snow.

Plans were made to transport three units of four men to the Glacier. Two

112

of these, as supporting parties, could help the polar party get within a reasonable distance of their goal.

The first part of the plan was carried out successfully. The two teams that went forward were led by Scott and Evans. By January 1912 they were getting closer. Petty-Officer Evans's party was sent back, with the exception of Lieutenant Bowers.

When Scott's team went on alone they were 120 miles from the Pole. Exhaustion began to take its toll for they were dragging heavy loads at over 10,000 feet above sea level. Progress was slower than anticipated and food was in short supply. Scott's realization that he had chosen the wrong animals to help lighten the burden of the arduous expedition came too late.

His men were hungry. As a dog-lover, Scott refused to kill and eat his dogs. During the drive to the Pole it was the ponies that were slaughtered to provide meat for both men and dogs – Scott's precious ponies, the very ones he had stubbornly set his heart on to help him make a success of his historic mission.

On 13 January, they still had 60 miles to go. The next day they covered 20. The dog team was dispatched back to the base camp. Now, as well as their own loads, the men had to pull the sledges too.

On 16 January, they experienced a feeling of triumph, then of despair. They had set off in reasonably good spirits, certain of reaching the Pole the next day. But on the last stretch of their journey, they came across the remains of a camp with a sledge track and the prints of dog paws. Amundsen, relying on his experienced dog teams, had been that way before.

In fact, his arrival, which marked him down in history as the first man to reach the South Pole, was 34 days before Scott's. Scott and his team dutifully continued until they reached the Pole, but they were despondent at evidence of the Norwegian victory. They knew it would be a bleak return trip. Food was even scarcer on the way back. Captain Oates and Petty-Officer Evans were early victims of frostbite. Wilson strained a tendon. Scott fell and bruised a shoulder. Somehow they managed to leave the tortuous plateau and reach the Glacier. Edgan Evans was by now very ill, and he died on 17 February. The four survivors struggled on, getting weaker by the hour. Then Captain Oates became seriously ill, his feet black with frostbite.

By the beginning of March the brave men knew the situation was hopeless – yet not one dared voice his gravest fears. Oates knew he was holding back his friends. He sought their advice. They said: 'Let's keep going together.' Wilson gave each man enough opium should a painless death be the only option.

On 15 March, brave Oates chose the ultimate solution without consulting his friends. He told them to go on ahead and let him sleep on. They would not hear of it. The thought of abandoning him to certain death was too much for the gallant band to bear. So Oates slept that night. He awoke to see a blizzard raging outside their tent. It was then he spoke the immortal words: 'I am going outside and may be some time.'

In a rare moment when he had the strength, when his hands had eased a little and the pain was not so bad, Scott wrote: 'We knew poor Oates was walking to his death, but though we tried to dissuade him we knew it was the act of a brave man and an English gentleman. We all hope to meet the end with a similar spirit and assuredly the end is not far.'

He was right.

The next day, Scott's right foot was completely eaten away by frostbite. He hardly noticed.

By 19 March, they had got within 11 miles of their food depot. But fate would once more dash their last, dwindling hope of survival.

Another blizzard blew up, blocking all attempts to push ahead. The men huddled together on 21 March to agree that Wilson and Bowers should go on, but they had to wait for the blizzard to die down. The heroic team were not to know it would keep tight its blustery, lethal grip for 11 days. They died before calm came to the Antarctic. Scott was still alive on 29 March, the day he made his sad last entry in his diary.

No one back home knew what had become of the men. It was eight months later, in November 1912, that searchers found the bodies.

Dr Wilson, it was reported, 'died very quietly with his hands folded over his chest.' Bowers lay 'in the attitude of sleep'. Scott himself lay between them, his left arm over Wilson, his oldest friend. His diaries were under his bag. Letters for Kathleen, his son and other close ones lay beside him.

The searchers did not disturb the bodies. There was something too moving about the sight of brave men, literally frozen in time.

A burial service was held and a pyramid built around the bodies. A cross was placed on it.

It was a tragic end – so near to glory, and yet so far.

Innocent victims

An American war plane homed in on its target – a fortification where Grenadian troops were believed to be stationed. But the fort turned out to be a mental hospital, and 50 innocent people died when the aircraft bombed it in error.

The tragedy happened during the US invasion of Grenada in 1983.

The Pentagon admitted the 139-patient hospital had been mistaken for the fortress, Fort Fredericks: 'Our personnel were unaware that a hospital was located at St George. Our troops observed the entire area was marked as a military area.'

Grenadian nurse Alice Celestine said later: 'We believe the Americans mistook the hospital for the fort when they saw the Grenadian army boys running towards it when the bombing started.'

A massive rescue operation was launched to find survivors in the rubble of Richmond Hill mental hospital in Grenada's capital of St George.

Rail disaster

Britain's greatest train tragedy ever occurred in the days when speeds were slower – but there was no advanced technology to ensure passengers' safety. Much of it depended on human judgement and efficiency. On one occasion, when that failed, five trains rammed into one another and more than 200 people died. It was a horror two men had to live with for the rest of their lives.

The morning air was still fresh as dawn broke over Quintinshill, Scotland on 22 May, 1915. Trains weren't running on time that morning, but that was not unusual. Scotland-bound expresses had left Euston station in London at 11.45 pm and at midnight and the two trains were expected to

115

approach Carlisle half an hour late. As was customary practice, a local train which normally followed them was sent on ahead to Quintinshill, where it was to be stopped to allow the faster trains to overtake it.

This arrangement was not new to signalmen Meakin and Tinsley.

When Meakin learnt of the local train's arrival, he had to decide where it could safely be shunted. The down loop already had a goods train from Carlisle standing there. So he directed the local train to the up main line. Business was getting a little too brisk, Meakin decided, especially when he was then asked to take on an empty coal train too. That went into the up loop. His last signal before handing the box over to Tinsley was to accept the first express train.

Both men only half listened when a message came that a special troop train carrying a regiment of the 7th Royal Scots from Larbert to Liverpool was making its way towards them on the up line.

For Meakin and Tinsley had been working a little fiddle between them. It had long been agreed that Meakin would tip off his mate Tinsley when the local train was stopping at Quintinshill. Tinsley would then take it from his home at Gretna Junction so that he could come on duty later than he should have done. While he was travelling down, Meakin would jot down train movements from 6 am onwards on a separate sheet of paper so that Tinsley could copy them into his train register, making it look as though he had never been late. Tinsley went on with his copying and Meakin settled down to read his newspaper.

No signal was ever sent to Kirkpatrick, where the coal train had come from, to say it was occupying the up loop. Staff at Kirkpatrick say what they did receive was a signal giving the 'all clear' for the troop train.

Tinsley went about organizing the expected trains.

At 6.38 am, he pulled off his down signals for the Scottish express. At 6.42 am he accepted the troop train.

He pulled off all his up main line signals. Three minutes later, the first of a double disaster shook the area as the troop train hurtled into the stationary local train.

Coaches from the local train were flung back 136 yards in the powerful head on collision. The engine was pushed back 40 yards. The engine from the troop train ended up lying on its right side across both through running lines. The 15 coaches of the troop train were smashed to pieces, the front ones shooting right over the engine and coming to land some distance in front of it.

Within moments a 15 coach train 213 yards long was crushed to almost half its size. It was carnage. But the tragedy had not ended. The second express train was making its way to Quintinshill.

116

Meakin rushed to the down signals to warn the oncoming train driver. A guard and other railway staff made a frantic dash along the line to give a warning. The driver could not believe anything was wrong. He was travelling at high speed under clear signals. Though he desperately tried to shut off steam when he saw the crazed waving in front of him, there was nothing he could do to pull up a 600-ton train in only 270 yards.

The express ploughed headlong into wreckage already littering the line. Survivors of the first crash, making a bid for escape, were felled as they ran. More people died as they tried to rescue other injured passengers. The troop train was struck again, right through the wagons of the goods train on the down loop. Coaches telescoped into each other.

The second smash had happened just one minute after the first. There were now five pulverized trains at Quintinshill – and barely nothing left of the troop train.

Eight people died in the second express train, and 54 were injured. Two people died in the local train. No one ever found out exactly how many perished on the troop train because the list of passengers had been destroyed. It was estimated about 215 soldiers and two railway servants died. About 190 men were seriously hurt. The accident inspector Colonel Druitt blamed the accident entirely on the 'inexcusable carelessness' and inattention to duty of signalmen Meakin and Tinsley.

Burnt-out coaches at Quintinshill after the collision.

117

They had made fatal mistakes that morning. Firstly, Meakin forgot to put safety collars on the signal levers controlling those parts of the line that had trains standing on them. These collars served as a reminder to the signalman and were designed so the levers could not be moved again while the track was occupied. The fireman of the local train, Hutchinson, had entered the signal box to check that this had been done, but Tinsley simply gave Hutchinson a pen to sign the book and carried on making the false entries in the train register.

Colonel Druitt also discovered the two men had overlooked the presence of the local train standing on the main line a mere 65 yards away in broad daylight. They had been too busy chatting with two brakemen who had popped in from the goods trains.

Hutchinson should never have left the box until he was satisfied the proper precautions had been taken to protect his train – the local which had made the fatal stop at Quintinshill that day.

The report stated that if the Caledonian Railway Company had installed inter-locking devices on signals at Quintinshill, the disaster may never have happened. But it was argued that the track layout was so simple that only human error could turn a relatively safe system into a lethal one.

It took almost 24 hours to extinguish the burning wreckage of the five-train pile up. Coals from the overturned engine of the troop train ignited gas cylinders used for lighting – and the flames spread with terrifying speed as the gas escaped under high pressure. Water was used from the tenders of the two goods trains but to little effect. A pump and hose were connected to a stream on a nearby farm to help fight the fire. The firemen from Carlisle arrived at 10 am. All that day and throughout the night the mighty train fire of Quintinshill raged.

When the fire fighters left exhausted at 9 am the next day, the 15 coaches of the troop train, four coaches of the express, five goods wagons and all the coal in the engine tenders had all gone up in the blaze.

The disaster happened because Meakin and Tinsley had not carried out their duties. Hutchinson deserved some of the blame, but it was the two signalmen who had to watch in horror as people died before their eyes in a tragedy of their making.

The horror led Colonel Druitt to introduce stricter safety measures. He strongly urged the abolition of gas lighting on trains, and recommended that steel rolling stock should be introduced, with more wrecking tools and fire extinguishers on all passenger trains.

Meakin and Tinsley could not fail to realize that these measures were the result of their own fatal carelessness.

118

Tampa Bay tragedy

'It was raining cats and dogs. It was dark. The wind was blowing like a hurricane. I was doing about 25 miles an hour, the Greyhound bus passed me doing about 35 miles an hour. As I came to the very top of the bridge I saw the rest was out. I applied my brakes within two feet of going in . . .'

The motorist, 60-year-old Richard Hornbuckle, was one of the lucky ones. For 35 people perished as their vehicles plunged 140 feet into deep waters in the great Tampa Bay tragedy. They were scattered like children's toys as a 600-foot ship ploughed into a massive section of the dual-carriage Sunshine Skyway Bridge linking St Petersburg and Florida's Central Gulf Coast of America.

The disaster happened on 9 May, 1980 as gale force winds and rain lashed the area. The *Summit Venture*, a phosphate freighter, was literally heading for a port in a storm.

'I was looking straight ahead,' the vessel's captain John Lerro was to recall later. 'I just didn't want to go barging through with all that rain. The next thing I saw was the bridge. It took me a moment or two to determine that it was not the centre of the bridge where ships are supposed to pass under.'

The Sunshine Skyway Bridge hit by the freighter *Summit Venture*.

119

What followed was the sickening sound of a crash and tearing metal as the freighter hit the bridge and brought down a 1,400-foot section of the Sunshine Skyway Bridge. For drivers making their way across the Tampa Bay span, there was little chance. All 21 passengers and the driver of the Greyhound bus were killed when it sank and became tangled in the twisted steel from the mangled bridge. At least five vehicles crashed into the waters.

John Lerro described his nightmare on that wild, windy day. 'Orders to reverse the engines and drop anchors were just too late. There was not time. The bridge fell down in sections, just seconds apart.' He had grabbed the ship's radio telephone and called the coastguard with a desperate Mayday alert. 'I looked up and saw the bridge was still falling. There were cars driving off.' Lerro said he considered dropping anchor before he reached the bridge but another vessel prevented him from turning left and leaving the channel. Turning right would put the *Summit Venture* broadside to the fierce wind and the ship would have been hard to control.

'The best thing to do was to head for that 306 foot gap,' the 37-year-old Lerro said, referring to the space between bridge piers on either side of the 600-foot wide channel. The empty, high-riding ship was pushed out of the channel by the wind. 'I felt sure she'd make the centre span,' Lerro said. But Lerro and his crew were misguided by buoys marking the channel, which seemed to 'appear, disappear then reappear on radar'. Seeing the buoys, Lerro thought he was on course and could safely pass under the bridge. But he was disastrously wrong.

Pulling out the dead from the mess of twisted bridge and crushed cars took three days. Each day brought divers the grim discovery of more bodies, buried deep under the wreckage. An eye-witness gave this graphic description of the mighty bridge that had toppled: 'The superstructure was torn and spread like a giant spider's legs against skies that were black and weeping.' A 56-year-old truck driver had a miraculous escape from death. Wesley MacIntyre was driving to work when he noticed the bridge 'swaying'. Then his truck hurtled into space, bouncing off the crippled ship and plunging into the swirling waters.

'As I approached over the high point of the bridge it started to give way. I couldn't stop. I just slid and hit the ship. Then I dropped into the water. I figured it was all over,' Wesley recalled. He escaped with a head wound and even managed to swim to the *Summit Venture* to be hauled aboard. He was the only survivor of those who were thrown from the bridge.

Today, locals of Tampa Bay and 14,000 commuters have a brand new, multi-million dollar bridge, but they are reminded daily of the tragedy of the original Sunshine Skyway Bridge. The death gap is still there, and grass grows on the approaches at either end of the sad structure.

CHAPTER SIX

ERRORS OF JUDGMENT

Simple errors of judgment have been the cause of things going badly wrong in countless walks of life since the beginning of time. This chapter contains a heady mix of some diverse examples of this, including military blunders, elaborate hoaxes, marketing fiascos and misinformed murder trials.

Holy or hoax?

elievers fell to their knees to give prayers of thanks when the news
was announced. The Holy Shroud of Turin, the sacred cloth of
Christ revered by millions, was to be displayed in public for the
first time in 45 years.

The 14-foot length of linen was to be viewed on the high altar of Turin
Cathedral in 1978, in a case with specially controlled atmosphere, to protect
the precious religious relic from the slightest risk of damage.

In one month alone, more than two million pilgrims visited the cathedral
to stand awestruck before this material evidence of the Crucifixion,
miraculously preserved. The cloth showed the shadowy outlines of Christ's
face, his eyes closed, and his forehead gashed by the crown of thorns. His
arms were crossed and a mark on his right wrist showed where he had been
nailed to the cross.

Ten years later scientists announced that the holy shroud, which had
strengthened the faith of millions over the centuries, was the work of a
14th-century forger. Their pronouncement, backed by indisputable proof
obtained by using the latest technology, ended long years of controversy
and debate. Cardinal Anastasio Ballestero, the Archbishop of Turin, broke
the news in October 1988. Technology had proved that millions of
believers had been mistaken.

Scientists in Oxford, Zurich and Arizona had used carbon dating to check
the age of historically authenticated samples of cloth and cuttings from the
shroud and were '95 per cent' certain of their findings: the blessed item of
Christendom was in fact a piece of linen woven between AD1260 and
AD1390. It could never have covered the body of Christ. When the news
was announced, Dr Michael Tite, keeper of the British Museum research
laboratories, and Professor Edward Hall and Professor Robert Hedges of
Oxford, all confirmed there could be no doubt about their scientific
findings.

The news, though deeply disappointing to the faithful, did not come as a
great shock to sceptics. As long ago as 1389, the Bishop of Troyes had
described the shroud as a cunning forgery. He said his predecessor had met
the forger!

The Holy Shroud which provoked so much Christian controversy over
the centuries has a fascinating history. The first reference to its existence

was found in St Mark's Gospel. The disciple stated that Christ's cloth was found in his empty tomb after the resurrection. Later, pilgrims to Jerusalem mention 'the shrouds of Christ'. It was later rumoured to be in Turkey, then in France and finally in the possession of the Savoy family in Italy during the 14th century. About this time, the first doubts about the authenticity of the mysterious and revered item were being expressed.

The Bishop of Troyes complained to the Pope of the time: 'Canons have falsely and deceitfully, being consumed with the passion of avarice and not for any motive of devotion but only of gain, procured for their church, a certain cloth cunningly painted, upon which by clever sleight of hand was depicted, the twofold image of one man, that is to say the back and front, they falsely declaring that this was the actual shroud in which our saviour Jesus Christ was enfolded in the tomb.'

In the late 15th century, the shroud was given for safekeeping to Louis I who built a chapel at Chambéry to house it. It was rescued from destruction in 1532 when fire gutted the castle, and was plunged into water. The signs of the burn marks are still visible. Early records show the shroud was once boiled in oil – but no one knows why.

The treasure was moved to Turin in 1578. Before its much publicized showing in 1978, the shroud had been taken from its hallowed casket on only five occasions. It was displayed for the marriages of Vittorio Emmanuele III in 1896 and of Umberto of Savoy in 1930. The third occasion was in 1933, a Holy year, marking the 1,900th anniversary of the death of Christ. When Italy entered the war, the shroud was hidden for safety in the sanctuary of Montevergine near Avellino in southern Italy. In 1946, the Archbishop of Turin cathedral, Cardinal Fossati, went to Montevergine to return the shroud to its rightful home.

In June 1970, the shroud had its fifth airing – at a secret gathering of Italians whose names were never revealed. They included an archaeologist, a chemist, a biologist, and church dignitaries. Dozens of photographs were taken and powerful microscopes were used to examine the cloth. The investigation was to herald many years of raging controversy and more scientific analysis.

The shroud's main surface is almost black, with the visible outline resembling a photographic negative, of a human face and body of a man 5ft 10½ inches tall. There appear to be bloodstains from the hands, feet, and a wound in the side. The torso bears the imprints of flagellation wounds and the eyes show the imprint of coins placed over them, a death ritual at the time of Christ. Early examination of the imprints revealed the coins had been minted shortly before Christ was crucified. This finding convinced experts in the early 1970s that the shroud could not be an ingenious hoax.

The Turin Shroud.

An amateur photographer, Secundo Pia, was allowed to take the now famous picture of the mysterious wrap in 1898. The photographic process created a clearer and more dramatic face, and Pia was greatly moved by what he saw. His photograph added more weight to the theory that this was indeed the linen cloth in which Christ's broken body had been wrapped for the three days before the Resurrection.

In 1931, the shroud was photographed again by a professional, Guiseppe Enri. The result convinced many more people that the shroud was indeed a holy relic.

And in 1981, American scientists using modern technology felt confident the shroud was authentic. Examination by experts in Santa Barbara, California, showed blood on the shroud to be human, but the Vatican would not allow them to use a special radiocarbon test which would have settled the issue conclusively.

In 1988, the Vatican finally gave permission for the carbon-14 tests to be done to date as accurately as possible the cloth, a blend of cotton and linen woven in a herringbone pattern. It was an earth-shattering decision.

The tests showed conclusively that the Shroud of Turin was not the burial cloth in which the body of Christ had been wrapped. It was the cunning fake of a 14th-century artist.

Even then, the results were contested by many who refused to believe they had been paying homage to a fake. Surely the same burst of energy which had resurrected Christ could have altered the composition of the cloth? Others felt the results confirmed their long-held doubts.

The confusion has been cleared up but the mystery remains unsolved: who perpetrated such a hoax? Was it the French knight Geoffry de Charny who 'discovered' the shroud in about 1350 and put it on display in the church he had just built? This would have attracted vast numbers of pilgrims – all willing to leave gifts in the collection plate. Even the great Leonardo da Vinci came under suspicion at one time. His genius was such that he could have easily fabricated a magical material – and myth.

'The church has nothing to fear from the truth,' declared the shroud's keeper, Cardinal Ballestero, before the results were announced. He stressed that the faith of the church did not depend on the shroud or any other religious relics.

Pilgrims and sightseers still flock to the Turin Cathedral in great numbers. 'I have been coming here for 30 years and nothing will persuade me that the holy shroud is not genuine,' said one.

Professor Robert Hedges, a scientist involved in the conclusive dating tests, commented: 'It is a shame that science gets involved in the testing of holy relics. It is like the loss of innocence in the garden of Eden, but once the

125

question comes up, science has a responsibility to provide the answers.'

But belief is a powerful thing, and although a master forgery has been unmasked, it will make little difference to those who kneel before the Holy Shroud of Turin.

An ill wind for the jolly met men

It was the most devastating storm on record in Britain. Gales of up to 100 miles an hour swept the country killing 13 people, causing widespread destruction, uprooting hundreds of thousands of trees, robbing three million homes of electricity, and paralysing a quarter of the country. Yet only hours before, Britain's weathermen, equipped with all the latest technology, failed to warn the public.

Telly weather expert Ian McCaskill confidently predicted nothing worse than 'breezes' and 'a showery airflow'. BBC weatherman Michael Fish scornfully dismissed rumours of a storm brewing. 'A woman rang and said she heard a hurricane is on the way,' he told millions of viewers. 'Well, if you are watching and waiting, it isn't.'

A few hours later, meteorologists had to admit they had blundered badly.

The killer winds whipped up at 4 am on Friday, 16 October, 1987. There had been earlier signs of a strong gust, but no one alerted the country to what was to be the worst hurricane for 284 years.

Two fire officers on their way to answer an emergency call which turned out to be a false alarm were among the first victims of the storms. Ernest Gregory, 47, and Graham White, 46, died when an 80-foot oak crashed on to the cab of their water tender as they drove through Highcliffe, Dorset.

Patricia Bellwood was one of several people who were killed in their beds. She died when a chimney crashed through the roof as she slept at the Harte and Garter Hotel in Windsor, Berkshire. 'She probably never knew what hit her,' a policeman said later.

126

Firemen recovered the body of Ronald Davies as they cleared debris of the Queen's Hotel, Hastings, Sussex, which had blown down 'like a deck of cards.' Cyril Homewood, 59, died as the roof of his farmhouse in Biddenden, Kent caved in. Fisherman James Read was fatally injured when he was hit by a beach hut swept up in the gales in Hastings. In London, a tramp was crushed to death when the tree under which he had been sheltering toppled over. William Bennister is believed to have died as he tried to stop his garage doors from blowing away.

Road accidents provoked by the force of the gales claimed other victims. Sidney Riches, 37, from Highfield Farm, near Tottenhill in Norfolk, died on the A10 near King's Lynn. Police said his car collided with a lorry after first hitting a tree. James McCullum, 25, of Toxteth, Liverpool, was killed as his motorcycle was blown into the central reservation of the M62. Others died at the wheel of their cars as trees and debris crashed down. Two seamen from Singapore drowned after their British-registered bulk carrier capsized in Dover Harbour. There were lucky escapes too. The earth really did move for two couples making love during the storm. Winds howling at 90 miles an hour caved in the roof on Nikki Long, 23, and Matthew Dutton, 27, as they cuddled at home in Colchester, Essex. In Barnes, London, Aussie tourists Garry Buchan and Barbara Lewis only just fled their creaking camper van before a 30-foot tree flattened it. Said Garry: 'We've heard of being caught with your pants down, but this is ridiculous.'

Emergency services were unable to cope with the destruction. At the height of the hurricane, the London Fire Brigade was receiving a call for help every second.

Ships were sunk, a ferry ran aground, roads and railways were blocked with uprooted trees and farms were flattened. Houses had their roofs ripped off, tower block residents were evacuated, overhead cables were torn down. Hundreds of thousands of ancient trees were destroyed. 'It was as if a giant had walked through the gardens, kicking over everything in his path,' was how the curator at Kew Gardens described the devastation. Smashed, upturned trees stretched as far as the eye could see, each a unique part of the world-famous botanical collection.

In central London's three royal parks more than 1,000 trees were felled. A further 1,000 were lost at Hampton Court and Bushey Park. In Kent, the town of Sevenoaks lost six of the oaks it was named after.

Farmers counted the cost in millions of pounds. At one poultry farm in Essex, 17,000 birds died. In East Sussex, a tree fell across a building containing dairy cow and calf pens. Grain store roofs were ripped off as far north as Peterborough, Cambridgeshire. Recently harvested crops exposed to the storms were damaged, and power cuts disrupted milking operations

After the storm.

and cold stores. Any fruit still left on trees had to be destroyed.

In the major horticultural area of West Sussex, between Worthing and Chichester, whole glasshouses were flattened. Damage in that part alone was estimated at nearly £3 million.

In the calm after the hurricane Britain was faced with massive transport disruption.

Commuter services were virtually at a standstill as more than 500 staff in the Southern Region toiled with army workers and volunteers to clear 5,000 trees from the region's lines. Over 170 trees lay across the 21-mile stretch of track between Tunbridge Wells and Battle.

More than 500,000 pupils from schools in London and the South-East stayed at home. Some school buildings had lost their roofs, temporary classrooms were blown away and playground walls collapsed.

Bus and railway stations were eerily deserted for a Friday as commuters stayed at home, trying in vain to call their workplaces on telephones put out of action by the storm.

Householders who had managed to sleep through the storm awoke to a landscape of both rural and urban devastation. Not even a reassuring cup of tea could be made as they considered their insurance cover. The electricity supply had been cut by the storm.

Sports fans were robbed of their pleasures too. Racing at Newmarket was called off – for the first time since 1908 – when the weather claimed another Newmarket fixture.

Head greenkeeper at the hallowed golf course at Broome Park near Canterbury, John Latham, viewed what had once been his pride and joy. Five greens had almost disappeared from sight, trees had been tugged from the ground, 12-foot holes gouged out of the turf.

Six craft were damaged at the Johnnie Walker world sailing speed record attempts at Portland Harbour.

Britain's top brass started to ask questions. Furious Tory MP Teddy Taylor described the lack of warning about the hurricane as 'incomprehensible'. Home Secretary Douglas Hurd chaired an emergency meeting on 'the storm crisis'. Prime Minister Margaret Thatcher and the Queen, both in Vancouver for the Commonwealth conference, wanted to return to Britain immediately. A state of emergency was declared as the full financial impact of the storms hit home. An estimated £200m worth of havoc had been wreaked. Insurance companies geared themselves up for a payout of £100m, the biggest single loss caused by a gale.

In the normally bustling City of London the Bank of England and the Stock Exchange closed down.

'It's the end of the world,' a gloomy stockbroker muttered sadly.

Why had there been no early warning of the killer winds, the nation demanded to know. The French Meteorological Department had been wide awake and had warned on the Tuesday of winds up to 90 miles an hour. Dutch television viewers were warned on Wednesday night of freak storms expected to hit the English south coast two days later.

At the European Centre for Medium Range Weather Forecasting in Reading, Berkshire, French scientists asked radio stations to put out a warning – but this was disregarded because it later contradicted with the British Meteorological Office computer at Bracknell, Berkshire.

The Bracknell computer had predicted a depression over northern France the day before the storm hit Britain. 'Later information is usually more accurate but in this case it was not,' said a rueful forecaster.

The storm had been caused by a collision between a belt of exceptionally humid air from the west of Africa and cold Arctic air drawn down over the Atlantic. The resultant depression, the worst recorded in Britain, deepened rapidly, passing west of the Brest peninsula and the Channel Islands, before centring on Britain in the small hours of the morning of Friday, 16 October.

The London Weather Centre issued a warning to the London Fire Brigade at only 3 am of a wind expected to reach a force of 80 miles an hour during the following hour. A spokesman at the centre admitted: 'We forecast strong winds overnight but nobody thought it would be anything like as bad.'

The British public made up its mind that night about the weather experts who had let them down disastrously, but it took a year to declare that the weather was no joking matter. The jolly television met men had to stop the wisecracks and concentrate on saving lives if abnormal weather was on its way.

The Meteorological Office in Berkshire responded by announcing the introduction of a computerized Amber Alert weather warning to be given to the police and other emergency services up to four days before bad weather was expected. A red warning would alert the public to dangerously heavy rain, snow, fog, blizzards and icy roads.

The system cost the forecasters £5m. They had learnt a costly lesson.

Dashed hopes

Brigadier-General Jean Louis Jeanmaire epitomized everything the Swiss Army could hope for in a top-ranking officer. He was fine, upstanding, honest and totally loyal to his country – the perfect patriot and soldier. When he retired the Swiss Government was proud to award him full honours.

Just 18 months later the same government learnt they had honoured the worst traitor in the history of Switzerland – a Russian spy.

The ending was not quite what Jeanmaire had planned and hoped for. It was a long way from his childhood when he dreamt of becoming a dashing, daring military man. He let his daydreams take him away from the reality of his strict upbringing in the Swiss town of Biel.

Jeanmaire knew he could make use of his degree in architecture to secure a commission as a regular army officer. In 1937 he joined the influential and elite unit of career officers, the core of the Swiss Army, who serve both as commanders of the country's home force and instructors in the reserve forces.

He was determined to win recognition by his superiors and missed no opportunity to air his views and to prove himself true and faithful to his country and the army. People listened respectfully when he listed the many virtues of Switzerland – and the evils of communism. By 1957 Jeanmaire had been made a full colonel and was becoming accepted in Switzerland's upper circles.

Then came the turning point. Although he had never seen action, he believed that as long as he was in the fighting force, he could consider himself a soldier with a reputation of courage and leadership in battle. His ideas were shattered when he was transferred to the civil defence forces.

Jeanmaire's personal life was desperately unhappy too. It was increasingly difficult for him to turn a blind eye when Marie-Louise, the woman he married 14 years before, flaunted her affairs. He was disappointed in his son, in whom he had invested more money than he could afford on the best schooling in an attempt to mould him into a satisfactory heir.

But soon Jeanmaire met the man who would change his life and lead him to betray his people and country.

Colonel Vassily Denissenko, the Soviet air attaché and a professional intelligence officer, greatly impressed Jeanmaire at a foreign diplomats' gathering. Jeanmaire was surprised when the Russian telephoned him a few days later and invited him and his wife to dinner. That night an apparently warm and sincere friendship was formed.

As Jeanmaire came deeply under the influence of Denissenko he chose to ignore the fact that his 'friend' was sleeping with his wife.

The portly little Swiss colonel suffered another blow to his ego when a personal rival won the promotion to brigadier he had hoped for. That was when the Russians knew their prey was ready for manipulation. Denissenko moved in. He told Jeanmaire he felt he should make a greater effort to get to know other Swiss officers. Could Jeanmaire help? A few nights later Jeanmaire handed over a telephone directory containing classified listings of Swiss military personnel.

He knew he was breaking the law and violating highly sensitive army security. And the Russians knew there could be no turning back for their chosen traitor, but they wanted him to be fully aware of the power they had over him.

On one occasion Denissenko gave Jeanmaire an envelope crammed with money. The Swiss soldier reacted with deep felt hurt, and he screamed at Denissenko that he could not be bought. The Russians never had to offer Jeanmaire money again. They had his services for nothing.

Denissenko continued to ask his prey for more documents, more specialized army information. Jeanmaire's excellent memory enabled him to report almost verbatim to Denissenko the contents of official documents and files he was unable to steal, and his training as an architect was useful for drawing accurate and detailed sketches of military equipment and installations.

The Swiss Army expected Jeanmaire to meet foreign attachés and, because he was known as a life-long anti-communist, had no reason to suspect his liaison with Denissenko.

By 1964, the Soviet hold over Jeanmaire was such that there was no further need for Denissenko to work on him. He was replaced by Viktor Issaev who knew exactly how to handle the Swiss traitor: he flattered him as his equal.

Guilt began to gnaw at Jeanmaire. He threw himself into his army duties with renewed enthusiasm and his apparent devotion and commitment were rewarded in 1969 when he was promoted to Brigadier-General in charge of the country's civil defence forces.

By this time Jeanmaire's divided loyalty was making him ill. There was only one thing to do – tell the Russians he could no longer work with them.

They responded by sending in yet another Soviet attaché, Colonel Vladimir Strelbitzki, who had a different way of dealing with traitors.

When the frightened Swiss officer announced his intention to break off the relationship, the Russian threatened to expose him.

In return, Jeanmaire told Strelbitzki all he knew. The Russians learnt of the exact sites of missile targets, top secret fortifications, storage depots and command centres. Jeanmaire was valuable to them, because he was in a position to discover the weaknesses and scandals of prominent people which would make them vulnerable to Soviet blackmail when necessary.

Jeanmaire retired at the end of 1975, when he was 65, and delivered his last report to the Russians. He was awarded full military honours at a glittering retirement ceremony, and believed his evil past would somehow fade into oblivion, as he was doing.

But early on 9 August, 1976, agents of the Swiss secret service posted themselves near the Lausanne block of flats where Jeanmaire lived. They watched as the balding, solitary figure emerged for his regular morning walk. Then they pounced.

On 17 June, 1977, a Swiss court sentenced Jeanmaire to 18 years in prison, and to 'degradation and expulsion from the army'.

What led security officers to Jeanmaire? He desperately tried to find out. So did his lawyer during the trial. No answer was forthcoming from the grim-faced Swiss authorities. And who could blame them? They had successfully unmasked the man who gave his country away to an enemy – for nothing.

Dropping a bombshell

Millions froze in horror at the radio announcement – America was about to bomb Russia. They clearly heard President Ronald Reagan say: 'My fellow Americans, I am pleased to tell you I have signed legislation to outlaw Russia forever. We begin bombing in five minutes.'

President Reagan thought he was doing a sound check before taking part in an American radio show. He did not realize his little 'joke' had been picked up on audio tapes by radio stations across the country.

President Reagan's pointer.

White House Press Secretary Larry Speakes hurriedly called two networks, CBS and Cable News, to ask them not to disclose what had happened, but someone, somewhere, leaked the blunder, made during a warm-up to a Reagan broadcast. The world's press and TV made a meal out of the president's foolery, but Americans were by then used to Reagan's radio repartee. In a similar sound check two years earlier he had called the Polish government 'a bunch of bums'. During a visit to Venice, Reagan made a tasteless Irish joke, overheard by broadcast technicians.

The president always liked a little bit of innocent fun. As a young radio baseball commentator in Illinois, early in his career his link-up with a match broke down. So rather than have listeners switch to a rival station he invented a game and pretended to be continuing a live commentary.

The president often seemed to get it wrong. In November 1985, when he was involved in a cancer scare, he sort of forgot his own diagnosis. The growth taken from his colon was malignant, but he told a BBC interviewer firmly that it was benign. When the BBC collected the tape from the White House the error, though fiddled with by Reagan's staff, could still be heard.

In Brazil, Reagan told baffled dinner guests how pleased he was to be visiting Bolivia. Receiving Lee Kwan Yew of Singapore at the White House he bade him 'Welcome to Singapore Mr Yew.' He gaily addressed President Doe of Liberia as Chairman Moe, and called the boxer Sugar Ray Leonard and his wife 'Sugar Ray and Mrs Ray'. Reagan often forgot his official lines and replaced them with the script of one of his old Hollywood movies instead. Once, when presenting medals of honour, he recalled as fact an act of bravery he had performed – but only on celluloid in an old film called *Wing and a Prayer*.

As a young governor, Ronnie Reagan predicted confidently: 'I just wanna say the Beatles have as much chance of getting the MBE as I have of becoming President of the United States.' He was destined to eat his words.

Battle of Blenheim

For more than two years the War of the Spanish Succession had been raging in Europe between England, Holland and Austria on one side, and France, Spain and Bavaria on the other.

Now both sides were preparing for a decisive battle in which England was determined to rid its Austrian allies of the marauding French. It was the Battle of Blenheim, and the French may well have been able to stand their ground and claim a historic victory had it not been for the blunders of the French Marshal Tallard.

The Duke of Marlborough had in fact expected the French under Tallard's command to win. Instead, the French leader simply goofed off.

On the evening of 12 August, 1704, the English were very uneasy. Their enemy, the French, had advanced almost as far as Austria's capital Vienna.

The Duke of Marlborough realized that Austria had to be saved, for without her help England would never win the war. He planned a daring stratagem. At the beginning of the year the Duke had led his army away from the Netherlands and into the heart of Germany, conquered Bavaria and joined the Austrian army under Prince Eugene in preparation for a great attack on the French. The French had been completely hoodwinked by

135

Marlborough's daring march and it was not until he was well on the way to the River Danube that it was realized he was marching to relieve Vienna. A French army hurried to the defence, teaming up with the Bavarians, and established their camp near the village of Blenheim to await the approach of their enemies.

The scene for the Battle of Blenheim was set.

The armies of Marlborough and Prince Eugene had halted to the north-east of Tapfheim, a small village close to Blenheim.

The Duke was studying a roughly marked chart in his tent. He knew if he failed, his country would be in danger from the French, and he himself would be ruined.

Prince Eugene joined him to discuss tactics. One thing they both agreed on was that their enemy leader, Marshall Tallard, would make mistakes. This gave them some hope of victory.

At dawn, on 13 August, the morning mist prevented the French and Bavarians from obtaining a clear view of the approaching armies, but later, when it cleared, they realized the hour of reckoning had struck.

By midday, Marlborough had reached a river, the Nebel, which flowed across the plain into the River Danube and separated the opposing armies.

Blenheim was packed with soldiers under the Marquis of Clérambault, who hoped to make an attack on the rear when the English advanced. Marlborough had anticipated that the French would occupy Blenheim and had already issued instructions to make an assault on the village as soon as the battle began. Meanwhile, Prince Eugene was making slow but steady progress through the wooded country to the west to take up his position on the right wing opposite the forces from Bavaria.

The signal was given and Marlborough's army advanced. At first the French fought back fiercely, weakening their attackers' line as men fell dead to the ground. But as the fighting continued, reinforcements swelled the English ranks and the French were driven back inside the village.

Now Marlborough took advantage of a great tactical error made by Marshal Tallard. He had reached the opposite banks of the Nebel, where Tallard cunningly offered no resistance while his enemies crossed the river. His own scheme was to launch an attack on the English before they had time to line up after reaching the other side and then to drive them back to the adjoining marshy lands.

The tactic failed dismally. Although the French army leader did in fact give the order for a charge to be made, Marlborough's army was prepared to stand its ground against the attack.

Then Tallard made a fatal error. He left the scene. His inexperienced men had to carry on the defence as Tallard foolishly went to see how the fight against Prince Eugene's forces was progressing. Unfortunately, he decided to take the Marquis of Clérambault's 3,000 fighters with him.

The Duke of Marlborough took full advantage of the confusion among his enemies. He determined victory would be his before nightfall, and mustered his army for a final attack. Thousands of panic-stricken French soldiers scattered. It was too late for Marshal Tallard to try to regain command of the fearful army. He was among those forced to surrender, and was taken prisoner.

Among those who died was the Marquis of Clérambault, who abandoned his men in Blenheim and plunged to his death in the waters.

The hapless Tallard was treated with courtesy by his enemy despite his military blunders. He was even taken in the victorious Duke of Marlborough's coach from the battlefield under escort, and sat out the bumpy journey in despondent silence. He had handed the British victory on a plate.

The most expensive hole in the world

It was the biggest hole ever dug – and at £14 million the most expensive. And because no one wanted it, it had to be filled in again.

The saga of the unwanted hole began in 1973, when the Department of Energy under Anthony Wedgwood Benn, decided to capitalize on the fast growing North Sea oilfields. What was needed, the department felt, was giant concrete oil platforms which would require massive excavation work.

The area earmarked for the innovative construction work was picturesque Portavadie overlooking Loch Fyne on Scotland's west coast.

Not only was the location a bad choice, but fate was against the project. The roads leading to the isolated hamlet were poor, and someone should have noticed that the outlet from the loch to the sea wasn't deep enough to accommodate any oil platform, concrete or not.

The government had grossly overestimated the demand for its massive £250-million platforms. And just then, the oil industry took a dive. No one wanted oil platforms, the government had to admit.

You couldn't blame one elderly resident of Portavadie for being particularly upset. Miss Munro had had to move her sheep off what had once been fine pasture land and all she had for her trouble was a hole 450 yards long and 50 yards wide. 'My view has been spoilt,' she said, somewhat politely under the circumstances.

Another victim was farmer Robin Watson, hired as transport manager for the ill-fated project. His efforts had been all in vain. The excavation work cost £11 million and a further £3 million was spent on constructing a village for the 700 workers involved in the project. But no one actually lived there. In 1976, the government conceded defeat.

Robin Watson explained: 'They never issued a compulsory purchase order on the village, even though it was built with government money. And under Scottish law the buildings belong to the landowners.'

The village was eventually sold off to a mysterious off-shore company in Curaçao – and resold days later to another company based on the South American island.

The Department of Energy and the Scottish Office came in for a drubbing from the Commons Public Accounts for squandering 'substantial sums' of public money.

But that was not the end of the world's costliest cavity. The bulldozers moved in again. They breached the sea wall and the waters of Loch Fyne flooded in to fill what was now known as Benn's Black Hole. Landscapers arrived to try to restore the shoreline to its original state. That was to cost taxpayers another £1 million.

But for Miss Munro, who had seen the area she'd lived in all her life spoilt for ever, the money was not important. 'It will never be the same again,' she said sadly, from behind a line of washing carefully placed to block out the blot on her view.

Amy

A ir ace Amy Johnson became a legend in her own lifetime, hailed around the world for her brave pioneering flight from Britain to Australia, when she was 26, in May 1930. A heroine's welcome awaited her in Melbourne when she landed there after her epic 19-day flight in her single-engined, secondhand Tiger Moth.

Yet this intrepid pilot, whose courage and determination were legendary, inexplicably ran out of fuel on a short flight from one British airfield to another. The mistake cost her her life and she plunged to her death in the icy waters of the Thames estuary on 5 January, 1941. No one could understand how a pilot as skilled and experienced as Amy Johnson could have made such a basic, fatal error.

Amy had taken off from Squire's Gate airfield near Blackpool earlier that day to deliver a twin-engined RAF Airspeed Oxford to RAF Kidlington in Oxfordshire. It was a vitally needed wartime aircraft and Amy was well aware of the importance of her official Air Transport Auxiliary mission.

The weather on that day in midwinter was not ideal for flying, with a dangerous inversion of warm air above cold air. This could have caused her aircraft to ice up dangerously and as an experienced pilot Amy would have flown at a higher altitude than normal to rise above the bank of cloud covering the country.

Experts later pieced together the sequence of events leading up to Amy's death plunge. When she reached Oxfordshire, she would have known that there were hills and radio masts which posed a hazard to low-flying aircraft. She would not have been able to drop any lower, and the presence of cloud would have made it dangerous for her to attempt to get her bearings visually.

There is little doubt that Amy's best bet would have been to turn east to head for her usual base at Hatfield. She knew the area well and from there she would have been able to fly on to southern Anglia's flat lands and drop safely lower under the clouds to plot her onward course.

The next news of Amy came when rescuers fished her body out of the lonely Thames waters. She had baled out, but instead of parachuting safely to the ground, she had plummeted into freezing water, too shallow to allow rescuers to pick her up by boat, even though valiant efforts were made to reach her. One man died in the attempt.

Amy Johnson and the plane in which she made her last flight.

The fuel gauge in her aircraft showed empty, which explained why she had had to bale out. Tragically for her, she mistook a line of barrage balloons stretched across the seven-mile width of the estuary for a land marker.

She ran out of fuel because she had been flying for four and a half hours, the maximum range of an Airspeed Oxford without refuelling. It is likely that Amy got herself lost in poor visibility and was too proud or stubborn to turn back, but no one will ever be able to confirm this scenario, or be sure about the motive that drove her on while the indicator on her fuel gauge dropped inexorably. There is no record that she made any attempt to land and refuel.

It seems likely that her unnecessary, tragic death fulfilled a macabre wish for the introverted air ace. She suffered most of her life with depression over love affairs that had turned sour.

If one relationship in particular, with a Swiss businessman she met when she was 18, had gone well, Amy would not have taken to the air in the first place. But her love married someone else and Amy, with the twisted reasoning of a woman scorned, decided to take up flying, a dangerous activity which, she was well aware, could easily kill her. It was the most dramatic way she could think of to make her hurt and rejection known.

So she became a pilot and a pioneer, risking her life, and winning fame and adulation. And eventually her bitter wish came true.

The dingo baby trial – and error

T he early evening sun beat down on the Australian desert resort and holidaying campers were happily making preparations for a barbecue under the welcoming shade of a few trees. Suddenly, the heart-twisting screams of a frantic woman rent the air.

'A dingo has taken my baby!'

Those words were to launch a macabre, chilling Australian murder trial which held the world spellbound for several years. The 'Dingo Baby' story began as a terrible family tragedy, turned into a mystery, and finally ended when a mother jailed for killing her own infant was freed – after the mysterious death of a young man.

The scene of the drama was the mystical Ayers Rock area in the centre of the Australian outback, the site of ancient and powerful aboriginal rites and beliefs. Over the years the rock, a natural world wonder, has exercised a strange fascination over visitors from all parts of the world.

The leading character in the drama was Lindy Chamberlain, whose terrified screams were heard at the campsite on 17 August, 1980. Her husband Michael, a Seventh Day Adventist pastor, played a supporting role in an eight-year nightmare which threatened to destroy the family after the mysterious disappearance of their baby daughter, nine-week-old Azaria.

The Chamberlains' ordeal of trials – and grave error – ended in September 1988 when Lindy was freed after 40 months' imprisonment for allegedly murdering her baby with a pair of scissors. The costliest trial in Australia's legal history involved five gatherings of legal and forensic experts whose findings at first condemned a mother for allegedly slashing her own baby's throat, and later set her free as an innocent woman.

Lindy Chamberlain's own unwavering version of the tragedy was that a vicious dingo, an Australian wolf dog, had seized baby Azaria as she slept in her cot in the family's tent. She maintained that the dingo had gripped the child's head violently between its teeth and had dragged her off to its lair. All that remained was the infant's pathetic shredded, blood-drenched jump suit. The matinée jacket Lindy swore the baby had been wearing at the time could not be found anywhere.

142

The infant's disappearance prompted a search of the area in which 300 people took part without finding a body.

Alice Springs coroner Des Sturgess found at the first inquest on Azaria's death that 'Mr Chamberlain went to the barbecue area and was there for some considerable time in the presence of witnesses when Mrs Chamberlain cried out "A dingo has got my baby!"

'In the time they went to the campsite and the time Mr Chamberlain was at the barbecue area, the death was caused.'

That was the only hard fact which could be established during the inquiries which were to follow.

Lindy and Michael Chamberlain believed the first inquest would end their ordeal, since they had been cleared of any blame in the tragedy. But a year later, the nightmare began all over again.

The Northern Territory police in Australia were not happy with the coroner's findings. They produced new forensic evidence which was laid before a second inquest in 1981.

The incriminating evidence Sturgess now had to consider was a woman-sized handprint on the baby's clothing and evidence that the baby's little suit had been handled with hands wet with blood.

Blood was to play a large part in implicating 33-year-old Lindy and her 37-year-old husband in a crime they did not commit. Blood was found on the door handle of the Chamberlains' car, under hinges, on the carpet and under the dashboard – in places not clearly visible or accessible, the experts stated. Some of the traces were fetal blood, consistent with that of a baby's.

Blood traces were also found in a camera bag belonging to the Chamberlains, in 'nooks and crannies' and on the clasp. There were minute bits of baby hair in the bag.

British forensic expert Professor James Cameron of London Hospital Medical College had been called in. His theory was that Lindy had slashed her baby's throat, possibly with a pair of scissors, as she sat in the front seat of the car. The baby's jump suit, recovered several days later behind the camp site, showed evidence that the child had been held by human hands: the bloodstains were not consistent with an animal's attack, the experts maintained. There were no signs, the inquest heard, of saliva or fur on the clothes. Although the body has still not been found, the sum of the evidence pointed an accusing finger at Lindy and Michael Chamberlain. On 2 February, 1982, at Alice Springs, coroner Gerry Galvin ordered Lindy to stand trial for the murder of her baby Azaria, and indicted Michael as an accessory.

Even before the sensational trial started, horrified followers of the macabre story were convinced of the Chamberlains' guilt. Their case was

The Chamberlains after the charge of murder was made.

further weakened when both inquests revealed that Ayers Rock was a sacred site used for centuries by aborigines in initiation and childbirth ceremonies, and that Lindy and Michael had visited other aboriginal sites in the same area. These included a site called Cut Throat Cave.

Because of its sensational and controversial aspects, the authorities decided the trial should be moved from Alice Springs to Darwin where the jury was more likely to be impartial.

The trial began on 19 April, 1982. The Chamberlains had been granted bail of £3,000 each. The next seven weeks were to make Australian legal history as a jury of nine men and three women listened intently to evidence which first damned, then exonerated the couple, then provoked a six-hour summing up by Mr Justice James Muirhead. The evidence of campsite witnesses, forensic scientists, lawyers and police, was led. Professor James Cameron stood by his initial claim. He said that, from the state of the baby's jump suit, death had been caused by an incised wound on the baby's neck, in other words a cut throat, inflicted with a cutting instrument across or around the neck held by a human element.

Prosecutor Ian Marker accused Lindy of killing her baby, burying the body in the desert and then, with her husband, digging it up again to remove the clothing and place it near a dingo lair. Lindy's dingo story was a 'fanciful lie' he said.

The defence called 28 witnesses, including 10 who said Lindy had been loving and caring towards Azaria and one holidaymaker said Lindy had a 'new mum glow about her'.

Two witnesses gave evidence that the day before the baby disappeared two other children at the campsite were confronted by a dingo that showed no fear and grabbed the seat of a teenager's trousers. Another said a dingo had seized her six-year-old son by his bottom, causing bad bruising, teeth marks and bleeding. A month before Azaria's death, a dingo was shot as it tried to snatch a three-year-old child from the seat of her parents' car.

It was also considered unlikely that Lindy would be able to slit her child's throat, wash her bloodied hands and return to join her husband at the barbecue site in the ten minutes she was absent.

There were gasps in court as another witness, Kyth Lenehan, told that he had been in an accident in June 1979, and the kindly Chamberlains had taken him in their car to hospital. He had bled quite heavily from a head injury.

During the trial, the entire court was flown to the death scene at Ayers Rock. Two women jurors wept during the proceedings when shown the baby's bloodstained clothing – Lindy wept too. Films were shown of a dingo snatching a doll, savagely gripping its head between its teeth.

Melbourne consultant biochemist Finely Cornell said blood samples were less reliable when examined a year after the blood was shed, as had happened with the second inquest evidence.

He stated that six samples of carpet taken from the Chamberlains' car bore no traces of blood at all, and that the baby's jump suit, singlet and nappies had marks consistent with those made by dingo teeth.

Dr Hector Oram, reader in dental surgery at Melbourne University, said the holes in the baby's clothes were consistent with those in material bitten by dogs and dingos he had examined.

Things looked very good for the Chamberlains. The jury was out for a long time. Lindy and Michael displayed no emotion when they were declared guilty.

Judge Muirhead told Lindy: 'You have been found guilty of murder and there is only one sentence I can pass upon you within the law of this territory and that is imprisonment with hard labour for life.'

Michael was found guilty of being an accessory and was given 18 months suspended sentence, and was bound over in the sum of £300 to be of good behaviour for three years.

Lindy's sentence caused shockwaves, not only because she had been found guilty of slaying her own child, but because she was eight months pregnant when sentence was passed on 29 October, 1982.

An appeal was immediately lodged. Lindy gave birth to another little girl, Kahlia, in prison, two days before she was freed on bail pending the appeal.

Conditions of bail were that she lived with her husband and sons Aidan and Reagan and her parents at a Seventh Day Adventist Church in northern New South Wales.

On 30 April, 1983, Lindy's appeal was rejected. She was delivered back to Berrinah jail in Darwin to 'resume her sentence as soon as possible.'

She lost a second appeal the following year and seemed destined to spend the rest of her life working in the prison laundry.

Then came a dramatic twist which was to clear her name at last. In February 1986, by an almost psychic coincidence, climbers searching for the body of a British tourist who had jumped to his death on Ayers Rock found Azaria's bloodstained matinée jacket in an inaccessible place where the couple could not possibly have placed it. Police were later to find 'organic material' near the jacket which could have been the baby's remains.

This was a blow for the prosecutors who had steadfastly maintained that the jacket Lindy claimed had gone missing in the dingo snatch was a figment of her imagination. But the sad little garment corresponded exactly to the description she had given police at the time of the inquiry. Lindy was freed from prison to allow her to have access to legal advisers to prepare yet another inquiry.

In May 1986, the Royal Commission Inquiry began 11 months of proceedings. Heading the inquiry, Mr Justice Morling found many faults with the case presented by the couple's accusers. He blamed unreliable and wrong forensic evidence, and said important witnesses had not testified at the trial. 'Bloodstains' under the family car's dashboard had probably been caused by an insulation problem, Judge Morling found.

The couple were granted a pardon.

But this was not enough for Lindy: 'There is no satisfaction in getting a pardon for something you didn't do in the first place.' She and Michael wanted the world to know they were not to be forgiven for a horrendous crime they didn't commit. They wanted their names cleared once and for all.

The legal wheels were set in motion once again while Lindy and Michael were reunited and picked up the pieces of the long months apart during which he had cared for their three children.

'Lindy is quite new to me even though we lived together for 13 years before all this happened,' Michael told the world.

Lindy spoke of her time in jail. Of how she feared violent action from fellow inmates; of her vegetarian diet and her jogging to keep fit; of the prison slang; the rules. 'If you let your self-esteem go, if you lose your self-respect, you lose your grip on everything else. I didn't. I'd fight first.'

On 15 September, 1988, three judges in Australia declared Lindy and Michael completely innocent. They immediately went into hiding to pray.

Said Northern Territory Senator Bob Collins: 'This has been the gravest miscarriage of justice ever experienced in this country. The Chamberlains' reputations have been destroyed. One thing I hope is now going to come out of it is that there are enough fair-minded people about to say "Well, yes. We were wrong."'

It took just ten minutes for a packed court in Darwin to declare Lindy and Michael Chamberlain had never committed any crime. As soon as the verdict was announced, the couple's lawyer announced he would institute further proceedings – to win compensation for all the years they had lived under sentence of killing their own baby, whose name meant 'Blessed of God'.

In a television interview Lindy gave at the height of the Dingo Baby headlines, she said: 'If you've ever seen dingoes eat, there's no difficulty for them to remove clothes. They never eat the skin. They use their feet and hands and pull back the skin as they go – just like peeling an orange. I knew my baby was dead. It was God's will.'

If the public had believed what Lindy had claimed all along, the nightmare would never have been, and the Australian taxpayer would have been £15 million richer.

Slip-up

Russian manufacturers were tripping over themselves to live up to their leader's demand that all Soviet goods should be of first-rate quality. But one hapless shoe factory slipped up on the job by sending out a strange batch of boots which had high heels attached to the toes.

The Russian people saw the funny side of it. Mikhail Gorbachev didn't. And the tipsy-toed footwear was put on show in the Ukraine to shame the shoddy shoemaker.

Return to sender

The whole world warmed to the story of a little boy called Buddy who was fatally ill with leukaemia. The plucky eight-year-old had expressed one last desire: he wanted to earn a place in the Guinness Book of Records by collecting the largest number of postcards in the world.

It was a moving wish, one even the American President couldn't ignore. Ronald Reagan wrote a letter of encouragement to Buddy in Paisley, Scotland. The touching story soon spread around the world. Scandinavian newspapers and television companies organized appeals on Buddy's behalf. Australia joined in; the Canadian Navy printed Buddy's address in its monthly house magazine to circulate it to forces worldwide. In Britain, a note about Buddy was pinned up on a House of Commons notice board. It appealed to MPs and their staff to become involved.

Cards of all sorts flooded in at a rate of 20,000 a day – until it was discovered that Buddy did not exist. The whole charity project had been a waste of time. It had started in all innocence when Cameron Black, a retired security officer from Paisley, heard Buddy mentioned on the crackling airways of a citizens' band radio in 1982. Someone had said that a little boy dying of leukaemia was collecting the special 'eyeball cards' CB enthusiasts send to each other after making contact on the air.

Without feeling the need to check it out, 60-year-old Cameron Black offered his own box number as a mailing address for the cards. Within a few months he had 180 bags of mail clogging up his house. Eventually he became uneasy about his errand of mercy. When he called hospitals and schools throughout Scotland they could find no trace of a child called Buddy. By then, the whole thing had got out of control.

Only Britain's hard-pushed Post Office knew the score, after handling a similar appeal for a non-existent eight-year-old called Mandy who was said to be mentally handicapped and wanted to acquire a record-breaking card collection too. When Buddy's appeal started to snowball, sorters shook their heads again. The cards were marked 'return to sender' or burnt.

Officials checked and found out that the *Guinness Book of Records* had never included an entry for the greatest number of postcards collected by one person. 'Buddy has become a pain in the neck,' a spokesman for the publishers said. But the little boy who never was had also become famous.

The finger of suspicion

It was a gruesome discovery and the finger pointed firmly at foul play. Twenty policemen with tracker dogs scoured the Bristol countryside looking for the body to whom the severed finger found in an adventure playground belonged.

An experienced Home Office pathologist had stated categorically that the finger belonged to a body that had been dead for a month. The severed digit was sent for further tests while police officers pressed on with their hunt.

Back came the report: 'It's a joke finger!' Police at Bristol were reluctant to reveal the name of the man who had sparked off the Bristol murder fears, but semi-retired pathologist Dr Derek Johnson 63, admitted: 'Oh dear. This is extremely embarrassing. The finger was given to me in a very casual way and I did not make a full examination.'

He had picked it up, he said, turned it over and had only a brief look. It appeared to be a mumified human finger; the skin seemed elastic and a bone was missing. 'I did say you couldn't state exactly how old it was but that it would take a human finger about four weeks to look like that,' Dr Johnson explained. 'But I was puzzled there was no blood.' He added that it was a very sick joke to play on anyone.

The finger had been found one Sunday by a woman out for a stroll, and was examined by a local fox expert, Dr Stephen Harris from Bristol University. He, too, thought a ghastly deed had taken place and that a fox had later torn the finger off a dead body. 'It looked realistic, but it did in fact remind me of a rubber joke finger,' he said. 'But it stank to high heaven so I didn't want to look too closely.'

Police called off the hunt.

The Sinclair C5

N
o one had seen anything quite like it. Right from the moment the Sinclair C5 was unveiled, on 10 January 1985, by its balding, bespectacled creator, Sir Clive Sinclair, the little battery-powered tricycle created controversy.

The idea seemed a good one at the time. Manufacturers had been scratching their heads for years trying to develop a motor vehicle which was quietly electrically-powered, pollution-free and cheap to run and Sinclair's C5 seemed to fit the bill perfectly. The three-wheeler had a top speed of 15 miles an hour, a lead-acid battery providing a 20-mile range and a compact, plastic, light-grey body.

For the £399 purchase price you also got a battery charger and a safe-driving book from the Royal Society for the Prevention of Accidents. The battery took 300 recharges through a domestic power point.

The inital plan was to sell the machine through mail order – then through electricity board showrooms, and finally through a supermarket chain. The C5's critics refused to take the project seriously, but Sinclair won support from prestige sports car makers Lotus. The unconventional vehicle, which used an adapted washing-machine motor, was built at the Hoover factory at Merthyr Tydfil in South Wales and was to be serviced by Hoover dealers.

Motoring experts were invited to test drive the machine, which was hailed on its launch day as 'an example of brilliant lateral thinking'. They discovered the pedals were useful when the battery ran flat up a steep hill, but most of them just felt embarrassed at being seen in the three-wheeler.

Initially, the Welsh factory turned out 2,000 trikes. Eventual production was targetted at 100,000. Then the problems started. Four days after the controversial launch, marketing consultant Guy Pearce drove the machine to work and found it would have been quicker by bike. He was left high and dry a mile from his Streatham office in London when the machine ran out of juice.

What should have been a quick, commuting trip from his Chelsea home – just four miles away – turned into an embarrassing journey during which Guy had to pedal furiously to get to work on time. 'At first,' said Guy, 'the trip was great fun. A lot of people were shouting and waving.' But when the trike came to a standstill, he was furious. Sinclair agreed to give him his money back.

The same day, Transport Minister, Lynda Chalker, told the House of Commons that the Road Research Laboratory was monitoring the safety aspects of the C5.

Four weeks later, enthusiastic purchasers of the C5 were not so ecstatic. Student Nicholas Botting was the first person to be arrested while driving the C5. He had gallantly offered to drive the vehicle, which a girlfriend had won at a St Valentine's Day raffle. 'I wasn't paralytic or sloshed, just a bit tipsy. I had a bit of trouble wiring up the battery so I just started pedalling along behind her car,' said Nicholas. 'But I sort of wobbled . . . and that's when I caught the attention of these policemen.'

They charged him with driving a tricycle while unfit through drink. Luckily, he was acquitted a couple of months later. Said Nicholas after his acquittal: 'I don't want anything more to do with the C5. It's quite a comic little thing isn't it? I wouldn't be seen in one again.'

By this time, motoring organizations such as the Automobile Association had aired reservations about Sinclair's cycle-cum-car. Richard Ballantine of *Bicycle Action* magazine tested the C5. His conclusion was: 'As a concept it is brilliant. As a vehicle it is nowhere.'

In March 1985, production of the C5 was halted. By this time, 5,000 of the C5s had been sold by mail order. But there were rumours that the revolutionary machine was in trouble. Sir Clive Sinclair had deferred a decision to invest up to £2 million in a second production line. The 1,700 workers at the Hoover plant in Wales had staged a one-day strike, called to coincide with a visit by the Prince and Princess of Wales, in protest against overtime.

Questions were being asked: was the little plastic pedal machine, aimed at bringing a bit of economic joy to London commuters, fun – or folly? Was the electric vehicle – unique but controversial – really a landmark in motoring history? Or were we better off with having just our 27,000 electric milk floats?

People still gave the C5 some benefit of doubt. There was still the fact that it was the first electric runabout. Sir Clive himself was surprised that demand for his creation was not greater. He blamed the press for lack of foresight and pessimistic reporting. A special team of teenage testers was recruited. Their job was to take the C5s around London to 'increase public awareness'. For a fee of £20 a day the teenagers drove and pedalled the Sinclair tricycle around the City and answered questions from curious passers-by.

Sir Clive attacked established motor manufacturers for holding back the development of the electric car to protect investments in the internal combustion engine. But his problems would not go away.

152

Sir Clive Sinclair before the C5's troubles began.

At least, the workers at Hoover went back to work. They accepted a four per cent pay offer, ended their two-month overtime ban and agreed to the company's £10m investment package which would modernise the factory. It would also mean up to 500 job losses.

There were further problems when it was decided more people in the world should have the benefit of a C5. Changes were needed to bring the vehicle in line with laws in Europe.

By October 1985, two receivers were called in by Sir Clive to sort out his troubled C5 car company. The news was even more dismal by November.

Sir Clive's dream of tomorrow's motoring became 'the ideal Christmas gift' at a special mark-down price of £139.99 (including VAT, the batteries and accessories).

The offer was made by Woolworth's, arm of the Comet Discount firm. It was a sad bargain. The original price had been slashed by 65 per cent.

What its harshest critics called 'that most useless of vehicles, the washing-machine motor-powered C5 trolley' did make a minor comeback three years after it drove into obscurity. Do-it-yourself enthusiast David Burton thought he was doing his sister a favour fitting a C5 engine to her baby's pram in hilly Exmouth, Devon. But the Department of Transport declared it illegal.

The final sad saga for the C5 became a desert song.

Oil-rich sheikhs could see its merits in a hot climate, where the rest of the world, it seemed, had not. Orders came flooding in from the Middle East, boosting business for Maurice Levensohn of Liverpool, who had snapped up the last 7,000 models to be made and sold them for £100 to the Sheiks.

They may have lost Sir Clive a fortune, but they made money for Maurice.

'I'll be keeping at least one C5 back as a collector's item,' he said.

Missile mistake

A Russian cruise missile flew dangerously off course after the wrong flight plan was put into its computer by mistake, and had to be shot down in Finland.

The missile was launched on December 28, 1985, from a frigate of the Soviet northern fleet on test trials in the Barents See, north of Norway. It was meant to land at the Russian's land testing site at Novazemia, but because of the accidental computer programming it headed for northern Norway.

The Russians immediately dispatched two MiG interceptors with pilots specially trained to shoot down cruise missiles. 'For God's sake, get it!' they were commanded. One of them did, complying with instructions to ensure it was done from within Soviet territory.

The missile had passed about two miles south east of Kirkenes, a busy airport in the north of Norway used by businesses with iron ore mining interests.

The missile, chased by the MiG 25, first climbed to 13,000 feet at 600 miles an hour.

It was first monitored going over a small Norwegian fishing village, Jakobsleve, then across Sholpen Bank, past Kirkenes and on towards Skogfoss, a village on the border between Norway and Russia. Though not armed with a conventional or nuclear warhead, experts later worked out from its speed and line of path that it was heading for Hamburg or Bremen, West Germany's two largest ports.

That was when the Russians really began to worry. They had just 25 minutes to stop the missile.

The MiG 25 jet pilot managed to hit the missile somewhere near Skogfoss. Most of the wreckage came to rest in Finland. Five weeks later, Finnish air force investigators were still finding bits. Finnish authorities clearly recognised Soviet lettering on the fallen pieces. But no-one in the area was officially given a reason for the 'supersonic boom' they heard that December morning.

The Finns issued an official statement that what had been found was Russian flight-testing equipment, even though witnesses on the ground described seeing a turbo jet thundering across the sky.

'The Finnish authorities did not want to upset the Russians by calling

155

them liars.' Diplomacy was the wisest policy on this occasion.

The Soviet authorities had in fact immediately contacted the Pentagon to warn the Americans about the rogue missile.

Because arms control talks were due to begin in Geneva only ten days later, America asked Norway, into whose air space it had wandered, not to take action. The Soviet ambassador to Norway at the time, Dmitri Poliansky, conveyed a discreet message of apology to the Norwegians.

The decline and fall of the French emperor

Napoleon was at first a true and loyal leader of the French. His revolutionary slogan 'Liberty, Equality, Fraternity' which once echoed throughout Europe, was finally debased. The people of France had come to realize just what a tyrant Napoleon Bonaparte really was.

His obsession with conquest, dictatorship over a country which once revered him and an alliance between his enemies were to bring about his downfall. A decision to complete his empire–building by invading Russia in 1812, was the greatest military mistake he ever made. We must first look at the early days of the man who was to become master of most of Europe, to see into the mind of Napoleon.

Born at Ajaccio, the capital of Corsica, in 1769, Napoleon Bonaparte received a military education as a humble pensioner of the King of France. By 1792 he was a captain of artillery. The brilliance of his first fight with the English at the siege of Toulon in 1793 marked him out as the French Revolution's finest general. Within three years he was head of an army – helped along by his marriage to the influential Creole widow, Josephine de Beauharnais.

When in 1796, General Bonaparte launched his campaign against the Austrians in Italy, he was just 27. His rise had been meteoric.

Napoleon returned from his Italian triumphs to launch new schemes of conquest. He would conquer Egypt, turn the British out of India and crush the power of Turkey on his way back.

Napoleon's fatal weakness was that he always underestimated the strength of England and the importance of sea power. ('The Channel is a ditch which it needs but a little courage to cross,' he once boasted.) His victories in the Egyptian expedition of 1797-98 were nullified by Nelson's destruction of the French fleet in Aboukir Bay – the Battle of the Nile – and by an unsuccessful siege of Acre – 'The key of Constantinople or of India' Napoleon once confided to a companion.

Napoleon returned to France at an opportune moment. The currents of the Revolution needed direction. Anarchy threatened and a second coalition had been formed by the enemies of France, whose armies had many able captains but lacked a master mind. Napoleon, assisted by his grenadiers, seized the reins of civil power, became First Consul and made his home in the magnificent palace of the Tuileries. It was only a short time before his next move for conquest. Crossing the Alps with an army of 40,000 men, he launched a lightning strike against the Austrians who were advancing in Italy and overthrew them at Marengo in June 1800.

In 1802, the Treaty of Amiens temporarily ended hostilities between England and France. But a year later, war between the two countries broke out again. Napoleon plunged into battle, both political and military. He made himself Emperor of France and from 1805 to 1814, led the French armies in a series of campaigns in many of which he displayed the soldier's supreme genius.

Napoleon's aggressive policy alarmed the rulers of Europe for he had annexed territory and established control in northern Italy. Again, he had to face a European coalition backed by Britain with ships, money and men. His plans for invasion of Britain were wiped out by Horatio Nelson's victory over a combined French and Spanish fleet at Trafalgar in 1805. Napoleon broke up his camp at Boulogne where intense preparations had been made for crossing to "perfidious Albion" and marched across Austria.

At Austerlitz in 1805, the emperor won a victory which caused British prime minister William Pitt to say: 'Roll up that map of Europe. It will not be wanted for ten years.' But Europe was in arms against the conqueror. Prussia mobilized for war and paid for it dearly. Her armies were overwhelmed at Jena and Avestadt in 1806 and Napoleon entered Berlin in triumph. He concluded the Treaty of Tilsit, which reduced Prussia to the position of a conquered state.

Napoleon's next move was not so victorious. He captured Madrid and left his brother Joseph to rule as king. The Spanish began to join in the hate-campaign against Napoleon.

In 1809, Austria collected her forces for another blow against the conquering Corsican. But Napoleon triumphed once more with a victory at Wagram.

By 1811, Napoleon was at the height of his power. So long as Russia remained his ally, he was virtually master of Europe. But the 'continental system' by which Napoleon sought to close every European port against the goods of his relentless enemy, Britain, began to break down. The French were deprived of cheap British textiles, of such comforts as coffee, sugar and tobacco. There was heavy French taxation and the requisitioning or commandeering of food and other stores.

The people of Europe were disillusioned. They recognized Napoleon for what he really was – a ruthless, power-crazy dictator – and they were more ready to support their rulers whole-heartedly in fighting the French.

More importantly, the Russian Tsar, Alexander, broke away from the imposed economic bondage and thus brought about the fatal rupture which ended with Napoleon's great invasion of Russia in 1812. The more cautious of his ministers frowned upon the invasion project. 'He will ruin us all,' Admiral Decres told a friend.

Napoleon paid no heed. He assembled a mixed army of 600,000 men and set forth to conquer Russia. His idea was to 'melt the states of Europe into one nation'. The Russians had their own, softly, softly campaign. They would draw the invaders deeper and deeper into a country deliberately left barren of supplies or stores – and encourage defeat through sheer exhaustion and absence of resources.

When Napoleon reached Russia he found a bitterly cold and hostile environment. There was nothing for him to seize to ease the fatigue of his soldiers. There were no people to be bullied into co-operation. And the cold! It tore an icy cut through the French soldiers' inadequate uniforms. But worse was to come. The army marched on to Moscow. Although the city was home to a quarter of a million people, it was virtually deserted! A fire broke out around midnight, waking the weary men. They beat out the fire, but then another broke out, and then another. The Russians' careful, calculated campaign to break the back of the French army was working well!

Napoleon waited for weeks, expecting Tsar Alexander to approach him to talk of peace. No word came. The weather got colder, supplies totally ran out, the men ailed. Reluctantly, the crushed conqueror decided to retreat. But he had left it far too late. The French army, perpetually harassed by the Cossacks, was caught in the iron grip of winter. As they tried to cross the Beresina, the conditions were so appalling, many died there and then.

Napoleon in a blue study.

From Napoleon's original Grand Army of 600,000, only 1,000 emaciated figures came back from the Russian wilderness. Apart from the appalling-numbers of the dead, Napoleon suffered losses of about 3,000 soldiers, who deserted or stayed behind as prisoners. It is said that Napoleon's heroic Marshal Ney, ragged, dirty and blood-stained, staggered into the town hall of a border town and when asked who he was, shouted: 'I am the Grand Army!'

This ruinous campaign gave heart to the allies. It was followed by a revival of the coalition against Napoleon. Austria, Prussia and Sweden joined forces with the Russians. Overtures for peace were made. But the emperor would not listen. The French were defeated at Leipzig, the 'Battle of the Nations', in 1813. In the spring of 1814, Napoleon was forced to abdicate.

You would think that was the end of his ambitions for conquest. But on March 1st, 1815, Napoleon returned to the south of France with a few hundred soldiers. The famous Hundred Days began that were to end on June 18 – at Waterloo. Austrians, Russians, Germans and British were assembled ready to move towards the French frontier. Soon the news of Napoleon's defeat reached Paris.

Napoleon was still ranting about raising more men, more weapons. But enough was enough. France's ministers convened and when Napoleon joined them he discovered he was no longer in charge of France's destiny. The people wanted no more fighting. He offered to abdicate. The offer was accepted the very next day.

On June 22, 1815, Napoleon ceased to be emperor. He was banished to St Helena, an island off the west coast of Africa. Napoleon died of cancer six years later.

The man who wanted to rule Europe, instead turned his country against himself and died a lonely figure.